THE BEST OF THE REVIEW — 1

NOTES ON THE

SPIRITUAL EXERCISES

OF

St. Ignatius of Loyola

Edited by
David L. Fleming, S. J.

Imprimi Potest: Paul F. Distler, S.J.
                  Executive Assistant

Imprimatur: Most Rev. John N. Wurm, S.T.D., Ph.D.
                  Vicar General of St. Louis
                  December 23, 1980

                  ISBN 0-924768-01-0

Fourth Printing, November 1989

the WORD
among us®
The *Spirit* of Catholic Living

This book was published by The Word Among Us. Since 1981, The Word Among Us has been answering the call of the Second Vatican Council to help Catholic laypeople encounter Christ in the Scriptures.

The name of our company comes from the prologue to the Gospel of John and reflects the vision and purpose of all of our publications: to be an instrument of the Spirit, whose desire is to manifest Jesus' presence in and to the children of God. In this way, we hope to contribute to the Church's ongoing mission of proclaiming the gospel to the world so that all people would know the love and mercy of our Lord and grow more deeply in their faith as missionary disciples.

Our monthly devotional magazine, *The Word Among Us*, features meditations on the daily and Sunday Mass readings, and currently reaches more than one million Catholics in North America and another half million Catholics in one hundred countries around the world. Our book division, The Word Among Us Press, publishes numerous books, Bible studies, and pamphlets that help Catholics grow in their faith.

To learn more about who we are and what we publish, log on to our website at www.wau.org. There you will find a variety of Catholic resources that will help you grow in your faith.

Embrace His Word, Listen to God . . .

www.wau.org

Foreword

A rich contribution to the study and understanding of the Spiritual Exercises of St. Ignatius has been made in article form over the past ten years. REVIEW FOR RELIGIOUS has had the privilege of publishing a good number of such articles.

Because of the great interest in directed retreat work, with all its implications concerning prayer, discernment, and spiritual direction, a collection of articles from the *Review* promised to be a very helpful contribution to directors and retreatants alike. With the support and cooperation of its editor, I have endeavored to go back over the period of eleven years of the *Review*—the years 1967-1978—in order to group together some of the articles which have proved to be enlightening, stimulating, and encouraging.

The book is structured in the following fashion. To introduce the whole subject of the Ignatian Spiritual Exercises, I have written an original article focusing upon the dynamic or movement in the retreat method. Then I have grouped together articles which provide a certain background and method that is incumbent in the directed retreat model based on the Ignatian Exercises. Next, those articles which help explain the content and provide some insight into the retreat experience form the second unit. The third collection of articles deals with prayer in its various forms and the topic of discernment. Following this section, I have drawn together some articles dealing with social consciousness and action related to the Ignatian retreat.

In a final postscript, I have included those articles that are wide in their application—one on the notion of adaptation of the Exercises, a second on the Nineteenth Annotation Retreat, and a final article which questions the use of the thirty-day retreat and identifies some qualities desirable in both the retreatant and the director if the full Ignatian model of a thirty-day retreat is to be used well.

Various weaknesses are evident in a book of independently written articles such as this. There are many aspects of the *Spiritual Exercises* and its adaptation into the shorter retreat style which are not handled. When a subject is taken up in many articles, such as those on prayer and on discernment, there can be a certain amount of overlapping of ideas and approaches. The quality of depth in insight and the difference of style in writing can be a disruptive factor in the flow of reading. But overriding these various negative elements, there still remains the richness of personal experience and understanding found in the wide variety of articles and authors brought together in one volume.

A special word of thanks is owed to Sister Eva Maria, O.S.F., novice of the Sisters of St. Francis of St. George Martyr (Alton, IL) who undertook and stayed with the tedium of seeing the manuscript through the printer to the final product.

It is my prayer that many men and women, touched in some way by the Spiritual Exercises of St. Ignatius, will find this book a treasury of resources that will deepen their faith and understanding and stimulate their apostolic lives.

David L. Fleming, S.J.

Table of Contents

Introduction

The Ignatian Spiritual Exercises: Understanding a Dynamic

David L. Fleming, S.J.

The *Spiritual Exercises* of St. Ignatius of Loyola has received many interpretations over the past four hundred years. Although these various studies are good and helpful for a deeper understanding of the *Exercises,* I want to focus my own reflections upon the movement or dynamic present in this small book by St. Ignatius. For the Ignatian gift to the method of retreats available within the Church shines out in this special way: what characterizes every element in the *Exercises* is the sense of movement—described more fully as a movement forward as well as a movement in depth in a personal commitment to Jesus Christ.

By a study of the history of spiritual developments within the Church, we learn that there are many styles of retreats or what we might more generally describe as concentrated prayer or personal spiritual-renewal periods. We could set aside a certain number of days, for example, to center our prayer and reading on the three theological virtues of faith, hope, and love. What results from this kind of retreat may be a greater personal understanding of these virtues and perhaps some greater desire is excited for their integral place in our lives.

By contrast, Ignatius spent some twenty years constructing the book of the *Exercises* in order that it might embody a certain movement—what we traditionally call a "conversion experience." He found this movement or dynamic significant for his own commitment to Jesus Christ as well as for the commitment or conversion of many others with whom he worked. The movement involved these personal elements: a person making these experiences (a retreatant), a person giving them (a director), and God present to both persons. The *Exercises* themselves are focused primarily on passages from the four gospels of Our Lord Jesus Christ, with certain key structures presented by Ignatius at precise intervals as a distillation of a particular movement or call within the gospels. The carefully constructed content of the *Exercises* was written down specifically as a help for the person giving them in order to facilitate the response to God's special grace and call in an individual Christian's life.

A variety of words or expressions has been used to try to capture central aspects of the *Exercises*. All of them are drawn in some way from the Ignatian text. *A growing freedom* is one important way of describing the experience brought about by the *Exercises. A process of ordering our life-values* is another expression of this dynamic. *Indifference* or *detachment* is sometimes seen as the permeating ingredient of a person's life, if it has been influenced by the *Exercises. Putting on the mind of Christ* or *the ability to see and make decisions the way in which Jesus sees and makes decisions* is another way of capturing the new quality nurtured by the making of the *Exercises*. The common element in all these descriptive phrases is the sense of dynamism—not so much a newness measured by something we have come to learn through the *Exercises* so much as an introduction into an abiding attitude towards life, an all-inclusive way of going about living.

From the outset of these reflections, I would like to make one caution. What appears to be a rigidly structured approach, so meticulously ordered in hours of prayer and examination, in positions for prayer, in the use of food, sleep, penances, and so on, can only be studied with comprehension by someone who has had the experience of making the Exercises. A study of the *Exercises* which is not grounded in the personal experience of them is akin to a blind person's braille-reading all about the color *red*. In both instances, there is a certain comprehension of the words and expressions used, but still no real ability "to see" can take place. My own reflections, then, do presume that we have had the experience of the *Exercises*. Although many people have experienced the full Exercises of thirty days in a group-style through a preached or guided presentation, I would like to consider the text of the *Exercises* as it is presented in a personally directed retreat over a thirty-day period. Influenced by Ignatius' own meticulousness in setting down the order of the elements which make up the *Exercises* text, I will try to reflect an orderliness myself as I attempt to shed light on the flow of the contents of his book. The numbers enclosed within brackets within the text which follows refer to paragraph numbers found in most modern editions of the *Spiritual Exercises*.

1. The Prayer "Soul of Christ"

What we find printed first in the book is not a part, strictly speaking, of the Ignatian text. Ignatius of Loyola has long been associated with the prayer *Soul of Christ,* so much so that at times he has been identified as its author. We know that Ignatius did not formulate this prayer, but it *is* a great favorite of his and he refers to it expressly in the text of the threefold colloquy [e.g., 63, 147] and in the Three Methods of Prayer [253, 258]. Although this prayer was not prefixed to either the original Spanish, or the early Latin editions, since the edition printed in Vilna in 1583, there has been an almost universal custom to include it in the text of the *Exercises*. In a true sense, we can say that the prayer is a summing up of the whole movement of the Exercises in terms of their Christ-centeredness. The *Soul of Christ* focuses line by line upon our getting ever more totally within the person of Christ so that he really becomes our life—or, better stated, we live only in him. This prayer, like the movement present in the Exercises themselves, centers us so much upon the person of Jesus Christ that, with St. Paul, we are meant to exclaim "the life I live now is not my own, Christ is living in me" (Ga 2:20a). It is because of this spirit, and Ignatius' own references to the prayer, that this formula takes its integral place within the *Exercises* text.

2. Annotations or Helps

The *Annotations* (called "Introductory Observations in Puhl; nn. 1-20) introduce the Ignatian text as he perfected it. These twenty observations of Ignatius, along with the various additions and adaptations which he suggests in accord with the content material of the various weeks, provide the basic directions on how to proceed in the giving of the retreat. Throughout the years, many books—some of the early ones were called *Directories* of the *Spiritual Exercises*—have been written to give aid to the retreat director and to the retreatant. But Ignatius' own pithy observations within the text remain the most essential tool for the good progress of the retreat. Even when the *Exercises* are adapted to various styles (preached, group-sharing, private) and to various time limits (three-day, eight-day, and so on), these observations maintain an essential place in accommodating the movement of the Exercises.

The fact that we find these annotations or helps first in the text stresses the overriding importance of adaptation. Ignatius intended that the *Exercises* which he presented to the Church and to the Society of Jesus were to be only sketchy outlines always accommodated by the director to a particular retreatant [18]. In these first directions, then, we are always reminded that there is no such thing as a "pure" presentation of the Exercises. There is only the unique adaptation of the movement of conversion to a particular retreatant. Since the true director of the retreat is God alone [15], the human director must try to remain his instrument. This he does by listening carefully to the retreatant in the review of a retreat day and then proceeding to follow out the lead of the Spirit as best as he can by the suggestions of such exercises as will further the movement of conversion. The Ignatian retreat director, as a result, cannot be caught up in a lock-step presentation of a text. The same kind of freedom is demanded of him in his role of retreat director as is sought by the retreatant through the methodology of the *Exercises*.

What promotes this kind of freedom of movement is found especially in the proper application of Ignatius' Rules for the Discernment of Spirits [313-336], as he himself suggests in [8]. These reflections of Ignatius capsulize for the director guidelines for following out the spiritual forces in our lives which tend to lead us towards God or away from him. As a person comes more adept at making use of the means which these rules provide, the dynamic of the retreat flows all the more smoothly.

3. The Title and Presupposition

After the Annotations, we find a brief statement which acts as a summary description of the *Exercises* in terms of their purpose [21]. Ignatius desires that each person come to a true sense of freedom—the freedom of a child of God. When we are ordering conflicting or competing values in our lives, we must not be at the mercy of our emotions or our prejudices if we are truly to seek and find the will of God. This freedom is clearly called upon when we are faced with decisions and choices especially those which affect our life-orientations.

It is also within this context of freedom that Ignatius sets the tone for the relationship between the director and the retreatant [22]. As usual, the progress or movement of the retreat itself is his major concern. Because mutual trust and openness is essential in the relationship between the director and the one being directed, Ignatius stresses how each person should be ready to give a more positive interpretation to the other's statement even if what is said or done should appear strange or even disedifying. The whole attempt to clarify, or possibly even correct, is pursued with Christian tact, understanding, and love. This principle remains the Ignatian base for all Christian ministry.

4. The Foundation

Most retreatants have found that their first taste of the Exercises came in the consideration of the *Principle and Foundation* [23]. It is commonly accepted that the Principle and Foundation became an essential part of the Exercises about the time of Ignatius' theology studies at the University of Paris. For Ignatius, these few brief paragraphs capture the truth about human existence. The statements appear so basic about our relationship to God, to our fellowmen and women, and to our world that we are tempted to pass over them lightly. Ignatius' own experience in giving the Exercises proves that there can be no progress or movement unless this base is truly a firm foundation. Before a person can even begin to look at sin and his own personal rejection of God at the Ignatian level where it calls forth gratitude in the retreatant, a basic trust and experience of God's creating and sustaining love must be present. Sin itself is a faith concept, and so to realize its meaning we need first to consider the firm foundation of our faith in God and in his creation. Otherwise a very unhealthy introspection and self-centered shame can become the focus of the First Week. What Ignatius intends to provoke in the retreatant is an unflinching gaze at the aspect of sinfulness which results in a response of thanks to a God who loves so much, both in his first creative moment and in his faithful constancy to his creation.

The little evidence we have of the use of the Foundation in Ignatius' time indicates that it was a brief consideration by the retreatant on the first evening or day. What is deceptive in this evidence lies in the rather long preparation time which Ignatius himself usually presumed before a person was ready for the Exercises. Although we do not know the content of this preparatory process, it evidently enabled the retreatant to feel "at home" with this kind of summary statement about the basic Christian catechesis found in the Principle and Foundation. From this starting point, the movement or progress which is involved in the unfolding of all that lies hidden in God's salvation plan can begin. In fact, the very consideration of the way of living called for in the Foundation often rouses the sense of personal inadequacy in exercitant's response. This inadequacy, or even failure, commonly introduces the movement towards the matter of the First Week.

5. The First Week

If we remember that Ignatius wrote down his text for use by the person who gives the Exercises, we will have a better sense for the ordering of the two pieces which form the content of the *First Week*. Ignatius first presents the matter dealing with the methodology of *conscience-examination* [24-43] and then describes rather briefly the five prayer exercises [45-71].

The process of the Ignatian retreat is predominantly a reflective one. We review or reflect upon our experiences—the prayer of the past hour, the integrating or disrupting factors affecting the retreat during this past half-day, the pattern of our tendencies in our past life, and so on. An unreflective person is not an apt subject for this kind of retreat. Consequently, the director must first help a person to be reflective about his experiences.

When Ignatius places the method of examination first within the text, he stresses the necessary importance as well as the practical ways of being reflective for the essential progress of the retreat. The examination of conscience also has a significant place within the context of the First Week matter which deals with a person's rejection of God by sin and God's continuing response of mercy. Both the review of our own past sinfulness and the possible preparation for the sacrament of reconciliation [44] are facillitated by this practical introduction to examining one's conscience.

Ordinarily a temporal priority is not needed or desirable for introducing a retreatant to the process of examination before involving him in the exercises of the First Week. The movement which carries us from the Foundation consideration to the matter of the First Week calls for a simultaneous interplay between the kind of instruction involved in fostering the practical method of being reflective about oneself and the kind of direction given in prayer as indicated in the five exercises. The director must be the one who determines how best to integrate the flow between these two pieces which form the matter of the first week.

Ignatius makes evident in [4] of his annotations that a *Week,* as he is using the word, does not of itself signify any set number of days. The length of time spent within each of the Four Weeks of the Exercises has to be adapted to a particular retreatant. He observes only that the total time to be spent in the Exercises is about thirty days. In the light of this orientation, we can understand the rather mysterious presentation of five exercises making up five one-hour periods of prayer as the total content of the First Week prayer time. The richness of the material as outlined by Ignatius demands time for assimilation.

The necessity of repetition allows a deepening realization to develop which produces the "intimate understanding and relish of the truth" [2] described by Ignatius. Two important aspects are made apparent in the text: the content matter itself and the progressive simplifying of the matter within the five prayer periods of a day in the First Week. What is also apparent is the dynamic of the Week; it is reflected in the grace sought, as expressed in the second *prelude* and in the *colloquies* indicated by Ignatius.

The first exercise [45-54] focuses on the awfulness of a single sin as revealed in the account of the angels' rejection of God, in the story of the first man and woman's sin, and in the faith understanding which we have of a person's freedom which allows him to reject God for all eternity. Ignatius has a retreatant look objectively at the effect of a single sin which disrupts the whole purpose of life, rouses hatred and division, and leads to a self-enclosed death apart from the only source of life, God.

The subjective entrance of the retreatant into this exercise comes in the *colloquy* or intimate conversation between the retreatant and Jesus hanging on the cross concerning the consequences of a single sin [53]. Ignatius suggests that we retreatants remember that more than a single sin has touched our lives. If Jesus, our Creator and Lord (by this title Ignatius connects explicitly these reflections to the preceding Foundation consideration), takes on temporal life only to die on a cross for our sins, what can we sinners say about our own response—in the past, even now, and in the future? The actual praying centers here in the conversation between the retreatant and God about various points stimulated by the matter under consideration.

This first exercise, with its three different focus points, stresses thinking and reasoning. Traditionally we have called the method of prayer which involves this kind of thinking *meditation*. This meditative style of praying forms the basic approach described by Ignatius for entering into the First Week.

The second exercise [55-61] turns the retreatant's eyes more upon his own history of sin. This exercise moves us from the more objective stance of our first prayer period to a subjective stance of deep involvement in this present one. But Ignatius carefully directs the focus away from despair because of one's faults and their effects and to the continuous support and love given by God directly and through the gifts of nature and the concern of our fellowmen and women. The colloquy aims outward from self by giving thanks to God for all the ways in which he continues to pour life into us, even as we feel the effects of our sin [61].

The third exercise [62-63] is described as a *repetition* of the material from the preceding two exercises. Besides interrelating the subject matter of the two preceding exercises, this third exercise makes clear that the emphasis is always on the colloquy—the subject matter being the stimulant for this conversation with God. In this exercise, Ignatius suggests that the conversation be directed to Mary, to Jesus, and to the Father.

Ignatius has two ways of inciting in the retreatant the intensity of a particular desire. Five prayer periods in a single day obviously show such an intensity. What is called the *triple colloquy* is another way. In a childlike way that only makes sense for a person of deep faith, Ignatius encourages us to line up all the help we can in terms of the grace-gifts which we need. He has us go to Mary in order that she might support us with her son, then to Jesus that he might support us before the Father, and finally we come to the Father to repeat again our own request. Here in this third exercise [62-63], Ignatius would have us plead for a depth of knowledge, an insight of understanding, and an ability to act against the tendencies in ourselves and in our world which lead us away from God.

The fourth exercise [64] is a time of even further refinement in terms of the matter which is still the same and in terms of our response in the form of the triple colloquy. The fifth exercise [65-71] continues the same simplifying movement of prayer within the day. In the Ignatian vocabulary, this fifth period of prayer in the day is ordinarily designated as being an *application of senses*. A number of interpretations about the meaning and methodology of this prayer-form have been proposed over the years.

From the viewpoint of a dynamic, it is clear that the usual pattern in the retreat day is the presentation of a certain amount of material for consideration, which in successive prayer periods less and less occupies the head as the heart more and more responds in colloquy. By the time of the fifth exercise within the day, there has arisen such an easy presence to God within the context or atmosphere of the matter that a method of praying seems difficult to describe. In some ways, this prayer-time can be called the most passive way of praying. It is akin to the passive way that our five senses take in the data of the environment around us. Here in this First Week, it is a total experience of being a sinner, weighed down by our personal sin, and feeling the oppression of the history of sin and its continuing presence in our world. From this sense of immersion into sin—so complete an experience is like to *hell*—we once again speak out our thanks to Christ for being so loving and merciful to us [71].

I have noted that there is movement in the retreat day as described by Ignatius. In the First Week, it is a movement from thinking and reasoning to a lessening of reflection with the head and more a responding with the heart. This same kind of movement can be traced within the structures of an entire Week. For example, in the First Week, if a person were to continue to repeat the five exercises outlined by Ignatius over a three or four day period, each day would tend to be a bit simpler than the preceding days in terms of the matter reflected upon. What would likely grow stronger and more intense would be the emotions or affections of the retreatant in making a response.

From the direction of the dynamic present in the First Week, and expressed through the prelude that requests a certain grace, and through the colloquy, it is clear that the sense of "finishing" the Week would come from the God-given peace of at once experiencing oneself as a sinner and being loved and saved as such by God. God's abiding mercy is a real experience, deeper down but just as factual as our own sinfulness. The stress which Ignatius puts on gratitude in the First Week is significant in making a judgment about a retreatant's readiness to move on to the Second Week.

6. The Second Week
The Call of Christ the King

Ignatius nowhere in the First Week indicates a mercy meditation with a base such as the gospel parable of the prodigal son in St. Luke. Some commentators find this quite curious. But besides the fact that he has laid stress on the response of gratitude throughout the Week, I believe that he concretizes the mercy of God in the exercise entitled *The Kingdom of Christ* [91-98].

There is a way of showing love by doing something for another person, as a father can send his child gifts while living afar. But a far greater sign of love is shown by being present and mutually involved, such as a father spending time with his child and together building a treehouse. It is in this second way that Ignatius presents the parable of a king calling to all the inhabitants of his kingdom.

The parable is intended to be a pale image—though it has been repeated many times in actual human history—of the call which Jesus Christ gives to each person. He not only identifies himself as our personal savior but invites each man, woman, and child to be involved with him in the salvation of their fellow men and women and their world. The victory has been won in Christ, though it is still in process in us and in our world.

Ignatius would have us understand even more deeply the mercy of God as it is extended by the very means of this call to work with Christ and to follow him in all the ways that our devotion to him can draw us. Ignatius proposes that we consider the response which a very generous person would make to Jesus, but he very carefully does not demand that we make the same response [97-98]. In fact, no colloquy is outlined, though a grace has been sought in terms of hearing and responding to the call of Christ [91].

This exercise—one of the structural pieces put together by Ignatius to introduce us to the present and risen Christ and to his call as it is addressed here and now to us—is best described as a consideration. In presentation, it is more akin to the Foundation than to the exercises of the First Week. Without trying to draw too hard and fast a distinction, I note that the evident logic involved in a consideration does not demand the kind of reasoning process which the meditation form does. Both prayer forms, however, ultimately call for some response from us.

Often commentators identify the call of Christ as the "Foundation of the Second Week." As Ignatius gives the directions for this day, he indicates that this exercise should be gone through twice [99]. The common practice of the repose day or breakday between the Weeks of the Exercises apparently drew its inspiration from the relaxation from the five exercises of a day in the First Week to the two exercises of this day on the Kingdom.

Although there are only the two exercises on this day, with the same material about the Kingdom repeated twice, the day itself is a most important one for the dynamic of the retreat. The Call of Christ is meant to rouse in the retreatant not only a generous response of gratitude but the commitment to the person of Jesus and to his work. The Kingdom exercise, then, acts as a bridge between the gratitude for the mercy of God seen in Christ in the First Week and the study of his person and his work in the succeeding Weeks. The Kingdom exercise at the same time is an encounter with Jesus as he is now—our risen Savior—who continues to invite each one of us to be his apostles for our own time and place.

The Contemplations

Ignatius opens up the *Second Week* proper with three days of exercises on the incarnation, birth, and hidden life of Jesus. The structure of each day is similar to the day described in the First Week, with new matter being presented in both the first and second exercise period, followed by repetitions, with the final exercise being identified as an application of senses.

The grace sought (expressed in the third preludes) and the colloquy again give us the sense of direction or movement within the Week. The grace consistently desired is "to know Jesus more intimately so that I can love him more and follow him more closely." The colloquies tend to sharpen up the desire according to the particular mystery of Christ's life which has provided the matter for prayer.

The way of praying found in the Second Week and in the succeeding Weeks most clearly bears the special mark of Ignatius' insight. Ignatius describes this kind of prayer as *contemplation,* and he gives to it his own special traits. His style of contemplation takes for its content various incidents (which are also called mysteries in Christian tradition) of the life of Christ as depicted in the gospels. Every incident recounted in scripture by the evangelist is potential matter for this kind of praying.

In the first and second exercise of the Second Week [101-109, 110-117], Ignatius describes two ways of approaching this kind of contemplation. The perspective of the Father, Son, and Spirit looking upon our world provides the entrance into the scene of the annunciation of the angel Gabriel to Mary. With God, we watch Mary's response and know that the Son has become man for us. For Ignatius, the idea of contemplation is to enter into the gospel scene so completely that we drink in the atmosphere, hear the nuances of what is said, and sense the meaning of gestures and actions at a depth which only a loving presence can penetrate.

The nativity of Jesus at Bethlehem is the mystery presented for the second exercise. Here Ignatius expands the simple scripture setting by relating the circumstances of Jesus' birth to a comprehensive view of his life of hardship leading to death on a cross. The simple way that Ignatius would call each retreatant to be fully present within a particular mystery of Christ's life is at the same time made more whole or integrated by his suggestions for expanding realistically the perspectives as, for example, from the viewpoint of God or from the viewpoint of Christ's whole life leading up to his death on the cross for us.

It is by means of this style of contemplative prayer that Ignatius has discovered a way of the retreatant imbibing Jesus' attitudes and approaches to God, to men and women, and to his world. The more we enter into gospel contemplation, the more we heighten the connaturality of our own way of living with the way that Christ lives. By the grace we seek and by the prayer-method we use, we find ourselves drinking in the experiences of Jesus, so that we begin to assimilate his values, his loves, his freedom. This style of praying provides the necessary context of decision-making or discernment which forms an essential part of the Second Week and is meant to be an abiding part of a Christian's life that is shaped by the Exercises.

The Two Standards

On the fourth day of the Second Week, Ignatius outlines a structural meditation once again which capsulizes the identity and mission of Jesus. This meditation is called *The Two Standards* [136-147], and together with The Three Classes of Men, supplies the matter for the prayer of this particular day. The exercise of the Two Standards is to be repeated three or four times [148], so that the final prayer period is given over to the matter presented in the Three Classes of Men.

Ignatius bluntly interprets the third contemplative day on the hidden life of Jesus at Nazareth and the incident of his being found in the temple at the age of twelve [134] as an indication of the life direction which each person faces before God [135]. Is God's will for our life to be found in the ordinary life of a Christian represented by Jesus' life at Nazareth or are we called to a life of special service hinted at in Jesus' being about his Father's business? Ignatius distills the experiences and choices made by Jesus throughout his life into the structural exercise of the Two Standards in order to help us answer that question for ourselves.

This fourth day stands out in the Second Week because the prayer is meditative and scripture itself does not form the matter for the exercise. The grace sought is one of recognizing and understanding how the power of evil leads us more away from God and how Jesus proposes to lead us ever more surely toward him [139]. These exercises are aimed at understanding the choice of values inherent in Christ's life and to which he calls each of us.

Ignatius presents Satan as the personal epitome of all that is evil and inimical to human well-being. He depicts him as an enslaver who entices men and women to make what they own or possess the measure of their personal value or worth and on which their identity depends. The next step is to look for and demand the adulation and honor by others for a personal sense of worth and selfhood. Finally there is the self-conceit of pride by which we try to assert our independence of everything and everyone, including God.

Only by examining this pattern of enslavement by the power of evil do we come to some insight into the mysterious values by which Jesus lives his own life and which he invites us to follow. He calls to a poverty which will not let us measure our worth or identity by what we have or possess. He calls to a humiliation which will permit us to be free from the flattery or fawning behavior involved in the quest for worldly reputation and esteem. Finally he calls to humility which must be the basic grounding or foundation of our lives: just as Jesus' own identity and personal worth are in being Son, so that same truth does he share with each one of us—men and women who can glory in calling upon God as "Abba." Why we can pray for and desire poverty, humiliations, and humility becomes apparent through the structuring of this meditation. But the depth of understanding which is necessary for living it out causes Ignatius to employ the threefold colloquy with Mary, Jesus, and the Father in which we beg for such an important grace-gift [147].

The Three Classes

It is not enough to understand the strategy of Christ in choosing poverty, humiliations, and humility and so calling us to follow. We must have a readiness of will and desire to be able to follow. In order to facilitate the movement between the understanding sought in the exercise of the Two Standards and this readiness of will, Ignatius proposes the exercise entitled *The Three Classes of Men* [149-156].

The exercise is simply presented as a parable of men who come at a decision in three different ways. None of the persons involved actually makes a decision. But the attitudes represented by the first two approaches demonstrate a way of avoiding any kind of decision which might seem to be called for. Personal preference or attachments seem to get in the way of doing what is necessary. The third approach is seen in the openness and willingness to follow out any choice or decision indicated by God. The third class, too, acknowledges the strength of certain attachments or preferences, but persons of this class do not allow themselves to be bound. They maintain their freedom to come to a decision made in terms of being better able to serve God our Lord.

By means of this exercise, Ignatius has us consider and reflect upon the way people come to decisions when their affections are involved. From the objective example presented in this meditation form, he suggests that we be aroused to intensify our own desire for freedom so that we are encouraged to express our desire by means of a threefold colloquy with Mary, with Jesus, and with the Father [156]. This final prayer exercise of the fourth day is meant to move a retreatant from the understanding of Jesus' values to a readiness for acceptance of his call in whatever way it comes.

The Three Kinds of Humility

Ignatius has one more structural piece to add at this point of the retreat. It is in the form of a consideration similar to the Foundation. The reflection deals with the many degrees of closeness to Christ, who sums up in himself the truth of what it is to be human—the humility of being son. Humility, as Ignatius uses the word, is our foundational virtue—what truly grounds our identity and consequently our way of living and working. In the gospel, Jesus wants us to learn of him because he is humble; he knows where he comes from and where he is going, for he is "son," "the beloved one." That sonship is what he has shared with us, giving us his Spirit so that we too might be one with him in calling upon God as "Abba." As we have been considering Jesus' value system by which he lives his life, we are drawn to reflect on how closely we want to be identified with him. The uniqueness of the relationship between Jesus and each one of us indicates that there are as many kinds of humility as there are people.

Ignatius draws in broad strokes *three descriptions of humility* which can be found in the spectrum of close relationships [165-167]. The first kind of humility is that of a person who would do nothing to break the relationship and yet can act in ways that neither build it nor strengthen it. The second kind of humility describes a person whose whole way of living is found in the relationship with Jesus and his life-orientation of doing the will of the Father. This person has been pictured in the third example given in the exercise on The Three Classes. Ignatius goes on to outline another level of closeness found only in those lovers whose very external appearances and experiences seem to mesh into a unity. The person described in the third kind of humility desires so close an identity with Jesus that if the externals of his life, especially in terms of the poverty that Jesus experienced, the rejection he received, and ultimately the crucifixion he embraced, were to be mirrored in this person's life, only delight and joy would be the result. What Ignatius pictures here is the madness of martyrs like St. Lawrence or St. Thomas More who truly delighted in a suffering and death that, because of their love, brought them into the closest of relationships with Christ. This madness, of course, finds its source in the grace-gift of God.

After having the retreatant consider these notions about intimacy in following Jesus over some period of time, Ignatius suggests that the retreatant might pray to be given the grace of this third kind of intimacy with Jesus, if it would be God's will and if it would give God greater glory [168]. The intensity of the request should be reflected in the threefold colloquy with Mary, with Jesus, and with the Father.

It is clear that Ignatius in these three structural pieces—The Two Standards, The Three Classes, and The Three Kinds of Humility—has strongly prepared the retreatant for the contemplations concerning the following of Jesus in his public life. We have an understanding of Christ's identity and values, a readiness and willingness to follow, and even a deep desire for the grace to be admitted to such a close intimacy with Christ that, if possible, even the externals of his life might be reflected in our own.

The Public Life of Jesus

With this kind of heightened interior state, the retreatant enters into the contemplations of Jesus' public life beginning with his baptism by John at the River Jordan, the temptations in the desert, the call of the apostles, and so on. Once again because of differences in retreatants, their desires, and the ways in which God works with them, the number of scripture passages which form the content of this Week varies greatly.

Two aspects of the Ignatian approach, however, should be noted. The mysteries of Christ's public life which are chosen by Ignatius are *ordered* in terms of the direction of the retreat. The selection of passages is not based simply on the chronological sequence within the gospel or on a random choice of a director's or retreatant's favorite gospel-incidents. The mysteries chosen are always ordered to the progress of this particular retreatant's response to the lead of God. In addition, Ignatius is not a man who thinks the more passages suggested by the director and the more covered by the retreatant the better. Rather just the opposite is indicated by the directions which Ignatius himself gives. In view of the importance of this particular retreat for the possible life-orientation of the retreatant, Ignatius suggests only one scriptural passage a day [159], with either three or four repetitions of the same matter. A central purpose of the contemplations is to allow a retreatant to live so closely with Jesus that there is more an immersion into his very person than an insight or discovery into all the activities he does which might come from examining many scriptural passages. The Ignatian dynamic inherent in the contemplations lies in fostering a depth of the relationship which gives relish to the companionship and following of Jesus which we are seeking in the retreat.

The Election

The structural pieces of the fourth day within the Second Week clearly mark out the natural flow towards a practical decision-making about our life in relationship to the following of Jesus. It is obvious from the placement of the material on election in the text of the Second Week, as well as from the historical evidence of Ignatius' conduct in giving the Exercises, that the choice of a state of life or the reformation of life is a central aspect of the retreat [169-189].

But as we see in the Third Class of Men and in the Third Degree of Humility, Ignatius provides a far broader purpose in the retreat, one that subsumes any particular decision or reform of life. By means of the contemplations, he expects a certain connaturality to develop in us such that the way in which Jesus responds to his Father, to his fellow men and women, and to events becomes more and more our way of response. It is only when this atmosphere is nurtured that the Ignatian method of discernment can properly take place. For him, the way to live life and the way to make decisions in accord with the will of God does not come from a human logic or even from a praying about them. It is the continuing process of "putting on the mind of Christ Jesus"—a process brought about by the focusing on Jesus through contemplation.

7. The Third Week

The sense of some resolution about the Third Kind of Humility or about a life-decision provides the usual indication that the time has come to move on to the *Third Week*. In general, this movement is subtler and more gently concluded than the flow between the First and the Second Weeks.

Contemplation remains the style of prayer. Ignatius introduces a difference through the identification of six points rather than the three points common to the Second-Week exercises. All three added points [195-197] focus upon a greater interiority in the approach to the mystery of Jesus' life under consideration. These added focal points are supplemented by Ignatius' review of the meaning and method of the colloquy, with a stress now not so much on the familiarity of conversation as on the intimacy of compassion [199].

By means of these different emphases, along with the grace sought in the Third-Week exercises, we know that there is a stress now not so much in terms of the activity of following Jesus but more in view of "staying with" or "being with" him in his passion and death. To be able to enter into his sorrow and to enter beyond the observation of exterior pain to the inner suffering of Jesus expresses the grace asked for in this Week [193]. One other element which Ignatius underlines for this time is the notion of "all this for me." He is most concerned that the redemptive act of Jesus be not drawn in cosmic terms, to the detriment of the unique and personal love for this particular retreatant which moves Jesus to spend his life for even one person's sin.

The intensity of the Week comes out in the five prayer periods and in the suggestion that the triple colloquy with Mary, with Jesus, and with the Father may be the common practice throughout the Week. There is a greater freedom of approach used in this Week, even to the suggestion of whole days being spent in the total account of the passion rather than in its division into individual mysteries [209]. Whatever seems best in view of the particular retreatant receives a continuing greater emphasis as the retreat progresses.

At the conclusion of the text for the Third Week, we find the *Rules for Eating* [210-217]. Although there may be legitimate speculation as to how exactly these rules are to be integrated into the dynamic of the retreat, it seems foolish to deny that Ignatius took as much care to place these rules at this juncture of the retreat as he did with all the other structural pieces. By their very title in the text [210], these rules look to the future—the Fourth Week and thereafter. They present a practical pattern for developing the means to living as Jesus lives, taken to the most common and everyday experiences such as eating.

Ignatius give us here a model of practically carrying out our following of Christ throughout the totality of our day. He begins the process of having us consider the means which we must use in our ordinary lives to continue to live as closely with Christ as he has drawn us in this retreat. Some things we can begin to do even now in the context of the remaining days of the retreat, which look to the present and risen Christ and the ways in which he makes himself present in our world. The Rules for Eating, then, are a consideration providing a kind of bridge into our following of the contemporary Christ of the Fourth Week.

8. The Fourth Week

The *Fourth Week* of the Exercises deals with the risen life of Jesus. Contemplation remains the style of the prayer-exercise. Although Ignatius continues to call for the freedom of approach used in the Third Week for adapting the movement to a particular retreatant, this is the only week in which he does not encourage five periods of prayer and repetitions. Instead he presumes a new mystery is to be used for each of the first three periods of prayer, with the application of senses remaining the method for the summation of the prayer experiences of the day [227].

The emphasis in these contemplations is not so much on the persons with whom Jesus deals or the activities he does. Rather the consistency of Jesus in his risen life is stressed—in his desire to dispel fear, to give his peace, and to send out with the good news. Jesus stands forth as one who consoles and strengthens.

The grace sought and the colloquy proposed again give us clues to the direction of this Week. We pray for the grace to enter into the joy of our risen Lord—one who has broken the chains of death, has defeated the power of sin and evil, and is the firstborn of the new creation [221]. The compassion with which we could labor with Jesus in his suffering and death is now changed over into the joy we share in his victory, even though we ourselves still experience the struggle towards the fullness of that new life. From our contemplations of the risen Christ dealing with frightened men and women so like us, we gradually come to appreciate that we ourselves and our world have been radically changed by Jesus' resurrection.

It is in this light that we better understand the exercise entitled *The Contemplation on the Love of God* [230-237]. The movement, seen in the grace desired, returns once again to the notion of gratitude to a loving God—a gratitude which empowers us to live a life of service in following our Lord and God [233]. There is a certain review of the dynamic of the Four Weeks of the Exercises present in the four focal points of this exercise. Because this material is not new, it does not require a reasoning process, and the prayer period can truly be a contemplation.

Each of the four points continues the dynamic found in the gospel-contemplations of this Week. Just as the Lord's activity is to console and share his joy with his mother and disciples, so he continues that effort with us today. Ignatius focuses that consoling activity of our Lord and God in terms of his gifts of nature and grace to us, the gift of his irrevocable identity with us, the gift of his continuing compassion for us in our labors and struggles, and the permeating flow of his life all around us in this new creation.

From Ignatius' own prenote to this exercise [230-231], he has made clear his understanding of lovers as being people who want to share whatever they have. The response which forms the colloquy embodies our own gift of self to God. As God has shared his life with us, so we desire and ask him to receive the sharing of our life with him.

This gentle expression of our love marks the continuing dynamic of a life now permanently affected by the *Spiritual Exercises:*

Take, Lord, and receive
      all my liberty, my memory, my understanding,
            and my entire will—
      all that I have and call my own.
You have given it all to me.
To you, Lord, I return it.
Everything is yours.
Do with it what you will.
Give me only your love and your grace.
That is enough for me.

I. BACKGROUND AND METHOD

The Nature and Value of a Directed Retreat

Herbert F. Smith, S.J.

REVIEW FOR RELIGIOUS, Volume 32, 1973, pp. 490-497.

During the last decade there has been a rebirth of the directed Ignatian retreat. The directed retreat is a marked departure from the familiar preached retreat in which we customarily spent some two hours a day hearing the word of God as it was spoken and interpreted by the retreat master.

Origins in Experimentation

The successful return of the directed retreat can almost certainly be credited to that widespread phenomenon of our day, the passion for experimentation. The experimental approach springs from a twofold conviction: that we can produce something *better;* and that, in an age wherein proliferating options are overloading our decision-making powers, we must discover what is most *relevant.*

We have all benefited from the experimental approach. Consider agriculture. Ten years ago there was widespread talk of the impossibility of feeding the world's people. Today there is not. That is largely because, in the interval, agricultural experimentation was carried on in the Philippines to produce a new strain of wheat. The first objective was to produce a *better* wheat, one that would give a greater yield per acre. The second objective was produce a more *relevant* wheat, one hardy enough to flourish on poor land in cold climates. The result is IR-3. It is revolutionizing the growth of wheat, turning traditionally wheat-importing countries to wheat exporters.

In the field of religion, we have similar problems and similar inclinations. How can we raise up better Catholic Christians, people more in contact with

God, more committed to Him, more faithful to the Church, more productive in the service of the kingdom? How can we form more relevant Catholic Christians, people who can responsibly handle the increased responsibility laid on each today? Enterprising men and women in the Church are presenting the directed Ignatian retreat as one answer.

Is it? I think it is, but my objective here is not to give proof of that. My objective is rather to give information concerning the nature of a directed retreat. Judgments can come later.

What is a directed retreat? I will proceed to answer that question by giving a series of progressively improving definitions until we ultimately reach the most illuminating definition I can provide.

One-to-one Relationship

The directed retreat is a retreat made neither alone nor in a large group; furthermore, it is made without the help of several talks a day. This incomplete definition is meant to clarify the manner in which the directed retreat departs from the familiar preached retreat. The directed retreat involves one director and one retreatant operating in a one-to-one relationship. The director may or may not be directing other retreatants simultaneously, but in any case he guides each retreatant as though he alone were on retreat. Of course, there may be some interplay between retreatants. They may celebrate Mass together. They may do shared prayer.

Smallest Possible Community

The directed retreat is a concerted effort to seek God in the smallest possible community. In a directed retreat, everything is set up and directed to help the retreatant *find God.* All irrelevant and distracting persons and entities are withdrawn. That leaves us with the smallest possible community, a community of three, in the likeness of the Trinity. The community of three which results can be described in various ways. It can be seen as composed of the retreatant, God, and His Spirit; God is the goal, and the Holy Spirit is the agent. He guides the retreatant to God, and He is the Love between the retreatant and God. There is, from another viewpoint, the triad of the retreatant, the director, and the Holy Spirit. The retreatant and the director work out the retreat in concert, and the Holy Spirit is the one Guide of both. From a still more comprehensive viewpoint, the tripartite community is made up of the retreatant, God, and the Church (whom the director embodies and represents).

The reason for setting up this smallest possible community is to promote the total personalization of the retreat. All transactions are aimed directly at the one retreatant and his unique personal needs here and now. While it is true that God always can and does work as personally with an individual in a group as with an individual off by himself, the retreat director cannot. And conversely, the retreatant cannot. The fact that God can is the saving grace of group retreats. The fact that retreatant and director cannot is the reason there is at times no substitute for a directed retreat.

The tiny directed retreat community favors intimate contact that helps the retreatant to come to know his God, himself, and his Church in an intimate new way. By *intimacy* I mean an attentive, healthy, open, and receptive relationship with another that is productive of a mutual identification in joys and sorrows.

Directed to Spiritual Exercising

The directed retreat is the engaging in spiritual exercises under the daily guidance of a director who has the twofold role of retreat director and spiritual director. The function of the retreatant is to do spiritual exercises. The function of the director is to guide and monitor the exercises.

In the directed retreat, there is emphasis on the activity of the retreatant. We have all seen the retreat master of the preached retreat deliver his four and five talks a day, hear confessions, hold interviews, and stagger out of the house exhausted six days later. The directed retreat, on the contrary, demands much more of the retreatant and focuses on what the retreatant is doing more than on what the director is saying. If the retreatant's activity still involves a great deal of active listening, it is not a human being he spends a lot of time listening to, it is God.

St. Ignatius himself stresses the activity of the retreatant, whom he calls the *exercitant*. He introduces his little book for retreat as "spiritual exercises which have as their purpose the conquest of self and the regulation of one's life in such a way that no decision is made under the influence of any inordinate attachment" (#21).

The director gives the retreatant *daily* guidance. Generally, the two meet once a day. The director provides spoken or written points for meditation, and they are generally given very briefly. If the director has more than one retreatant, he may give points in common to save time, where this is not to the disadvantage of the retreatants.

The retreatant gives the director a faithful account of the inner experiences and responses which take place in the course of his meditations. He tells of joy or sadness, peace or unrest, hope or fear, and so on. This account of one's personal experiences is always given in a private interview. This account is at the heart of the directed retreat, as is the response the director makes to it. The practice of making this report develops the retreatant's ability to discern the movements of good and evil that play in man's mind, heart, and feelings. The guidance of the director helps the retreatant learn how to distinguish between the good and evil influences more successfully. Most important, it helps him distinguish the divine call from every other influence on him. This knowledge frees him from old slavery to whims and emotions and nagging feelings of guilt. It helps him to put on the mind of Christ.

Functions of the Director

From what has just been said, it becomes manifest that the director of the directed retreat has two clearly distinct functions. *First,* like the director of a preached retreat, he provides the retreatant with input for the meditations. Let it be added that, both in the brief way he provides this material and in the selection of the material he provides, he himself is guided in a general way by his source material, *The Spiritual Exercises* of St. Ignatius. The director feeds in this input in harmony with the retreatant's *actual accomplishments,* thus moderating the advance and flow of the retreat in a fully personalized way. The director is fully aware that the graces sought in each meditation are necessary graces which have to be built up in their proper order like the parts of a building: sorrow for sin is the excavation, forgiveness the foundation, and so forth. This careful control of the process of the retreat is certainly one of the great advantages of a directed retreat.

Second, the retreat director is the retreatant's spiritual director. The great religions of the world, even in their most mystical traditions, all teach the need of a guide, be he a guru, a starets, a roshi, a spiritual director. Without a director, there can be no making of the *Spiritual Exercises,* as a reading of the introductory observations will establish. Without a director there has not been set up the necessary mini-community described in the second definition.

The Discerning Process

The director helps the retreatant to discern the mysteries of the interior life in a practical way that is meant to lead to practical decisions and practical service of Christ. The retreatant himself is always the primary discerner, and the director the auxiliary discerner. Only the retreatant is present to his own inner experiences. Unless he gives a good and faithful report, the auxiliary discerner cannot give the help he is meant to give.

The retreatant, then, is the subjective discerner. The director is the objective discerner. As objective discerner, he interprets the experiences of the retreatant in accord with the Biblical and doctrinal expressions of revelation as it is guarded and developed and handed on by the whole Church. If the retreatant too is learned in theology, and sometimes even if he is not, he may be able to interpret his experiences quite authentically himself. But in accord with the wisdom of the Church and of revelation, the People of God do not rely on themselves individually, but depend on one another in the effort to understand the meaning of God's communications, even the individual and personal ones. If the retreatant is guided by the Holy Spirit to come to a certain decision, the director can hope to be guided by Him to confirm the decision.

The Priest-confessor and the Retreat Director

The role of the director as auxiliary discerner is made even clearer if we consider the distinction between the role of the *priest-confessor* and the role of the *retreat spiritual director*. The confessor in the sacrament of penance is concerned primarily with the moral order, with the person's conscious, sinful rebellions against God's will. The retreat spiritual director is concerned with the retreatant's inner experiences, his moods, attractions, and repulsions, even before he has made any deliberate free responses to them. The confessor wants to know what a man has done of good and evil. The director wants to know to what seeming good and what seeming evil the retreatant is being drawn through his inner experiences in prayer and meditation. St. Ignatius himself makes this distinction, and even makes it clear that the retreatant' should feel free to go to a confessor other than the director:

> While the one who is giving the *Exercises* should not seek to investigate and know the private thoughts and sins of the exercitant, nevertheless, it will be helpful if he is kept faithfully informed about the various disturbances and thoughts caused by the action of different spirits. This will enable him to propose some spiritual exercises in accordance with the degree of progress made and suited and adapted to the needs of a soul disturbed in this way (#17).

It might be pointed out here that the director need not be a priest. He or she need only be a spiritually gifted person experienced in living the spiritual life, possessing the developed capacity to guide others, having a good knowledge of the faith, and knowing the *Spiritual Exercises* through exercise in them. This is a fact to be underscored, since if the one-to-one retreat is to proliferate, many directors will have to be drawn from religious men and women and other members of the laity. Sisters and laymen are in fact already active in directing retreats.

The retreatant needs openness and courage to give his director the necessary account. Still he does not need to steel himself to bare his whole soul, as he sometimes finds it necessary to do with his regular spiritual director, and certainly finds it necessary to do with his confessor.

Direct Communication with God

A directed retreat is a retreat in which one is guided by a director to do spiritual exercises which will purge him, illumine him, and dispose him for direct communication and communion with God, direct guidance from Him, and the readiness to do His will. This final definition gives a comprehensive idea of the directed retreat. The Ignatian directed retreat is divided into four parts or *weeks*. It was Ignatius' hope that the retreatant would really spend a whole month, apart from all other business, in making his retreat. Thirty-day retreats *are* being conducted today. More often, however, the retreat is condensed and made in a period of eight days. The first *week* provides spiritual exercises of purgation. The second *week* provides spiritual exercises of illumination which call the retreatant to a more wholehearted commitment to Jesus. The third and fourth *weeks* invite one to share Jesus' experience of passion and resurrection as a preview of one's own future in His service and life. In everything, Christ is the retreatant's life, his light, his salvation, his motivation.

The directed retreat is a search for *direct communication and communication with God.* To miss this would be to miss the meaning of the directed retreat. The preacher of the preached retreat is not really replaced by the director. He is replaced by God who Himself gives His message to the retreatant here and now. The retreatant hears God, not by words in his ears, but by the various movements in his inner life which have been described in this article as the experiences which call for discernment.

To come into a retreat with this expectation calls for deep faith in both the director and the retreatant. No doubt this faith frequently falters in both, perhaps most when they are least aware of the fact. Some directors may not even have the conviction that this direct communication and communion with God should take place, but then they are betraying their trust, for it is inescapably clear that this is the expectation and absolute conviction of the author of the *Exercises.* He writes:

> The director of the *Exercises* ought not to urge the exercitant more to poverty or any promise than to the contrary, nor to one state of life or way of living more than another. Outside the *Exercises,* it is true, we may lawfully and meritoriously urge all who probably have the required fitness to choose continence, virginity, the religious life, and every form of religious perfection. But while one is engaged in the *Spiritual Exercises,* it is more suitable and much better that the Creator and Lord in person communicate Himself to the devout soul in quest of the divine will, that He inflame it with His love and praise, and dispose it for the way in which it could better serve God in the future (#15).

What Ignatius expects is that the retreatant will, by making the *Exercises,* repeat some of his own experiences of God guiding him. Those experiences were so vivid that Ignatius called God his "Schoolmaster."

Let me point out here by way of example that we customarily describe the attraction to the priesthood as a "vocation," a "call" from God. St. Ignatius is simply broadening the base of that belief by affirming that God calls us directly to many things, to little things, every day, if we can hear His voice and if we will respond to it. God's call is experienced through the inner movements of love, joy, peace, attraction to a better way, and so forth. According to Karl Rahner, S.J., this is a case of grace breaking into consciousness. In essence, therefore, the directed retreat is meant to be a mystical retreat. It is a series of spiritual exercises and prayers and contemplations in search of the experience of God and the reading out of His will. It is a transcendental relationship breaking into consciousness.

Directed versus Preached Retreat

It should be of help to add a brief comparison of the directed and the preached retreat. The directed retreat is the authentic presentation of the

Spiritual Exercises. This is a fact of history, but it also stands from an examination of the introductory observations in the *Spiritual Exercises.* Still, that does not mean that the directed retreat is always best for everyone, in every set of circumstances. St. Ignatius makes it clear in the *Exercises* themselves that not everyone is suited for them or ready for them. Nor are they necessarily better for anyone, year after year. They have a certain inherent advantage in that they guide the retreatant to listen directly to God Himself. On the other hand, there are times when God Himself sends us to men, as He did Paul after his conversion experience. Many factors must be weighed in determining which type of retreat will be best: the level of human maturity; the level of religious maturity; the personal needs at the moment, such as the need of making a decision concerning a state of life; the level of generosity, of restfulness, of vitality.

The preached retreat remains of immense value when it is well conducted.

I support this simply by appeal to the years of experience which most of us have had in making such retreats and which some of us have had in conducting them. Furthermore, preached retreats are excellent opportunities for hearing the word of God, and men always remain bearers of that word. There is no substitute for the preached word of God, just as there is no substitute for the inner experience of God. Then, too, the preached retreat is an opportunity to share the personal faith vision and synthesis of the retreat master who can often communicate his experience with the help of some specialized theological, sociological, or psychological competence.

What it comes to is that the preached and the directed retreat are two species of retreat. Each has its own unique value, and each addresses itself to unique needs. The directed retreat is of unsurpassed value for times when serious decisions have to be made. It is also of unsurpassed value in providing a guided and formative experience in living the interior life. It has great value in helping a person find direct communication with God and in coming to other primary religious experiences.

The preached retreat is especially valuable for broadening and articulating our knowledge and vision of the faith. This helps us overcome our personal limitations and biases, so that we can formulate a more comprehensive response to God. It helps us supply for our personal lack of initiative in overcoming our deficiencies. It can stir new faith in us, for belief is communicated by believers; and it can stir new love of God in us, for love is communicated by lovers. In brief, the preached retreat is especially valuable in those times when for one reason or another, we need the word of God preached to us through the agency of men.

If this information and these norms do not yet make it clear which retreat you should prefer, I would offer one piece of advice. Experiment. Try the one you haven't experienced. For St. Ignatius, the need for experimentation was one of the fundamental principles of the spiritual life.

The Retreat Director in the
Spiritual Exercises

Paul J. Bernadicou, S.J.

Volume 26, 1967, pp. 672-684.

The book of the *Spiritual Exercises* is a rich compendium of Christian spirituality. From its contents whole treatises could be developed on the manner and progress of prayer, on the role of penance in Christian asceticism, on the methods of Christian decision-making, on the appropriately Christian image of God, on discerning God's true action within one's spirit.

But the particular focus of this paper is not directly on this carefully wrought spiritual doctrine: our concern is more with the one who is responsible for the use of it: the retreat director.[1]

The book itself would seem to have been written with the director, not

---

[1]At the outset, I should express a very personal gratitude to Fr. David Asselin, S.J., (Regis College, Toronto) whose enlightened understanding of and instruction on the role of the spiritual director started me in pursuit of this topic. He has suggested most of the relevant insights which I attempt to express.

There is reason to question whether the title "retreat director" (or "spiritual director") is the best choice for the one who gives the *Exercises*. To my knowledge, the term is never found in the *Exercises* themselves—usually we find "he who gives the exercises" (*el que da los exercicios*). The title "instructor" seems better suited to the nonauthoritarian role he assumes in the *Exercises;* even though he instructs and guides, he must be a supple instrument of the Spirit who is the actual director and guide of the exercitant in an individualized encounter of love. Charles Jacquet, whose excellent article I have followed in the latter half of the paper, has in fact opted for this title. "Spiritual counselor" may also have some appeal as a choice since it too underlines the instrumental role of the retreat giver, but its shortcoming is that it seems too passive for the actively instructional side of the retreat master's task. I have decided to retain the more conventional title of director if only to clarify its properly instrumental meaning in the context of the *Exercises* and to divest it of a false aura of authoritarianism.

the exercitant, chiefly in mind. That it was composed at a time when printed books were still a very costly rarity would lead one to suppose this was the case. The text itself corroborates this supposition; its prenotes (called Annotations), which form a kind of preface for its use, are addressed to the director who is to control the unfolding of its exercises and contents for the exercitant. Indeed it is explicitly stated in these Annotations that it is better if the exercitant does not know the matter which is to come, so that he may concentrate his full attention on what has already been given for his consideration (11).[2]

We investigate in the first section what the *Exercises* themselves say or imply about the role of the director. The next section attempts to describe somewhat more fully the two main functions of the director which follow from what the *Exercises* say about his role.

Throughout this paper, we have in mind the full exercises of thirty days, as envisaged in the book itself. The translations from the text are the writer's own from the Spanish autograph copy.[3]

What the *Spiritual Exercises* Say about the Director

It is especially in the twenty Annotations (or prenotes) to his *Exercises* that Ignatius spells out the role of the director, for they control the use which the director makes of the book's contents.

Here is an outline of the main statements which these Annotations make on the role of the director:

(1) It is his task to plan and adapt the progression of meditations and contemplations during the course of the Four Weeks according to the needs of the exercitant; and his narration of the history for these exercises should be faithful to the mystery they present and brief (2).[4]

(2) If he discovers that there have been no spiritual motions within the retreatant, that is, no experience of desolation or consolation,[5] he should

---

[2] The numbers in parenthesis refer to the paragraph numbers of the *Exercises* which were introduced by Father Codina in his 1928 edition of the *Exercises*. They have been universally adopted since that time.

[3] The text I have used is the simplified Spanish autograph text of Jose Caiveras, S.J., *Ejercicios espirituales, directorio, y documentos de S. Ignacio de Loyola* (2d ed., Barcelona, 1958). The translation is quite literal, except where a more literary translation sufficed for the point which was being made.

[4] If Ignatius' thought is to be fully understood, there are a whole series of terms which must be invested with the meaning with which he uses them. This understanding will have to be taken for granted or bypassed in the course of this paper. One such term is the "history." It refers to the short factual or doctrinal digest on which a particular mediation or contemplation of the retreat is based and about which the director is told to inform the exercitant briefly and faithfully, (that is, saying on the point which the word, in the case of the Scriptures, communicates).

[5] "Consolation and desolation" are again Ignatian terms which must be understood with that fullness of meaning with which Ignatius uses them. An explanation cannot be given here, but

find out if the retreatant is making the exercises properly and at the appointed time; he should particularly inquire if the Additions (that is. Ignatius' suggestions on how to dispose and prepare oneself for prayer) are being followed (6).

(3) He should treat an exercitant who is suffering desolation and temptation with mildness and kindness; he should encourage him, alert him to the stratagems of the enemy,[6] and help him to prepare and dispose himself for the consolation which will come (7).

(4) When he discovers that the retreatant is undergoing various spiritual motions, he should give him the Rules for the Discernment for either the First or Second Week, depending upon his need, so that he may recognize the origin and direction of these motions and respond to them accordingly (8-10).

(5) He should caution a retreatant who is experiencing consolation from taking a vow or promise precipitously (14).

(6) He should let the Creator and Lord communicate Himself to the retreatant, "embracing him in His love and praise, and disposing him towards the way in which he can the better serve Him"; consequently, the director should maintain himself in a balance, neither urging poverty nor a promise, and allowing "the Creator to act without intermediary with His creature, and the creature with his Creator and Lord" (15).

(7) He should insist that the exercitant devote an entire hour to each exercise (12, 13).

(8) Finally, "it very much helps him who gives the exercises, while neither seeking to ask or to know the free *(proprios)* thoughts or sins of him who receives them, to be faithfully informed of the various motions *(agitaciones)* and thoughts which the various spirits cause *(traen)* him. Because, according as whether his progress is more or less great, he can give him certain spiritual exercises useful and adapted to the need of a soul so moved" (17).

Annotation 17 has been quoted in its entirety because it defines the subject matter for the dialogue between the director and the exercitant. The other Annotations provide many helpful hints for the general orientation of

---

one might refer to Ignatius' own description of what he means by the terms as given in 316 and 317 of the *Exercises*.

[6]Today we would have difficulty in throwing all the blame for our evil impulses on the enemy or "evil spirit" as Ignatius calls him. We would want to make some distinctions on how these terms are to be understood and applied. Karl Rahner has expressed the situation very succinctly and hinted at the solution: "Can we so easily admit the bad thought to 'come from without' (n.33)? Can we consider that compulsive thought to be simply suggested by the devil (n.347;349)? . . . We shall see presently that one can, without qualms, make excisions here and yet preserve the real kernel of Ignatius' idea of the divine origination of certain experiences 'from outside,' without on that account attributing to God equally and indiscriminately all that is morally unobjectionable simply because it is good, which is not what Ignatius has in mind." Karl Rahner, S.J., *The Dynamic Element in the Church* (New York, 1964), p. 121.

the director towards his role or on how he should meet particular problems which the exercitant may encounter. But our investigation particularly bears on Annotation 17 because it establishes the ground of dialogue within which all the other Annotations and directions operate so that spiritual direction achieves the end Ignatius has envisaged for it in the *Exercises*.

Let us first take notice that a distinction is implied in the Annotation between the exercitant's *"proprios pensamientos ni pecados"* (that is, his own free thoughts and sins) and *"las varias agitaciones y pensamientos, que los varios espiritus le traen"* (that is, the various motions and thoughts which the different spirits bring about in him). Ignatius explicitates the foundation for this distinction further along in his *Exercises* when he speaks of the three types of thoughts he finds in man: "the first, properly my own, which come merely from my freedom and will; and two others which come one from the good spirit and the other from the bad" (32). Although he here makes a threefold division, the distinction is basically the same: thoughts and motions that are free, and other thoughts and motions which the exercitant receives outside his free, deliberate choice from "good and evil spirits."[7]

Matter of Direction: Non-free Thoughts and Motions

Ignatius indicates that it is especially the non-free thoughts and motions in the exercitant which constitute the matter for spiritual direction. This implies that the spiritual director's role is not simply identified with that of the confessor, since the confessor, by reason of his office, is essentially concerned with absolving the *free and deliberate* failings of his penitent. In the autograph Directory for *Exercises,* Ignatius in fact differentiates the roles of retreat director and confessor: "It is better, if he [the retreatant] can do so, to confess to someone other than to the one who is giving the exercises."[8] For the respective concerns of confessor and retreat director are different. Unlike the confessor who is told the free and deliberate sins of a penitent, the director should instead be informed of the non-free movements and thoughts that the exercitant experiences, the movements and thoughts which he receives and feels rather than deliberately generates. Although the roles of confessor and spiritual director may be exercised by one individual for reasons of expediency, there is for Ignatius a fundamental distinction in the type of matter which essentially concerns them.

The *Exercises* provide many confirmations that Ignatius considers these non-free thoughts and feelings the essential terrain of spiritual direction. The whole carefully and subtly nuanced scheme for analyzing the spiritual movements with the exercitant which is formulated in the Rules for Discernment of spirits is based on the supposition that these motions are

---

[7]See the earlier note under 6.
[8]*M.H.S.J., Mon. Ign.* II, (Madrid, 1919), p. 779.

outside the exercitant's directly free decision; they *"se causan"*—are caused—within him, as the introduction to the Rules states (313). The point and purpose of the Rules is to provide a methodology through which the director and exercitant can trace the origin and spiritual value of the attractions and repugnances the exercitant experiences spontaneously welling up within himself. By the skillful sifting and discernment which these Rules teach, the exercitant comes to recognize the true action of God within himself among the many forces which play within his mind and feeling.

The passive, received character of these motions—whether from the side of good or evil—is supposed or implied throughout the Rules. For instance, "the enemy of our human nature" is compared in his manner of acting to a false lover, "who would wish to remain secret and not be discovered"; he wants his guile and insinuations kept hidden. "But when one uncovers them to a good confessor or to another spiritual person who recognizes his deceits and perversity, he is very vexed. For he concludes that he will not be able to succeed with the malice he has begun since his manifest deceits have been discovered" (326). The retreatant is here imaged as a recipient of a disturbance, however attractive to lower appetite, outside his own freely conscious design; and this is what constitutes matter for discernment and spiritual direction. It is of just such non-free spontaneous tendencies in himself that the exercitant is asked to inform the director so that with the help of his expert guidance, the exercitant may learn to experience and recognize their evil source in the very act of feeling them.

With respect to God's action within the soul, Ignatius speaks of consolation without cause; that is, spiritual consolations "which come only from God and Lord" (336). The exact meaning of this term is still a matter of discussion,[9] but we need only take notice that a distinction between non-free, received motions—this time from God—and the free intellectual activity of the exercitant is once more operative and supposed by the context.

These non-free responses and motions in man are also very significant in Ignatius' directions on prayer. It is not the matter which has been a source of intellectual clarity and insight that he recommends to the exercitant for further rumination in succeeding periods of prayer. He suggests

---

[9]In his essay, "The Logic of Concrete Individual Knowledge in Ignatius Loyola," Karl Rahner speculates on the meaning of this phrase, "consolation without cause" (*consolación sin causa precedente*), *op. cit.*, pp. 132 ff. "What is decisive is not any particular suddenness of the experience but, to put it quite plainly, its absence of object. . . . The absence of object in question is utter receptivity to God, the inexpressible, non-conceptual experience of the love of the God who is raised transcendent above all that is individual, all that can be mentioned and distinguished, of God as God. There is no longer 'any object' but the drawing of the whole person, with the very ground of his being, into love, beyond any defined circumscribable object, into the infinity of God as God himself. . . ."

rather that the exercitant direct his prayer according to the consolation and desolation which he has received during the previous exercises; that is, on the basis of his non-free, received feelings and thoughts and not as a result of his own free intellectual efforts and discursive consideration (see 62,118).

Importance of Non-free Thoughts and Motions

But in Annotation 17 Ignatius has more than stated the area of concern for spiritual direction, which we have seen verified in other places in the *Exercises*. He has also indicated the reason why he assigns such non-free thoughts and feelings to the director's charge. It is so the director might adapt the exercises to the needs of the exercitant according to the non-free motions he experiences within himself. This means that the director, as we have just seen Ignatius suggest to the exercitant, should adapt the matter and approach of an exercise of prayer to the pattern of consolation and desolation which mainfests itself in the retreatant. But it further requires that the spiritual doctrine and the program for discerning spiritual motions which he imparts to the exercitant should also be adjusted to the exercitant's experienced need (8-10).

The purpose for making these adaptations is of course to better attain the ultimate end of the entire *Exercises*. Adaptation results from the director's respectful attention to the individualized personality and grace of the exercitant so that each be led to his individual spiritual maturity at his own true pace under the personal guidance of the Spirit. This spiritual maturity which is the end of the *Exercises* is variously described in its pages; at the very start, before the exercitant has experienced much conscious awareness of the Lord's loving activity in his life, it is described in the rather negative and indeterminate phrase of ''conquering himself and ordering his life without being decided by any attachment which is disordered'' (21). But a more positive expression of what is to be expected has already been indirectly stated in the Annotation to the director in which he is told that he should allow the Creator and Lord to communicate with His creature and that he should not obtrude himself when the Creator acts on His creature and the creature with his Creator and Lord (15); in other words, Ignatius implies that he expects an intimate relationship of familiar love between the exercitant and his heavenly Father to be the result of the *Exercises*.

This intimate relationship of love, which is personalized and indivivualized by the adaptation mentioned in Annotation 17, becomes more and more particularized as the *Exercises* run their course. The retreatant makes his very personal and unique prayer for this grace at the beginning of each exercise and in the colloquy (that is, the dialogal prayer between the exercitant and his Lord) which terminates each exercise (for example, 91 and 98, 104 and 109, and so forth). In Pauline terms, the exercitant personally experiences and realizes his covenanted love with his God who comes to him in the person of His Son and who transforms him into the likeness of his Son through the power of His Love. Or it might be described as a profound experience of creaturely truth, of the *anawim* of the Old Testament, or of the spiritually poor of the beatitudes who respond in humble yet confident love to the God who has first loved them. It is the result of having personally experienced and lived through the mystery of salvation re-enacted within oneself during the successive contemplations of the *Exercises;* in the terms of the first Annotation, the exercitant has sought and found "the will of God in the disposition of his life, for the good of his soul." What is most to our purpose is to note that this result is an experience, not just intellectual insight; it is an *affectively felt response* of love for the person of a loving God and not simply clarity of vision on the content of the Christian message of salvation. Rightly, then, do the *Exercises* conclude with a Contemplation for Obtaining Love which epitomizes the lived love of a Christian who "beholds how all good things and gifts descend from above; and also justice, goodness, piety, mercy, etc, as rays descend from the sun, and water from a spring etc." (237). The retreatant has entered into complete familiarity with his heavenly Father, finding Him in all things and all things in Him. And he continues after retreat on a new plane of lived and convinced (because experienced) Christian love. The director adapts the exercises with a view to disposing the retreatant's affectivity for this experience of true order and loving openness to the visitation of the Lord who made him for His love.

To open the affectivity of the retreatant to this experience means to apply Annotation 17. In order that the cooperative effort of director and exercitant effect the exercitant's transition from self-centered disorder to a lived and affective appreciation of the Lord who loved him unto death and who handed over the Spirit on his behalf, self-knowledge and discernment of God's love within his life must intervene. How else can the exercitant disengage his affectivity from self-concentration to a full and open regard of his Lord? And enlightened awareness of his spontaneous, non-free tendencies and affective responses reveals his basic personality and the measure of God's action within him; it manifests his unique configuration of nature and grace within which he finds the Lord. For he must discern and experience, *"sentir y gustar,"* (2) feel and taste, the superiority of the Lord's peace, order, and tranquillity (334) over the narcissistic pleasures of self. By discerning the origin and tendency of his non-free thoughts and motions, which Annotation 17 indicates is the especial matter for dialogue in spiritual direction, he will come to see his genuine self and the way of true consolation and peace amid the maze of alien forces which would suppress or circumscribe his freedom.

The director is the guide on the voyage into self-discovery, and the vehicle for the journey is the knowledge on the non-free thoughts and impulses which move within the exercitant.

The Functions of the Director

In the light of the Annotations we have just studied, it is clear that the director of the thirty-day *Exercises* cannot conceive of himself as a preacher of a retreat even though it is his task to "propose to another the manner and order for meditation or contemplation" (2). Ignatius immediately adds that if the retreatant "advances and reflects for himself and if he finds something which explains or causes him to feel the history[10] a little better, either by his own reflection or because his intelligence has been illuminated by divine grace, he finds more taste and spiritual fruit than if the director had abundantly explained and developed the content of the history." A preacher-director would not foster such initiative in the exercitant and would not allow the Spirit to guide the exercitant in an individualized dialogue of love and response. The director is therefore cautioned to narrate the "history"—the factual or doctrinal data of the mystery to be meditated or contemplated—faithfully and briefly.[11]

Neither should the director conceive of himself as a conference giver. There is obviously a vast sum of doctrinal and ascetical knowledge that is imparted in the course of a thirty-day retreat. But the *Exercises* are not a classroom; they are a school of prayer, of finding the Lord in the intimacy of personal dialogue. Instead of talking learnedly about God, the director's job is to guide the exercitant to a personal discovery and experience of God. The program of contemplations of the mystery of salvation is meant to be lived through and personally experienced. The exercitant will thus personally enter into an intimate friendship with Jesus Christ which will express itself in a loving concern for Him as He is found in the Church and in his fellowman.

The retreatant will doubtless have acquired a great fund of knowledge about the Christian life during the retreat: about prayer, the attractiveness of Jesus Christ, the operations of the Spirit in himself and in the Church. But these instructions will not have been the main objective of the director, and neither will they be the main and most important result of the *Exercises*. For the exercitant will have been initiated into the experience of loving the person of God in Jesus Christ and of serving Him in his brothers and in the Church.

The Annotations, particularly 17 as we have seen advise the director on how to set up the environment in which this personal experience of God can develop and mature. Reductively, they call for a twofold effort on the part

---

[10]See the earlier remark on Ignatian terms under note 4.

[11]In developing the thought of this whole article, I have very closely followed an excellent article by Charles Jacquet, S.J., "L'instructeur de la retraite," *Christus*, 1956, pp. 208-24. Of a more general nature but also helpful have been: Joseph Stierli, "L'art de la direction," *Christus*, 1960, pp. 22-46; Jean Laplace, "La formation du directeur," *Christus*, 1960, pp. 47-63.

of the director: he proposes the matter of the exercises for the prayerful consideration of the exercitant, and he interprets the action of the Spirit in the exercitant's life.

The Director Proposes

The director is the one who introduces the exercises one after another, Week by Week, to the exercitant. He follows the pattern of the Four Weeks, gradually unfolding to the exercitant the mystery and order of salvation in which, as a son of God, he participates. In this enterprise a very creative effort is required of the director. He is expected to initiate the exercitant into an individualized experience of the Spirit; this is the real aim of the thirty-day retreat, not just to offer a list of exercises which are suppose to automatically produce a guaranteed result. To achieve his aim, the director must himself be versed in the way of God, must know how to interpret His way of acting with a human being so that he really adapts the exercises to His action in a particular retreatant.

Clearly, there is no simple technique which will lead everyone to a personal experience of God. Each such encounter is a unique instance, unprecedented and never to be repeated in the whole history of human encounter with God. But at least the willingness of the retreatant to participate in this dialogue should have been ascertained as a qualification for making the full *Exercises* (18,19,20). No one can consciously experience intimacy with God, unless he freely opens himself to His presence and call. This is the very first condition for making the *Exercises*. A retreat made under constraint is necessarily a poorly made retreat.

But to those who "undertake these Exercises with a large heart and with generosity towards their Creator and Lord, offering to him all their will and freedom" (5) the word of God speaks. It will be the director's task to make this word intelligible to the retreatant by presenting it in a very personalized fashion, adapted to the need and capacity of the exercitant. This form of pedagogy characterizes the *Exercises* throughout their Four Weeks. It means that the director's presentation must be simple and taylor-made. Its lived application will, as a consequence, be authentic and vital, true to the individual person for whom the director molds his instruction.

With Charles Jacquet, let us take for an example the practical bit of advice that Ignatius gives for prayer: Before commencing my contemplation or my meditation, at a step or two removed from the place of prayer, "I will stand for the space of an Our Father, my mind raised upwards, considering how God our Lord looks at me etc., and I will make an act of respect or of humility" (75).[12]

When the director explains this practical recommendation, he is helping the retreatant to see by a very simple method, what proper reverence for

---

[12]Jacquet, "L'instructeur," p. 216.

God means: it is a gesture if filial respect "in His presence." Otherwise it is merely a façade which we project, consciously or unconsciously, for ourselves or others. By such simple, practical, and inductive means, the Exercises lead to authentic religious experience in a way that is immediately and fully intelligible to every exercitant.

The director moreover realizes that what he proposes is only a framework in which God Himself should be expected to intervene. He therefore disposes the retreatant psychologically and religiously for these unpredictable but expected and awaited interventions which alone accomplish the divine will within the exercitant. The director's job is to orient the retreatant for this experience so that he "looks for the divine will, which the Creator and Lord Himself communicates to the soul devoted to Him, embracing it in His love and praise, and disposing it for the way which it may the better serve Him" (15). The director expects this action of God upon the soul. His very words and manner are an expression of this hope. His one aim is to orient the retreatant towards a personal encounter with the Lord, an experience which transcends what can be predicted at any step as it subsumes within a present advance in intimacy all the progress of the past. Is there any reason to be astonished at such happenings? They are after all the intended goal and purpose of the *Exercises*.

An essential ramification of this new personal experience of intimacy with God is described by Jacquet:

> . . . there is question not only of an art of prayer, but more broadly of an art of living. The retreatant who has met the Lord is henceforth more faithfully attached to His steps, as a companion and friend. The instructor not only proposes methods of prayer but also methods for making decisions. He aids the soul of good will to concrete its light and generosity on the precise points to which the honor and glory of the Divine Majesty call it.[13]

The *Exercises* are in a real sense a course in Christian decision-making, of finding God in all things, "of looking for and finding the divine will in the orienting of his life (*'en la disposición de su vida'*)" (1). It is part of the director's task to make the exercitant aware of this dynamic union between light received and lived response. As occasion allows and indicates, in obedience to the spirit's lead, the director helps the retreatant to realize that his love finds its adequate expression only in the service of the church and fellowman.

The Director Interprets

The director however misses an important function of his office if he only proposes the exercises for prayer and decision-making, even though these exercises be adapted to the needs of the exercitant's own individ-

---

[13]Ibid., p. 217.

uality. He would then perform like a very clever but detached observer.

He must in addition be the *interpreter* of God's action in the soul of the exercitant; he stands beside the exercitant as a witness to the dawn of a new life within this exercitant and he must help him translate his newly discovered fidelity to the Lord into action and lived love.

Just as the exercitant has come to the retreat master in order to get an account of the matter for his prayerful consideration, so he must now, in his turn, relate to the director what has transpired as the result in his inner experience. The director must be informed of his spiritual experiences—or of their absence—if he is to interpret their source and meaning.

It may be—in fact, in the context of the thirty-day retreat it will almost always be—that the retreat master is not normally the director of the retreatant's conscience, since he will go back home to his regular director. If so, the director's mission is clear: he assists this particular Christian at an important time in his spiritual development; in a time if struggle and crisis, in a moment of grace, he aids the retreatant by his understanding of the manner and ways of God. This function, in a less intensive degree outside the time of retreat, applies to every director of souls; he acts as instructor and interpreter in the ways of God with man.

He ought to be informed then of the interior movements which the *Exercises* provoke. Every day, during the course of the Four Weeks, he should speak with the exercitant, for a brief session, to find out how he is doing and what his experiences have been, to suggest to him the appropriate matter for meditation or contemplation and to encourage him in more difficult periods:

> It is important that he should obtain his [the exercitant's] confidence. Let him offer the exercitant the support of a friendly and assured presence; let him be "more kindly than austere." But, by general rule, their conversation will be brief: it is well to respect the silence of the soul and especially the action of the Holy Spirit, the principal artisan in the work which has been undertaken. Servant of a baptized soul and of the operations of the Spirit in it, the instructor is the "helper of divine grace" who attracts this Christian to a distinguished service of Christ and of the Church."

This action of the Spirit should be the focus of all his attention. And for this reason, as we have seen, St. Ignatius recommended that, except in a particular case of need, the director leave to another priest the care of the retreatant's confessions. The interior events in the exercitant, to which the silence, the solitude, the contemplation of the mysteries of salvation in an atmosphere of intimate friendship with his Creator and Lord give rise, must be traced back to their source, to their orientation for good or for bad, to their ultimate effect on his life in the true Spirit. In this task of discernment, the director uses his knowledge of theology and his experience, both personal and from directing others, of the spiritual life. But most especially, he

---

[14]Ibid., pp. 219-20.

uses St. Ignatius' Rules for the Discernment of Spirits:

> The series of twenty Annotations, and especially the double series of Rules for the Discernment of Spirits, constitute without a doubt the most remarkable effort to put in simple formulas the practical science of discerning the ways of God. These sections, which are among the most original in the *Exercises,* are properly addressed to the director who is constantly inspired by them in his mission of interpreter.[15]

We cannot here go into a detailed study of these efficiently simple yet carefully nuanced Rules.[16] If the director learns to apply them in a skilful docility to the movements of the Spirit, he plays a privileged role in advancing the history of salvation, for he actually assists the spirit in filling out a unique page of human history. In the measure that he succeeds, he will respect and marvel at the fidelity and grace of God Who never ceases in His love for men, each of whom He calls by name.

Conclusion

Thus the *Exercises* attain their aim. They will have mediated a personal relationship of love between the exercitant and his Lord and have helped the exercitant to find the individualized nature of his call from God. The *Exercises* put a person in possession of himself, insofar as it is possible in our human state; more exactly, they put one in possession of his personal grace so that he accepts, lucidly and consciously, his full role in the service of Christ in the Church.

The director has the privilege of being an instrument in this new work of God's gracious love by fulfilling his role as advocate and interpreter in this action. His can be the joy of serving the Spirit in His mission of love and fulfillment for men.

---

[15]Ibid., p. 220.

[16]Many excellent articles have been published in *Christus* on the subject of the discernment of spirits, particularly by Maurice Giuliani, as for example, "Les motions de l'Esprit," *Christus,* 1954, pp. 62.76. A very enlightening article is also by Jean Laplace, "L'expérience du discernment." *Christus,* 1954, 4, pp. 28-49.

Growing Freedom in the Spiritual Director

George P. Leach, S.J.

Volume 32, 1973, pp. 834-842.

In the past few years there has been a great surge of interest in spiritual direction. The re-birth of the personally directed retreat, the keen interest in spiritual discernment, both personal and communal, and the concern for ongoing, personal direction and guidance in spiritual growth are all evidence of this renewal and revitalization within the spiritual life. Countless religious women, many diocesan priests, and a number of Canadian bishops have made the thirty-day Spiritual Exercises of St. Ignatius. Numberless priests, sisters, and laymen have experienced shorter prayer encounters. Different communities, especially at chapter proceedings, have adopted a communal discernment process to discover the Father's will in their present situation. Flowing from all of these experiences is the great awareness of God's Spirit in the life of the Church with its concomitant need for spiritual direction, the discernment of God's Spirit in His People.

The Spiritual Director

With this new awareness of God's action in men's lives the importance of a spiritual director, a discerning, faith-filled person, receives increasing emphasis. In a retreat the director is called upon to help clarify and discern where the Spirit is leading the retreatant. In community discernment the leader prays and reflects in order to be aware of the movement of the Spirit in the whole group. In continuing, personal direction the director calls the person to see the Lord's action in his daily life so that he might grow through responsible decisions and a developing commitment. The spiritual director meets the person at the deep level of faith, at the core of his spiritual experience. At this meeting point spiritual direction emerges.

Within this interpersonal relationship there are many levels of engagement. There is always the possibility of a friendly chat, a sharing of experiences, or an informative session. This is not spiritual direction. There are all the psychological dynamics that arise between any counselor and counselee, doctor and patient, or director and directee. A certain knowledge of these is very helpful. There are many movements, both spiritual and psychological, within the person desiring direction but there are equally as many movements within the director. This is my focal point. What is happening within the director? Within himself, what is he aware of in the directing situation? How does he grow in his own freedom in order to assist the other to grow in freedom and response to the Lord?

Varied Awarenesses

There are many experiences that arise in a directing relationship. The director will quickly realize that some people wish to be assisted in their spiritual growth but spend all the time talking around the pertinent points. They are hesitant to respond to any questions and find it very difficult to share at the faith level. But what is happening in the director at this time? Or, is the director talking all around the point himself? When the director becomes aware of this problem from discerning his own reactions to the situation, what can he do if the person still continues to speak loquaciously and avoid the point? Sometimes the director meets a person who is terribly frightened and can hardly speak at all. Other people will try to dominate or control the director. Needless to say, angry people pose another problem, as does the quiet person, the "joker," the touchy man or woman and the myriad of other personalities that surface in the directing relationship. What does the director do when he becomes conscious of these or similar dynamics in the relationship?

When the director discerns within himself that some dynamic is hindering the direction, he must act to correct it. If he is conscious of what the basic dynamic is, for example, if he realizes that the person is retiring and fearful, then he will move to alleviate this fear. If he perceives that the person is angry, then he will move to meet the anger. The important factor lies in how he handles his own reactions to the fear, anger, or whatever is emerging. He must be conscious of his own feelings, thoughts, and mode of action in each situation. He must be in touch with himself so that he is *not re-acting to* the person but *acting for* the person.

The directee's mood, attitude, or presence must not control or manipulate the director; rather, he must be ready to meet each person where he is and in the state of being in which he is expressing himself. His aim is to develop a trusting relationship in which the other person can speak freely and openly. This may take days, weeks, or months depending upon the persons involved. But, as this rapport grows, the person is able to share more easily his faith experiences, his prayer encounters, and the movements of the Spirit within him. This is the dawning of spiritual direction.

A Trusting Relationship

In any situation of spiritual direction a trusting relationship is primary. If the person does not trust the director, spiritual direction is well nigh impossible. But where does the trusting relationship begin? How does it grow?

Any relationship starts when the two people meet. There are the natural exchanges and pleasantries but there is also the non-verbal, what is not said. As a person talks and begins to dialogue, he is revealing himself. The director must be aware of what is going on in himself during these initial stages of the meeting. What is the directee speaking about? What is his tone of voice? What is he revealing? And more important, what is all this saying to the director? What is he experiencing during these moments? Is he comfortable? Uncomfortable? Peaceful? Uneasy? What is happening inside him?

Of course, there is also all the non-verbal communication. How does the person sit? What are they doing with their eyes, their hands, their feet, or anything else that may be communicative? The director attentively receives all these communications, discerns how they affect him, and then moves to appropriate action.

If the person is fearful, he meets him with love and concern. If the person is slow and lethargic, he waits patiently, especially if he is having difficulty expressing himself. If the person is lively and energetic, he listens quietly and peacefully meeting him with stillness and calm. In whatever state the person is, the director must call him to meet the Lord. This will usually be done by calling him to a balanced stance of life and to do this the director rests at a point of equilibrium and balance himself.

As the relationship continues, the trust will grow as the directee experiences regard, respect, and reverence from the director. As the director listens, questions, dialogues, he does so with deep caring and real concern. The person begins to sense this regard. The trust is growing. As the relationship progresses, the director will be respecting more and more the person as a person, a creature loved by the Creator into whose spiritual life he has been invited. As the openness comes and the person speaks more freely, the relationship deepens and trust grows even more. A profound reverence for the person naturally grows in the director as he unfolds the mystery of God's presence within himself. This often produces wonder, awe, and gratitude in the director.

The basis for this growth in regard, respect, and reverence in the relationship rests upon a loving acceptance of the directee by the director. If the directee has a theological question, for example, some doubt in faith, or struggle with a moral question, the director accepts the problem and responds. If the directee presents a personal problem arising from community tension or personal stress, the director accepts the person and meets him in his present reality. It would obviously be very disturbing in a retreat context if a person came to pray but had a very pressing problem and failed to face it. The director must meet the person in the reality of his life with loving acceptance. This provides the ground for the trusting relationship from which emerges spiritual discernment and direction.

Self-knowledge: For Freedom

From varied direction encounters the director can learn a great deal about himself. There are many opportunities for his personal growth in freedom. Through personal reflection and honest feed-back from others he will find frequent occasions to grow as a person and develop as a director. Through coming to know himself honestly, through his personal and communal prayer, through the integration of all his activities of life and, of course, through personal discernment and direction, he comes to wholeness in Christ. He attains a new freedom in the Spirit which enables him to direct others more freely towards the Father.

His freedom to respond to the Spirit makes him conscious of how the Spirit is moving and how he is responding. At the same time as he feels the Trinity drawing him, his growing self-awareness sharpens his sense of his own needs, disorders, and sinful tendencies. He realizes that there are shades and shadows in himself that can hinder his direction and the work of the Spirit in others. He becomes attuned to his own reactions in situations. He realizes that he is unfree, chained, and bound up in himself at times. He knows when he is nervous and begins to realize what that can do to another. He catches his fearful tendencies before they hurt the relationship. He holds his disappointment or hurt quietly within, not to distract the other. These are but a few of the spontaneous reactions that the director can and ought to be aware of if he is to keep the spiritual direction in its proper perspective and grow in freedom.

Of course, there can be deeper needs or disorders operating in the director. A director may have a great need for approval; he may have a deep rooted desire to be liked; he may have a dominating need to talk about himself; he may have to control the situation or be in the power position at all times; he may have a great fear of failure; or, it may be some other deep need or disorder that is running the relationship. The important fact to face is what need is operating and whose need is it? There is a basic and crucial kind of self-knowledge that is paramount in any directing relationship. Without it his spiritual direction of others suffers and his personal discernment is questionable.

Growth in self-knowledge, in awareness of the various movements in one's heart, is a basic requirement in directing others. This, of course, does not mean that a director should not have needs or cannot have disorders, but it does point to a knowledge of himself so that his needs and disorders do not dominate or control the situation. Rather, they create an opportunity for growing freedom in the director to assist the directee to grow in Christ. The director realizes very quickly that he does have disorders, but they need not be obstacles to the other. In fact his own awareness will assist him and at times make him more sensitive to another's need. This self-knowledge can be a source of freedom to the director which can greatly aid him in his direction of others.

Shared Responsibility

This growth in personal freedom allows the director to be free in his direction. As he personally experiences his own freedom, he desires to call forth the freedom in another. As he tastes his own expansion of person and personality, he hopes for an opening up in others. The seed of freedom may rest dormant but its awakening is very much part of his direction. He calls to growth by gentleness, by understanding, by cajoling, by teasing, by confrontation, or by whatever way he is led by the Spirit to invite the person to a free response to the Father. He is ever aware of the delicacy and tenderness of the garden of the soul in which he has been invited to be, to act, to direct. This is his responsibility and he is freely responding.

In exercising this responsibility the director ought to be aware of a balanced or perhaps what we might call a "shared responsibility." He may have the tendency to take all the responsibility. For example, in a directed retreat he may find himself making many of the small decisions about the retreat and determining countless other tiny details. But if the retreatant makes most of these decisions himself he will be acting responsibly even at this level. From the outset of the retreat the director should ask the retreatant to exercise his freedom and decision-making ability. This shares the responsibility and both are ready to move as the Spirit leads.

The need for shared responsibility rests on the conviction that a person is free, can change, and will grow in Christ with the presence of the director as a catalyst in this development. The director must believe this deeply and act accordingly. To avoid the danger of spiritual spoonfeeding, he encourages the directee to take an active participation in the relationship. He discerns with the person, not for him; he makes suggestions, looks for options, and at times directs; but he leaves the responsibility with the person.

The director should always distinguish an overly dependent relationship from a freeing and expanding one. If his needs or disorders are blocking the way, he could unconsciously be controlling the person and placing him in a very passively dependent position. Obviously, this will cause problems.

Although there are many possible reactions, the directee could respond in two basic ways. The passive person will fall naturally into the direction and give over all the responsibility for decision-making to the director. He could appear as a very good retreatant or directee but when the experience concludes, where does he turn, or to whom, for his decision-making? Take the religious who wants the director to tell him to leave his religious community. This would be crippling and passive dependence at its worst since it would be robbing the person of his responsibility.

A second reaction comes from the active person. If the director begins to make too many of the decisions, usually this person reacts negatively. There can be a struggle, a verbal battle, and a tense situation. The clash can come for many reasons but the director must be aware that he is meeting this type of person. Such a person will need more leeway, more freedom to orient the growth towards and in Christ. Both persons, however, will need careful discernment but from different viewpoints. Whoever the person is and whatever kind of personality he has, the director must always be free enough to allow him to assume the responsibility for his own life so that he can grow in his response to Christ.

The Director's Faith

Trusting faith is a strong and necessary factor in the life of the director. He has great need of this gift of the Spirit. As he responds, discerns, and directs the person, his faith comes to the fore, at least in his own consciousness. His personal trust in the Father, his realization that Christ is the only true director, and his dependence upon the Holy Spirit for inspiration quickly surface. His faith in the Trinity to effect this growth in the directee is essential.

The true grace and growth for the director may be to realize how weak his own faith is; but as he trusts in the Father, Son, and Holy Spirit, so he will be ready to meet the person and move with the Spirit acting in him. He realizes how much and with what longing the Lord wants to move in this person and in himself. He must believe this and at times call the person to this same kind of faith. Many times the moment of conversion, the time of grace, comes when the person also believes this. When the person experiences the love of God that Paul speaks of in Romans 5:5, through His grace, the act of faith becomes easy—the experience is real, and faith flowers. The director rejoices at the re-birth of a Christian, as the Spirit touches both uniquely.

The Director and Prayerfulness

It seems unnecessary to say, but prayer is essential for the director. That the director present himself to the Father in total dependence, as eminently poor in spirit, that he relate to Christ as his guide, and that he remain open to the movements of the Spirit are all obvious enough but often forgotten. The director's habitual and prayerful presence to the Trinity brings a tone, an attitude, a deeply spiritual dimension to the relationship. It is actually a sine qua non for direction.

This prayerful presence to God overflows in a personal presence to the person. It assures a faith foundation in the relationship. It focuses the attention on the Trinitarian awareness in the person. It fosters faith and places the relationship at the level beyond psychology, within or without, above or below, but very much in a presence that, on the one hand, includes the dynamics of human psychology but, on the other, goes beyond and transcends it. It is the reality where the believer meets the believer, where both meet Christ in the other and in himself. Prayer, then, calls forth faith as the director guides the person in his personal discernment.

Growing Maturity

Of the many qualities in a director a certain maturity greatly assists spiritual direction. A psychological, theological, and spiritual maturity provides an integrated base upon which the director himself can grow and direct others in their growth. While I realize that there are multiple factors in psychological maturity, I would like to suggest two important elements: the ability to sustain a trusting relationship and the openness to grow in affective balance.

Each person must accept the other, have patience, be willing to wait, and above all move with loving concern in the relationship. Any sign of rancor, anger, fear could jeopardize real growth unless the director discerned a necessary confrontation or expression of feelings for the good of the directee. This would obviously come from the need of the directee and not from a frustration of the director. The director needs the ability to move, develop, and sustain the relationship.

Secondly, he has affective balance when he has a mature emotional life outside the retreat or directing relationship. If the director has his emotional needs met in his community, with his relatives and friends, then he is more able to meet the needs of the directee. If not, there is the danger that he will use the directee to meet his own personal needs. The dangers are obvious. Thus, the director needs a basic psychological wholeness.

Theological Knowledge

In the integration process of the director there is a certain prerequisite of theological knowledge and maturity. In retreat work he will need a basic Scriptural knowledge with a desire to stay abreast of developing Scriptural trends. He also ought to have a basic knowledge of dogmatic and moral theology. Scripture may or may not play a part in ongoing direction, but dogma certainly will. That a person have a solid foundation in Christology, especially the Incarnation and Redemption, is central. For Christ to be born in poverty and called to the ultimate poverty of the cross is the reality beckoning each Christian. That each of us passes through the Passion to the Resurrection is the core of Christian living. As Christ said to the disciples on the way to Emmaus: "Was it not ordained that Christ should suffer and so enter into his glory?" (Lk 24:26). Whether we are in a retreat or in our daily life, this reality of the paschal mystery is with us. It is the foundation of our Christian lives.

I might add more about many areas of theology, but my final thought is to invite the director to theological openness. He quickly realizes that he cannot stay abreast of all the developments in theology. Since he knows that this is impossible, he must remain open and free with a readiness to listen and learn. He will need resources when problems arise. His openness will take him to consult experts and scholars. His humility will keep him reading and in dialogue over theological and spiritual matters. This approach will reveal his interest in a method or process, rather than a solution orientation to every possible problem. Hopefully he will have this dynamism, this search orientation, to continue to grow, change, and develop as he directs others from this theological base and personal integration.

Spiritual Maturity

To be spiritually mature is our third integrating factor. There is, of course, a theoretical level which is directly related to his theological awareness. This arises from reading, studying, and dialoguing about spirituality. It goes without saying that this is important. There is also, however, a lived spirituality. The director who actually prays, lives poorly, obeys freely, and loves chastely becomes a viable sign, a living reality. This too is equally fundamental. The Father invites him to this authentic wholeness in Christ; He calls him to be like His Son; He prompts him through the Spirit to be totally supple and free. Indeed, the director experiences the invitation to grow spiritually in directing others. It becomes a mutual growth, a two-way-spiritual-street, a shared faith which urges the director to continued spiritual integration and freedom.

Expanding Freedom

The director's freedom expands as he lives his loving fidelity, experiences his poverty of spirit, and prays for continuing, personal discernment to assist himself and others in their spiritual life. His personal freedom to respond in faith to the Trinity and to God's People increases as he lives his faith lovingly each day in each situation. His freedom also deepens as he accepts himself as a creature dependent upon his loving Creator. The Lord meets his spiritual poverty with His riches. He patiently awaits the movement of the Spirit, the grace of discernment, the wisdom with which to direct. He is sometimes deeply humbled to be so near and so much part of Christ's Spirit in others, but this is His call, His invitation, His gift.

The fear to move with someone in this spiritual labyrinth is a temptation. The courage to move quietly and cautiously, however, is a grace. So many people are aching to speak of the Spirit and of spiritual movements in their being, but so many priests seem to be hesitant to enter this realm of reality. That a priest would fear to speak of the holy, the sacred, the sacramental, the Spirit, or that a sister would shy away from sharing faith, inviting to prayer, or speaking of Christ, or that a director would never ask specific, spiritual questions about prayer, about life, about love, all reveals a great poverty. The Church is certainly in need of spiritual persons who value prayer, live faith, discern experiences, and move with a Trinitarian view in the ebb and flow of the Christian life.

Appealing to Strength in Spiritual Direction

William J. Connolly, S.J.

Volume 32, 1973, pp. 1060-1063.

The term "spiritual direction" has many meanings today. It can refer to the precepts of a religious superior, advice, the offering of a willing ear, and to many other situations involving the discussion of religion and morality. Its primary intention may be personal growth, observance of law, relief from anxiety, or any one of a number of other goals.

For the purpose of this article I will see spiritual direction as an attempt to help a person to grow in prayerful response to the Spirit. This attempt will include the willing ear, may include advice, and may well result in relief from anxiety and more respectful observance of law. But its primary goal is growth, the development of lived dialogue with the Lord. Understanding spiritual direction in this way, the article will suggest that there is an approach to "direction" that concentrates primarily on a person's strengths and another that concentrates primarily on his weaknesses, and that the choice between these approaches is a crucial one.

A Concrete Case

To propose the question in concrete terms: A priest in his 40's is a member of a religious community and a successful college professor. He has no worries about his professional future, but finds himself frequently at odds with communal decisions made in the house where he lives. He is irked, too, by the presence in his house of a group that meets regularly for shared prayer. These and other difficulties have led him to think of moving to another house. His present house, however, is convenient, and the prospect of a move forbidding. During his annual retreat he goes to one of the retreat-house staff to talk over these questions.

Immediately, two options open for the director. He can confine himself to discussing the problems as they are presented, or he can help the man to situate them in his life context by encouraging him to ask himself: "Who am I? What do I want from life? What do I want to give to life?"

The problems, impasses, and difficulties represent the person's weak side. This is not to say that they are unimportant. Concentration on them rather than on the identity questions will not, however, make him a gospel person but will instead weaken his confidence and sense of identity. For there is something infinite about problems. The more we concentrate on them, the more of them there are. The danger in discussing the community problems without confronting the identity questions is that once the man has solved these problems he will be faced with new problems and will be no closer to developing a core of strength from which he can solve or avoid them.

Facing the Lord

"Who am I? What do I want?" on the other hand develops in prayer into "Who is the Lord to me? Who am I to the Lord?" The Lord's own strength and generosity come to be seen more clearly in the dialogue of prayer and come to have a deeper, more personal meaning. The person sees the Lord's love as his own strength, as accepting him in his weakness, and as calling him to creativity. He comes to identify himself as recipient of the Lord's love and generosity and to see his own freedom and creativity as given and guaranteed by the Lord.

As he faces the Lord by listening to His word and personally reacting to it, he becomes simpler, deeper, broader. The fact of letting the Lord become more real to him and of letting his deeper feelings emerge in prayer brings about this simplifying, deepening, broadening effect—a result which is not brought about by the mere solving of problems.

From this core a person can grow. Whenever he begins to be enmeshed in his weaknesses, he can draw again on this point from which growth takes place. He will observe that while he is in contact with it he has a sense of peace and confidence. Away from it he tends to be aimless and floundering.

If the priest with community problems can put himself before the Lord and converse with Him as giver of life, freedom, healing, and spiritual sight, and can see himself called to share the experience of Jesus, he will begin to develop resources that will enable him to deal with or healthily ignore these problems, and in doing so develop strength to deal with other problems in the future.

Strength from the Lord

The strength a person discovers in prayer is not his own natural talents —his intelligence, his physical strength, his poetic or musical ability—

although his discovery or rediscovery of these talents often follows on the finding of himself which takes place in prayer. His real strength is from the Lord and is seen in prayer as coming from the Lord. The Lord's love for him with all his scars and mutilations is the core of this strength; his recognition of this love gives him the assurance to acknowledge his weakness, claim it as his own, and go to the trouble of learning to deal with it.

The key danger in encouraging a person to plunge about among his weaknesses lies in the enmeshing, fascinating effect produced on each of us by our own problems. He may become so preoccupied with them that he will never let himself look at the Lord. Conflict situations for instance, with the pull they exercise on his fears, angers, and guilt can keep him so fascinated, even for years, that he never directs attention to who the Lord is for him. However, a person must be in contact with his own reality if the Lord is to be real to him, and this means he must not exclude his weaknesses from his awareness.

Eventually, as the person finds assurance in his strength-from-the-Lord, both his natural talents and his strength-from-experience will come together with his weaknesses as a new constellation in his awareness. He will see himself in a new way, with realism and hope.

His strength will show itself in creativity, increasing breadth of mind and affection, deepening reflection. A person's weakness appears in his lack of creativity, in narrowness and shallowness. We are called to a compassion that is as broad and deep as the Father's, so that any lack of breath or depth of sympathy is a sign that we are not yet wholly alive.

Our strength is our link with the Lord; our weakness is our failure to receive fully from Him, our tendency to be someone we are not with Him.

Strength shows itself in a growing integration, weakness in a scattering of forces. Strength moves toward submission to the Lord, toward a willingness to do what we would prefer not to do; weakness guards itself, takes care of itself. Signs of strength are an undogmatic assurance, flexibility in change, interest in others, an ability to pray without great difficulty, freedom to choose distasteful courses of action, an earthy hopefulness.

A Matter of Crucial Importance

The choice between emphasis on strength and emphasis on weakness is one of the elements of spiritual direction in which the director's view of his role is of crucial importance. If he sees himself primarily as a defender of law and order, he will focus on violations of law and so distract the person he is directing from the development of strength. If he is fascinated by problems, he will allow and even encourage an emphasis on them. If he likes to tell people what to do, weakness will be an opportunity for him. The director has to remain aware that because helping a person to grow offers few quick rewards to either the director or the person seeking help, he will often be tempted to try the short cut of problem-solving, telling the client what to do, or invoking the law. If he develops and maintains the role of helping persons to grow, he will do so, with the help of much self-criticism, because he sees the enduring value of this kind of help.

Application to the Spiritual Exercises

Up to this point we have spoken of emphasizing strength or weakness in spiritual direction in general. All that has been said is applicable to the giving of *The Spiritual Exercises* of Saint Ignatius. In giving the First Week of *The Spiritual Exercises* the retreat director appeals to strength by suggesting to the exercitant that he not concentrate on his sins, but rather let the Lord meet him and heal him, free him, make him alive. This healing, freeing, making alive may take some time. A waiting on the Lord will be necessary, and although this waiting does not directly imply a length of time but a spiritual attitude, time may pass before the attitude is adopted, especially with an achievement-oriented person. It may also take time for angers, fears, guilts that lie a little below the surface of awareness to come into the prayer, for the person to become real to himself, in other words, so that he can present himself as he really is before the Lord. The result is worth the time.

A person making the *Exercises* often experiences, during the First Week or before it, a great deal of difficulty in realizing what he does feel and does think. He may concentrate instead on what he thinks he should feel, should think. Much of the director's time will have to be given, if this is the case, to helping the person recognize and acknowledge his own reality. His strength will lie in his recognition of that reality, inadequate as it may be, and his acceptance of it. Here the freedom of the retreatant is of crucial importance, since he will often be tempted to accept the director's reality rather than seek out his own.

In the Second Week of the *Exercises* the retreatant's strength is the reality of Jesus to him and the reality of his response to Jesus. It becomes the director's task to help him patiently to face the Lord. The person's bravest resolutions, his loftiest ideals, may be his greatest enemies here; what looks best can turn out to be his most insidious illusion. The director has to help him to contemplate the Lord rather than his own ideals, engage in dialogue with Him, and allow his own truth, rather than abstract truth, to appear.

Helping a person by appealing to his strength can involve a director in a long, meandering journey, fraught with uncertainties. Who, after all, can comfortably trust another person to see and recognize the Lord? But the journey is worth it. It enables a person to be himself with the Lord, to respond to Him as himself. From this relationship comes a new and rich creativity.

The Contemplative Attitude in Spiritual Direction

William A. Barry, S.J.

Volume 35, 1976, pp. 820-828.

In a number of articles both William J. Connolly, S.J. and I have referred to contemplation and the contemplative attitude as the kind of prayerful attitude which spiritual directors try to encourage in those who seek spiritual direction.[1] We have tried to describe what we mean by these words. Suffice it here to say that we use the word contemplation in its etymological sense; we mean to refer to the act of looking at or listening to something. Webster's first definition of "contemplate" says some of what we mean: "to view or consider with continued attention."

In our earlier articles, I believe, we have not been sufficiently precise in our use of the word contemplation and contemplative attitude. We have spoken of contemplating the Lord in Scripture and in nature and have not sufficiently distinguished between the contemplation of Scripture and nature and the contemplation of the Lord. Perhaps we have also not sufficiently attended to the nuance that one can have a contemplative attitude and yet not be contemplating the Lord. It is the purpose of these notes to attempt some clarification of the meaning of and use of contemplation in spiritual

[1]Barry, W. A., "The Experience of the First and Second Weeks of the *Spiritual Exercises*," pp. 95-102. Barry, W. A., "The Necessity of Contemplative Prayer for the Teaching and Study of Theology in a Ministerial School," *Church Society for College Work,* Vol. XXXIII, No. 1 (1975), pp. 6-10. Connolly, W. J., "Contemplation and Social Consciousness in the Context of the Directed Retreat: An Experiential Approach." An address at the 8th National Workshop on the Spiritual Exercises, Cincinnati, August 25-28, 1974, and published by The Program to Adapt the Spiritual Exercises, Jersey City, New Jersey 07302. Connolly, W. J., "Contemporary Spiritual Direction: Scope and Principles, An Introductory Essay." *Studies in the Spirituality of Jesuits,* VII, (1975), pp. 95-124.

direction.

The Contemplative Attitude and Its Relation to "Transcendence"

Have you ever been so absorbed in watching a game or reading a book or listening to music that you have been surprised at the end of the passage of time, by how cold or hot you are, by the anger of a friend (who has been asking you something for ten minutes)? Then you know the power of paying attention to something, and you have a personal example of the contemplative attitude. The most telling examples come from reports of how parents have been so concentrated on their children's safety in a fire or accident that they have only at the end felt the pain of their own wounds.

Thus, one effect of the contemplation of something outside ourselves is that it can make us forget ourselves and our other suroundings. Contemplation leads to, or rather, is an experience of transcendence, of self-forgetfulness of everyone and everything else except the contemplated object.

Conversely, we find that self-absorption makes the contemplation of anything or anyone else very difficult, if not impossible. Thus, a starving man may well be unable to enjoy a sunset. One of the key elements to ministry in a hospital is the attempt to help the sick to become interested in others around them and in the outside world, that is, to help them to do something that will enable them to forget their own pain and suffering or to put it in another perspective.

Another aspect of the examples we began with should catch our attention, namely that the responses of absorption, joy, pain, sympathy, love, gratitude which are associated with contemplation are not willed acts or willed emotions. They are elicited from us by what we see and hear and comprehend. (Of course, these responses do not arise from a blank tablet, but are conditioned by our own past experiences.) Here we have an important element to consider in all spiritual direction. Responses that are elicited by contemplation are not experienced in the first instance as willed acts. The clearest example, perhaps, is the response of love when one looks at the beloved; it seems to be a gift, something that arises because of the other, not because one has decided to love or fall in love. What one can do is to look at and to try to pay attention to the other, but one cannot will one's response. At most one can hope that one will respond a certain way.

This last point leads us to a further consideration. The person who contemplates in the way we are describing has to have an attitude of reverence and wonder before the other, especially if what he/she wants to see or hear is within the power of the other to grant or withhold. In this case all one can do is to ask the other to reveal himself or herself and wait for it to happen. This insight is behind the prayer for what one desires which Ignatius of Loyola puts at the beginning of every one of the exercises of the *Spiritual Exercises*. For example, in the *Exercises* I pray that the Lord will reveal to me my sinfulness, that I may have shame and confusion, that the Lord make himself known to me in order that I may love him and follow him.

Here we see even more clearly the relation between contemplation and transcendence. When we are dealing with another person, we are not in the same position as we are when we are dealing with an object. Saint Exupéry's Little Prince on his small asteroid only needs to move his chair a bit in order to see another sunset, but he is powerless to see the reality and uniqueness of his flower until she chooses to reveal herself to him.[2] But when the free other chooses to reveal him or herself, then the genie is out of the bottle, as T. S. Eliot said,[3] and the mystery of the other is upon us.

Thus we have a further observation on the relation of contemplation to transcendence. We try to control our perceptions. We are threatened by newness and strangeness. As a result we often see only what we "want" to see or what our perceptual and cognitive structures let us see. To try to contemplate means to try to let the other be himself or herself or itself, to try to be open to surprise and newness. To begin this process means to open oneself to mystery, ultimately to the Lordship of the Other. It is to let oneself be controlled by the other; paradoxically, one finds oneself free. The upshot most often is that one becomes less incapacitated by fear from accepting the mystery of life.[4]

The experience of transcendence is, I believe, one of a continuum from total self-absorption to total absorption in the other—with the two ends of the continuum being ideal states not found in nature. In any human experience there is bound to be an admixture of both self-consciousness and awareness of the outside world. The boundaries of the continuum might well be circumscribed by referring to the narcissistic person on the one hand and the enraptured mystic on the other. It might also be a help to those who are praying to realize that the contemplation of the Lord is no different from the contemplation of any other person in this regard, namely that one can be in the intimate presence of a very dear friend and still be or become aware of the ache in one's feet, of wondering whether one put out the lights in the car, of the work still to be done for school tomorrow, and so forth. "Distractions," in other words, are a part of even the most intimate relationships and should be expected in prayer too.

Finally, in an intimate conversation reflection on what is happening

---

[2]Antoine de Saint-Exupéry, *Le Petit Prince*, New York: Harcourt, Brace and World, 1943.
[3]"But let me tell you, that to approach the stranger
Is to invite the unexpected, release a new force,
Or let the genie out of the bottle.
It is to start a train of events
Beyond your control . . ." T. S. Eliot, *The Cocktail Party*
[4]See W. J. Connolly, "Freedom and Prayer in Directed Retreat," pp. 61-67.

or on how well one is doing, especially with the idea of writing about it in one's journal or using it as an example for an article like this, can disturb the communication and be an instance of self-absorption. It happens, but it is better not to program it this way. Thus, the wisdom of the tradition in spiritual direction of advising the person praying to do the reflecting after the period of prayer is over.

Contemplation of the Lord in Nature and in Scripture

Perhaps now we can clarify what we mean by contemplation of the Lord in nature and in Scripture. The Lord is invisible, and so hard to look at; he also seems pretty silent, and so hard to listen to. Often enough, therefore, we try too hard to pray, try too hard to listen and look. Too often prayer is seen as self-absorbing; our natural reaction when someone says, "Let us pray," is to bow our heads, close our eyes, and get serious—all of which is proper in its place. But we rarely get the impression that prayer can be an enjoyable experience, that it can be a conversation, a dialogue, a relationship. The spiritual director is confronted with the problem of helping people to the enjoyment of God when much of their past experience of prayer is one of labor, seriousness, brooding, and self-absorption.

Many of us who do spiritual direction have hit upon the idea of helping people to forget themselves for a while. We ask them what they like to do, what helps them just to forget their problems (besides going to sleep), and we try to help them to see that they already do contemplate in the way described in the first note. We suggest that they spend a certain amount of time—each day, if possible—doing whatever it is that they like doing that is contemplative, and that they consider this time as time with the Lord (i.e. prayer) in much the same way that they might want to share the same experience with a close friend. We also suggest that they ask the Lord to make his presence known, to reveal himself. Then they look at and/or listen to whatever it is they enjoy. After each period of doing this we ask them to reflect on the experience: What happened? What did they experience? Did the Lord make himself known?

It is surprising what happens when people begin to do something like this. They often have objections at first: they feel it cannot be prayer. Moreover, being so conditioned to think that brooding and insights and resolutions are what prayer is all about they often need time and patience to get the hang of it and to find out that the director really means what he says. But then they begin to find such "prayer" times enjoyable and relaxing; they find themselves surprised by feelings of joy and gratitude and a real sense that Someone is present who loves and cares for them. They find that they can admit things to themselves that they were always afraid or ashamed to look at—and they feel better for it; they feel freed, healed.

Agnes Sanford in her book *The Healing Gifts of the Spirit* gives very similar advice. To people who say "I can't find God," she suggests doing some simple things, especially things they like to do, that will put them in the way of God, as she says, so "that he can find you."[5] That is the point, of course; as we saw in the first section, the only thing we can do when we want to get to know another person is to put ourselves near and ask the person to reveal himself or herself.

These reflections bring us to the question: Are there any privileged places or privileged events where we can go to put ourselves in the Lord's way? The traditional answer has been that there are, and that these places and events include the sacraments, especially the Eucharist, the church teaching, the Scriptures, and the works of the Lord, especially nature. I will say something later about additions to this list, but now I would like to take up nature and the Scriptures.

Traditionally people have found peace and refreshment in the beauties of nature. The fact that most retreat houses, houses of prayer and monasteries have been located in or near scenes of natural beauty testify to the belief that God is found more easily in nature and in solitude than, say, in cities. Traditionally, too, we have spoken of God revealing himself in the things he has made, "in plants and animals and in men, the wonders of Your hand," as the canon written by John L'Heureux puts it.[6] I do not want to counter this tradition although I do believe that the Lord can be as present in the city; rather, I want to examine how the Lord is met and how we can help people to meet him in nature.

First of all directors should suggest looking and listening, not give ideas about God's continual creation, his indwelling, and so forth. We have to remember that most of us are conditioned by catechism, philosophy and theology classes to have beautiful thoughts about how God is in all things, but that few of us have ever looked long enough at a flower to let God reveal himself as the maker of that flower for me. Before a tree can become a symbol of God, it must first be seen and touched and smelled as a tree. The first suggestion then is that people look at and listen to what is around them.

The second suggestion is that looking at natural beauty can in itself be a way of relating to the Lord without any words being said. Just as I relate to an artist by taking interest in what he has made, by taking time to look at it or listen to it, so too I can relate to God if I take time to contemplate what he has made. Creators like to have people show interest in what they have done. All the better if I like what I see and smile or sigh or express

---

[5]Sanford, Agnes, *The Healing Gifts of the Spirit* (New York: Lippincott, 1966), esp. pp. 25-32.

[6]In Hoey, R. F. (ed.), *The Experimental Liturgy Book* (N.Y.: Herder and Herder, 1969), p. 97.

delight in the presence of the artist. Such responses are elicited by what I contemplate, not willed by me, and they are communications to the artist; in the case of God they are then called prayers of praise. They do not have to be couched in "prayer language." Indeed, the prayer is often made before a word is formed. The spiritual director might then be able to point out that the responses of the directee are similar to the responses that the poet who wrote Psalm 104 must have had and then tried to express in poetry. Not everyone is a poet, but almost everyone can be thrilled by a dazzling sunset or sunrise, the sun's light on fall leaves, and so forth, and feel a deep sense of wonder.

Thus far we have been stressing the need to look and listen, the contemplative attitude. As I contemplate, I can also have desires, one of which is that the Lord reveal himself to me while I am looking at his works. If I begin my period of contemplation with a prayer that this desire be granted, then it is liable to happen. I do not want to rule out high mystical experiences—because they do happen and more frequently than we tend to think—but here I would rather concentrate on the more ordinary ways the Lord reveals himself in answer to this prayer.

One can be walking along the beach at night and see a touch of silver from the moon on the crest of a wave and besides delighting in it suddenly feel at peace and in someone's presence who himself delights in such things. Unaccountably one may feel that one is still loved, even though one does drink or eat too much or get angry with one's community members too often or even though one has just lost one's best friend or has just been turned down for graduate school or was not elected superior or whatever, and one may feel free to face oneself more honestly and with less self-pity. Or a person may sense her insignificance under the stars, and yet feel her own importance in the whole scheme of things. Or another may sense a call deep inside himself to change his life style. In all these instances the person may be hearing or sensing the voice of the Lord revealing himself. When these kinds of experiences are real and exciting and challenging as well as comforting, then the Lord has begun to take on a new reality for the person. Perhaps now he or she can also pay attention to him and not just to his creatures. And here may lie the dividing line between contemplating the Lord and contemplating his works.

The work of the spiritual director now becomes one of helping the person praying to discern, that is, to figure out what is going on, what is God's voice, what not. The discernment of spirits begins when there are inner movements and the question is: Is the Lord revealing himself, and if so, what is he saying? The genie is out of the bottle, and now it is important to follow the genie's movements.

We can look at the contemplation of Scripture in a similar way. Scripture is not the Lord, but a privileged place to meet him. However, one must pay attention to the Scripture itself just as one has to pay attention to trees or sunsets or mountains. That is, it is necessary to have a contemplative attitude toward Scripture, to let the Scriptures be themselves and to listen to them and to ask that the Lord reveal himself while we are listening to these words.

I do not intend here to delve into the arguments as to whether any other religious texts might be privileged places for meeting God; they could be and indeed people have met God while paying attention to St. Augustine's *Confessions,* to the prayer of St. Francis, to many other works of religious literature, and even to secular literature. I am accepting as a given that Scripture has primacy of place over all other literature as the Word of God. But we must listen to the Scriptures themselves, and not our projections onto them.

One sometimes hears that modern scripture scholarship with its demythologizing and its form criticism has been a blow to piety and has made it more difficult to use Scripture for prayer. Scripture scholars, it is sometimes charged, have taken the mystery out of the infancy narratives of the gospels and other stories. We are not sure what Jesus actually said, or whether he actually did everything the gospels say he did. "How can we ever know him then?", people wonder.

Those of us who take scripture studies and spiritual direction seriously have had to ponder these questions and charges as well as to take seriously our own and others' experiences in praying with the Scriptures. I think that we have not always been careful in our way of speaking, and it is my hope that this note will contribute to the clarification of our thought and expression.

I want to focus on the contemplation of the gospels and hope that the principles enunciated here can be analogously translated to the use of other scripture texts. The first point is obvious: It does little good for prayer or Christian living to base both on a delusion. Hence, it is important to see the gospels for what they are. They are not biographies of Jesus, but four different expressions of the faith of the early Church and what it remembered in faith about Jesus. Each gospel has its own point of view, its own theological focus, its own *Sitz im Leben.* Contemplation of Mark's gospel, for example, means taking Mark's work on its own terms and trying to listen to his work of art.

Secondly, it should be said that one need not be a Scripture scholar in order to be able to use the gospels for prayer. The Lord can still reveal himself to someone who believes that angels actually did sing "Glory to God in the highest" at Bethlehem as long as one is open to having the living Lord reveal *himself.* But I do believe that the more one knows about the gospel, the better one can look at and listen to it and not to one's own cultural and personal projections of it. Thus, I believe that scripture study can be a help to contemplation. In other words, it helps, I think, to be able to contemplate Mark's Jesus and know that it is Mark's Jesus and not necessarily the "real article" in all his historical reality. For one thing, one is not going to be thrown so much out of kilter by new discoveries of scripture scholars. More importantly, one is more likely to realize that the person one wants to meet is not the Jesus of the past, but the present living Lord (who, of course, is continuous with Jesus of Nazareth).

Here we are at the heart of the matter. The purpose of contemplating the gospels is to come to know the living Lord Jesus. Here again we can see the wisdom of Ignatius of Loyola. Before every contemplation of events from the gospels Ignatius has the retreatant pray for what he desires, namely "an intimate knowledge of our Lord, who has become man for me, that I may love him more and follow him more closely."[7] Then I listen to the gospel text and treat it for what it is, as imaginative literature. I try to take the text seriously, and try to let it inspire my imagination, as it was written to do (as well as to enkindle my faith). But my desire is not to know the scripture text better, but to know the risen Jesus better. I want him to reveal himself to me. And when he takes on reality and shape for me (not necessarily in a picture, by the way), then I talk to him, not to the text, and I listen to him, not the text. Those who have not had this experience will not know what I am talking about, but hopefully they will be open enough to listen to the experience of those who have. The purpose of contemplation of Scripture is not to see Jesus walking on water or to see him in Galilee or hear him say to Peter "Feed my lambs." The purpose is to hear the risen Jesus say to me: "Your sins are forgiven you" and to know he means me; to hear him say to me: "Come, follow me and be my friend" and know that it is the Lord and that he is talking to me. Once again, discernment becomes a necessity when I begin to feel moved by the Lord himself.

I hope that by now it is clear that contemplation of nature or of Scripture is not in itself contemplation of the Lord, but that the former is a privileged way to the latter. Indeed, one can say that contemplation in the first sense is a technique or method, where contemplation in the second sense is relationship itself and no methods are needed.

Finally as to the list of privileged places, it may be well to indicate that those mentioned earlier are still privileged places and also that different eras and different people may prefer one of the privileged places to others. It may also be that new privileged places may come into prominence. I am thinking especially of a shift from nature to man-made works of art or technique, a suggestion made by Josef Sudbrack, S.J.[8] In our modern urban culture we may well find that human artifacts as well as human persons themselves may be more privileged than natural beauty. There should be no difficulty here since the works of humans are ultimately God's handiwork.

---

[7] *Spiritual Exercises* (Puhl Translation), No. 104, p. 49.
[8] Sudbrack, Josef, *Beten ist Menschlich: Aus der Erfahrung Unseres Lebens mit Gott Sprechen* (Freiburg in Breisgau: Herder, 1973).

On the Question of the Utility of Contemplation

Recently in a discussion of contemplation someone mentioned that many people were advocating the techniques I have labelled contemplative for problem solving in management, for conflict resolution and that they worked without reference to God or the transcendent. That is, the contemplative techniques we mentioned in the earlier notes were being used for secular purposes, and people were feeling better, were more creative, more integral, and so forth. There is no question that the technique of contemplation by itself is very salutary. We need not bemoan that fact. But then what is the need to bring in God and prayer?

Here the only reply is to ask oneself to what end one uses contemplative techniques. If the answer is to solve problems, to feel better, to be more creative, then perhaps there is no need to refer to God and prayer. But for those for whom contact with the living Lord and the relationship itself with him are the goals, the question loses significance. It is like asking someone what he gets out of time spent with his wife that he could not get from others just as well. For those who seek the Lord, these techniques would be worthless no matter how good they made them feel if in the process they did not find their Lord. Throughout these notes I have stressed that the purpose of contemplating nature, Scripture, or anything else is to meet the living Lord. When he is engaged, or rather when he engages me, there is no need of techniques or even of asking what the utility of prayer is. I want to be with him, and that is enough. Without effort utility comes; one becomes a better person and Christian. But relationship is what is sought.

Freedom and Prayer in Directed Retreats

William J. Connolly, S.J.

Volume 32, 1973, pp. 1358-1364.

The interest in directed retreats that has developed among active religious in the last three years may at first glance seem a simple, easily-understood phenomenon, an attempt to get help in returning to former observance after the adventures of the early post-conciliar years. A renewal of prayer, however, is never a simple matter. Genuine prayer is too rich and multi-faceted a reality for easy explanation. It is affected by too many influences and leads to too many life consequences.

If, instead of explaining away the reality, we let that reality speak to us, we will find that it raises at least one question that may well be crucial for American religious life: How basic is freedom to the development of a life of prayer? This in turn leads to a second: How high a priority should individual freedom be given in directed retreats?

Three Paradoxes

A number of paradoxes have appeared in the extensive experience of directed retreats we have had in Cambridge at the Center for Religious Development in the last two years. The most surprising is the kind of person who has come for directed retreats. Not at all the quiet, reserved person often called "contemplative," he or she is far more often independent, energetic, adventurous, frequently an initiator and sometimes a prophet. Of six religious making directed retreats independently of one another at the Center during one recent week, for instance, one was an instructor at a black college, another was beginning a new campus apostolate, a third initiating a new program in formation. In the directed retreat movement as we have known it, it has tended to be those who have gone into the inner city, formed small communities, started independent apostolates, been outspoken in the government of their communities—the kind of person you would expect to "have no time for prayer"—who have been willing to take this step to grow in prayer and the prayerful life.

A second paradox. Those who look for directed retreats at the Center do not take this step because they feel obliged by a rule to pray or because they are conditioned by structures. They have made a free decision to pray. Sometimes the freedom of the decision is accentuated by a previous lack of prayer or even of inability to pray. A few years ago the spiritual director often heard: "I'm a religious, so I ought to pray." Now, he will more frequently hear: "I've thought it over, and I've decided to do something about prayer."

A third paradox. The prayer developed is non-conformist. It does not begin with, or depend on, the habits of a group. It begins with and depends on the convictions of the individual. It develops in varied directions, follows its own rhythm, is integrated with the individual's life experience. It tends to be Scripture-oriented, very pragmatic in that it stresses what works rather than what sounds good, and is little influenced by the latest books on prayer.

Free Enough to Pray

From the vantage point of these three paradoxes, then, the directed retreat has the look of an adventure in Christian freedom. But it is the experience of the person while he attempts to pray that bears out most clearly the basic role of freedom in this renewal of prayer. The person who is controlled by fear, anger, a fixed idea of his future, finds himself incapable of more than superficial prayer. When he begins to be freed of that control, he becomes capable of a deeper prayer.

The person whose life is defined by structures, who wants nothing more than to hold a teaching job, or be acceptable to his superiors, or not be regarded as an oddity by his community, finds great difficulty with prayer until he is free to have his own desires and hopes.

The religious whose life is so hemmed in by regulations that he cannot make significant decisions for himself also finds prayer hemmed in and dry. He cannot face a free God. The divine freedom is too much of a challenge to his own mind set.

Repeatedly, people who learn to make their own decisions and shape their own lives begin to experience a deeper prayer. As the freedom grows, their ability to commit themselves in a vital way to Christ also increases.

The problem of not being free enough to pray is only partially a problem with dominating structures. A person's anger and fear limit his freedom and therefore his prayer more severely than structures can. The difficulty is that he often cannot become free of inner chains until the structures have been loosened. The only way to become free is to make decisions. Thus structures will enable and encourage prayer only when they are loose enough to encourage decision making.

Fostering Freedom in the Spiritual Exercises

At every stage of the Spiritual Exercises, inner freedom is necessary. The person must be free enough to be himself before the Lord, to look at the Lord, to receive from the Lord, to commit himself to the Lord, to grieve with the Lord, to let himself be consoled by Him. The more freely and expansively he enters into these stages, the more deeply he is likely to experience them.[1]

If freedom is essential to the experience of the Spiritual Exercises, what can be done to foster it? First, it must be recognized that giving priority to personal freedom is no easy matter. For one thing, the director will encounter obstacles within himself. Spirituality is a heady discipline, and a tendency to think he knows what is best for everyone is an occupational hazard every spiritual director must deal with, some of us frequently. More perhaps than other practitioners who depend on communication for the success of their work, he must listen to the person he is trying to help, for only by listening can be come aware of the person's inner reality, a reality the person himself is hard put to understand. It is in this reality that the Lord calls a person to his unique vocation, and it is here that the person responds or refuses to respond. Yet, the intellectual content of spiritual theology, sacralized by its close relationship with the most mysterious of God's actions and therefore more fearsome, may make it difficult for the director to be a listener. He has the truth; what can he hope to gain from the long dreary business of paying close attention to the evolution of thought and feeling? Short-cuts come to look attractive, individual attention to seem wasteful, especially when there is too much to do to begin with. Rules and commands come to seem regrettable perhaps, but necessary; individual freedom important, but in practice too time consuming.

The director of a personalized retreat must combat within himself five major enemies of the other person's freedom: the director's own desire to have others dependent on him; his fear that he may lose control of the retreat if the retreatant exercises freedom; the worry that he may not know what to do if the retreatant takes a path he himself is not accustomed to; his desire to achieve results in the retreat; inflexibility in his own spiritual life, with the tendency to feel his personal spirituality threatened when the retreatant goes his own way.

---

[1] See the following articles: William A. Barry, S.J., "The Experience of the First and Second Weeks of the *Spiritual Exercises,*" pp. 95-102; William J. Connolly, "Story of the Pilgrim King and the Dynamics of Prayer," pp. 103-107; "Disappointment in Prayer: Prelude to Growth?," pp. 191-194; and "Appealing to Strength in Spiritual Direction," pp. 48-51.

Resistance to Freedom in the Director

What are the practical consequences? Insecure people should not be directing one-to-one retreats. Success is too important to them, and so they are too dependent on structure to allow the retreatant his freedom. This would mean that the very young should not give directed retreats, and that older people who give them should not be dependent on them for a living or a sense of their own usefulness. Part-time spiritual direction, combined with some other work at which the director is successful, is usually the best situation for developing the freedom the director must have. His other work then provides him with whatever security he needs, and thus leaves him free enough to give personalized retreats without worrying excessively about failure. He can afford to let the Lord act in His own time and His own way, and can afford to leave the retreatant free.

The freedom of the retreatant will often be protected by the director's colleagues if he works with a team. They will frequently detect rigidity in his approach before he does and can point it out to him. If he is to benefit from a team approach, the team must have agreed to criticize one another's practice, and he must be open to criticism.

A director's reliance on a method and his reluctance to depart from it is one of the more obvious banes of the directed retreat. Obvious because spiritual life, both spirit and life, could never be confined by a method and an attempt to do so is bound to be harmful. But addiction to method dies hard in the recent, attenuated tradition of the *Spiritual Exercises;* and directors are still found who believe, for instance, that the four "weeks" of the Exercises have to be given in every eight-day retreat. Their belief may well be costly to the retreatant who faces the Two Standards before the Lord has begun to free him from radical personal fears, or who tries to empathize with the Jesus of Calvary before he has a sense of His person and mission. He can easily fall into depression or anger that it may take several years for him to overcome. Or, he may never overcome them. After all, he has made the *Spiritual Exercises,* hasn't he? And they didn't take.

If the retreatant's freedom is to be fostered or even safeguarded in a directed retreat, the director must be primarily familiar not with a technique, but with what happens while a person is making the Exercises. He must listen carefully to the person and not categorize him as "priest," "sister," or even as "retreatant." He must avoid relying on lists of Scripture passages, charts of expected reactions, mimeographed sheets to be distributed before each day's prayer. He must scrap every technique he has if that will help him to meet the person in the person's actual situation. If he can do these things, he will probably be free enough himself to help the retreatant to be free. If he cannot, he has reason to fear that he will do the retreatant more harm than good.

Resistance to Freedom in the Retreatant

The person who applies to make a directed retreat will find resistance to freedom within himself too. Everyone finds the word "freedom" attractive, even compelling. A person seeking direction will always agree that he wants to be free, but may seize the first opportunity to become dependent. "Am I getting what I'm supposed to get out of this prayer?" "What's the homework for today?" "I was thinking of taking another Scripture text that struck me a lot, but since you hadn't assigned it . . ." There is a natural reluctance to letting ourselves face God and letting Him face us, and dependence on someone else's ideas and techniques becomes a convenient way of escaping this encounter. So it is common for a person both to ask for freedom and yet seek, at least subconsciously, to avoid it.

There is deep within us 20th century Americans, too, a hope that we can be saved by a method. We are impatient with being ourselves before the Lord and looking at Him. Contemplation does not give us enough to do. "I'm just sitting around doing nothing" is familiar to everyone who has tried to help people toward more contemplative prayer. "I don't know how to pray," which sounds so beguilingly humble at first, can later show itself to express an anxious hope for a technique that will excuse the person from the necessity of being himself before God.

Whatever valid uses techniques may have, they fall short of usefulness and may be harmful when they are substituted for the rich and varied dialogue that the free God seeks to initiate and develop with the free human person. The *Spiritual Exercises* are intended to further that dialogue, not substitute for it. When they are reduced to a method, or are allowed by negligence to become that, their purpose is frustrated. It is, then, a primary responsibility of the director to help the retreatant to recognize and exercise his freedom during the retreat itself, and to combat any tendency to withdraw from this exercise.

Helping the Retreatant to Freedom

The director will find that he must go out of his way to help the retreatant here and will have to spend time at it. His own attitude will be essential, but to overcome the conditioning that a lifetime of dependence on secular and religious structures has deposited, he will have to be explicit and persistent. The interview that takes place before a person is accepted for a directed retreat thus has high importance. Neither the director nor the prospective retreatant has committed himself to anything. They have a chance to look one another over and decide whether they want to work together. The director has an opportunity to ask why the person wants to make a directed retreat and how he understands such a retreat.

There may be a discussion of the person's religious history and of the director's experience. In this way a free and knowledgeable decision can be made to undertake or not to undertake the retreat.

Ancillary circumstances can also help the prospective retreatant to be aware of and deepen the freedom of his decision. If he has to plan a 500 mile trip to make the retreat, and live in unfamiliar surroundings while there, he is more likely to give himself energetically to prayer than he would be if he did not have to leave his own house. A man who makes his own decision to seek out a retreat director is more likely to be serious and deliberate about it than one who makes a retreat because his friends are making it. A director who is aware of the importance of a free decision on the part of the retreatant will take such circumstances into account before he decides to give a retreat. Otherwise, he may pay the price of having to work with people who have not fully decided to pray.

No Imposition of Regulations

If the director really wants the retreatant to be free, he will not impose regulations on him. Imposed silence, refusal to allow the retreatant to receive mail or telephone calls, insistence that the retreatant pray in a particular place—such behavior would limit the retreatant's freedom and thwart the single factor on which, after the action of God, the success of the retreat most depends: the retreatant's mature ability to make his own decisions.[2] This is not to say that there should not be quiet in a retreat situation, or that the retreatant should receive telephone calls. But the decision should be the retreatant's, not the director's.

It can be helpful to discuss some of these matters either before or during the retreat. The retreatant, too, should, before an agreement is concluded to make a retreat, inform the director of anything he intends to do that may affect the director's decision to give the retreat. If he intends to study, teach, conduct an extensive correspondence, or attend social functions during the retreat, he should inform the director so that the latter can decline to give the retreat if he does not want to contend with these preoccupations. Such communication is expected between responsible adults and leaves both retreatant and director free people.

Some of these measures cannot, of course, be easily adopted in retreat houses. Previous interviews may not always be feasbile. There may not be enough personnel to deliver telephone messages, sort mail, provide flexible arrangements for meals. But instead of allowing the physical plant to dictate the terms of the retreat, perhaps both serious directors and serious retreatants should first decide what measures are necessary for an adult retreat in which director and retreatant deal with one another as peers, and then

---

[2]William A. Barry, "Silence and Directed Retreat," pp. 68-72.

find a situation in which such measures can be adopted.

It has been observed that the more free a person is, the more likely he is to be capable of prayer. It has also been observed that deep personal prayer makes a person more free.

Two Crucial Questions

These observations raise two questions that are crucial for the directed retreat movement as they are crucial for the future of the American Church. Will we keep the directed retreat and other forms of help in prayer available to free, creative Christians or will we effectively deny such helps to them by clothing them in an atmosphere that free people cannot accept? Will the directed, personalized retreat actually help to develop Christian freedom? Those of us who have experienced the powerful pressures that militate against genuine freedom know how difficult it is going to be to withstand them. But it is also clear that unless we can withstand them a powerful instrument for Christian growth will lose its effectiveness.

Silence and the Directed Retreat

William A. Barry, S.J.

Volume 32, 1973, pp. 347-351.

It seems clear to me[1] that in the spiritual theory and practice of today we are in danger of throwing out the baby with the bath water in a number of areas. No doubt, we are seeing an understandable reaction to the mindless imposition of rules of the recent past. It may be necessary to fix blame for all I know; I suppose that at the least it keeps historians busy and does allow a healthy outlet to anger. But blame-fixing does not change the fact that many excellent spiritual ideas and methods are in danger of being lost because of the reaction to our past. Moreover, because of the anger in many of us at what we were forced to do we cannot ask reasonable questions without evoking ghosts of the past. Thus, to ask whether regular times for daily prayer may not be a good thing receives angry outbursts about regimentation and confining of the Spirit. Again, for some time it was difficult for a religious superior to ask a subject whether he should have a spiritual director without causing an explosion. And the feelings afflict all of us, superior and subject alike, so that there is real difficulty in having a rational discourse. One topic that especially raises these feelings is the question of silence during the making of the *Spiritual Exercises*. And here, I think, we have thrown out the baby with the bath.

When the idea of silence on a retreat is broached, all sorts of ghosts of the past are touched. We remember the strained silence and the downcast eyes of our early years of training; we remember the tensions we felt during

---

[1] I wish to thank my colleagues at the Center for Religious Development for their critical reading of the first draft of this paper and for their helpful suggestions.

retreats and the almost maniacal laughing jags that let the tensions out; we remember feeling guilty and ashamed when we were "caught" talking by a superior; we remember the feeling of being watched by others; we remember the furtive looks and smiles and whispers of friends. We may seethe at the inanity of it all. Perhaps we are ashamed of ourselves for what in the name of "silence" we did to other members of the community. Few of us, I wager, can look back at those years without some feelings of anger and shame and without a determination not to let ourselves get trapped into *that* mentality again. Silence is a dirty word.

Since retreat directors are also a product of the same formation and have the same feelings and questions about silence and since they are understandably reluctant to submit themselves to the anger they know will wash over them if they raise the question, they have tended not to raise it—or at most have been content to leave it up to the individual to decide. Rarely do they put themselves on the line by stressing its positive advantages. Are there any?

There are none if by silence we mean the silence that led to the effects described above. That kind of silence is detrimental to prayer since it can keep the focus off the Lord. If I am tense, I cannot look at or listen to the Lord any more than I can listen to a friend if something is bothering me. Moreover, that kind of silence seriously interferes with the relationship between the director and the retreatant by introducing an extraneous element, namely the cops-versus-robbers' relationship. It is too easy for the retreatant to see the director as the enforcer of silence—and, mind you, too easy for the director to see himself or worry that he is seen as the "cop." That kind of silence really is a trap.

The object of the *Spiritual Exercises* is prayer and the experience of God. Everything has to be ordered to that end. Moreover, the *Exercises* presuppose that the particular encounter with God they aim at will come about in private prayer—up to five hours of such prayer a day. The prayer is basically contemplative, not analytic; St. Ignatius wants the retreatant to look at the Lord and what He has done and to respond. The presumption is that during the days of making the *Exercises* the retreatant will experience the Lord and will have interior movements of consolation and desolation. I have already described elsewhere[2] the movements experienced during the four "weeks" of the *Exercises;* for the argument here I need only point to that article and reiterate that there is in each "week" a dynamic that operates in the retreatant who gives himself to this kind of contemplative prayer. Our experience is that the dynamic can be thwarted both by the director who does not trust the experience and by the retreatant who defends himself against the experience by using his usual modes of evading desolation. It

[2]See William A. Barry, S.J., "The Experience of the First and Second Weeks of the *Spiritual Exercises,"* pp. 95-102.

is the latter which bring up the question of silence and the particular kind of silence which we have in mind for such a retreat.

The encounter with the Lord which the *Exercises* aim at requires a belief that He will show Himself during these days, that His Spirit will be operative in the experiences of prayer. The "first week experience," for example, is one of being a saved sinner, of experiencing in the prayer salvation from our own alienation. The experience is precisely one of being saved by the Lord, and not by any other means. But desolation is difficult to bear, and we typically avoid its pain by turning to others for consolation, or to drink, or to amusement, all of which may be good in their place. The period for making the *Exercises,* however, is a time for turning to the Lord alone for salvation. Perhaps now the value of silence can be seen, not as a tense kind of ascesis for its own sake, but as a way of giving the Lord a chance to show His love and grace. The retreatant, in other words, chooses this kind of retreat to let the Lord operate within him, to let the Lord save him from his desolation and his sense of alienation. The retreatant himself chooses to spend these days with the Lord, and the silence we are talking about is the mind-set of spending the days with Him, and of not turning to others for help.

It is important to be clear about what I mean here. I am not denigrating the seeking of help from others; I am not advocating an individualistic Christianity. I am talking about a particular, and very valuable, dimension of a person's life, that of facing the Lord alone. This dimension requires a choice of separation from ordinary life and from friends for a period of time. The choice is to let myself go into the mystery of contemplation for a period in the belief that God will reveal Himself and in revealing Himself also reveal me to myself. But experience teaches us that we do get scared or bored or desolate when we let ourselves go in this way and that we will be tempted to give up too soon, that is, before the Lord has a chance to reveal Himself. Hence, we need the help of the director and our fellow retreatants to stay with the Lord; we need an atmosphere of recollection. If we do stay with the Lord and experience His grace, then we will come to a deeper trust in the Lord, and we will not have to keep our deepest feelings to ourselves.

One further argument presents itself. The major part of the *Exercises* consists of contemplations of the life of Jesus as it is presented in the Gospels. The aim is to get to know Him and love Him in order to follow Him. Again, it is not easy to get to know anyone intimately unless you really spend time with him alone. It is like a honeymoon; it does not mean that life will always be like this, but this period is necessary in order to grow in intimacy. Again the choice is to spend *these* days (not all days) with the Lord as much alone as possible. The silence sought for is this time alone.

The kind of silence we are here talking about does not require absolute quiet, abstention from all conversation. It does require a realization that I may use others as an escape from the Lord, and hence it does require an ascesis of some sort that aims at avoiding escapes. Thus, the retreatant chooses to be alone most of the day. Moreover, he should also realize that there may be days when it is particularly urgent for him to be totally alone because of the dynamic he is involved in. The ideal, therefore, is a retreatant who is free of obligations to a group or to individuals for the time of the retreat; this freedom means internal freedom, the freedom to use these days for one's friendship with God without feeling guilty for avoiding others or pressured to participate in fellowship. Such freedom does not necessarily require the desert, by the way; it only requires a retreatant who chooses freely this kind of retreat and others who respect his freedom without themselves feeling guilty or left out. Truth to tell, such ideal circumstances are not easy to come by, and especially when retreatants make the *Exercises* in large groups.

Indeed, directed retreats in large groups constitute the problem. The question of silence can be readily handled with an individual retreatant; it becomes a problem when a number of people gather together to make directed retreats with one or several directors. Then the ghosts of the past may be evoked.

I believe that the feelings about silence are there in many, if not most, of our retreatants whether or not they are voiced. Hence, I advocate an open discussion of the issue of silence (or recollection) with the retreatants before the retreat rather than a laissez-faire attitude or a notice on the bulletin board announcing silence. The discussion allows the feelings to surface if they are there. The director (or directors) should explain the nature of this kind of retreat as a time for working out things with the Lord and the kind of relaxed and quiet atmosphere that is needed for this. They should ask everyone to help create this atmosphere, and they might even bring up the issue of how to help a fellow retreatant who seems to be escaping into too much talk and activity. Perhaps, too, they should be frank in saying that this kind of retreat with its great investment of time on the part of retreatant and director should only be made by someone who has the attitude of wanting to be with the Lord alone for a time; otherwise both director and retreatant risk wasting time, and the atmosphere in the house may be less conducive to prayer for the others. In our experience an hour or two spent with the group beforehand has helped to create the atmosphere of recollection that is needed. Naturally, the directors should make clear that the recollection is for the benefit of the retreatants and not their own and that they will not, therefore, police it.

A frank facing of the issues involved in the question of silence can be very helpful to all concerned. The directors will have stated their hopes for the retreatants and the conditions which experience has shown are helpful. The retreatants will be able to air their anxieties and other feelings about silence and will, perhaps, realize why silence is recommended. Thereby we may be saving one of the babies, a noble enterprise in itself.

On Asking God to Reveal Himself in Retreat

William A. Barry, S.J.

Volume 37, 1970, pp. 171-176.

In Ignatius' *Spiritual Exercises* the retreatant is advised to ask for what he desires as a prelude to every period of prayer. Retreat directors of every tradition often spend a great deal of time helping those they direct to know what they want of God in prayer and to ask for it. The contention of this essay is that most of these desires are for the personal revelation of God.[1]

People sometimes come to retreat with rather vaguely thought-out hopes and desires: "I want to get back to prayer;" "I need to recharge the spiritual batteries;" "I want to pray about a decision I have to make;" "I just want to be alone with God for a while." When the directors probe a bit into these desires, they regularly find that retreatants want to experience the closeness and care of God, but hold little hope that God will make his presence felt. In other words, some retreatants expect too little of God, have an image of God as being more niggardly with his favors than God has revealed of himself. This image of God may stem from a sense that God cannot be bothered with the "likes of me." It may stem from a sense that God is a distant and almighty figure. With such an image, whatever its source, retreatants will not have those great desires that Ignatius hopes

[1]This article is the fruit of work with retreatants and directees at the Center for Religious Development. It may be seen as an expansion on certain points made in an earlier article in this journal. See William A. Barry, "The Experience of the First and Second Weeks of the *Spiritual Exercises*," pp. 95-102.

for in the exercitant. Such retreatants need a different picture of God. However a new view of God is not attained from theological lectures or homiletic exhortations as much as from a different experience of him. Thus, a retreatant with such an image of God is helped if he is guided to ask God for what he wants and needs, namely an experience of God that will enable him to expect great things of God.

An example may help. A forty-year-old priest began a thirty-day retreat with a good deal of apprehension. He wanted to rekindle his devotion. But the prospect of praying four to five hours a day for thirty days was not a little daunting. The idea that God would speak intimately to him seemed foreign to him. He expected to "grunt his way through life" with God at a distance. At the same time part of him wanted intimacy with God. In the first few days he was surprised that the contemplation[2] of natural beauty came easy to him and that the days did not seem to drag. But he still could not believe that God would speak intimately with him. He did ask God to help him to believe this. About the fourth day he was "surprised by joy," as it were. He had had an up-and-down day of prayer. When he woke up in the morning he got into a conversation with God and felt that God was saying: "You are precious in my eyes." In the following few days he seesawed between believing in the experience and the possibilities it evoked and still doubting its validity. Finally about the eighth day the reality of the experience, and of other like experiences sank in. Here was an experience of God he had secretly hoped for, but also did not expect. From then on he had great hopes and a great desire for God, only occasionally dampened by a return of his old image of self-in-relation-to-God. His image of God—and correlatively of himself—was changed by this experience.

A retreatant may be a "house divided" as he begins the retreat. He may desire closeness to God, but he may also be afraid of him. He may fear that he will be terribly demanding. He may fear that he will come close as a condemning judge who frowns on his actions. A retreatant like this needs help to put his ambivalent self before God. What he wants and needs is an experience of God that will overcome his fears. He might be encouraged to begin his periods of prayer by asking God to reveal himself in a way that will not frighten him away. Then he does something that will give God a chance to answer his request. He may take a walk in a park or along the shore; he may quietly read Psalm 139. But he wants a revelation of God that will help him to overcome his ambivalence.

Retreatants may also be helped to know God better by knowing how he has been present in their lives up to the present. In the first days of a retreat the desire to know one's personal salvation history often surfaces. One approach that many have found helpful takes this desire as a desire for

---

[2]See William A. Barry, "The Contemplative Attitude in Spiritual Direction," pp. 56-60.

God's self-revelation. At the beginning of a prayer period the retreatant asks God to reveal in detail how he has been present throughout the retreatant's life. Then he recalls some place or person or incident from childhood and allows the memories to come freely. The idea is to try not to control the thoughts and images and memories, but to trust the process and the Spirit who dwells in our hearts to bring to mind what God wants to reveal at the present time. One period of prayer might be spent on childhood, another on school years, and so on through one's life, with repetitions where appropriate. A day or two or even longer may be given to this exercise. Some retreatants fruitfully spend many days in such prayer; one man we know spent almost all of a thirty-day retreat on his salvation history.

Naturally enough, not every thought, memory, or image is equally important or a revelation of who God has been for the person. But it is extraordinary how fruitful such prayer-time is. It often allows the retreatant to "own" here and now reactions, attitudes, and feelings locked in the past. For instance, a retreatant may cry for the first time for his father who died years before and realize that one of the blocks to intimacy with God was his inability to own his feelings of loss and anger. Most people finish a day or two of such prayer able to say, sometimes for the first time with conviction, the words of Psalm 139: "It was you who created my inmost self, and put me together in my mother's womb; for all these mysteries I thank you: for the wonder of myself, for the wonder of your works" (Ps 139:13-14, Jerusalem Bible).

Once again we see that the desire of the retreatant is for a personal revelation of God, a revelation which will also disclose to the retreatant who he or she is before God. When such desires are answered, then the retreatant "knows" (in the Johannine sense which combines faith, knowledge, and love) that God is *his* God and that he is his son. He can affirm from inner conviction the Principle and Foundation of Ignatius.

The Revelation of Sinfulness

Once retreatants have had a rather deep experience of God's personal love and concern for them and have acknowledged the centrality of God in their lives and hearts, they often begin to think of examining their consciences. The director needs to help them to recognize their desires and to discern where they come from.

We have become so used to seeing the examination of conscience as a thorough self-scrutiny that we can forget the theological truism that only God can reveal sin to us. The sinner, precisely as sinner, is blind to his state. The conviction of sinfulness is a gift of God, an act of his love. Thus, when the desire to examine sinfulness arises, it is important for the director to take time with the retreatant to clarify where the desire comes from. Examination of sins can become an exercise in self-absorption. It may even be a way of resisting the light of God's love, his view of one's sinfulness. The clearest example of such resistance is the self-scrutiny of the scrupulous person. What such self-scrutiny effectively blocks out (albeit without conscious awareness of such intent) is God's revelation of himself as lover and of the scrupulous person's real sinfulness, namely the unwillingness or inability to accept that love. Concern for "my sins" may effectively keep the light of God's scrutiny from illuminating the need for conversion.

If retreatants have come to a deep trust of God's love and concern, they may spontaneously ask God to reveal any wayward ways, or they may be encouraged to do so by the director. They make their own the words of Psalm 139: "God, examine me and know my heart, probe me and know my thoughts; make sure I do not follow pernicious ways, and guide me in the way that is everlasting" (Ps 139:23-24). God is being asked to reveal his ways, to root out all that hinders intimacy. When the prayer begins this way, the retreatant often is surprised to find that "sins" expected to be on the docket are not even brought to mind. But something else is revealed and becomes the focal point for conversion, for example, an attitude of self-righteousness or an unwillingness to receive. God has been allowed to reveal himself, and he turns out to be different from what was expected. Where, for example, a retreatant expected him to come down hard on his occasional indulgence in sexual fantasies, he instead came through as revealing how weak the retreatant's trust in God's love was. Retreatants often discover that their sinfulness is not so much in their acts of commission or omission as in their unwillingness to be open and honest with God about these acts. They find out that God wants intimacy with them, warts and moles and all, and that they have been preventing that intimacy by being unwilling or unable to speak the whole truth to him. Their sin, in other words, consisted partly in not believing that God would forgive them, that he does love sinners. They also find out that their unwillingness to be open with God stems from their reluctance to look honestly at their lives in his presence. The revelation of sinfulness reveals who we are, but it also reveals who God is and wants to be for us.

Even when retreatants have experienced the forgiving love of God, they may have difficulty facing in its stark reality the fact that Jesus died for them. That he died for all human beings is accepted and affirmed, but the sticking point comes when one faces the very personal experience that "he died for *me* in the full knowledge of who I am." Retreatants want to believe this truth, but they can also be afraid and sometimes even terrified of approaching in imagination Jesus crucified. Whatever the source of these fears—whether they arise from the reluctance to accept such love or the apprehension that he will not be looking at *me* with love or the fear of the demands such love will make—the fears are real enough, and the prayer can be very difficult. The director does best not to argue with retreatants, but to help them to ask Jesus to reveal himself in such a way that they can accept such love. They are encouraged to share with him their fears and to approach him as best they can. It may take days, but they should not be moved on, because this point is crucial for their subsequent relationship to God and to Jesus. If this stumbling block is removed by the grace of God, then they will experience at a profound level the free and freeing love of God for them precisely as who they are. They will know that they are loved sinners and they will also know that God really is a lover of sinners.

The Desire to Know Jesus

The desire of the "Second Week" of the *Exercises,* "an intimate knowledge of our Lord . . . that I may love him more and follow him more closely," is obviously a desire for revelation. One can only know Jesus intimately if he reveals himself. One asks for this grace and then contemplates the gospel stories, not in order to understand the gospels better, but because the gospels are privileged writings to contemplate in order to give the living Lord Jesus a chance to reveal himself. The purpose of contemplating gospel scenes, in other words, is to make it easier for the living Lord to show himself. "And when he takes on reality and shape for me (not necessarily in a picture, by the way), then I talk to him, not to the text, and I listen to him, not the text."[3] As Jesus takes on more and more reality for retreatants, they may find him more challenging and daunting than they expected. He may show himself as having desires for them which they resist. He may desire that they give up everything and follow him in apostolic discipleship. They may recognize that they can freely respond "yes" or "no" and that they will not jeopardize his love for them by saying "no." They, too, develop new or different desires towards him; they may desire to be chosen for apostolic discipleship realizing that he is free to choose them or not. The experience of many retreatants in this week, in other words, is that they are developing an adult relationship to the living Lord Jesus.

A desire for a more intimate revelation of Jesus is the way many retreatants express the grace of the "Third Week." They have come to a personal knowledge of Jesus, and now they ask that he share with them his suffering self, that he let them into that suffering and death that made him who he now is. It is important for directors to point out that the "grace of the Third Week" is precisely that, a grace. Many think that they can easily enter the contemplation of the passion and death of Jesus only to find that their prayer is dry and difficult. One cannot enter into another's sufferings unless the other reveals himself. So retreatants need to ask Jesus to reveal himself so that they can be sorrowful and compassionate with him. When he begins to reveal himself, they may well find that they have asked for more than they expected and that they resist strongly letting this revelation penetrate to their hearts. The "Third Week" very often is a struggle.

The desire that Jesus reveal his triumph, his joy, the experience of having

---

[3]*Ibid.*, p. 827.

come through to resurrection so that one can rejoice and exult with him is the grace of the "Fourth Week." Here again the director stresses that a grace or a revelation is being asked for. The "Fourth Week" experience is not automatic, the climax that can be experienced just by contemplating the resurrection narratives. Jesus must reveal himself. Moreover, the retreatant may well resist this self-revelation of Jesus just as he has resisted earlier self-revelations. Resurrection, for example, does not mean sweet revenge on one's enemies. The triumph may not be as one had expected. Once again we find that the desire for revelation is an ambivalent one because God and his Son are surprising mystery.

Conclusion

When directors and retreatants look at the graces asked for in retreat as a request for revelation, perspectives change. For one thing, people realize more clearly that prayer is a matter of relationship. Intimacy is the basic issue, not resolutions "to be better" or answers to problems. Many of life's problems and challenges have no answers; one can only live with and through them. Problems and challenges, however, can be faced and lived through with more peace and resilience if people know that they are not alone. A man's wife will not return from the dead, but the pain is more bearable when he has poured out his sorrow, his anger, his despair to God and has experienced God's intimate presence to him. Secondly, retreatants recognize more clearly that will power alone cannot achieve "success" in prayer. It is much clearer that what one desires is a gift which only the Other can supply.

Freedom is at the heart of the process. No one can coerce personal revelation or intimacy. God cannot be forced, but neither can the retreatant. There are some graces that God has bound himself to give. He wants to save and liberate; he has loved us to the point of letting his Son die for us, and he wants us to accept that love. But the call to apostolic discipleship has not been promised to anyone who asks for it. It may also be that there are certain desires we have, such as to be let into the suffering heart of Jesus, that are not granted or only granted after a long time of waiting. On the other hand, we need to recognize much more clearly that freedom also means that we are free before God. Directors should not try to coerce retreatants to ask for what they do not (yet) want or are too ambivalent to desire honestly. God does not seem to want dumb submission. He wants spontaneous love.

The relationship to God and to Jesus tends to take on a more adult flavor when people begin to look on prayer in this interpersonal way. They realize that they are not asking for graces, much as a child asks for candy, but for intimacy. While they wisely approach such an enterprise with fear and trembling, they nonetheless can do so as adults who know that intimacy requires relative maturity on their parts.

The Eighteenth Annotation of the *Spiritual Exercises* and Social Sinfulness

Bernard J. Bush, S.J.

©*Soundings* (Washington, DC: Center of Concern, 1974).

The Spiritual Exercises must be adapted to the condition of the one who is to engage in them, that is, to his age, education and talent. Thus exercises that he could not easily bear, or from which he could derive no profit, should not be given to one with little natural ability or of little physical strength.

Similarly, each one should be given those exercises that wold be more helpful and profitable according to his willingness to dispose himself for them.

Hence, one who wishes no further help than some instruction and the attainment of a certain degree of peace of soul may be given the Particular Examination of Conscience, and after that the General Examination of Conscience. Along with this, let him be given for half an hour each morning the method of prayer on the Commandments and on the Capital Sins, etc. Weekly confession should be recommended to him, and if possible, the reception of Holy Communion every two weeks, or even better, every week if he desires it.

This method is more appropriate for those who have little natural ability or are illiterate. Let each of the Commandments be explained to them, and also the Capital Sins, the use of the five senses, the precepts of the Church, and the Works of Mercy.

Similarly, if the one giving the Exercises sees that the exercitant has little aptitude or little physical strength, that he is one from whom little fruit is to be expected, it is more suitable to give him some of the easier exercises as a preparation for confession. Then he should be given some ways of examining his conscience, and directed to confess more frequently than was his custom before, so as to retain what he has gained.

But let him not go on further and take up the matter dealing with the Choice of a Way of Life, nor any other exercises that are outside the first Week. This is especially to be observed when much better results could be obtained with other persons, and when there is not sufficient time to take everything (18th Annotation: Puhl translation, *The Spiritual Exercises of St. Ignatius,* Loyola University Press, Chicago).

It should be noted that the language of the Eighteenth Annotation seems belittling and condescending to the types of retreatants described, and for this reason, I believe, the annotation has not received the study it deserves. No one, director or retreatant, is willing to admit that the retreat is being given to "one who is illiterate or of weak constitution, poorly educated, or a poor subject, of little natural capacity or one from whom there is not much fruit to be looked for." Peters, in his commentary on the Spiritual Exercises, does not consider the retreatant of the Eighteenth Annotation, since they are "... the many who are of little natural capacity and limited understanding and yet long for peace of soul."[1] However, if these descriptions are taken as inclusive rather than exclusive, the annotation can take on quite a different flavor. If, that is, Ignatius is saying that for people at the low end of the spectrum of talent and awareness, so to speak, the Exercises in certain forms can profitably be given. It is surprising that adapted forms of retreat are so overlooked in view of the great insistence that Ignatius himself placed on them.

Screening and Adaptation According to Ignatius

I wish to cite here some documentary evidence from the writings of Ignatius in support of the contention that the principles enunciated in the Eighteenth Annotation should be reconsidered.

1. *Constitutions of the Society of Jesus*

They could begin by giving the Exercises to some in whose cases less is risked, and by conferring about their method of procedure with someone more experienced .... Generally, only the exercises of the First Week should be given. When they are given in their entirety, this should be done with outstanding persons or with those who desire to decide upon their state of life [409].

The Spiritual Exercises should not be given in their entirety except to a few persons, namely, those of such a character that from their progress notable fruit is expected for the glory of God. But the exercises of the First Week can be made available to large numbers, and some examination of conscience and methods of prayer (especially the first of those which are touched on in the Exercises) can also be given far more widely; for anyone who has good will seems to be capable of these exercises [649].[2]

2. *Autograph Directories of St. Ignatius*

It does not seem wise to encourage anyone to seclude himself to make the exercises unless he has these dispositions or the most noteworthy of them: ... and simply speaking, to the degree that he is suited for the institute of religion and for the Society, he is the more suited to seclude himself to make the exercises (no. 394).

Those who do not have these dispositions ... because there is no hope that they might bring themselves to a balance in such things ... should not be given the exercises .... But adequate help should be given them such as the First Week .... He is able to give them fur-

---

[1] William A.M. Peters, S.J., *The* Spiritual Exercises *of St. Ignatius: Exposition and Interpretation* (Jersey City, 1968), p. 11. See also pp. 10, 12, 18, 170.
[2] *St. Ignatius Loyola, The Constitutions of the Society of Jesus* (St. Louis, 1970), pp. 203, 283.

ther help in the form of different exercises from the other weeks, the method of praying and examining the conscience and other similar things (no. 395).

[regarding]...[in the case of] those who are not yet resigned into the hands of the Lord, ... but enter with certain plans and intentions, it is very fitting that all diligence be exerted in order that they might be rid of such imperfection, because it ... does not permit one to know the truth by any means. And he who is known to be very obstinate in this way before entering the exercises, should not be encouraged to make them, nor admitted to them until by frequent confessions, as has been said, he should become more mature (no. 416).

Nevertheless, after he has entered to make them, it is necessary to try to help him, and for this it helps much to delay him in the consideration of the Foundation *(marginal note in the Roman Codex III:* "On this point, our father put no little emphasis) ... and in particular and general examens, and in the awareness of how he has sinned in thoughts, works and words, for three or four days or more, until he grows in maturity. And when he has remained very obstinate for the First Week, it seems to me that I would not go forward with him, or at least I would give him the exercises that remain as briefly as possible (no. 417).[3]

3. *Letters of Ignatius*

Recall that only the exercises of the first week are to be given to all in general, unless you are dealing with very special persons *(raras personas)* who are disposed to regulate their lives according to the elections (To the Fathers at the Council of Trent, early 1546).

The exercises of the First Week could be given to many; but the other weeks only to those whom you find suitable for the state of perfection and who are truly willing to be helped (To Father John Pelletier, June 13, 1555).

Help them with examinations of conscience and with the Spiritual Exercises, especially at the beginning with the exercises of the First Week, and leave them some methods of prayer suited to each (To Father Ponce Cogordan, Feb. 12, 1555).

The First Week could be given to many along with some method of prayer. But to give them exactly, one should determine precisely to find subjects capable and suitable for helping others after they themselves have been helped. Where this is not the case, they should not go beyond the First Week (To Father Fulvius Androzzi, July 18, 1556).

If I were giving the Exercises in their entirety, I should give them to very few, and they educated, or persons who are very desirous of perfection, or very prominent, or who might be thinking of entering the Society. As a rule, I would give only the exercises of the First Week together with the general confession, and some of the examens, but would not go further.

I would rarely give the elections, and only with persons who are educated and very desirous of making them, or to persons who are not likely to cause us any embarrassment. It sometimes happens that, when they come out of the Exercises without having made all the progress hoped for, they are tempted, and say out publicly that Ours wanted to reduce them to poverty by urging them to religious poverty (To the Members of the Society in Portugal, undated).[4]

In the light of these texts, then, it is evident that Ignatius was quite insistent that the full exercises generally not be given. More to the point, whenever he couples his instruction to give only the First Week with forms of examen and

---

[3] *Ejercicios, Directorio y Documentos de San Ignacio,* ed. José Calveras, S.J. (Barcelona, 1968).
[4] *Letters of St. Ignatius Loyola* (Chicago, 1959), pp. 95, 247, 366, 434, 442.

methods of prayer, especially the first method, he is explicitly recommending the Eighteenth Annotation. Within the body of the Exercises the only place where the first method of prayer on the commandments, capital sins, etc., is recommended is in the Eighteenth Annotation. Ignatius is very interested in the dispositions of the prospective retreatant before the exercises are adapted to meet his or her needs. This certainly raises some questions about the current practice of giving "full" exercises to many. Perhaps many of the long retreats being given today are in fact Eighteenth Annotation retreats given in disguise.[5]

Experienced directors confess that their retreatants sometimes remain in some form of the First Week for the whole of the thirty days. Other Jesuits who are widely experienced in making and directing retreats question whether they themselves have in fact ever experienced the "full exercises." Even when material from the other three weeks has been covered and meditated upon deeply, the retreat still may not have gone beyond the first week. There is evidence within the first week that all other weeks are contained germinally. A whole retreat could be made from the colloquy on the first meditation on sin. There one can be present to Christ alive in mystery (Fourth Week), on the cross dying for my sins (Third Week), being Creator (Principle and Foundation) who came to make himself man, passing from eternal life (Incarnation, Second Week) to corporal death.

The Eighteenth Annotation in Today's World

In addition to the simple and uneducated people already referred to and prescribed for, there is another group of people described in the Eighteenth Annotation:

> . . . [to one] who desires to be helped to get instruction and to attain to a certain degree of contentment of soul, there may be given the particular examen, subsequently the general examen, together with the method of prayer on the commandments, the deadly sins, etc.... recommending him to confess his sins every week and receive communion . . . but not to get further into the matters of election, nor into any other exercises beyond those of the first week....[6]

This sounds like persons who just want to be a little bit happier than they are presently, but I do not think it should be seen so restrictively. Over and over we meet people, lay and religious, who are confused about living life religiously and need an experience of God's love and personal loveableness. We give retreats to women and men who have a poor self-image, who are adrift in their prayer-life, oppressed by Church and community structures, and who have little social consciousness and yet feel helpless and guilty in the

---

[5] David L. Fleming, S.J., "The Danger of Faddism and the Thirty Day Retreat, see below," pp. 311-315.

[6] *Spiritual Exercises,* [18].

face of the world's evils. So "one who desires to be helped to get instruction and to attain to a certain degree of contentment of soul" describes in a brief way a great many of the people who are coming to us today. For these Ignatius prescribes a variety of consciousness-raising spiritual exercises. These exercises are designed to guide a person to become more deeply aware of himself and the various influences he responds to, the good and the evil, under the enlightenment of the Holy Spirit. How could a retreatant possibly mediate, for example, on the commandment not to covet the neighbor's goods or the deadly sin of gluttony without considering that, as an American, he or she is one of the 6% consuming 40% of the world's resources? This is an inordinate affection which determines our responses, produces social desolation, and is generally accepted unconsciously. It would be unwise to attempt the full exercises with a person who does not have an awareness, or who does not have the capacity or the desire to have such an awareness of sin in his life. This type of person might even be considered the unlettered, the illiterate, the culturally ignorant that is considered in the Eighteenth Annotation.

Although we are speaking of those who desire or need instruction and a certain degree of contentment of soul, we are not proposing, nor does Ignatius, that the exercises become times for indoctrination, teaching, or covert preaching. These considerations should be proposed in such a way that the retreatment is exposed in prayer to that which causes the loss of peace — sin and inordinate affections, and to the redemptive action of Christ revealing them and himself as savior simultaneously. This revelation is what is asked for in the triple colloquy of the third exercise of the First Week. There the retreatant prays for a knowledge of the world which will reveal to him his unfreedoms and complicity in evil in the form of cultural addictions, sinful social structures of which we are members, and disparity of national lifestyles reflecting personal injustice.[8]

Formation of Conscience

Anyone who attains a "certain degree of contentment of soul" apart from the dimensions of life mentioned above has a false conscience. One need only advert to the frequent and insistent calls of the Church directing our attention and prayer to these issues. Far from being an alien influence on a retreatant in the exercises, considerations of social consciousness must be seen as the authentic voice of the Holy Spirit through the magisterium. Furthermore, it is

---

[7] *Ibid.*, [63].
[8] For a fuller treatment of these issues, see W. J. Byron, S.J., "Social Consciousness in the Ignatian Exercises," pp. 272-285; W. J. Connolly, S.J., "Social Action and the Directed Retreat," pp. 286-290; W. A. Barry, S.J., "The Experience of the First and Second Weeks of the Spiritual Exercises," pp. 95-102; Thomas E. Clarke, S.J., "Holiness and Justice in Tension," *The Way*, 13 (1973), p. 184; Peter J. Henriot, S.J., "The Concept of Social Sin," *Catholic Mind*, LXXI (1973), p. 38.

absolutely essential to form a correct conscience and thus attain freedom through these exercises before one can form the empathic identification with Christ in the contemplations of the subsequent weeks. Clarke notes, "...today, no adequate spirituality is possible which does not integrate into its viewpoint the insight we have been describing. Whatever the limitations of the past, a contemporary spiritual way which attends not at all to the social and cultural embodiments of sin and grace must be dismissed as inadequate, as not fully Christian."[9]

Segundo, in his development of a theology for artisans of a new humanity, observes:

> ...[society] is not the end result of juxtaposing already constituted individuals,...from the very start it is a system of human reactions and interrelationships that constitute the individual and form part of his total human condition. Thus we cannot talk about two types of conscience or human awareness: i.e., an individual conscience and then a social conscience....
>
> The social sphere, viewed as a dimension constitutive of man rather than as the content of conscience, confronts man with a new source of determinisms. And these determinisms are all the more dangerous in that they are normally lived inadvertently....
>
> But there is more involved here. These norms, values, attitudes, and behavior patterns which form the basic consensus of a given society, are an expression of the way in which the society's members conceive and experience their relationships with others—whether they realize it or not. And at the same time, they are a justification of these relationships which are imposed and perpetuated by existing structures. In other words: the established moral code takes on the characteristics of an ideology justifying the situation.
>
> As we said before, the established morality (or the social conscience) is the complex of values and behavior patterns which a society communicates to its members....It is not just that it confronts the individual with a new fount of determinisms are also prejudiced in favor of the vested interests within the society.
>
> Man's liberation must necessarily involve his conscious realization of the unconscious determinisms that surround him....In short, it is concretized in ideological transformation and political action.[10]

It is the work, then, of the exercises of the Eighteenth Annotation type of retreat to lead into the experience of conversion spoken of here. It is a faith-filled reflection on life as it is being lived, and a turning to Christ who liberates from sinful determinisms. The retreat experience should be filled with consolation, empowering to action coupled with a deep desire to go forward with Christ responsive to his invitations. Premature social action based only on restlessness, anger, or guilt feelings perpetuates the evil.[11] The mission of the retreat director in the apostolate of the Exercises will then be to offer concrete living witness through his own life and sensitivity to the alternative ways of living which Christ can offer. These alternate ways of living challenge the existing sinful structures and ideologies from within our own experience of

---

[9] T.E. Clarke, S.J., *op. cit.*, p. 188.
[10] Juan Louis Segundo, S.J., *Grace and the Human Condition* (New York, 1973), pp. 38, 39.
[11] Bernard Longergan, S.J., "Religious Commitment," *The Pilgrim People, A Vision With Hope* (Villanova, 1971), pp. 45-69, esp. p. 66.

them. It involves a change of a world-view and sense of self in relation to God and others which is dominated and infused in faith, love and the gospel values. Our screening and preparation of potential candidates for the "full" exercises should, according to the policy of their author, be reserved for those who are capable of such a transformation. They should have the mental ability to comprehend these vast and complicated dimensions of our life today, the emotional stability to face them, however helpless and poorly equipped he might feel himself to be, and a desire to do something about them, involving whatever personal changes might be called for by Christ. For such, the Exercises adopted according to the Eighteenth Annotation can be seen as preparatory to the full experience of the thirty days. For others who lack this capacity, these exercises can be seen as terminal, with the goal of achieving that certain degree of contentment of soul.

Conclusion

Finally, the title of the book of the Exercises itself gives support to their use for conscienticizing evangelization.[12] It states: "Spiritual Exercises, which are for overcoming oneself and ordering one's life without being determined by any affection which might be disordered."[13] This ordering means being caught up in and working to bring into perfect reality the orientation of the entire universe to the Father through Christ. It is impossible to be of this dynamic order without personal freedom from the cultural and social sinful determinisms which have formed our consciences. Becoming aware of them through instruction, examination, and meditation is the work of redeeming social grace. St. Paul describes the experience: "What a wretched man I am! Who can free me from this body under the power of death? All praise to God, through Jesus Christ our Lord! So with my mind I serve the law of God, but with my flesh the law of sin."[14] The liberation we seek does not occur in isolation from the real world where sin is embodied in persons and institutions. The Eighteenth Annotation provides the *locus* for the consideration of adaptation of the exercises, including the First Week, to meet the needs of a great many of the men and women who are presenting themselves to us for retreats today.

---

[12] The term, "conscienticizing evangelization," comes from Gustavo Gutierrez, *The Theology of Liberation* (New York, 1973), p. 116. In that context it refers to the need for the Church to support the cause of liberation of the oppressed to free, better, and humanize people through the recovery of a living faith committed to human society. On the same theme, see the statement of the Synod of Bishops, 1971, *Justice in the World.*
[13] *Spiritual Exercises,* [21].
[14] Ro 7:24,25.

II. CONTENT AND EXPERIENCE

The First Week of the *Spiritual Exercises* and the Conversion of Saint Paul

Carolyn Osiek, R.S.C.J.

Volume 36, 1977, pp. 657-665.

The title says in a general way the topic of this article. Actually, however, it is somewhat the other way around, for another way of expressing the topic would be: Paul's decisive "First Week" experience, or, the "First Week" in the life of Paul. The present investigation will be an attempt to focus, examine, and understand the personal experience of Paul which parallels and reflects the process experienced and planned by Ignatius for his followers in what he later came to call the "First Week" of the *Spiritual Exercises*.

There are some obvious limitations to such an undertaking. First, if as is generally accepted, Paul's initial conversion experience took place sometime between 33-36 A.D., and if what is preserved of his Philippian, Galatian, and Corinthian correspondence was written between the years 54 and 57 from Ephesus, there is a 20 year gap between the experience and the description.[1] Second, Paul had no intention of writing an autobiography. He alludes to his own spiritual experience only insofar as it helps him convey his point to others, usually in terms of the bankruptcy of the Mosaic law vis-a-vis the grace of Christ—a religious situation far removed in actuality from the experience of most of us, whatever figurative applications can be made. Third, the one source in which Paul's spiritual conversion is graphically and formally portrayed (in triplicate)—Acts 9:22 and 26—could be utilized in a consideration of New Testament theology of conversion, but

---

[1]The chronology of the letters is disputed. Here I follow J. A. Fitzmyer, "A Life of Paul," *Jerome Biblical Commentary*, ed. R. E. Brown, J. A. Fitzmyer, R. E. Murphy (Englewood Cliffs, N.J.: Prentice Hall, 1968), pp. 218, 221.

in the light of modern scriptural source criticism cannot responsibly be used to shed light on Pauline spirituality or spiritual experience. Some of the elements picked up by Luke in his triple narrative will be used as illustrative of the Pauline experience in the wider dimension of familiar religious symbols, but it must be kept in mind that for Paul they are secondary.

This brings us to a statement of the broader scope of the present undertaking. The purpose of the investigation is not historical. If it were, it could well stop with the Pauline data. Rather, the full scope is an attempt to understand Paul's wounding and healing as exemplary of a common spiritual journey through death to new life for a purpose. The expanded articulation of that process is drawn from personal experience as retreatant and as a spiritual director.

It might be well to begin by describing the structure of the "First Week" process as it will be treated here. Basically it is a movement of entering into death in order to have life, of descending into the depths only to find there new inspiration to arise, of going down with the old and familiar and coming up in newness, as the ancient ritual of baptism by immersion so clearly portrays. It is wounding and healing, alienation and reconciliation as the person comes face to face first with human evil and then with divine goodness. Precisely where these two currents cross is the point of greatest pain because the comparison becomes nearly unendurable. But out of the conflict engendered by that pain comes the energy to begin anew, and thus the paradoxical cycle of death and rebirth is once again lived out.

Ignatius' term "confusion" is not a bad word to describe the growing sense that something is wrong, both in its literary meaning of "shame" and especially in its more common sense of "losing one's bearings." There are three stages that can occur as defenses are stripped away and the sense of confusion sharpens. Ignatius described these three stages one way in n. [63] of the *Exercises:* first, a deep knowledge of personal sin and a feeling of abhorrence; second, an understanding of the "disorder of my actions" and a resulting feeling of horror; third, a knowledge of the sinfulness of the world and, again, a sense of horror. Abhorrence and horror are strong enough terms, yet they imply a primacy of activity on the part of the retreatant—though, it must be added, the grace to have such feelings is clearly seen as something to be asked of and freely bestowed by God.

The terminology used by Ignatius here, at least as we can understand it four centuries later, does not adequately describe the passive nature of the First Week experience as it is sometimes encountered when, without active pursuit of desire for sorrow for sin, and so forth, rational defenses and affective supports previously relied upon suddenly disappear. Disorientation deepens as awareness of sin increases. The revelation of sinfulness progresses, as Ignatius described it, in three stages. The first is that of felt guilt over specific acts for which the person is responsible, guilt that has been accumulating perhaps over a long period of time, the full impact of which suddenly bursts forth with unexpectedly painful sharpness as the retreatant faces God and himself in solitude. Confusion is balanced only by the firm witness of the mercy and forbearance of God in allowing the person to come to this point.

The second stage occurs if the layer of the conscious mind can be sufficiently peeled off to reveal the underlying basic tendencies to evil for which a person is only partly responsible at the conscious level. The feeling of confusion, pain, and alienation increases and a new factor enters in: helplessness—the inability to do what one would want to do about vast areas of life. The realization deepens that one is unable to consciously regulate tendencies to grab for security, love, and control that diminish both victims and subject. The person is painfully aware of not being in control of his own motivation. At this point feelings of guilt mix with a newly discovered fear of one's own innate destructiveness. Mistrust of oneself can be countered by trust in the God who has kept him from becoming worse than he is.

In the third stage the probe of the Spirit goes deeper still until it reaches the level at which personal responsibility is no longer at stake. It is the experience of total powerlessness, helplessness, total inability to act in any way to save oneself. The forces of disintegration seem to be triumphing and God seems to have left the person totally to his own resources which have consequently crumbled. Here it is no longer a question of guilt and mercy, but of the ability to live with fear and to cling to some memory of the love of God. The familiar theological maxim that God sustains all things in existence at every moment becomes a crushing reality, for the person is sure that nothing within himself is preserving his being, and yet it seems to be God himself who is crushing him. Ignatius understood [53] that only the total powerlessness of Christ on the cross as he is destroyed by forces beyond human control can give any meaning to this experience. W. de Broucker describes this state of soul in a way that sums up the whole triple movement:

> This "confusion," flowing from the sense of being judged by God, is not the result of a rational process: it is total loss of face before a situation which cannot be long endured with the usual supports of reason and prudence. We find ourselves confronted by the cross in the presence of unmeasuredness itself, that which is "madness to the world" (1 Co 1:23).[2]

---

[2]"La 'confusion,' fruit spirituel de ce jugement divin, n'est pas le résultat d'une argumentation logique: elle est perte totale de contenance, devant une situation qui précisément ne peut être plus longtemps supportée avec les ressources habituelles de la raison et de la prudence. Nous voici, devant la Croix du Christ, mis en présence de la démesure même, qui est 'folie pour le monde' (1 Cor 1:23)" "La première semaine des Exercices," *Christus*, vol. 6, no. 21 (1959), pp. 22-39 (translation mine).

It is precisely the attitude expressed by the dying Christ that marks the beginning of the movement upward: "Into your hands I commit my spirit." Surrender into the hands of God, the cessation of struggle against the force that seems to be annihilating the self, goes against the basic instinct of human nature. It is natural for us to fight for life, to hang on tenuously to the familiar. If the shred of self that is left can be given up, a new self can be formed. With surrender comes trust that there is someone or something to surrender to, and that something other than total chaos can result. Once trust has been given, a dim hope can begin to arise, an assurance that dawn will come and that a reason for the suffering and death of the experience may be that something greater is coming to birth.

With a new confidence given to the force that is at work within, further insight into one's personal responsibility may result. There may be deepened realization of how one's total helplessness before God, now a vivid reality, creates subconscious defenses in the form of root tendencies to turn away from God in order to avoid pain, conflict, or unwelcome truth. New awareness of personal orientation away from God then leads to a whole new outlook about personal sinfulness. The avoidance, neglect, anxiety, and self-seeking expressed in everyday life as sin are seen with much more understanding and insight into one's personal motivations and weaknesses. At this point a healing of pain and guilt can take place and the mercy of God becomes an invading presence bringing with it the experience of reconciliation leading to a deep sense of peace and eventually of joy.

The new clarity of understanding leads inevitably, for the person who remains faithful in following the new way where God is leading, to a transformation of attitude and behavior. This transformation is a psychic and spiritual change that invades the whole person, but rarely does it happen all at once. It involves the abandoning of certain accepted values and untried assumptions regarding personal autonomy, perception of truth, or need for affectivity. Realization of what God is asking in these areas and consequent surrender and acceptance of change usually happen gradually over a period of at least several months. What is happening simultaneously is the acquisition of a new set of personal values to replace the old ones, values usually founded on sharpened awareness of the fragility and weakness of the self and a deep sense of awe and gratitude at the ways that God's power is at work in weakness. Mary Esther Harding describes the psychological change that is taking place at this point:

Whenever there is an upsurge of highly activated unadapted material into consciousness, the task of assimilation becomes urgent. This holds true whether the new material is valuable, creative stuff or merely archaic phantasy that bespeaks more a morbid exuberance than a prolific creativity. The assimilation of the new material demands a fresh standpoint, which implies a recognition of the relativity of all former judgments. What was formerly considered unqualifiedly good must now be judged in the light of the new and enlarged understanding; the same must be done with that which has been considered bad.[3]

The whole experience might be summarized as an awareness of:

the goodness of God	gratitude
sinful actions	guilt
	need for mercy, forgiveness
sinful tendencies	fear
	struggle
	need to experience love of God
powerlessness	surrender
	trust
	hope

And a new awareness of:

sinful tendencies	new awareness of mercy
	love
motivation for sinful acts	power of God
	need to change

There follows a healing and reconciliation   peace, joy

and a gradual transformation of values, attitudes, behavior

As was stated at the beginning, the primary focus of this paper is the spiritual experience of Paul, and the previous discussion of the process is by way of setting the stage. Paul's change of heart is classically spoken of as a "conversion." The limitation inherent in the use of this term is the restricted sense in which the word is most often used: change of faith or religion or, somewhat more broadly, emendation of a wayward moral life, while the root meaning of the word "conversion" is really something closer to an "about face"—a total turning of the person from one orientation to another. While Paul's "conversion" certainly did entail a change of religious affiliation, though probably not a change of moral conduct, it must be understood primarily in the broadest sense of the term, as a complete overthrow and turn-about of personal values. Because of the ambiguities present in the word "conversion," it might be preferable to speak of the "transformation" of Paul in his encounter with the living Christ.[4]

---

[3]*Psychic Energy: Its Source and Its Transformation*, 2nd ed. Bollingen Series X (Washington, D.C.: Pantheon, 1963), p. 285.

[4]An important article on the structure and Western interpretations of Paul's conversion experience appeared long ago and attracted considerable notice in Protestant scholarly circles, coming as it did out of a Lutheran interpretation of Paul; I refer to Krister Stendahl's "The

Contrary to what much popular and undiscriminating piety (and perhaps even the author of Acts) would have us think, Paul's transformation did not happen overnight or even in three days as a careless reading of Acts 9:18-30 might suggest. Paul himself speaks of three years (Ga 1:18) transpiring before he began to preach Christ. There is no reason to suppose that the process moved along with remarkable speed.

We tend to clothe Paul's transformation experience in a thick covering of the miraculous, leaning too heavily on the clear triple account of Acts and too lightly on Paul's own illusive comments. The flash of light, the heavenly voice of the revealer, Paul's being struck to the ground, and the mysterious three-day blindness are all stock elements of narrations of divine epiphanies. For some, miraculous revelations are a stumbling block and a source of conflict. But for most people today, they are something else: an invitation to disregard. And so what happens is that someone like Paul, who leaps out at us so humanly in his own writings, becomes relegated to the dim past, to the gallery of "saints" who are not quite as human as the rest of us, to the realm of the "supernatural" dichotomized from that realm in which we ourselves live and struggle. The reason for all this is not surprising: we do not have to have the uncomfortable experience of seeing ourselves reflected in such a "saint."

The ways of God with humanity are as varied as are the persons who seek to know them, and yet there are qualities of our common humanity that remain very much the same. It is for this reason that an analysis of the transformation process as given above, and an attempt to see that process as it happened in Paul are worthwhile. We may be able to see something of ourselves in him and so better understand the ways of God in us.

It is a mistake to think of Paul as changing from hardened persecutor to enthusiastic mystic, from his blind cruelty to a Christian sensitivity, as though his transformation were from sinner to saint. Paul was not a hard man; he was a sincere and generous man. His pursuit of Christians sprang not from cruelty but from enthusiasm in the service of God. He was the good and upright man whom the Lord loved, and because the Lord loved him so much, he called him to give more. Paul says of himself (Ph 3:5-6) that his family and religious credentials were impeccable and that he had done

---

Apostle Paul and the Introspective Conscience of the West,'' *Harvard Theological Review* 56:3 (July, 1963), pp. 199-215, an article well worth reading. In recent conversation between the author and myself there was agreement about Paul's ''clear conscience'' regarding his former way of life in Judaism (see especially pp. 200-201); however, I would not want to stress the idea of ''introspection'' as the search for personal sin, but would rather emphasize the seeking after awareness of God's action within the person. In contrast to Dean Stendahl's interpretation (pp. 204-205), I would distinguish two aspects of Paul's change of ways: first, a personal transformation, and second, the directing of that new energy toward evangelization of the Gentiles.

far more than the minimum required to be a son of the Law. He was without fault in its regard, fully aware of its value as gift bestowed upon Israel as a proof of God's love. His sincere thirst for justice must have led him periodically into the self-scrutiny of the just which produces an awareness of personal failings and sinful tendencies that only deepens devotion as it deepens an appreciation of God's mercy.

Then something happened. Whether his encounter with the living Christ was as dramatic as Acts 9 portrays it is doubtful, for Paul nowhere alludes to his experience as containing elements of the sensational but rather describes it quite simply: "Have I not seen Jesus our Lord?" (1 Co 9:1); "I did not receive [the gospel] from a human source nor was I taught by any but a revelation from Jesus Christ" (Ga 1:12); "God who had set me aside from my mother's womb called me through his grace and revealed his son in me" (Ga 1:15; see Is 49:1; Jr 1:5). There is an undeniable sense of personal encounter and call, even for a specific mission, but very little impression of fanfare. He found himself at point zero, knocked off his horse more internally than externally, with no patterned defenses or conditioned responses to fall back on that had not been stripped away by a new presence that was relentlessly pursuing him.

When the realization of what had happened began to take hold of him, Paul knew he had been changed. Luke's image of blindness approximates in physical terms what must have been his psychic state for a period of time: confusion, loss, fear, inner chaos, spiritual paralysis, the terrifying feeling that his whole world was coming apart. As he began to surrender to the force that was invading him, he would have become aware that it was a new and unwelcome presence—that of Jesus of Nazareth, suddenly intruding upon his well-ordered world. This is in fact the heart of the experience of brokenness: that Christ manifests himself in a new and unexpected way, and before his demanding presence all pre-conceived structures of life must be put aside.

Once he had accepted what was happening, he would have begun to see himself in a new way, feeling within himself the slowly-dawning and terrible realization that he had misplaced his devotion and misdirected his zeal, the frustration of knowing for the first time that he had been turned in a direction which, in the light of a new awareness, he had to judge as the wrong way. New understanding would have brought about new self-knowledge and a new capacity for radical honesty about the movements of his life, enveloped in deepened awe at the sustaining and patient love of God revealed in Christ who was now calling into question the whole meaning of his life.

The realization that the love of God has been constant when our response has been anything but constant, that his forgiveness was extended even before we knew for what to ask it, can be a crushing blow from which the security of the ego never fully recovers. The wound inflicted on it is not *cured,* as if the tearing never happened; rather, it is *healed,* brought to new wholeness not in spite of, but because of the rending. As is often the case, Paul's healing and reconciliation with God were not for his sake only, but that he might lead many others to the same point: "The love of Christ overwhelms us when we realize that one died for all . . . so that the living should no longer live for themselves but for him who died for them and was raised again . . . for everything is from God who has reconciled us to himself through Christ and given us the ministry of reconciliation" (2 Co 5:14-18).

What is cautiously born then is a self that must undertake the painful task of shedding and leaving behind as so much debris much that the former self deemed of value, in order to make room for new value to come. In the case of Paul the reversal which he had to endure to be faithful to newly-given grace was dramatic and loaded with not only personal but also social consequences: "But whatever was formerly gain to me, I have come to consider it loss because of Christ; moreover, I now consider everything loss because of the overwhelming knowledge of Jesus Christ my Lord, for whom I have let go of everything and consider it rubbish in order to gain Christ and be counted with him" (Ph 3:7-9). For him it meant giving up a worldview, religious affiliation, a certainty of being right, a reputation, family and friends, the whole fabric of personal and social relationships that had formed the pattern of his life. Few are called to so drastic a change.

Yet the most fundamental change must have been one with which many can resonate: the need to reconstruct from broken fragments a new self, a much more fragile self, like an earthenware jar hollowed out at the center in which "the overflowing power comes from God and not from us" (2 Co 4:7). It is the need to understand and accept the voice of Christ addressed to the prostrate human spirit, "My grace is enough, for strength is brought to fullness in weakness," and to respond by saying, "Joyfully then I will openly share my weakness so that the power of Christ may be revealed through me" (2 Co 12:8-9).

It might be argued that the above account of Paul's conversion and transformation is a fanciful extrapolation based on insufficient data. Yet the essential human experience underlying it is so basic and universal that no matter in how many myriad forms it is manifested, a true experience of transformation from one spiritual state to another (as opposed to a superficial "conversion" that is only temporary because self-induced) has certain fundamentally similar components. Certainly Paul's experience was a transformation of this kind. Though he leaves many things unsaid, the pain and fear, the bewildering search, and ultimately the ecstasy of discovering that it is precisely in crucifying weakness that the power of the risen Christ is manifested, come through in the few literary traces he has left.

For Paul transformation meant a radical break with the past, with family, home, and faith. For most of us, the break is not so abrupt, and yet the need to abandon old habits of thinking and feeling to make room for new ones still only dimly perceived is a common element. Spiritual directors are plentiful these days, but guides and models in one's spiritual experience are not always easy to come by. An ability to find echoes of one's own life in the jolting experience of Paul may give encouragement and be a cause for that movement of hope in darkness which affirms with him that no matter how chaotic may be the experience of finding out what we really are, for the person who continues trying to hang on the way Christ has hung onto him neither height of blind pride nor depth of despair—both of which can co-exist in the same person—nor any creature of the imagination can ever wrench us away from the love of God that is expressed to us in Christ Jesus our Lord.[5]

---

[5]See Ph 3:12; Rm 8:39.

The Experience of the First and Second Weeks of the *Spiritual Exercises*

William A. Barry, S.J.

Volume 32, 1973, pp. 102-109.

The directed retreat is rapidly becoming a preferred method of making the *Spiritual Exercises* of St. Ignatius Loyola. Thousands of individuals have by now made such retreats under the guidance of a director who tailors his direction to the needs and experience of the individual. Enthusiasm for such direction is running high. It seems the appropriate time for directors to begin sharing in print their experiences and methods—if for no other reason than to subject our practice to the scrutiny and critique of others. This article is an attempt to begin the process and to contribute to the development of technique and theory in spiritual direction.

In this essay I would like to share one reading of how retreatants experience the *Exercises*. The reading is based on the directed retreats given by six staff members of the Center for Religious Development.[1] Hundreds of individuals have been directed by us over a period of years in various adaptations of the *Spiritual Exercises*. The basic model presupposed in the essay is the thirty-day closed retreat, but we have also given the full *Exercises* in the form of the nineteenth Annotation[2] and parts of the *Exercises* in shorter retreats of six to fifteen days. Over the years we have shared with one another our experiences and methods. The reading presented here is in the final analysis the responsibility of the author, but it is based on much

---

[1] I wish to acknowledge with gratitude the contributions of my colleagues at the Center for Religious Development to the ideas and experiences brought out in the article. In a real sense the Center is the author though only I am responsible for the final form.

[2] The text of the *Exercises* to which reference will be made is the translation by Louis J. Puhl (Chicago: Loyola University Press, a reprint of the Newman Press, edition of 1951). The nineteenth annotation retreat is described in no. 19, p. 8, of this edition.

experience beyond his own.

It should also be noted that the title limits the discussion to the experiences of the first and second weeks of the *Exercises*. The reason for the limitation is that we have had more experience with these two weeks than with the third and fourth weeks. Thus the remarks on the third and fourth weeks will be short and much more tentative.

A Pattern of Experience

The intent, then, is to describe a pattern of experience that we have discerned as characteristic for many of our retreatants and which seems to be consonant with what Ignatius hoped exercitants would experience. The pattern we have found is of particular interest because we have taken a stance of *not* leading retreatants through the *Exercises*. Let me explain. We begin the retreat by helping the retreatant to a kind of contemplative prayer that involves looking at the Lord and what He has done. Thus, we might suggest Psalms 103, 104, 105 as models of praying to God in praise and thanksgiving for what He is and has done; we might suggest looking at flowers, trees, sunlight, rain—smelling them, feeling them, hearing them, and then responding—or rather letting the response arise from within. For some retreatants, experiences with people might be the focus, and memories of loved ones and of events with them flood in; again we encourage the retreatant to let his responses come. We try, in other words, to help the retreatant to pray spontaneously, to enjoy this kind of prayer, and to find his own way and content. And, we make it clear that we have no program for him to cover in the thirty days, or eight days, or whatever number of days. The Lord will lead him, not we nor even the structure of the *Exercises*. Thus, if the pattern occurs, we reason, it is because there is a dynamic in this kind of prayer that is predictable.

In many ways prior knowledge of the *Spiritual Exercises* can be a disadvantage since many retreatants are programmed to expect certain meditations and a certain structure. Indeed, they even expect themselves to have the same responses as on previous occasions when they have made the *Exercises;* in this case the response expected could be an adolescent response because they were adolescents when they first made the *Exercises*. Since most of our retreatants have been exposed to the *Exercises* a great deal, our effort often has to be to keep them from structuring themselves out of contact with the living God. The "naive" subject is, thus, to be rejoiced over.

If a retreatant comes to the retreat with a "problem" he wants to solve or a decision he has to make, we tend to have him put the problem on the shelf for a while and just look at the Lord and react to Him. We point out that often a "problem" is a problem because we worry it too much, and so we counsel him to turn away from himself and look at the Lord. We also point out that he has thirty days or eight or whatever and that he should let the Lord lead him as to when to take up a problem or decision. We thus hope that the retreatant will give up any preconceived agenda items that he has and we assure him that we have none.[3]

The Experience of the First Week

The stance we take means that we do not introduce the "first week" ideas after a certain period of time. Rather we let the dynamic of prayer and of God's dealing with the person do the "introducing." What does this mean? We have found that many of our retreatants are led into what might be called a "first week experience" once they get deep enough into the kind of prayer just described. That is, after he has been praying in praise and thanksgiving for a while, after basking in the Lord, as it were, for a day or two or three, the retreatant begins to experience a sense of alienation, of impotence, of desolation. Where before, for example, he found the Psalms full of praise and hardly noticed the references to sinfulness or to the vanity of human hopes, now these latter references hold the center of his attention. He feels desolate, alienated from his God, unable to return to the consolation of the last few days. He may even begin to doubt the experience of the first few days of the retreat and to wonder if he has ever been able to pray for real. He feels himself unworthy of God.

Welling up in him is a sense of helplessness and hopelessness, a feeling of having botched his life, of being lost and lonely. Often enough he recalls all the times when he has resisted the call of God, all the times he has sinned. If a particular "sin" has been habitual with him, for example, doubts against faith, anger, sexual excess, he may not only recall this "sin" with great remorse but also find himself disturbed by the "temptation" to that sin— again a source of great discouragement. When experiences like these occur, we know that the man has been led by the Lord and his own needs into an experience of sinfulness.

Note that in these circumstances his experience is an experience in the present not just a memory. He experiences himself as alienated, desolate *now,* as needy *now.* And sometimes the experience can be deep and frightening, so much so that the inexperienced director because of his own anxiety may try to lift the retreatant's spirits and help him out of the desolation prematurely instead of letting the Spirit do it at the right moment. It is our experience that such an intervention (except perhaps where the desolation is clearly clinical depression) is disastrous in the long run. We have met men and women who have been "helped" to avoid real problems in their spiritual lives by a too directive spiritual guide only to have the problems arise years later with more virulence when the person has less resilience to bounce back from them. We find that many psychologically "normal," hard-working, faith-filled people have been staving off feelings such as those we have just described by overwork, alcohol, pills, the piling up of experiences ("effusio ad exteriora" in the old ascetical language), the continual seeking after companionship and even after spiritual direction. The first few days of prayer remove these "defenses," and the feelings come to the surface. If the director himself has experienced the saving power of God in his own life, he can now give the retreatant a chance to

---

[3]Of course, later on in the retreat we will ask him about the problem if he has not brought it up. Often enough it seems to have solved itself.

confront these feelings in the faith and hope that he will experience the "good news" of salvation, that he will be saved from this dark night. The director gives the retreatant this chance by helping him not to run away from these feelings, by pointing out that it is precisely here that he needs to stay and to turn toward the Lord in hope.

Sinfulness Experience

Many retreatants spontaneously see the misery of the world around them during this time of desolation; everything seems colored by their view of themselves as lonely and lost. We then help them to look at the actual condition of the world in all its misery and war and despair, and to recognize that this world is in the state it is because of men's choices. Thus, the triple sin meditation of Ignatius enters the retreat in the form of realizing that the present is the result of all past history, and the feeling very often is one of helplessness that the world and oneself are on a drunken career toward hell. The retreatant, in other words, feels the enormity of evil and his own helplessness to do anything about it.

Often enough he may be unable to experience and believe in the love of God for him or his world. Thus, he experiences the reality of sin as alienation, as flesh in the Biblical sense of man cut off from God and unable to restore the relationship to Him.

What is painted here is a typical picture of the first week experience of sinfulness. I believe that at some level this experience occurs in anyone who has a "first week experience." At the same time it must be acknowledged that I have painted the experience dramatically and in starker terms than many will perhaps recognize; I have done so because many do experience the "week" as painful and also to make clear what I mean. The experience may well be for some less dramatic, like the experience of feeling clumsy and dumb before the Lord and needy of His help.

Thus, each retreatant's experience of alienation is unique and governed by his own past and present. Each one of us has his own "history of sin," not so much in the sense of actual sins to be counted, but in the sense of sins against the light, ways in which each of us has alienated himself from God and neighbor and self half-unwittingly, has ignored signs and signals of trouble. For one man the "sin" could be running away from a sense of inadequacy by overwork; for another it could be a continual effort to win over people by avoiding any hint of reproval for their unjust actions; for another it could be the use of drink or sex or praise to bolster self-esteem, and so forth. Whatever the particular history, the underlying dynamic, we believe, is the one we have described. The director's role is not to become concerned with the particular history but with the dynamic and to help the retreatant to stay with his feelings and to open himself up to the healing love of God.

The Healing Love of God

We find that if a retreatant stays with his feelings of desolation and turns to the Lord for help, especially to Jesus who died for us sinners, then he does experience the "good news." This experience may take days to come, but it is well worth the time. Many experience tears of joy as they feel themselves to be loved sinners. And it is to be stressed that they *experience* this; they do not tell themselves they are saved. For many the experience is like a baptism, like a conversion, a new birth and now they know, perhaps for the first time, what it means to be saved. The knowledge is a deep, abiding, felt kind of thing ("knowledge" in the way John means the word in his gospel). It is the kind of knowing that leads to action and desire, the kind of knowing that wants to be shared and spread. It is "good news."

I would like to delay on this experience because it is central to the point I want to make in this essay. It is important to realize that the retreatant is not led into the experience by the director; if he prays and if he has need of this kind of saving experience, we maintain, he will enter the dark valley without being led by anyone else but himself and God. And we believe that there are many people who for fear of the "dark valley" waste energy and time trying to keep themselves away from it. We also believe that most of these people could experience great release and relief (that is, could come to fear no evil) if only they would let go because they believe in the God who walks with them. Moreover, the effectiveness of this "first week" experience in the *Exercises* comes precisely because both the alienation and the saving are experienced in the present. In the present—and in prayer—I experience my helplessness, my alienation—those things in myself I was running away from—and, *mirabile dictu,* I find that I have nothing to fear; God loves me with all my warts and moles.

It is often thought that therapy works because the patient grubs around in his past and finds the "cause" of his symptoms; but in actuality what happens, I believe, is that here and now in the therapy I find that I no longer need to fear myself or the other person as I had, and so I can deal with people on a more mature level. True enough, I come to realize that I have been dealing with people as though I were a five year old boy and I may even realize why I did that. But the real change comes when I realize *now* and experience *now* that I am an adult talking to and reacting to another adult. So too with the "first week" experience; it is not the remembering of all my past sins that heals, but the experience of being saved from my *present* alienation and spiritual desolation.

I would also like to stress the fact that there is an experience of sinfulness in this "week"; the retreatant comes to realize that he is at least partly responsible for what ails him; he did sin against the light. Once again let us use the analogy to therapy to clarify what is a very subtle issue. It is my belief that in every successful therapy with neurotics (successful in the sense of leading to deep change) there comes a point when the client comes to recognize his own complicity in his neurosis and his own covert gratification through his symptoms. That is, there is in some sense a recognition of responsibility; he does not have to confess by number the times he has deliberately or semi-deliberately "sinned against the light," but he has to recognize that he did it at least once. *Of course,* there have been traumatic incidents in his life; *of course,* he is often unaware of why he acts the way he does; *of course,* there are excusing causes. But at some level he recognizes his responsibility. In this day when we are so aware of diminished guilt, it is well to be aware of this subtlety because otherwise one can too quickly make excuses for another and too easily reassure him without allowing him to come to terms with his own sense of guilt and shame for his own part in his continuing "illness" or "desolation."

Finally, this experience of salvation leads most naturally to the desire to share with others the "good news," to do something for this Christ who has done so much for me; it leads in other words to a desire to be a disciple, to follow Jesus. This experience, thus, leaves a person at the threshold of the "second week" of the *Spiritual Exercises.*

The Experience of the Second Week

The retreatant who has had a deep "first week experience" enters the contemplation of the life of Christ with enthusiasm and gratitude. Contemplation of Jesus seems something brand new, enjoyable, and relatively easy. One retreatant said: "There doesn't seem to be enough time in the day." Prayer periods seem to go by in a flash.

In the initial enthusiasm the retreatant may concentrate on Jesus' kindness and sympathy, His care for the sick and suffering, His anti-legalism, His comfortable relation with the Father and His desire to bring others into that relationship. He is captivated by the positive aspects of being with Him, of answering yes to His "Come, follow me." The director may note that he does not advert to or take seriously the opposition Jesus encounters even if in the presentation of the matter for contemplation the director points out, for instance, Mark's intention in Chapter 2. One way to understand this phenomenon is to say that the retreatant prays out of his strength, that he concentrates on those aspects of Jesus' person and words and actions that fit his own needs and strengths.

After a few days (anywhere from three to six), it seems, the novelty wears off; the prayer becomes less enthralling; boredom can set in as it appears that Jesus just repeats cures and the same message. At this point the retreat director may be tempted to jump ahead in the gospel in order to get to the "third week," especially if the retreatant does not seem to have an "election" to make; the director may feel that he has erred in not choosing matter for contemplation that is more "challenging," or that brings out different facets of Jesus' character and call. But we have found that this "doldrum" period is a prelude to another conversion experience which we liken to the "first week experience" already described. Indeed, we venture the hypothesis that the "doldrums" are a form of resistance to entering this experience, that somehow or other the retreatant is becoming aware of "the cost of discipleship" and is resisting without even knowing it.

The Cost of Discipleship

If the director gives the retreatant time and does not move him too rapidly through the "week," and if the retreatant stays with the contemplations of Jesus, it soon becomes clear that the Lord is indeed showing him what discipleship means and how he, like the disciples in Mark, keeps missing the point. The retreatant becomes aware that there is one thing lacking to him, as to the rich young man, and a real choice opens up before him. The choice is not about whether to give up cigarettes or not, or whether to be a religious or not, but about whether to let one's life be ruled by the Lord and His plan as exemplified in the contrast between Herod's banquet and Jesus' banquet in Mark 6 and in the Ignatian distillation of the gospel in the Two Standards meditation.

We have found that retreatants who reach this point have a more or less hard struggle and that many of the same conflicts that came up in the first week recur at this juncture. The basic issue once again is one of trust in God and in Jesus' vision of what God wants. Again the issues revolve around one's self-image and one's image of God: Will this "death" lead to life for me? Will He take everything from me? Often enough the resistances come in the form of questions about asceticism and its negatives, especially as these were practiced in the past.

Here again the director has to be careful in his handling of the situation; he should avoid intellectual arguments and authoritative statements, but point to the issue at hand, the choice facing the retreatant. He should keep before the retreatant that there is a real choice here and a question for discernment. Thus, the retreatant should not be put down for his "resistances," but encouraged to take them seriously to see if they represent for him the will of God. He should be helped to realize that it is the Spirit who will show him what to do; indeed, it must be clearly pointed out that it would be presumptuous to declare himself a man of the third degree of humility[4] if the disposition is in fact not his. We make it clear that the consideration of the Three Degrees of Humility is aimed at discerning, at least as a first step, what is in fact, not in hope, his actual disposition, and we try to make sure that he recognizes the exalted religious position of even the first class.

It is important to realize what we are saying here, for we believe that many retreat directors have exhorted retreatants, and even shamed them, to make asseverations of love and desire which they had not the faith-ful disposition to carry through. There is a real question of discernment here, and we believe that the main issue is to discern clearly where one is and what the Spirit obviously wants of me. And this may well be to be a man of the second degree of humility—one who will take his chances with the Lord, but will not beg for sufferings with Him.

In our experience retreatants who reach this choice situation in the *Exercises* will receive the grace to say "yes" to the Lord at least to the point of wanting to walk with him "on the way" (Mk 10:52) and to throw one's lot in with him, and trust wholly in His Father. And when the retreatant does say yes, he knows that this yes is to follow Jesus and to live by His standards with the possibility that like Jesus he too will suffer. He is now, as one retreatant put it, at the gates of Jerusalem on the Sunday of Holy Week.

---

[4]*Spiritual Exercises*, nos. 165-167, p. 69.

The Experiences of the Third and Fourth Weeks

With this "yes" there is great consolation, and the retreatant is ready for the "third week" experience. We must admit that our experience here is limited since we have not directed a large enough number through the full thirty-days, where, it seems to us, the experience is most clearly seen. We have noted that retreatants who have reached the point described in the last paragraph experience very deep pain for Jesus; tears are not unusual. There does appear to be a similar experience, at a deeper level, to the ones that occur in the first two weeks, that is, a period of desolation or resistance or loss of that closeness to Jesus that was experienced at the end of the second week. Perhaps the enormity of what the Father might ask comes home; perhaps the old image of a God who wants blood reoccurs to awaken mistrust and anger. We have some indications that something like this does occur, followed once again by "consolation" (in its technical sense) if the retreatant is faithful to prayer. He can now walk with Jesus to Calvary and like the faithful women stay with Him to the end in trust and hope.

We have even less experience to rely on in describing the fourth week. There are suggestions that retreatants can experience some kind of "desolation" in this week before the very deep and abiding consolation occurs. We must confess to a lack of sufficient experiences here to be able to provide any explanation.

Conclusion

In this essay I have tried to describe patterns of experiences of retreatants making the *Spiritual Exercises* in the directed retreat mode. I hope that this essay will be a help to other directors and will lead to more dialogue among us and to corrections of what is said here or to further refinements of theory and technique.

One final word. If what I have written here comes close to being an adequate description of what happens to a person who makes the *Spiritual Exercises,* then it is clear that time is needed for each of the "weeks" of the *Exercises.* It may well be, therefore, that retreats of six to eight days would be best thought of as periods when the experience of a single "week" is the goal rather than an abbreviated tour through all four "weeks." On this hypothesis the director then has as his first—and difficult—task to diagnose where the retreatant is at spiritually, that is, to diagnose what experiences the retreatant seems now to need and to be ready for. It might be good, therefore, for the director to meet with the retreatant at least once before the retreat begins to take soundings of what is needed and to begin this process of mutual discernment which could be called "spiritual diagnosis."

Story of the Pilgrim King and the Dynamics of Prayer

William Connolly, S.J.

Volume 32, 1973, pp. 268-272.

Perhaps the most piquant question a religious encounters is: "How can I get into prayer?" It comes often and from a wide variety of people. Usually it is no longer intended merely as a conversation-opener to ease the first ten minutes of a counseling session, but as a life question in its own right.

There has been in the last two years, particularly because of the directed retreat movement, unusual opportunity to observe what actually happens when a person tries to pray with some concentration over a period of days or weeks. Spiritual directors, as a result, now have a more substantial empirical basis for their thinking about prayer. One of the lessons we have learned is that the more "traditional" instructions on prayer have often ignored the depth and richness of the personal resources a person brings to prayer. There are a number of possible reasons for this neglect. Perhaps the controversy of the early part of the century on "ordinary" versus "extraordinary" prayer focused the attention of seminary professors, and so of their students, too energetically on a notional issue and left too little psychic energy for a more empirical approach. We may have been too preoccupied with our civilization's sharp distinction between thought and feeling to be aware of what happens "at the intersection of thought and feeling." We may have been thinking like good rationalists and been unable to see what was happening outside our mental framework. Perhaps our students were too young. Whatever the reasons, the experience of many adults who were taught to pray ten and twenty years ago shows that they did not learn at that time to bring their most powerful personal resources—the ability to intuit, to react to symbol, to relate to other persons—into their attempts to pray.

Extensive prayer could and often did become a quasi-academic study of the idea of God, with reflections on our need for good resolutions and a steel spine if we wanted to be at peace with ourselves and with the Lord.

It was not always so, and need not be so today. Reflection on the famous parable of the king that appears in the *Spiritual Exercises* and the use made of symbols in the parable may help us to evaluate some of the resources that have been brought to prayer in the past, but have often been neglected during the last century.

The God we encounter in the Bible is not an idea to be pondered and analyzed. He is Someone who is and who acts. When the Biblical authors describe Him, they do so in terms of their experience. He is light, a rock, running water, rain on a parched land, like the doting father of an ungrateful son, the forgiving husband of a runaway wife. The reader is not permitted to turn Him or His action into ideas to be analyzed, but is faced with One who says "Let there be light" and who loves the world enough to send His Son to give it life. He is thought about not in the way a syllogism is studied, but in the way a friend is remembered, puzzled over, contemplated.

It is from this Biblical point of view that Ignatius sees the Lord. Jesus has freed him and given him life. He has asked himself what he should do about this Jesus who has done such prodigious favors for him. To answer the question, "What does His mission, His service mean to me?" he looks to his own experience for meaningful terms. He uses some of them in the parable of the pilgrim king.

The parable's central figure is described in a few strong strokes. He has been chosen by God, and his authority is recognized by all Christendom. The call he issues is an invitation to share knightly brotherhood with him on a crusade. In gathering recruits he pledges himself to endure whatever perils and hardships they encounter, and he promises victory.

To understand what Ignatius is trying to do in this parable, it is important to notice that no one like this king ever existed, and that Ignatius knew this as well as we do. There never had been a king or emperor of all Christendom; no Christian ruler had ever conducted a successful crusade against "all the lands of the infidels." Nor was there any likelihood that such a king would ever exist. Ignatius was deliberately appealing to dreams. When in preached retreats we used to compare the adulation given to heroic figures from Caesar to Napoleon and John Kennedy with the hoped for response to Ignatius' king, we could not have more clearly missed the point. The point of the parable is that the king never could have existed: His reality is the powerful reality of dreams where the symbols of our deepest desires and hopes stand clear of the mutations of external reality.

It is significant that Ignatius chose symbols that were not confined to the dreams of the devout. The universal ruler chosen by God who would finally overcome the infidel recalled figures who had inspired European civilization since Charlemagne's day. The brotherhood of knights was a military ideal that goes back at least to Anglo-Saxon times. The king who faces obscurity, danger, and hardship and who finally triumphs, appears in the tales about Richard the Lion-Hearted. Historical figures like Richard and Charlemagne had been aggrandized by attaching to them the power of the symbols. Even in the sixteenth century, when the symbols Ignatius used were less central to political and military reality, they still were powerful enough to be used by major poets like Spenser and Tasso, and the most powerful often prove attractive far beyond the era that gave them literary embodiment.

Dream symbols transcend the limitations of time and space. Recently the transcendent power of the symbols used in the Ignatian parable was illustrated by the startling success of J. R. R. Tolkien's *Lord of the Rings*. Tolkien is a contemplative writer. He gives the impression that he has not imposed his elves, dwarves, and hobbits on reality but has stared them into visibility. The reader comes to feel that hedges should contain hobbits. What else is a hedge for? And that no night in the woods should be without its traveling elves.

With the same patient intensity he has contemplated history. There he has seen the world blessed with an enduring goodness and threatened by persistent evil, wise men corrupted by their own power, "halflings" entrusted with tasks beyond their strength. Against this background the king appears, embodying the symbols of the Ignatian parable: a claim to leadership that is acknowledged by all who seek good for the world, an invitation to share both hardship and victory in brotherhood, a willingness to share hardship and danger with his companions, and a foreordained mission to bring about universal peace and justice.

Prayer does not seem to reach the depth that is possible to it unless it involves our deepest fears, hopes, and desires, feelings that are so deep we are not often conscious of them—the desire to live at peace with nature, for example, to communicate with all living things, to see destructiveness finally overcome, to live an unambiguous integrity, to take a significant part in a struggle that will finally establish justice in the world. It is to dreams, and the symbols that come clear in dreams, that we have to resort for the realization and expression of these longings. Prayer that does not allow these fears and longings to express themselves is necessarily more shallow than we are, and so we will be dissatisfied and ultimately bored by it.

The solution, it seems, is that we have to let ourselves dream. We have to let ourselves see what we want the world to be, not just for ourselves, but for everyone else too, and we have to let the Lord tell us that He will make our dreams of justice and peace come true. The lion lying down with the lamb and the swords being beaten into ploughshares have to become our own dreams as our fear that this can never come true must become our own nightmare before we can be challenged by the full strength of the gospel message.

The Ignatian parable spells out the dream of universal peace and justice in the figure of the king who is appointed by God to make all the infidel lands Christian. No "me-and-Jesus-and-forget-everyone-else" construction is possible here. The struggle is precisely for the sake of everyone else. I am involved in it not according to my own preferences, but in the way the king himself is involved. I wear what he wears, I act as he does. And I am no conscript. I am invited. And I am asked to recognize how I would feel if I refused.

We can plod on for years in prayer and still be shallow if we exclude from it our deep feelings and our dreams. We can also become very narrow and constricted in prayer, conversing with a well-edited picture of Jesus and allowing no hint of the world's need to intrude upon this dialogue, or picturing God as a champion of middle-class values, or as an unquestioning, unchallenging supporter of our own personal values. This is one of the difficulties the social activist has with prayer and with all religious practice: Prayer can shield a person from the challenge of social or political reality. It is also a difficulty that anyone who values the Christian life can have with prayer: Prayer may, when it is narrow, make it hard for a person to see that he is called to anything he does not want to do. The Gospels themselves can be subconsciously forced to serve the purposes of one's own egocentricity so that "Jesus loves me" and "He spent His time doing good for people" become excuses for moral vapidity and even for destructiveness.

It is the breadth of the gospel love—seeking out all men, no matter what their condition or class or sins, always striving to enter where it has not been before, challenging us to love the most disparate of our brethren and to put the interests of the kingdom before the demands of our own egotism— it is this breadth that overcomes our tendencies to limit our own interests. But how do we avoid the pull to cut back that breadth when we go off by ourselves to pray?

The first task of the spiritual director here is to give the person the freedom to recognize and elaborate the symbols that mean most to him. The director's willingness to discuss the relationship with God in whatever terms are most significant to the person will give him encouragement to go ahead with this recognition and elaboration. If several meetings are spent discussing a man's relationship with God in terms of the dependence of an oak tree on the sun, or of a mackerel on the sea, the time spent may give the person the assurance he needs to go to a new depth and breadth in prayer.

The director's task is to help the person evoke the symbols that have a meaning for him. This is precisely the opposite of imposing symbols on him. The symbol that is already rooted in the person's inner experience must be nurtured and tended, and not interfered with by the intrusion of symbols that may be more to the drector's own taste, or may seem more traditional. Someone else's symbols may be more handsome or better developed than the person's own, but they can never be as real to him and as integral to his prayer as those that are rooted in his own experience.

The director's second task is to help the person to believe in his dream, to trust the intuitions that take form there. This task is made easier when it becomes clear in experience that our reluctance to trust the dream is often based on memories of past disappointments and fear of being disappointed again. We have trusted our dreams in the past and have been hurt when they did not seem to be coming true, so we have decided to be satisfied with getting the daily jobs done and to resist as a waste of time or as non-incarnational thinking any suggestion that we move beyond the pragmatic.

Whether a person can live without dreams and still be at peace with himself and open to the gospel and the gospel community can be ascertained only by experience. The experience of Ignatius himself, however, should give pause to one who thinks he can live without dreams. So practical that he has seemed Machiavellian to some historians, he nevertheless had that dream of his that led him to picture the Trinity looking upon "the whole extent and space of the earth," and the entire "face and extent of the earth," and then to envision a religious community whose members would "go anywhere—whether among the faithful or the infidels—for the sake of matters pertaining to the worship of God and the welfare of the Christian religion." The question arises: Could he have been so practical if he had not been such a dreamer? The experience of people who are trying to pray has convinced many of us, in the New England area at least, that a work-oriented, problem-centered prayer too often results in losing sight of the gospel and the subsequent loss of its sustaining and challenging power. It may be just as true that without dreams we believe in and that help us to focus our experience, we cannot pray and work effectively as gospel persons.

Experiences of Darkness in Directed Retreats

William J. Connolly, S.J.

Volume 33, 1974, pp. 609-615.

Most of us bring to prayer the assumption that it will be either boring or bright and satisfying. When instead we meet with darkness, we are dismayed. There must, we think, be something wrong with us or with the way we are praying.

The Recurrent Problem of Darkness

Yet darkness is a common experience in prayer, especially extended prayer. Clearly different from the experience of distraction and of "nothing happening," it does not occur when a person is engaged in study or rational investigation, but only when he has become personally involved in some form of felt dialogue with the heart of reality.

The coming of darkness is not a shy, easily-overlooked phenomenon. On the contrary, it calls obtrusively for attention. Because it is common and distinct, it lends itself to reflection. Because it often puzzles and disturbs both retreatants and their directors, and yet frequently results in a deepened, more personal relationship with God, it deserves discussion. The experience of directed retreats, with its revelation of what actually happens in prayer, offers an excellent vantage point from which to carry on such a discussion.

Reflection on the experience of darkness in this context can also further our understanding of directed retreats. For one thing, it can help us to avoid thinking of the directed retreat as a method, four easy steps to peace of soul.

Darkness is so peculiarly our own, and method so obviously helpless in dealing with it, that even the most militant advocate of methods has to re-examine his allegiance after encountering it.

Then, too, as our experience of directed retreats grows, it becomes increasingly clear that a strong desire to share in the mission of Jesus to the world does not develop without a prior experience of darkness. Such a desire can never be the product of a reasoning process. It can result only from experience of some kind, and the deeper the experience the more personally gripping the desire can be. There seems to be, then, reason for concluding that, in the milieu of the directed retreat, the sense of mission often does not develop because retreatants have not been receptive to the experience of darkness. To move one step further: lack of radical response to the social dimensions of Jesus' mission may be a result of retreatants' failure to be receptive to the experience of social darkness, their refusal, for instance, to let themselves be shaken and dispirited by social evil.

Special Times of Darkness

We can encounter darkness at any time, in or out of prayer. However, for the person who gives time to prayer, it will often be most distinctly encountered when he has begun to let himself, without distractions, be himself before God, and has begun to let the Lord be Himself with him. As we can meet it at any time in life, so we can also meet it at any time in prayer and, during a directed retreat, at any point in the making of the *Spiritual Exercises.* There are two points in the *Exercises,* however, at which it is most often encountered: the earlier stages of increasing receptivity and the time of identification with the Jesus of the Passion—in the terminology of the *Exercises,* the First and Third Weeks.[1] This article will attempt to describe and discuss darkness as it occurs at those two points in the hope that the discussion will also contribute to our understanding of darkness as it occurs at other junctures of prayer, and, outside the specific focus of prayer, at other times in a person's life.

The First Week

There are experiences of darkness that bring quiet and tranquility: the gathering of shadows on a summer evening, the corners around a Christmas fireplace. Darkness can be a time of peace and confident waiting. The experience of darkness we are discussing, however, is different. This darkness is forbidding, the lair of fears, doubts, anger.

Yet the only way to avoid it is to withdraw from personal involvement with prayer. For it is personal involvement, with the opening up of our

---

[1] William A. Berry, S.J., "The Experience of the First and Second Weeks of the *Spiritual Exercises,*" pp. 95-102.

fears, guilts, and angers that it entails, that brings on this experience of darkness. If we can close off those feelings, the darkness will no longer enshroud us. However, it will not be replaced by light, but by a gray world in which God is distant and detached. It seems that, if we want the light, we have to explore the darkness in which the light shines.

"Everything is fine," a man says on the second or third day of a directed retreat. "The people I live with are admirable, though there are the usual difficulties. And I'm not perfect. Who is? I'm just like everybody else: there's always room for improvement. But I don't spend time brooding and feeling sorry for myself."

While his view of himself is this bland and featureless, his experience of prayer will be calm, rational, and detached. Because it is shallow, the prayer may also be badgered by distractions. Only when deeper feelings begin to emerge will his prayer become eventful. Among the events there will often be an awareness of darkness.

There are times when a person clearly knows he must choose to enter darkness or turn away from it. He feels like a traveler standing at the edge of a deep forest. He wonders whether, if he enters, he will ever come out again. He feels both attracted to go on because he knows he cannot find the Lord unless he does, and yet repelled because what lies before him is fearsome.

Resistance to Darkness

Resistance to entering the darkness takes different forms. "Life is hard enough," one person will say. "Why look for gloom?" Another fears he will become lost in introspection. Some think that entering darkness will mean concentrating on the "garbage" of their lives and believe that God wants only healthy enjoyment for us. Others see entering darkness as self-pity, undermining the courage with which a person must face life. Underlying all these objections is primitive fear, sometimes conscious, but often so submerged as to be almost imperceptible.

Another form of resistance is concentration on false darkness. We become so concerned with surface problems—the aggravations of family life, superficial colleagues, the irksome features of our jobs—that we give our deep hopes, desires, and frustrations no chance to come to our awareness. In a retreat, we may even take such a relentless grip on surface concerns that there will be no opportunity to experience true darkness.

The person moves in darkness from a sense of his fears, angers, and guilts, to a sense of his own insufficiency.[2] At this point he may feel he has come into a denser darkness. He sees no sign of relief, nothing that offers hope. Yet he often will not feel completely alone: The Lord is not experi-

---

[2] William J. Connolly, S.J., "Disappointment in Prayer: Prelude of Growth?," pp. 191-194.

enced as unhearing. He seems to be communicating nothing, however, and the lack of communication is painful. Often there is, without a lightening of darkness, a sense of being sustained. Then, gradually or suddenly the retreatant realizes that he must trust Someone other than himself. The struggle within him is not about the direction in which he is being led. It is really about recognizing himself as not self-sufficient, and accepting light from Someone else.

Darkness and the Lord's Freeing Action

The struggle between self-sufficiency and receptivity to the Lord can take place on different levels. Sometimes if a person is becoming aware of his fears for the first time, for example, deeper levels of negative feeling may remain untouched, yet he may be aware that the Lord is freeing him from the controlling grip of his conscious fears. His deeper feelings may be touched only some time later, frequently either during spiritual direction or in a subsequent retreat.

One of the most menacing beasts we encounter in the darkness is our realization that we have not and probably will not live up to our own ideals. The more deeply rooted the ideal is, the more entwined with family and cultural values, the more menacing is this realization. Central to the freedom given in this Week for some people is the realization that the Lord loves us even when we do not live up to our own ideals, or the standards of our family or our culture, that we can be cowards and still be loved, for instance, or not bright, or awkward. To live with this realization is to live with darkness. To deny or avoid it, however, will mean distortion and unfreedom.

The freeing action that takes place at this time in the retreat can leave this person able to live with his own darkness. Some gospel scenes are poignantly helpful in enabling us to receive the full impact of the Lord's freeing action.

Gethsemane, for instance, is a place of darkness. Fear, weakness, and confusion shroud the scene in the garden. But the Light shines there too. Through contemplating this scene a person can come to accept living with his own darkness. Denial that the darkness exists becomes needless and futile. Because the darkness does not overwhelm the Light, I can live with it. I may never be comfortable with it, but neither need I fear that it will overwhelm me. I can trust the Lord to touch my own darkness because He has experienced it Himself and is not thwarted by it. I can accept it in my own life because it is an acceptable condition in His.

The Retreat Director and the Exercitant's Darkness

At whatever level of awareness darkness is encountered, it is real enough, and the person is unable to provide light for himself. It must be given to him, and he must let himself receive it.

The issue of freedom becomes crucial for both retreatant and director when the decision is being made to explore darkness.[3] No one can be forced to this exploration. Because the darkness is threatening, the retreatant will be particularly wary of any pressure to enter it. It would be at best a waste of time if the retreatant at this point were to spend two or three days debating whether or not to succumb to pressure from the director. Any pressure at this point must come from the person's prayer. In practical terms, the director might well, instead of arguing about whether his approach is old-fashioned, or whether he is adhering slavishly to an out-moded text, or trying to impose on the retreatant grim thoughts he does not need, simply suggest that he use any alternative approach he chooses. If the invitation to explore darkness is from the Spirit, no alternative will be helpful. The prayer will become fixated, will not develop substantially until the darkness is explored. Eventually—though perhaps not during that retreat—the retreatant will see that any pressure that exists is coming from the prayer, not from the director. For retreatants particularly sensitive to pressures placed upon them by structures or persons, this exercise of freedom may be the most important moment of the retreat and the beginning of a significantly deeper and more personal prayer. It is vital, then, that the director when dealing with this issue be acutely aware of the retreatant's need for freedom.

The Threat of Unreality

Unreality is always a possibility to be guarded against in prayer, and the *Spiritual Exercises* give the director a number of expedients to use against it. Unreality threatens the whole purpose of the *Exercises,* would turn them from an approach to union with the heart of reality to a subtle form of escapism. The person's ability to explore his darkness and willingness to live with it instead of denying it is one of the clearest indications that his own reality, rather than an idealized concept of himself, has entered into the dialogue with God.

The dialogic attitude is the best criterion for determining that the exploration of darkness has not ceased to be prayer and become instead egocentric self-analysis. "Did you feel you were talking to yourself or to someone else?" and "Did you talk to the Lord about that fear, or anger, or guilt?" are questions that encourage the retreatant to develop and maintain an attitude of listening and response.

While the retreatant is in darkness, the director can do little but encourage. He has not produced the darkness and he cannot take it away. He may however become frightened by its impenetrability and be tempted to advise withdrawal, either from prayer altogether or into a prayer that will not engage his deeper feelings. However, if the retreatant has normal emotional strength, this suggestion would be ill advised. He would only have to return

---

[3]William J. Connolly, S.J., "Freedom and Prayer in Directed Retreats," pp. 61-67.

to the level of his conflict later. Often too, the retreatant intuitively knows that withdrawal would be an escape, and that the conflict will, if he sees it through, result in new growth.

The Third Week

There is another experience of darkness that often occurs later in the *Exercises*. In the Third Week a person asks to share in the feelings of Jesus during the Passion. The sharing that ensues may be highly existential. He may feel deeply alone. The Church's failings may probe him like searchlights, and her gifts seem of no consequence. " . . . but He cannot save Himself." "Is faith only a monstrous fraud?" he may ask himself. "How do I know my ministry is productive? Have all of us Christians been brainwashed into a massive illusion?"

The risk of faith tends to become intensely real through the experience of its intangibility. The darkness of faith is intensified, becomes an interior experience of the darkness "over the whole land" in which Jesus died.

No one goes into this darkness buoyantly. Here again we use a wide variety of excuses. "The suffering Jesus means nothing to me. His Passion is over and done with. It's the Risen Lord we deal with now." "Making a resolution in the Second Week made sense. But there's nothing here I can get my teeth into." And indeed there is nothing we can work at in the Third Week. There is no way a person can "work at" creating the darkness of Calvary. He lets it come or he doesn't. For the Pelagian in us, the Third Week is keenly frustrating. It is a time when nothing gets done, no resolutions get made. The task is simply to let something happen, and that is no task at all. The feel of the darkness, too, when it comes, says to the person that the experience of prayer has come to a dead end, that he has failed. And so the temptation to retreat into superficial good cheer or mind-absorbing work seems a call to virtue and Christian good sense.

These disturbing feelings will conflict sharply with the retreatant's expectations. He has been engaged in intensive prayer for some time, and, though he has not looked forward to sharing the Calvary experience, he has not anticipated doubts and a sense of futility. The director's encouragement to accept and admit these feelings will, then, be very important to him. Otherwise he may waste time by viewing the Passion as one would view a mob scene through a window: it is seen, but the viewer is not present to it, not involved in it.

The Director's Role

The darkness of the Third Week can be an alarming experience for the director. As in the First Week his task is to be with and to encourage but not to alleviate. Here, however, his own insecurities or his preconceptions of the Lord's ways are particularly likely to lure him into interference or withdrawal. The retreatant's doubts may, for example, be saying that the retreat has been a waste of time and implying that the direction has been poor. His doubts about the value of the apostolate challenge the value of the director's own work. The basic intuitions he has developed as a director will, however, serve him well if he listens to them. They will tell him again that he does not know the road the Spirit is leading the retreatant to travel, so he must not meddle. They will also tell him that, as that member of the People of God who happens or has been chosen to be with the retreatant on his journey, he must be with and not abandon him. If he obeys these intuitions, he will avoid both interference and emotional withdrawal.

The main current of his prayer will keep the retreatant's attention focused on being with the Lord. The director can help him significantly by encouraging him to respect this central intuition. This is not the time for either apologetics or an evaluation of the retreat. It is a time for accompanying.

For both retreatants and directors darkness in prayer, like darkness in life, is an experience they would rather avoid. They enter it only because the real issues of prayer, as of life, confront them with it, and because the price of avoiding it is shallowness and unreality. The result of entering is a deepened empathy with reality and with the Lord of reality.

Hidden in Jesus before the Father

George A. Aschenbrenner, S.J.

Volume 34, 1975, pp. 121-131.

The strikingly new dimension of Christian revelation is that God is Trinitarian. It is a dimension so fundamental and central that it shapes and directs the Christian vision of all reality and it therefore invites the Christian man and woman to find and to appropriate life for what it is: a Trinitarian experience. Yet, while the Trinity is not something that believers outright deny, it often does not enrich their actual, felt experience of life and reality. The Trinity is more like a piece of abstruse theological geometry—how many persons and how many natures in the one God?

This article will not be a strict theological reflection on the Trinitarian dimension of our lives. Rather, by looking at the hidden life of Jesus and by expanding a little our ordinary understanding of His hidden life, I hope to open up another avenue of appreciation of our own lives in Jesus Christ and thus bring us more fully to the Trinitarian dimension of the revelation in Jesus and of our daily life of faith in Jesus. I will describe three different though related understandings of the hidden life of Jesus as we find Him in the New Testament, and then I will trace some possible lines of development of just the last, or third, understanding I refer to. I will conclude with some practical reflections which suggest themselves in the light of these three senses or understandings of the hidden life of Jesus.

Hidden Life at Nazareth

We usually understand the hidden life of Jesus as referring to His rather ordinary, daily life for about thirty years at Nazareth. These years are seen as preparation for the work and public mission to which Jesus would give Himself

115

for the last few years of His life. In this understanding, hidden life means being out of the public eye and out of the mainstream of activity. There is an obvious truth to this understanding of the phrase, and it points to a great mystery. When we appreciate the challenge that awaited Jesus in His public life and the amount and extent of apostolic work that those last three years involved, we wonder why He waited so long to get started. There were so many people whose hearts were changed and enlivened through Jesus's human encounter with, his concrete touch upon, their lives. His life and spirit were so contagious for so many. And yet there were so many others into whose lives He did not walk and whose hearts He did not so personally touch—simply because of lack of time and energy—those inbuilt, human limitations. If He had not remained hidden for so long, couldn't He have touched more and had a more extensive and effective personal apostolate? There is an amazing mystery here which we must not pass over too lightly.

The mystery is not resolved simply in realizing some particular cultural situation of first-century Palestine. Still the mystery remains. What is the Father communicating of His view of life through the hidden life of Jesus? Jesus's words at the Last Supper to Philip give us a glimpse into the deepest identity of this man from Nazareth: "To have seen me is to have seen the father" (Jn 14:9). The remark, in a way, explains nothing. But it is a principle of interpretation for everything. It tells us who is revealing, and who and what is being revealed, in every moment and event of this Man's existence.

Hidden in these Nazareth years, then, is a whole vision in faith of life and of success and of true value revelatory of the way of our Father, a way very different from our own ways (Is 55:8-9), and waiting to be communicated to the carefully contemplative heart. And in our contemporary, aggressive, achievement-oriented culture, the heart of the believer needs to taste deeply and regularly the mysterious power and patience of Jesus with His Father in those hidden Nazareth years.

Ultimately, however, Jesus's hidden life remains too superficial and narrow if understood primarily as a preparatory period removed from the public arena of activity. The hidden life of Jesus can and does also describe the life of faith of Jesus in His humanity, and the faith life of each one of us too, in our following of Him. Thus, quietly but decisively, the hidden life of Jesus breaks out of the narrow confines of Nazareth. And it will grow, through many meetings, even to the deepest and most intimate experience of His Father, in the shockingly public spectacle of the cross.

Hidden before the Father

Paul's remark in Colossians 3:3, that our true life is a hidden one in God, points to a second understanding of the hidden life: a quality of heart and presence in the very midst of active involvement. In the actions and events of our lives together, we know a great deal about the discrepancy of interpretation, and of experience too—a discrepancy that occurs both within our own selves and between ourselves and others—depending on whether those actions and events are seen and felt in faith, or are done and discerned apart from faith. But there is a further, dark but beautiful discrepancy that occurs *within* faith: the magnificent distance between what our faith *sees* and *feels* and what our Father knows and is actually accomplishing in and through our lives. Our sensible perception of deeds of faith on this earth is always somehow blinded to the hidden fullness of that deed as motivated by faith and love of our God. The fullness of this deed of faith *must* now be hidden to the eyes of faith; it is what the life of faith is all about. But this fullness does register and is known *now* in all its brilliance and simplicity before our Father. One day our hearts will be expanded in revelation and know clearly and humbly before our Father the fullness of what has been our life of faith.

But now we live and work in the hiddenness of faith blinded to the full significance of our deeds and life. We ought not to be too preoccupied with this. An unduly anxious concern for how worthwhile our lives are and for what our lives of faith aré really accomplishing often destroys the simple unself-conscious zeal of an apostle. The apostle who loves and serves in faith must learn to act always in peace and in hopeful trust of the fullness of accomplishment before our Father. It may not always be easy for some to avoid such concern about results and to allow Jesus to be our peace in faith and expectation before His and our Father. For Jesus Himself, in His humanity, had to live this life of hidden faith and trust of all that was being accomplished before His Father. This hiddenness of faith kept His heart, and keeps our hearts, transcendently and trustfully open beyond ourselves, to the loving power of a Father who works and surprises us in our zeal.

This trustful openness to the Father in every part of our life, an openness called forth by the hidden nature of our faith perception, leads us to a third understanding of Jesus's hidden life.

Hidden Inner Intimacy with the Father

Here we touch a most profound understanding of Jesus's hidden life, and one which underlies the previous two understandings. For the special quality of heart, and the special presence to life described above in our second understanding, gets its ground and nurture only in a growing interior life of intimacy with the Father. It is this interior life of growing intimacy with the Father which is our third understanding of the hidden life of Jesus. And it brings us to the very heart of the life of faith in each of us.

At this point, let us trace briefly in the Gospels the growth in Jesus of this inner life of intimacy with His Father. I suggest we are talking to the most important theme in the life of Jesus and are at the very heart of the revelation that He is. In our treatment here we do not pretend to do full justice in length and thoroughness to a theme of such centrality. We mean simply to suggest a direction which the reader can develop further in prayer and reflection.

In the past few years Christians have taken more and more seriously the gradual, very human growth and development of Jesus the man as sent from the Father. This has brought many spiritual blessings and insights in its wake for those carefully contemplating the mysteries of the life of Jesus. Without necessarily being familiar with the subtlety of contemporary professional reflection on the self-consciousness of Jesus, individual believers at prayer have found much light, inspiration, strength, and peace for themselves in the various mysteries of His life. Without in anyway denying the divine, eternal sonship of Jesus as revelation sent from the Father, in our reflections here we will presume and deeply affirm this gradual human growth and developing consciousness of mission and of person—of His entire human existence—and in Him ours too—as being from, in, and toward the Father.

The Finding in the Temple

A remark of Karl Rahner in his *Spiritual Exercises* points our way here: "If His hidden life was not primarily a religious life, then it is impossible, with the very best will, to find anything really significant about it."[1] In the midst of the ordinariness of His early life in Nazareth, Jesus began to grow in religious experience. As would be true for any young Hebrew boy, Jesus was taught by His mother how to pray and come in touch with the revelation of the Old Testament. We can imagine Jesus at an early age able to mouth the human words and images of Psalm 139. But it was a special day, finally, when Jesus's own heart was touched in its originality and moved to pray as His own, Psalm 139 to Yahweh. Now those human words are significative of a sentiment in the heart of this young boy: the beauty of the beginning of a real religious sentiment in His heart. A conscious personal relationship to Yahweh begins to grow and mature. Those years in Nazareth hidden from the public eye are specially characterized by this religious growth in the heart of the young man Jesus.

The mystery of the Finding in the Temple pointedly highlights this development in Jesus. The beautiful and very understandable worry and care of Mary and Joseph is met with the mysterious word of Jesus there in the Temple. The verse in Luke 2:49 is translated in many different ways, but the core of meaning certainly seems to be: Did you not know I must always be where my Father is. It is a word about the religious experience and identity of Jesus which Mary and Joseph, and Jesus too, had to receive at that moment. This word of truth and identity must have come to them like a two-edged sword which revealed not only Jesus's identity, but also the identity of Mary and Joseph in relationship to Him. Perhaps Mary had to confront for the first time the reality that, although she was mother, her son did not in some real way belong to her. More accurately, perhaps, she had to ponder newly *how* he belonged to her (for, ultimately, the more He is from and for His Father the more entirely is He hers—and ours). One wonders also whether Jesus Himself did not have to ponder deeply the word of truth and identity that had been *given* to Him there in His Father's house.

Jesus's prayerful pondering for more than fifteen years would bring a definite religious growth which finally confronted Mary with her son's leaving

---

[1] Karl Rahner, S.J., *Spiritual Exercises* (New York: Herder and Herder, 1965), p. 157.

Nazareth. As His own religious experience and identity continued to grow, a greater interior intimacy with His Father developed. This inner intimacy of real love and trust had now become clear and decisive enough to call Jesus away from Mary and from Nazareth (as Abraham from Ur, and Moses from Egypt). It is a beautiful human scene, but surely with a touch of sadness. This woman, who had shared so much of life with her son, on a certain level perhaps not understanding why He must go off to the lonely life of a prophet separated from His whole clan, nevertheless renews her offering of the Annunciation and gives Him over to the world and to the Father. Jesus, knowing now that He must follow the light of His own inner religious intimacy with His Father, sets out very directly and decisively for the Jordan, but only after a tender farewell to His mother. That word of identity—did you not know I must always be where my Father is—calls Him forth to be where His Father is for Him. It is an identity that will finally bring Him to the cross. It is the hidden, inner life of intimacy with His Father, then, that calls Jesus out of those hidden years at Nazareth.

But we must look to the scene at the Jordan now to appreciate more fully why Jesus leaves Nazareth.

The Jordan Experience

Without any lingering, Jesus goes straightway from Nazareth to the Jordan to meet with the Baptist. It is precisely a call to the Jordan that has led Him away from all that Nazareth had been for Him. Perhaps parts of chapters 40 and 41 of Isaiah were in His heart as He made his way.

The Jordan is a scene of sinners of all sorts encountering the Baptist. Within this gathering of sinners the truth of the Baptist is bluntly calling to repentance and arousing the beginning, graced stirrings of conversion. The whole sinful scene focuses on the starkly prophetic figure of John.

Jesus strides directly into the action and enters it deeply. His words are few, but His behavior and His inner experience reveal the sense of mission and profound religious identity that is growing and moving within Him. Without a word, Jesus gets in line and awaits His turn for baptism—identifying completely with the brotherhood of sin. He takes on the sin of the world. He counters the Baptist's understandable desire to be baptized by Him with words about His need for baptism, that righteousness may be fulfilled.

Then it happens. Whatever the external manifestation precisely was, much more important is the interior experience of Jesus at His baptism: the power, clarity, and sweetness of His inner religious experience of being called by Yahweh: my son, my beloved, my servant. How it must have fired His heart and filled Him with the Spirit! This clear, core identity experience of Jesus results from, brings, and celebrates His profound intimacy with His Father. This core identity experience will be further tested and specified, but now it leaves Jesus deeply at prayer in this interior religious experience, even quite oblivious, for the time being, to all that is going on around Him. His prayer could so easily center on Isaiah 41:9-10:

You whom I brought from the confines of the earth
and called from the ends of the world; you to whom I said, "You are my servant,
I have chosen you, not rejected you,"
do not be afraid, for I am with you;
stop being anxious and watchful, for I am your God.
I give you strength, I bring you help,
I uphold you with my victorious right hand.

Propelled by the Spirit of this experience, Jesus leaves the Jordan with an even more intimate inner consciousness of His Father and a sense of His mission as servant for righteousness over sin.

Tempted

With His trust and hope so totally in His Father, Jesus is led by the Spirit into the desert region. The desert with its starkness and simplicity is not a place of superficial experiences. The depth of one's identity is often tested and experienced in the desert. And temptation is always an identity experience, nothing less. Whether in a quiet private area of our hearts or in a dramatically public situation, temptation reveals who we are, who we might mistakenly become, and, finally, who we are *meant* to become. What can often seem so harsh and bleak and austere about the desert can deceptively prevent a person from discovering the beautiful intimacy of the quietly profound, solitude experience of God. But Jesus is not so deceived, for it is the Spirit who leads Him into the vast silence for further confrontation with and specification of His own identity before the Father.

Jesus's experience of the temptations is highlighted when seen in relationship to His Jordan experience. While He is still in immediate touch with His religious experience of being called "my son, my beloved, my servant," in some special way, the three temptations described in the Gospels really challenge the authenticity of that Jordan identity. All the temptations somehow add up to the same thing: if you are the Son of God. Again, whatever the external trappings of this incident were, our chief concern here is the inner experience of Jesus in that growing life of intimacy with His Father. Is He really son-servant-beloved? Was that Jordan experience illusion? This direct attack on His own inner religious identity must have cost Jesus a great deal of inner reflection and struggle before He could once again choose His Father and, by going with the special experience of being son-servant-beloved, ratify the Jordan experience. The form of presentation of the temptations in the Gospels does not highlight this inner struggle and conflict of Jesus. If misunderstood, the Gospel presentation can make it all seem too easy. But in reality, the issue is tumultuous for the human heart of Jesus. He is asked here in risk and trust to ratify, and thus to embrace, at the level of mission and action, His own relation to the Father.

In each temptation Jesus is confronted with the alluring attractiveness of Satan's way of being son-servant-beloved. It is a way opposed to the way of His Father. Why not be son-servant-beloved by turning stones to bread? Why not begin the public ministry in this flashy and showy way? In each instance Jesus must interiorly reject Satan's worldly way of being son-servant-beloved. But this rejection is really a cover for something wonderfully positive: the beautifully intimate inner experience of choosing His Father and discovering some specification of His way. The scene ends there in the desert with Jesus having interpreted his existence and mission in the world at a newly decisive level—all lost in the awesome aloneness of a specially beloved son deeply with His Father and ready to serve with Him in everything. A Son with His Father, and nothing else matters for the moment—and yet, a whole life of love and of service definitively, however darkly, contacted in that moment. His hands and His heart and His eyes will continue their human search, but the breath of His Father is on His face here. And He will need to return here, as He will need to return to other experiences, like Jordan and Tabor, for strength to grapple with the darkness of that human search for His Father in the world.

The desert brings Jesus valuable enlightenment and profound growth in that inner life of intimacy utterly alone with His Father. And it is the experience of the *Father's* holiness which creates the imperative of a mission of justice, of peace, and of forgiving love. This inner life with His Father is creating a whole climate of heart which will continue to grow and to give a warm clarity and decisive direction to His life. Within that climate of heart alone all future decisions will be made.

The Public Ministry

Jesus comes out of the desert "in the power of the Spirit" and, in Luke's Gospel goes quite directly to the synagogue in Nazareth where He had been raised. In a dramatic scene Jesus carefully chooses to read a passage of Isaiah:

> The spirit of the Lord has been given to me,
> for he has anointed me.
> He has sent me to bring the good news to the poor,
> to proclaim liberty to captives
> and to the blind new sight,
> to set the downtrodden free,
> to proclaim the Lord's year of favor (61:1-2).

His own brief commentary brings a revelation of His identity. Father Paul Hinnebusch in one of his books says, "The Holy Spirit causes thirst for the Father."[2] That remark can be enlightening here. Jesus comes from that solitude experience in the desert with an all-consuming thirst for His Father, and there is within Him a towering desire to reveal His Father in serving the poor, the captive, the blind, the oppressed, and all who are in need. No wonder the crowds are amazed at the graciousness of His words! After the profound intimacy of His personal experience alone with His Father in the desert, His

---

[2]Paul Hinnebusch, O.P., *Prayer, the Search for Authenticity* (New York: Sheed and Ward, 1969), p. 22.

words have an unction and simple power of conviction that can come no other way. The Spirit of the Father is so obviously upon Him!

But even here the angry reaction of the crowd temptingly confronts Him and tries to deter Him from His Father's way. These moments of temptation and search kept him in touch with that inner climate of heart, that union with His Father which specifies for Jesus, gradually and increasingly, His Father's way for being son-servant-beloved. At Caesarea Philippi, Peter's confession of faith in Jesus's identity is revealed to be quite superficial and short-visioned when, with all "good will," he denies Jesus's mission of loving service to death by the way of the cross. Jesus rebukes Satan and, once again, rejects the worldly way by choosing His Father in openness to being with Him, even in the suffering of the cross. In the scene of the entry into Jerusalem on Palm Sunday, the jarring ambiguity between His Father's way of peace and liberation in Jesus's heart and the superficial, worldly way in the hearts and voices of the crowd perhaps expresses another searching confrontation for Jesus. This total life pattern of searching for and finding the Father in action—and of finding His actions in the Father—could be traced in greater detail. But this is enough for our purposes here.

Another phenomenon of the life of Jesus that is related to the growth of His hidden life with His Father is His frequent withdrawal to pray. Just as it is impossible really to know what Jesus's experiences were like when He was in that intimate presence of the power and love of His Father which was His prayer, so it is impossible to deny that He really needed this special kind of intimate touch with His Father. His own interior growth and sense of direction and mission depended very much on these times of prayer. That desert solitude and intimacy alone with His Father never died but was continually enkindled. It is important to keep these experiences of withdrawal in the context and rhythm of His very active and busy life. These experiences of prayer are frequently mentioned in the Gospels and are always oriented to His active life and presence in the world. We are told (Lk 6:12) that He spent a whole night in prayer with His Father before the important choice of the twelve whom he *wanted* as apostles. In that long night of prayer, as clarity slowly came, these men were truly *given* to Him by His Father. And at the last supper he would refer to them in that way in His prayer (Jn 12:6). The inner strength and clarity and zeal that came to Jesus from these times of intimate and intense prayer can be observed in the quality of His life and activity, although the fullness of what these times meant to Him can only be guessed at.

Tracing the total life pattern of His temptations, His searchings, and His experience of prayer alone with His Father, brings us to the floodtide of His hidden life and love: the Passion. But further prayer and reflection by the reader will reveal much more of this hidden life of Jesus with His Father in those years from the temptations in the desert to the Agony in the Garden—to which we now turn.

Gethsemani

After the raising of Lazarus, Jesus knows Himself to be a hunted man because the opposition has now decided to kill him (Lk 11:53) and has put out a warrant for His arrest (Lk 11:57). This burden in His heart, though it is interrupted in the beauty and directness of His uninhibited display of love and concern for His own men in the Cenacle, does give a quiet sense of foreboding to the scene.

Having gone to pray in the olive grove, He is given over completely to that inner burden. The inner experience of a sorrow and sadness verging on heartbreak must have registered on His countenance. Being given an inner revelation of sin and its horror in a way He never experienced before, Jesus is all but crushed at the perspective of what will be entailed for Him as servant for righteousness over sin. The intensity of the temptation shouts out for support and encouragement. And very little if any human support is present. But here in His lowest moment of tense anguish and loneliness, similar to that of a trapped animal, a gentle strength and a mighty patience is born: "Let it be as you, not I, would have it" (Mt 26:39). The choice of His Father and His way, in an intimacy of trust alone with His Father, reveals here a man with an even deeper awareness now of being son-servant-beloved. The intimacy of that desert moment has been renewed. And as He calls the Apostles to readiness at the end of the agony (Mk 14:41-2), there is no longer any sense of being trapped. Rather there stands and strides forward the Son, at one with His Father in obedience and confidence to the end.

Beloved and Trusting on the Cross

This intimacy is especially hidden in Jesus through His Passion, except for that patience and that power in silence which could come from nothing but His inner union with His Father. But it is on the cross that this hidden inner life of Jesus reaches its climax in a final trusting surrender—its climax of hiddenness and its climax as a life lived in God.

The jeers and taunts hurled at Jesus on the cross contain the full temptation of worldly unbelief. Once again the point is the same: "If you are the Son of God, come down from the cross" (Mt 27:39-43). Jesus must choose again to be son-servant-beloved according to His Father's way of love. The situation, in its external appearance, is the height of absurdity. A promising young Hebrew man at the height of His power and of His attractiveness for His people is being asked to disengage from life—the utter foolishness of the cross. Significance and redemption are found, here above all, only in the inner life of Jesus with His Father on the cross. The death on the cross gives final, definitive, and everlasting form to Jesus's intimate, loving trust of His Father. This disengagement from life by Jesus is His greatest act of trust in His Father. And it brings for Him, and for everybody, the fullness of life. Those words in the temple—"Did you not know I must always be where my Father is"—they have led to this. And Mary hears them differently here on Calvary. She has treasured them in her heart for very long.

Jesus's words from the cross are almost responses to the taunts hurled at the cross. But then He cries out in the inner bleakness of forsaken aloneness:

"My God, my God, why have you forsaken me?" There is a great mystery here. But He seems to be doing more than simply reciting the Twenty-second Psalm. Somehow His inner experience, just for a moment, finds Him utterly bereft of His Father. Sin now has had its way fully, and somehow Jesus seems and feels Himself to be without His Father. And this is the final gift. For this is a man who loved His human life and the exploration of His talents. And the cross is the destruction of all of that. Further, this is not only a man, but a Jewish man. And now He hangs repudiated and driven from His people. But if you go to the core of Him—as this article has hoped to show—the primary, growing definitive identity and consciousness of Jesus was to be His Father's son, His servant, His beloved. And here on the cross—for a moment—in the final foolishness of love, the felt experience of this too was given over: "My God, my God, why have you forsaken me?"

But even in that moment, Jesus does not really lose hope and trust. And so now sin's sway over the world is ended and broken by the loving trust of the Obedient One. And perhaps, out of the bleak barrenness of that dark moment, there sounds in the heart of Jesus the loving call of his Father in the words of the Song of Songs:

> Come then, my love,
> my lovely one, come.
> For see, winter is past,
> The rains are over and gone.
> The flowers appear on the earth,
> The season of glad songs has come. . . .
> Come then, my love,
> my lovely one, come.
> Show me your face,
> Let me hear your voice;
> for your voice is sweet
> and your face is beautiful (Song of Songs 2:10-4).

"Come, my beloved, my lovely one, come." It is the Father, calling Jesus home now, in a hidden intimacy that defies description, where "he will wipe away all tears. . . ; there will be no more death, and no more mourning or sadness" (Rev 21:4)—not only for Him but for the total world of all His brothers and sisters who are here, on the cross, taken up into His own final loveliness.

In this way, the light and joy of Resurrection is somehow present and beginning there, in the dying. For a man to die in that way is to be assured of new risen life. And so Jesus's last words on the cross are a response to His Father out of the profound, powerful, inner intimacy of His heart: "Father, my Father, into your hands I give over my heart." It is the Son who speaks, obediently and intimately beloved servant to the end!

Our Life of Faith

Let us now turn to some reflections on our own lives in the light of Jesus's hidden life with His Father. We are all called to share and live in some similar way this inner life. It is Jesus as Risen Lord who makes possible this inner life our Father desires to share with each of us: "Everything has been entrusted to me by my Father; and no one knows who the Son is except the Father, and who the Father is except the Son and those to whom the Son chooses to reveal him" (Lk 10:22). It is overwhelming but true that this is precisely what the life of faith is all about. Faith is not simply a matter of external actions, or words, or of certain thoughts. All these, without the inner intimacy of love and trust of the Father, turn faith into an empty shell. Thus faith requires a continual conversion of our sin-stained affectivity into the true, living affectivity of the Risen Jesus who is now entirely at one with His Father in the desire to console all of us by sharing with us their inner life together. It is this inner hidden life of faith that always distinguishes the true believer from the secular humanist.

The climate of heart that this hidden life creates should be the atmosphere within which all of our decisions become clear and out of which all of our actions spring. In this way, all our slightest interior movements are discerned in consonance with the peace and intimacy of our Father in our hearts. The inner, affective experience of peace in our Father becomes thus the birth place of an indomitable zeal.

This zeal and desire to do great things for God is often expressed quietly and humbly in the eager readiness to do the next deed as discovered through intimacy with the Father in Jesus. So this hidden life of intimacy is not simply a matter of prayer and of inner religious experience that is oblivious of our real world in its struggle for redemption and justice and peace. This hidden life inevitably takes expression in a special, vital quality of presence in our world and in the midst of the most active situations. It is a presence characterized in faith by peace, gentleness, joy, humble gratitude, and a decisive zeal. This quality of presence in the world requires careful contemplation of the mysteries of Jesus's life, a contemplation which brings an inner harmony with His own hidden life of intimate trust and love of His Father. This kind of presence in any situation of our troubled world is rarely easy, since it is often so counter-cultural. But it is always decisive in faith for the kingdom of our Father in Christ.

Finally, this inner hidden life of faith enriches our appreciation of the Trinity of God, and it reveals the Trinitarian dimension in even the most ordinary of our experiences. We can understand the Holy Spirit as all that inner richness of intimacy and love that is between Son and Father. And Jesus returned to His Father so we could live in His Spirit and continually grow in that hidden inner life of intimacy with His Father. He desires this, that the world may come to believe in Him who is our Father and in His only Son, Jesus Christ who, together, now send us the Spirit:

Out of his [the Father's] infinite glory, may he give you the power through his Spirit for your hidden self to grow strong, so that Christ may live in your hearts through faith" (Eph 3:16-7).

The Imitation of Christ Revisited

Charles J. Healey, S.J.

Volume 36, 1977, pp. 549-556.

*T*he *Imitation of Christ,* commonly attributed to Thomas a Kempis, holds a special place in the history of Christian spirituality. Since its first appearance in Latin in the early fifteenth century, this classic of devotional literature has gone through countless editions and translations. It has had the distinction of being the most well known and popular religious writing outside of the Bible in the western world, and over the centuries it has nourished the interior lives of people in all walks of life. In recent years, however, it has gone through somewhat of a decline in popularity and use. Many aspects of its piety did not fit in easily with much that was being stressed in contemporary spirituality. Its heavy emphasis upon the vertical dimension in the Christian life and upon such aspects as withdrawal from the world, self-depreciation, and a certain anti-intellectual tone did not sit well with modern trends which were placing a great emphasis on the horizontal aspects of Christian living. However, we do seem to be in a period where attempts are being made to achieve a more integrated and a more balanced view of Christian spirituality. In the present climate which does seem to favor a rediscovery and re-evaluation, it would be helpful to look again at this spiritual classic.

The purpose of this article, then, will be to "revisit" *The Imitation of Christ.* It will attempt to recall some of its strengths and limitations, as well as offering some reflections for its possible use and value in the nourishing of one's life of faith today. This should be done in the light of the historical context from which the book evolved, and for this reason, its historical background will be briefly reviewed before looking at the contents of *The Imita-*

126

tion of Christ itself. For some, this may be a case of getting acquainted with *The Imitation of Christ* for the first time, but perhaps for the majority, it will be a case of returning to a familiar but still somewhat elusive friend from the past. Still, rediscovery does play a very important part in the spiritual life and *The Imitation of Christ* deserves to be revisited continually.

Historical Background

The Imitation of Christ is closely connected with the movement known as the *Devotio Moderna* and the association known as the "Brethren of the Common Life."[1] The pioneer in this movement was Gerard Groote (1340-1384), a native of Deventer in present day Holland. After his conversion in his mid-thirties through his friendship with the Flemish mystic Blessed Jan Ruysbroeck, Groote gathered around him a number of disciples who devoted themselves primarily to the copying of books of piety. One of his disciples, Florentius Radewijns, conceived the idea of forming a community of copyists, and in 1381, three years before Gerard Groote's death, the association of the Brethren of the Common Life was formed. The members, who were not bound by any vows, devoted themselves to exercises of prayer and the copying of spiritual books. Later the Brethren also founded and directed schools for poor boys and these schools eventually became very successful and well known.

A further development found some of the Brethren going from Deventer to Windesheim to found a monastery. This group became religious in the strict sense, adopting the Rule of the Canons Regular of Saint Augustine. The monastery at Windesheim, which was approved by Pope Boniface IX in 1395, flourished and expanded, and by 1464 there were eighty-two monasteries connected with it. All of them were centers for the spread of devotional writings, for the members continued to excel as copyists. Gradually, original anonymous writings also developed from these centers and they manifested the spirit and tone of the *Devotio Moderna* movement. *The Imitation of Christ* would become the most famous of these writings.

It was the spirit of Gerard Groote and the *Devotio Moderna* that was very influential in the schools of the Brethren and the monasteries connected with Windesheim. Perhaps the best way to come to some understanding of the *Devotio Moderna* is to read over the pages of *The Imitation of Christ,* for its spirit is embodied there. In general, it can be said that the spirit of this movement is marked by two main aspects: first, there is a reaction against speculative spirituality; and secondly, there is a strong emphasis on affective piety. The fourteenth century, it will be recalled, wit-

---

[1]For a fuller development of the history of the *Devotio Moderna*, see P. Pourrat's *Christian Spirituality*. Trans. by S. P. Jacques (Maryland: The Newman Press, 1953), vol. II, pp. 252-264.

nessed a rich flowering of mysticism in the Low Countries, particularly with the writings of Meister Eckhart, Jan Ruysbroeck, John Tauler, and Henry Suso. However, the excessive speculation of later developments produced a strong reaction, and this reaction was evident in the writers of the *Devotio Moderna* school. There developed here a practical, empirical spirituality that was marked by a strong return to affective piety. The writings of the *Devotio Moderna* school were collections of pious upliftings expressed in detached sentences and spiritual maxims, rather than in any systematic treatises on spirituality. Thus, very little attention is given to doctrinal considerations. The primary aim was to respond to the needs of those seeking a fuller interior life by stirring up an ardent desire for the following of Christ.

One of the most famous writers of this school was Thomas à Kempis. After completing his schooling at Deventer in 1398, he was admitted by Florentius Radewijns into the community of copyists. A year later, he entered one of the monasteries connected with Windesheim where his brother was Prior, and it was here at the monastery of Mount Saint Agnes near Zwolle that he lived out his long life in calm and peace, surrounded with books. He copied books but he also composed ascetical and historical treatises of his own. It is to him that the authorship of *The Imitation of Christ* is commonly attributed, although this has not always met with universal agreement.

There is no need here to go once again into the age-old problem of the origin of *The Imitation of Christ* and its actual author.[2] There is common agreement that it was known and pondered at the beginning of the fifteenth century by the Brothers of the Common Life and the Canons of the Windesheim Congregation. They were the first to speak of this famous work and they did much to make it known and loved throughout Christendom with their copying of the text. In addition to Thomas à Kempis, it has been attributed at one time or another to such persons as Gerard Groote himself, Giovanni Gersen, a thirteenth century Italian abbot, and John Gerson, the famous chancellor of the University of Paris. However, the most solid scholarly opinion continues to associate *The Imitation of Christ* with the name of Thomas a Kempis. But again, this is not a point that need overly concern us here, for our main concern is with the book itself, regardless of the actual author.

The Imitation of Christ: Content

It is a little difficult to talk about the content of *The Imitation of Christ* because it is offered primarily as a treatise to be pondered over and read

---

[2]See Pourrat, pp. 262-264 and also the article "Imitation of Christ" by W. Jappe Alberts in *New Catholic Encyclopedia* (New York: McGraw Hill, 1967), vol. 7, pp. 375-377 for further background material.

prayerfully rather than discussed and treated abstractly. Yet some brief description should be given to recall with what we are dealing. The title usually given to it comes from the title of the first chapter: "Of the Imitation or Following of Christ and the Despising of All Vanities of the World." The text of the book as we know it has been traditionally divided into four books. Book I contains admonitions useful to the spiritual life; Book II speaks of admonitions concerning interior things; Book III treats of interior consolation and the inward speaking of Christ to a faithful soul; and Book IV is devoted to a treatise on the Blessed Sacrament.

There is no logical sequence between any of the books or chapters and, as a result, it can be picked up at any place and read at random. The various chapters contain unconnected spiritual maxims and other sayings which seek to arouse the reader to a greater knowledge and love of God and a knowledge of oneself. There are many allusions and references to Scripture and the author makes use of the writings that were being read at the time in the circles of the *Devotio Moderna*. With its stress on affective piety, the influence of such writers as Saint Augustine, Saint Bernard, Saint Gregory the Great and others is evident. There are frequent colloquies directed to God in touching terms, and often, particularly in the third book, there are moving dialogues between Christ and the individual.

The spirituality of *The Imitation of Christ* is predominantly inward looking. Although there is no systematic presentation of ideas, certain elements of the spiritual life are stressed. There is, first of all, the relationship between the individual and God, and in this sense, the vertical dimension of the spiritual life assumes the prominent position. Recognizing the importance of the knowledge of God and the knowledge of self for the growth and development of the interior life, it stresses Saint Augustine's prayer: "Grant, Lord, that I may know myself and that I may know thee." To attain this, there should be the continual examination of one's conscience and the consideration of one's position before God. Acknowledging our weakness and misery, we turn to God from whom comes all our strength.

Closely connected with this stress on the knowledge of God and the knowledge of self is the theme of renunciation of self or *resignatio*.[3] This involves a complete sacrifice of oneself and at the same time a trustful abandonment to God. It is a going out of oneself and embracing the divine will with all one's heart and strength; it is focusing one's eyes firmly on God in love and valuing him above all things.

There is also the theme of the following of Christ which is developed in a very beautiful and inspirational manner. Christ the Master is the way, the truth and the life, who invites us to follow him. He teaches us through his doctrine, but more through his example of renunciation of self and

---

[3] See for example characters 15, 17, and 37 of Book III.

resignation to the will of the Father. If we wish to follow Jesus seriously, we must enter courageously upon the royal road of the Cross, "for we shall seek him elsewhere in vain." It is only through obedience, humility, poverty, freedom from earthly goods, and especially patience in adversity that we will find him.

Perhaps the secret of *The Imitation of Christ* and its great strength lies in its ability to move the heart and inspire the reader to turn to God with renewed hope, dedication, love, and trust. It has a unique power to awaken in the reader a profound awareness of God and his reality. What makes it a spiritual classic is its ability to speak universally to the hearts of men. It seems to portray clearly and cogently the unexpressed moods and experiences of the soul, and people at so many stages can find themselves mirrored in its pages. It taps the deepest yearnings and desires of the human heart, the yearnings Saint Augustine expressed with his words: "Our hearts were made for you, O Lord, and they will not rest until they rest in you."

Often, too, one can find the right phrase or expression that is needed or helpful at the time, whether it is to console, to challenge, to stir up the conscience, or to inspire to turn to God anew. It seems to have a particular message for each reader, and that message is a hopeful and positive one. It is a book that one can turn to again and again. It has the marks of agelessness and inexhaustibility, for persons can ever approach it anew with their experiences and needs of the particular moment. At times it may oversimplify, but it is basically seeking to recall what really counts in life and what should really be of value and concern. "Vanity of vanities and all is vanity except to love God and serve him alone."[4] All of this is put forward in simple, straight-forward, practical language that is appealing primarily to the heart rather than the mind.

Some Limitations

And yet, *The Imitation of Christ* is not without its limitations, and this has often been pointed out.[5] It is only when we recognize these limitations and allow for them that the fullest fruit from this book can be reaped. Let us consider some of these aspects which I think can be best understood in light of the book's history and the particular context in which it was written.

There is, first of all, the charge that *The Imitation of Christ* tends to be anti-intellectual in its approach and attitude, and that its piety is not related sufficiently to doctrine. This orientation is certainly present and should be kept in mind, but it can be understood to some extent in light of the reaction of the *Devotio Moderna* school to the excesses of an overly speculative spirituality of the late fourteenth century. It must be kept in mind, too, that

---

[4]Book I, c. 1.
[5]See for example, Philip Hughes, *A History of the Church* (New York: Sheed and Ward, 1946), vol. III, pp. 216, ff.

this work by no means presents the whole of the Catholic faith and life. It only represents particular aspects and thus it must be supplemented by other readings and instructions.

Secondly, the "withdrawal from the world" aspect is very pronounced, and along with this is a certain negativism towards oneself and other created persons and things. The dictum, "As often as I have been among men, I have returned less a man" sums up this attitude as well as the well-known emphasis of staying close to one's cell. There is also a choice of words at times that does not resonate too well with the modern ear. For example, the expressions "vileness of oneself" and "contempt for oneself" do not sit well in a climate that recognizes the importance of a healthy self-image and the need of self-affirmation. Part of all this is due to the fact that the work was written by a monk and principally for other monks, and it makes use of expressions and ways of looking at things that were an accepted way in the devotional literature of the time. Still, it cannot be denied that the withdrawal element and the contempt for the world do tend to be over-stressed. There is no question that anyone serious about the interior life needs a certain amount of solitude and withdrawal, and this is a value that is being rediscovered today; but for the majority, this is a means and not an end in itself. And perhaps a more balanced spirituality will place the stress on the *right use* of things of the world rather than a *withdrawal* from them.

Thirdly, some have found the "vertical dimension" too strong with the emphasis on God and the soul, and it has been suggested at times that it is a "manual of sacred selfishness" with its strong individualistic outlook. It is true that the stress is placed on the interior life of the individual and his or her relationship with God. It is also true that little attention is given to the apostolate or the service of others. But this is by way of omission rather than denial, and to dismiss the work because it does not place more of a stress on the horizontal aspects of the spiritual life would be shortsighted. What is lacking should be noted and kept in mind. There is always the danger of selfishness and a sense of exclusiveness in the spiritual life and this must be guarded against. "By their fruits you shall know them" always provides a fine test for authenticity. Still, I do not see any danger of fostering any spiritual selfishness in *The Imitation* if used in a mature and balanced way. It must be kept in mind, too, that an effective and productive apostolate does call for a strong and vibrant interior life.

Such are the main limitations of *The Imitation of Christ*. They are mostly in the areas of emphasis or omission, and they should be recognized and taken into account. Like any spiritual book, particularly works of piety and devotion such as this, it is perhaps best to approach it and make use of it with an open, discerning mind, recognizing what is of great value and help and what is not particularly applicable. A certain freedom should be present to the reader of this work to seek and find what is particularly helpful and leave aside what is not.

Value for Today

In light of this brief historical background of *The Imitation of Christ* and some remarks on its strengths and limitations, we might now consider the question of its value and usefulness for meeting present day needs. Can it be recommended to and used with profit by those who seek to deepen their lives of faith, hope and love? I would suggest that it can be of great value if used in a spirit of discretion, freedom and openness.

First of all, I think the present-day climate is open to a spirit of rediscovery and re-evaluation. The tendency to react negatively has lessened noticeably and there is greater receptivity to some traditional practices, not in the sense of merely returning to the same old way, but rather in the sense of taking up again in light of one's own growth and experience. In the case of *The Imitation of Christ,* there is more of a tendency to see its limitations in a larger perspective and framework rather than merely reacting against it. This is the approach I would prefer to take, that is, recognizing and making allowances for its limitations while recognizing, too, its uniqueness and value. For this is a work that has nourished so very many in the past and one that can continue to do the same today.

Perhaps its greatest value lies in the help it provides for prayer, for it has the ability to make one aware of the reality of God and to awaken the spirit to the presence and transcendence of God in a special way. It speaks to the heart of the person seeking God. It has the power to shock one into an awareness of God, and a sense and awareness of the eternal. All spiritual reading seeks with varying degrees of success to make us aware of the transcendent reality of God and to nourish this awareness in our daily lives. Like all good spiritual reading, *The Imitation of Christ* gives God the opportunity to touch us and to be operative in our lives. It has the unique power to open our lives to God's grace and to bring us to God in a spirit of humility, simplicity and trust.

It is a book that can be read easily and with great freedom. It can be picked up and read at any time and place, either for shorter periods or longer periods. If something doesn't appeal, one can move on; if something moves us and stirs up feelings of devotion, it is best to linger and draw as much fruit as possible. In fact, it is important that it not be read hastily as though pressed for time, but slowly, little by little, in order to taste and savor what is read. A prayerful reading and pondering is what is called for, leaving to the Holy Spirit the particular fruit or message to be received. It is as a help, then, to raising our minds and hearts to God, rather than as any complete guide to the spiritual life, that *The Imitation of Christ* would seem to have its greatest value. For it is not to be taken as a complete explanation of the Catholic faith, or any systematic spiritual program, but as a series of spiritual maxims and meditations intended to deepen one's interior life. And we constantly have to be reminded of the importance of the interior life and its need for continual nourishment.

I would suggest, too, that this work can be used with great profit in connection with the directed retreat movement. It will be recalled that one of the books that touched Saint Ignatius Loyola deeply during his stay at Manresa was *The Imitation of Christ,* and it subsequently became the book of devotion he especially favored, constantly read, and recommended to others. He recognized its power to move and incite the heart to respond to God's grace. During the course of the *Spiritual Exercises,* where he is very reluctant about recommending outside reading, it is one of the books he recommends during the second week of the *Exercises.* At times, the director who knows the text well can recommend passages from *The Imitation of Christ* suitable for individual needs along with the suggestions from Scripture. For example, the chapter, The Royal Road of the Cross (Book II, c. 12), can be read and pondered in connection with the following of Christ and the third degree of humility.

Conclusion

So much, then, for talking about *The Imitation of Christ,* something the author never had in mind. He intended it to be read and pondered prayerfully, to be used in the presence of God. If read merely out of curiosity or out of historical interest, it will not have the effect intended. This article has merely attempted to revisit, to suggest some reflections, and to point the way. The rest under God's grace lies with the reader and the book itself.

The Graces of the Third
and Fourth Weeks

Dominic Maruca, S.J.

©*Soundings* (Washington, DC: Center of Concern, 1974).

I would like to situate this essay within the context of our Task Force's origin, objectives and preceding dialogue. Our remote origin seems to have been the concern first expressed to the American Assistancy Seminar of Jesuit Spirituality, as reported in the *National Jesuit News*: Is the current inward trend of Jesuit spirituality a healthy development or an unbalanced orientation? Is it leading Jesuits — and the persons whom they are guiding — to neglect a necessary outward thrust?[1]

This concern was spelled out in greater detail in the "Proposal" to establish this Task Force:

> During the last dozen years...there has been extensive growth in the social theology of the Church...This social theology has not been integrated into the present catechesis and spirituality of our Church...it is important that this social theology be integrated into the vision and practice of modern spirituality lest the person become trapped in an interiority of religious experience, while the exterior relationships of life are controlled and structured by the values of culture rather than by those of the gospel.

The objective which consequently governed our dialogue up to this point has been a single one: How can we develop a spirituality which takes cognizance of and integrates the social theology of the Church?

This essay will explore the possiblity of making our dialogue two-directional: granted that spiritual directors have much to learn from their socially-oriented brothers, can it be that social theorists can learn something from experienced spiritual directors? Specifically, we will ask a series of

[1] *National Jesuit News*, February, 1973, p.1.

related questions: What is the grace which God is expected to communicate and which the exercitant is expected to realize in some degree, during the making of the exercises of the 3rd and 4th Weeks of the Spiritual Exercises? Can a consideration of this grace contribute to our understanding of social theology? Can the mystery of the Cross and Resurrection teach us something about what our hope can realistically be?

Methodology

Various approaches could be taken in order to find answers to these questions. Through textual analysis and consultation of the standard commentaries on the Spiritual Exercises we could determine the specific objective or grace to be achieved at each phase of the Spiritual Exercises.[2] By surveying the school of "hope" and "liberation" theologians, we could learn from them where we have been and where we might be heading.[3] We could reconsider the classic antinomy of "involvement and disengagement," of "flight from and transformation of the world," and thereby devise an ideal position or posture.[4]

I decided to try a different approach: to consider the actual experience of persons whom I and other directors have been privileged to direct during the past four years both in the U.S. and abroad, with special attention to those who are involved directly in a ministry toward the poor and powerless. The limitations of such an approach are obvious: the sampling makes no claim of being representative in scientific sense, though it does draw upon extensive experience with priests and sisters in different cultural settings. Moreover, my perception was obviously limited, so that what I am reporting has been refracted through the prism of my own mind-set and relayed by what may be a selective memory, even though I have consulted colleagues who corroborated or corrected my observations. Since the lived experience of socially active exercitants is a valid theological source, I felt it should be consulted, despite these limitations.

Joseph Ratzinger has remarked that the hottest theological issues of the moment are two deeply related themes: politics (neo-Marxism, violence, the real meaning of liberation), and spirituality (the content of our hope, in what way God is the basis of life). "For me," Ratzinger continues, "priority must be given to the urgent question of how to discover God in our life. This is not an academic question; it is a radical question, which must somehow be answered before one can ask academic questions in theology, particularly those questions which relate to the political sphere."[5]

---

[2] William J. Byron, S.J., "Social Consciousness in the Ignatian Exercises," pp. 272-285.
[3] Thomas Clarke, SJ, *New Pentecost or New Passion?* (Paramus: Paulist Press, 1973), pp. 171-181; Walter Capps, *Time Invades the Cathedral* (Philadelphia: Fortress Press, 1972).
[4] Karl Truhlar, SJ, *Antino miae Vitae Spiritualis* (Rome: Univ. Greg., 1961).
[5] Quoted by Desmond O'Grady in "The Ratzinger Round," *The Month,* December, 1973, p. 411.

Clarification of the Notion of "Grace

Experience has led me to alter my understanding of the reality we call 'grace.' At one time I tended to think of it as a unit, as something either totally present or totally absent. Such an inadequate notion led me as a director to expect God to produce on a pre-conceived schedule, like a dispensing machine: the exercitant has gone through certain exercises, so now it is God's turn to come through with a corresponding grace. Gradually, I came to view grace as an *evolving* reality which is realized in a progressive manner, and as a *relational* reality which can be realized only in concrete circumstances. In asking whether a person had received the "grace" of the 3rd or 4th Week of the Spiritual Exercises, I now understood this to mean, "How is this person actually finding himself related to God? to the community of man? to the created universe? to the Paschal Mystery?" Not only, "How does he think about this mystery?" nor even, "How does he feel about it?" But most importantly, "How is he actually realizing his dependence upon God, his responsiblity for others, his share in the crucifixion and resurrection of Christ in the circumstances of his own life?"

A common teaching from sacramental theology may offer us an analogy. A person can be baptized, confirmed, married or ordained validly, but the actual grace of the sacrament may remain dormant for some time afterwards. In a given set of circumstances, God can actualize that grace when the person has become properly disposed to realize what it is that God has done for him. So, too, it seems that many graces envisioned by the Spiritual Exercises are communicated in a seminal form during the making of the Exercises; later they are actualized progressively as they penetrate to deeper levels of the personality, revivified as it were, or intensified as the person experiences the "task" aspect of the "gift" he has received. Grace admits degrees and specific qualitative differences as it grows within a person. One correspondent expressed this realization to her former director in this way: "I know that the work of the (30 day) retreat is still going on because I can now find God amid the barrenness, the muck and slime of the area in which I work and live."

We should also keep in mind that the graces to be "longed for and petitioned" during the making of the Spiritual Exercises have an organic and a *sequential* quality about them. There is a progressive building upon what has preceded. As we enter upon the 3rd Week, therefore, the exercitant has already realized, at least in a seminal manner, a series of graces. Though we cannot define them in a purely objective way, we can indicate certain features which bear upon our themes of social consciousness.

While considering the *Principle and Foundation,* the exercitant should

---

Ratzinger is also quoted as saying: "In prayer and meditation, we can find the tranquility and the transforming power of the presence of God...The type of committed detachment which is the byproduct of this interior liberty destroys the roots of all forms of exploitation including the lust for power inherent in political activity; and it opens the eyes to injustices that are concealed in every system."

have received a dual grace: (a) since God is the Lord of history, it is His prerogative to demand that we serve Him at each specific moment of history, cooperating with Him in directing the course of history; (b) since we are dependent creatures, we are relieved of the oppressive burden of autonomous agents serving rather as instruments of the Source of all being and activity. This balanced dual-grace enables him to be both accountable and yet not over-anxious. Moreover, he has acknowledged the relativity of all things; no thing is made absolute: neither wealth nor penury; neither health nor distress; neither honors nor disapproval; neither longevity nor a short life-span. He is truly free and fearless and yet conscious of his responsiblity to utilize the means and opportunities which God provides.

In dwelling upon the *enigma of sin* in history, he has been assured that the process of alienation from God began long before he came on the scene and that it will continue long after he has taken his leave. He has considered how this outcast state was compounded by subsequent sins of man which have woven a tangled skein of sinful structures in which we all find ourselves enmeshed as part of the human race. History, therefore, is not viewed as uninterrupted progress; there is much ambiguity in the culture which man has developed. In some respects man has grown more independent, more in control of himself and his environment; but in other respects he has become more enslaved and victimized. In addition to this original sin and its consequences, the exercitant has realized that the history of his own sinful past has added to this mess. Because he himself has failed to "act justly, love tenderly, and walk humbly before God" (Micah 6:8) he has distorted his relationship with God, with the community of man, and with material creation. In accepting God's judgement upon this past personal sinfulness, however, he has experienced God's healing forgiveness and been freed from oppressive guilt and the frustration of sheer futility.

With a sense of gratitude toward Jesus Christ, his liberator, he has felt the inspiration to enlist in a corporate enterprise, to enter into the mystery of how Christ is continuing his work of liberation through the joint efforts of many brothers. This grace of the *Call of the King* has several dimensions: the earnest desire to promote the Kingdom on a grand scale is balanced by the realization that his own person — body and soul — must be the immediate focus of his zealous concern, since the roots of all evil are lodged within himself.

Next, by entering into the mystery of the *Eternal Council* of the Holy Trinity, he has felt a sharing of God's own concern and compassion for mankind, which he views as wandering about lost in its own blindness and powerlessness. When he hears the words, "Let *us* work out the redemption of mankind," he has experienced them as addressed to himself, the co-worker of Christ.

Beginning with the mystery of the Nativity he has responded to the leadership of the Lord, praying for progressive incorporation into the mystery of his emptying-out and pouring-in. Christ's actions and attitudes have been contemplated as both models and energizing forces which are actually effecting his transformation. He has prayed to be associated with Christ more closely *mas actualmente,* "here and now," as Peters has translated it.[6]

To conclude this clarification of the notion of grace, we would note its importance for our essay. The graces of the 1st and 2nd Weeks are not something which were communicated *en bloque;* rather, each exercitant has *realized* them to some extent, depending on the lived experiences of his relating to the living God and his involvement in the course of human events. His *actualization* of these graces, however, will continue in a spiral-like fashion as he is progressively blessed and burdened with a new lived-experiences of sin and redemption. Grace is an evolving, relational, organic reality which God is continually communicating to each person.

Third Week: Composite Case-Study

With this understanding of "grace" as a background, the question I asked myself was a simple one: What has been the actual grace-experience of mature exercitants when they have repeated the exercises of the 3rd and 4th Weeks? How have persons of various ages and temperaments, who are now actually involved in social ministries, responded when praying contemplatively the mysteries of the Passion, Death and Resurrection of our Lord? What I will offer is a composite image that has formed in my mind as I listened to exercitants describing what they experienced when they considered Christ lamenting over Jerusalem, agonizing in the Garden, being arrested and tried, going to his death — while they themselves were actually suffering with Christ in their efforts to help him liberate people and bring them into some kind of unity.

Frequently there has been a feeling of great sadness; a rather diffused state of feeling stunned. Jesus has done all things well. All things — his words, his attitudes, his actions — measured up to the most sublime ideal imaginable. And yet he was rejected by his fellow-men. The most remarkable person ever to grace our world is being put to death by the ecclesiastical and political rulers of his day. What, then, in God's name am I trying to do? How can I possibly hope to accomplish anything when Jesus Christ himself failed to remedy man's ills? If he couldn't change men's hearts, how can I expect to transform them with the limited resources I have?

Some broadened their composition to include the history of the Church. The sight became even more depressing as they experienced the "social desolation" described by William Barry.

As they considered how from the earliest years and down through the centuries our history has been one of misunderstanding, envy, jealousy, rivalry, dissension, greed, violence, they found themselves asking a distressing question: Was it all — is it all — worth it?

---

[6] William Peters, SJ, *The Spiritual Exercises of St. Ignatius:* Exposition and Interpretation (Jersey City: Program to Adapt SpEx, 1968), p. 134.

Such an experience of "social desolation" seems to have been rather frequent among socially active persons who were, in a real sense, contemplating or sharing the Passion of Christ. Their description of the experience usually took the form of questions they found themselves asking: "What's the use of carrying on this useless charade? No one is really listening to what I am trying to say through my live. Everyone is so wrapped up on his own little world, his own petty concerns. How can I share my horizons when the people I want to help are locked up in the narrow prison of a struggle for survival? I had romantic notions when I came here. I thought I could help God shape a new human family, a family not turned inward on itself but willing to reach out and share God's blessings with others. I spoke bravely about fighting against dehumanizing forces in the culture; of establishing a community conscious of its solidarity and collective responsibility, of the unity and dignity of all men. I really thought we could succeed in our struggle to establish peace and justice."

A particularly poignant note was sounded with distressing frequency: "The attitude of my own brothers, my co-workers, is another source of pain. Not only don't many of them seem to share my vision, my sense of urgency, but they give me no support. They seem to be living in a different world, deaf to the drumbeat I hear, I go home looking for companionship, for the strength I need to carry on. I meet lethargy and dullness, complacency and a comfortable mediocrity. It hurts all the more when I recall the glow of hearts that once were fired with lofty ideals of generosity. Now I see, in so many instances, only cold ashes. Yet I can't blame them; I don't want to shift the burden of my depression onto their shoulders. God alone knows what they've been through. I don't know why they stopped dreaming and banked the fires. Maybe I'll be that way myself someday. Lord, help me, help us. Was this a part of your Passion, what I am going through?"

Colloquies such as these presume great intimacy. Peters tells us that they are the climax toward which meditation and contemplation should move.[7] The grace these exercitants were obviously experiencing was a real compassion with the Lord in anguish. Their lived experience was serving as a basis for the most intimate kind of dialogue. I seldom heard an exercitant speak of "talking over motives" or "begging for grace"; but this was obviously what was actually happening in their prayer.

What did the Lord say to such persons? Many seemed to hear him say: "I know just how you feel. I once felt that way myself. Stay with me for a while. Don't bother trying to figure it all out; just be with me."

The grace described by Ignatius as proper to our contemplation of Christ's Passion — "sorrow in company with Christ in His sorrow, being crushed with the pain that crushed Christ, tears and a deep-felt sense of suffering, because Christ suffered so much for me" (Sp. Ex., No. 203) — was experienced by most exercitants. As some watched and waited with the Lord, they reported

---

[7] Peters, op. cit., p. 132.

that nothing spectacular happened; there was no overwhelming burst of light, no uplifting insights. They experienced a quieting down, a sense of deep peace, a willingness to just be with Christ. It was still very dark and distressing, but they felt a definite sense of union, a gentle force enabling them to trust and surrender in faith to a mystery beyond their comprehension, a willingness to continue suffering with Christ, "here and now" in their effort to help the contemporary world. A remarkably large number acknowledged that in their deep communion with Christ, they became aware of the fact that they had been given, somewhere along the process, the gift of a preferential love for actual poverty and rejection together with Christ who was so treated. They had actually been placed under the standard of Christ in the highest degree of intimacy and association—something they had dreaded and feared had become an actuality in their lives; far from being a disaster, it was embraced as gift.

Other exercitants spoke of a new dawning. The darkness had not been totally dispersed, but their situation seemed to take on new contours within a new horizon of faith. Some, in witnessing the faith and singlemindedness of Christ, felt empowered to take a courageous stand. Despite fearful foreseeable consequences, they knew they had to do something; they knew they could do it. Others found that a fierce anger against "the whole system" was gradually being replaced with the courage to accept a very minor role, but a significant one, in God's mysterious design. Once again, they felt they had done so; they knew they could persevere.

The words and concepts that exercitants used to articulate their experience of contemplating the Passion, reflected the twofold mystery of grace as both a gift and a task. Some identified with the faithful servant of Yahweh and used vocabulary proper to this classical Old Testament image: they felt it was God's Holy War, a war which He alone could ultimately bring to a successful conclusion and in His own good time. Their language was that of traditional piety and mysticism: sacrifice, self-denial, the Cross, poverty of spirit, being among God's *anawim*. They accepted the mystery that "power is made perfect in weakness' (2 Cor. 12: 9), and that "as we share abundantly in Christ's sufferings, so through Christ we share abundantly in comfort too" (2 Cor. 1:5). They sensed that if there had been a better way, then Jesus Christ, who was of God, would certainly have chosen it himself and taught us to do likewise, as a Kempis has noted.[8]

Others did not deny this time-honored perspective of deep mysticism, but they still felt compelled to follow God's mandate and protest to the limit against the particular types of injustice and oppression in which they and their people were entangled. Their understanding of realized eschatology and their compassion for their people moved them to battle against every kind of man-made structure that was causing or perpetuating human misery. They had to put their lives on the line in order to live with themselves—and with Christ.

---

[8] Thomas a Kempis, *Imitation of Christ*, Book II, Chapter 12.

Worthy of note is the fact that at whatever point on this spectrum a person might be, he seemed to feel a peaceful tension, a tension that was at one and the same time both painful and hopeful, not unlike that of a woman in labor. There was also frequently a sense of emerging pluralism: the humble awareness that God must be illuminating different facets of this mystery to different people. Though they did not use Clarke's felicitous expression, they recognized the "complementarity and convergence of charisms."[9] If everyone were trying to row the boat from either the left or the right side, it would simply go into a circle.

Fourth Week: Composite Case Study

An integral part of the Paschal Mystery, of course, are the apparitions and assurances which the Risen Lord gave to his disciples and which he wishes to share with exercitants making the exercises of the 4th Week. This is ideally a time of "ectasy" in the technical sense of the word: a standing outside of oneself; not a loss of consciousness but of self-consciousness, as Joseph Whelan has expressed it.[10] My observation, for whatever it may be worth, is that women religious seem to have experienced this grace more frequently than the men I have directed. "To be filled with joy and happiness at the thought of Christ's great glory and happiness" (Sp. Ex., No. 221) is, perhaps, a grace still in store for many of us men.

Ignatius advises the exercitant to contemplate our Lord "doing the work of consolation, comparing it with the way friends are accustomed to console one another (Sp. Ex., No. 224). A common vehicle used by directors for disposing persons to experience this grace is the account of the apparition to the two disciples enroute to Emmaus. Most exercitants I have dealt with found it easy to identify with these two dejected disciples; they seem to have recognized their own distress mirrored in the disillusionment of these two earth-bound disciples. Many, as a result, took with them from the retreat the determination to continue asking the Lord in prayer to illuminate their minds with the words of the Scriptures, so that their hearts can know the joy and strength that those two disciples experienced.

A note of humor, I'm delighted to say, has frequently been introduced during these contemplations. It was almost as if the exercitant (usually a very serious and energetic person) were saying to himself (or hearing the Lord say): Don't take yourself so seriously." This has been truly a saving grace, a safeguard against morbid self-pity.

Many, as they contemplated the mysteries of the Risen Lord, came to realize that they had caused themselves unnecessary suffering by separating the two dimensions of the Paschal Mystery, seeing only the shadow of the Cross without the radiant Lord enthroned beyond it. A frequent prayer which

---

[9] Thomas Clarke, SJ, "Holiness and Justice In Tension," *The Way*, V 13:3 (July, 1973), p. 185.
[10] Joseph Whelan, *Benjamin* (Paramus: Newman, 1972), p. 63.

I and other directors have heard exercitants express is the simple desire, "If I could only keep this in mind!" Such a desire has led them to recognize the centrality of the Eucharist in the life of every active apostle, for both himself and for the people to whom he is ministering. What has struck many directors forcefully is the fact that those persons who are most intensely engaged in the nitty-gritty of the social ministry have been the ones most conscious of the inadequacy of their human efforts and the need of God's transforming power. They were determined to go on doing their utmost, working and suffering while waiting for God to crown their efforts. The celebration of the Eucharist helped them to keep it all together: to remember that Jesus walked this way; his faithful followers have done so down through the centuries; true believers are still doing so today, in a simple and joyful companionship. This grace of recognizing Jesus in the breaking of the bread is realized repeatedly during the exercises of the 4th Week.

A scripture passage which a colleague of mine, Gerard Campbell, has called to my attention as helpful in giving the exercitant a sense of continuing Christ's role as consoler, is that of John 14:12: "Truly, truly, I say to you, he who believes in me will also do the works that I do; and greater works than these will he do, because I go to the Father." The commentary of John Marsh illumines this astounding promise:

> This work, of bringing men to believe in Jesus Christ as the true Son of man, which has been the work done in his own works, would be continued in various ways, not necessarily in healings, by his disciples. But in one aspect the work of the disciples would be greater than that of the Lord, for it would be the privilege of the disciples to carry the grace of believing for the acceptance of the Greeks, and all the other Gentiles who as yet knew not the Christ. That they would come to belief at all depended, of course, entirely upon the "departure," the death of Jesus; if that did not occur, there would be no conversion of the Gentiles, but once it had occurred, the disciples would be able to do — to proclaim that his death as an historical event had been efficacious in bringing man and God finally together.[11]

The grace of the 3rd and 4th Weeks, as I and other directors have been privileged to witness it in numerous exercitants, has included the various dimensions which I have indicated. It appears to be a many-splendored thing: an evolving reality which is deepened as each exercitant is progressively incorporated into the actual living of Christ's Passion and Resurrection.

Conclusion

The aim of this essay was to raise and answer two questions closely related: What is the grace communicated during the making of the exercises of the 3rd and 4th Weeks? Can a consideration of this grace enhance our understanding of what is authentic social theology, what Christian hope can realistically be? By drawing upon the actual experience of exercitants who are very active in social ministry, we have seen that they have derived endurance and strength from contemplating the mysteries of the Passion and Resurrection of Christ.

---

[11] John Marsh, *Saint John* (Baltimore: Penguin Books, 1968), p. 63.

The observation is sometimes made that there is a disproportionate amount of despondency experienced among persons who are most deeply involved in effecting social reform. Do we have in the grace of the 3rd and 4th Weeks, properly experienced and understood, a preventive for discouragement? If we really believe that God is dealing directly with our exercitants, then we cannot ignore their experience of what he actually is saying and doing within them.

A blind-spot is defined by Webster as "as small area on the retina where the optic nerve leaves the eye and which is itself insensitive to the light." A secondary meaning is: "An area or subject about which one is uninformed, prejudiced or undiscerning." As a consequence, the eye is blind to its own blind spot; it is only someone else looking into our eye who can perceive our blind-spot and mirror it back to us. Our very strength, in a sense, is our weakness. What enables us to be perceptive of the world around us must itself be ministered unto.

It seems to me, in all frankness, that we who are serving as the very nerves which are mediating messages and signals to others run a high risk of ignoring our own blind-spot. In one sense, this might be a tribute to our zeal: an indication of how intense and singleminded we wish to be in our service of others. But in another sense, we could be failing to give others an opportunity to exercise not so much fraternal correction as fraternal clarification and enlightenment. To fulfill the purpose of our Task Force, communication will have to be reciprocal: spiritual directors must learn to integrate social theology into their spirituality, and social theorists must in turn listen to the actual experience of directors.

On Leaving Retreat: To Go Out Can Be To Go In

Charles C. Murphy, S.J.

Volume 34, 1975, pp. 975-986.

"Going out of retreat," especially a thirty day retreat, is an experience that the *Directory of the Spiritual Exercises* describes in terms of going from a warm to a cold place.[1] Some say that is an understatement. This is an extremely important transition period for the exercitant, however, and the dynamics of the *Exercises* can and should provide an interior thermal adjustment of some kind in preparation, for it.

The *Spiritual Exercises* have a richness that permits many vantage points from which to view them. One way is to see them as mediating the Divine Presence in ways that significantly change a person's life. A danger arises from the very fact that this Presence is very successfully mediated during the retreat and leads to "felt" change. It is a precious time when thoughts, words and

---

[1] *Directory* (of 1599). XL no. 1. From the days when the *Exercises* were first given it was realized that some directives other than those in the *Exercises* were needed to help directors. Ignatius himself worked at the composition of a directory. Because of dissatisfaction with the incompleteness of previously written directories this *Directory* of 1599 was commissioned and approved by Fr. Acquaviva, General of the Society at that time. It is known as the official directory of the *Exercises*. This directory is very faithful to the thought of Ignatius. One of its deficiencies is that it failed to include from the *Directory* of Polanco an explanation of the application of the senses leaning heavily on the "spiritual senses" of the soul as described by the mystics, particularly St. Bonaventure. See De Guibert, *The Jesuits: Their Spiritual Doctrine and Practice* (Chicago, 1964, Loyola University Press), pp. 243-247.

deeds can become "warm, clear and strong."[2] Ideally, this state should be taken right out of the retreat into the home, the school, the streets, and work. It is a time of vision, a time of getting in touch with a very important reality. And like good clean air it is a reality worth being in touch with continually. All too often, though, a serious attrition soon results in many of the benefits received during the retreat. But the *Exercises* are especially aimed at life, not three or eight or thirty days, and in a real sense they begin when the retreat ends. Properly understood they are a preparation to find God in all facets of one's life.

The prayer intended to aid in this difficult transition and designed to help find God in all things is the "Contemplation to Attain the Love of God," hereafter referred to as the *Contemplatio*. In this striking contemplation God is seen as giving, as laboring, and also as seeking love. For the presupposition is that love is a mutual exchange of gifts, so it is not attained until there is a return giving and laboring on the part of the one contemplating. Often enough one sees the world as not all that gifted and graced, so the exercitant prays for a special knowledge, an intimate knowledge of all blessings received. If he sees his arms, his life, his world filled with gifts of every kind and variety, and all very specially for him, his natural response will be to cry out, "What can I give in return?" If he has an intimate knowledge of all the blessings of creation and redemption that he has received, he will be alive with feeling for the wonder of it all. For all this divine lavishness he will want to respond with every fiber of his being in a resounding "Thank you! Here is my gift. It's everything I am and have. Take it all!"

Early commentators on the *Exercises* thought this contemplation to be appropriate for even the first and second weeks if the needs of the exercitant indicated it.[3] Eventually commentators put this contemplation later, with the *Directory* of 1599 suggesting that it be given for at least an hour a day during the last week of the retreat, or for the whole of the last day or the last two days.[4] At this later time it becomes an excellent preparation for *going out* of retreat, whereas the earlier use of it in the first and second weeks interrupts either the first week, which has a far different emotional content than that of the *Contemplatio* and as such would be discouraged by the text of the *Exercises*,[5] or the second week that is already "overloaded" with matter for contemplation.

As beautiful and as powerful as this *Contemplatio* is, there remains a very subtle obstacle to its full benefit, or even partial benefit, being realized. The ideas presented in the four points of this exercise may be reflected on, put to memory, their logic and truth seen and appreciated and cherished. But it might

---

[2]William J. Young, S.J., tr. *Letters of St. Ignatius of Loyola* (Chicago, 1959, Loyola University Press), pg. 181.

[3]*Monumenta Ignatiana*, II, 2, 322f; 416, 459, 560.

[4]*Directory*, XXXVI no. 2.

[5]*Exercises*, 73-81, esp. 78.

well be a "head trip" for the exercitant. In his *Grammar of Assent* Newman articulates this problem that very often is that of the exercitant making the *Contemplatio.*

> Logic makes but a sorry rhetoric with the multitude; first shoot round corners, and you may not despair of converting by a syllogism. Tell men to gain notions of a Creator from His works, and, if they were to set about it (which nobody does) they would be jaded and wearied by the labyrinth they were tracing. Their minds would be gorged and surfeited by the logical operation. Logicians are more set upon concluding rightly, than on right conclusions. They cannot see the end for the process. Few men have that power of mind which may hold fast and firmly a variety of thoughts. We ridicule "men of one idea"; but a great many of us are born to be such, and we should be happier if we knew it. To most men argument makes the point in hand only more doubtful, and considerably less impressive. After all, man is *not* a reasoning animal; he is a seeing, feeling, contemplating, acting animal. He is influenced by what is direct and precise.[6]

Even though we are dealing with a contemplation it is easy to approach the *Contemplatio* with a heavy emphasis on the reasoning rather than on the seeing, contemplating, feeling and acting that are better equipped to deliver the power inherent in this exercise. For this power to be realized it is necessary to reach the heart. And "the heart is commonly reached, not through the reason, but through the imagination, by means of direct impressions, by the testimony of facts and events, by history, by description. Persons influence us, voices melt us, looks subdue us, deeds inflame us."[7] This is what should happen in the *Contemplatio:* the heart should be reached.

The great contribution of this contemplation is that it prepares the person to find God in doing as well as in thinking. It is not necessarily true that to labor is to pray, but labor *can* be prayer. And when it does become a prayer, the transformation that the *Exercises* seek, and that is prayed for in the beginning of the *Contemplatio,* becomes a greater reality. There the prayer is that an intimate knowledge of all blessings received may be had, that in all things God may be loved and served.

A clarifying example of what this can mean comes from the life of Artur Rubenstein. On the *Today Show* on February 11, 1975, this great musician and wonderful human being described in an interview what happens when he plays. Queried about his statement: "When I make music I make love. It is the same thing," he replied: "It is. You see, when I come out I fall in love with the public who was good enough to pay money . . . to listen to me. So from the beginning, before even going out, I love them for it. And when I come out my job is to give them my emotions. I want to make them happy. I want to give them consolation. I want to give them everything I have in me . . . I sit there and love what I play, and it goes to my heart. I play with all my heart what I have to play, music which fills me completely with joy and happiness and emotion and everything, and I have to be able to transmit it by some secret antenna."

---

[6]John Cardinal Newman, *Grammar of Assent* (NY, 1959, Image Books), pg. 90.
[7]Ibid., pg. 89.

This lovely example from the life of a great contemporary speaks eloquently about what the *Contemplatio* is about. It is about making love. But its message is also that you do not have to be an Artur Rubenstein to do it.

The *Contemplatio* is about making love. You can be minimally gifted in all the areas of human endeavor. But according to the particular insight of this *Contemplatio,* expressed so succinctly in the *praenotanda,* you can make love by returning a gift for the gifts you have received. Of course, there is love and there is love, even as there are gifts and there are gifts. How does one fall in love to such a degree and depth that with and from all one's heart the response comes forth? Especially where this response is not just an action to be done once, or even repeatedly, but the whole of one's day, day after day? The *Exercises* are intended to lead to a progressively deeper falling in love, a state that begins during them and, hopefully, continues on after them. When the *Exercises* are lived this way, and repeated with great relish each year, there is excellent hope for continued growth in the quality of one's response in love and service.

In the life of the author of the *Exercises,* St. Ignatius, we find a continued growth in his facility to find God everywhere. Near the end of his life he confided to Father de Camara that "his devotion had always gone on increasing, that is, the ease with which he found God, which was then greater than he had ever had in his life."[8] This same growth is possible to all according to their own graces and gifts.

The experience of Cardinal Newman while he was making the *Exercises* can focus light on what the interiorization of this *Contemplatio* can effect in one's life in and out of retreat. In his *Apologia pro Vita Sua* he writes:

> What I can speak of with greater confidence is the effect upon me a little later of the *Exercises of St. Ignatius.* Here again, in a pure matter of the most direct religion, in the intercourse between God and the soul, during a season of recollection, of repentance, of good resolution, of inquiry into vocation, the soul was "sola cum solo"; there was no cloud interposed between the creature and the Object of his faith and love. The command practically enforced was, "My son, give Me thy heart." The devotions then to angels and saints as little interfered with the incommunicable glory of the Eternal, as the love which we bear our friends and relations, our tender human sympathies, are inconsistent with that supreme homage of the heart to the Unseen, which really does but sanctify and exalt what is of earth.[9]

He was writing about his experience in retreat, but the *Contemplatio* has very much to do with the supreme homage of the heart to the Unseen and the sanctification and exaltation of what is of the earth. How can this *Contemplatio* contribute to this hallowing of the secular and the profane into which the exercitant soon returns? The experience of Teilhard de Chardin, who was profoundly influenced by the *Contemplatio,* was that of more and more

---

[8]George E. Ganss, S.J. *The Constitutions of the Society of Jesus* (Institute of Jesuit Sources, 1970, St. Louis), cited on pg. 26.

[9]John Cardinal Newman, *Apologia Pro Vita Sua* (Image Books, 1956, Garden City, N.Y.), pp. 284, 5.

seeing all as sacred. For him to go out of retreat was not a diminution of the experience of the divine, but a continuation of it. For him to go out was to go in. The everyday world provided him with a rich interior and total experience of the Creator never absent from His creation.

> Throughout my whole life during every moment I have lived, the world has gradually been taking on light and fire for me, until it has come to envelop me in one mass of luminosity, glowing from within. . . . The purple flush of matter fading imperceptibly into the gold of spirit, to be lost finally in the incandescence of a personal universe. . . . This is what I have learnt from my contact with the earth—the diaphany of the divine at the heart of a glowing universe, the divine radiating from the depths of matter aflame.[10]

Is something similar possible in the lives of all who make the *Exercises,* or is this experience of finding God everywhere possible only in the life of an Ignatius or a Teilhard or some other extraordinary mystic? To his confessor at Alcala, Fr. Manuel Mione, Ignatius extolled the value of the *Exercises* in their power to transform the quality of his service. " . . . the *Spiritual Exercises* are the best means I can think of in this life both to help a man to benefit himself and to bring help, profit, and advantage to many others. Even though you felt yourself to be in no special need, you will see how they will help you to serve others beyond anything you ever dreamed of."[11] The great efficacy that Ignatius sees in the *Exercises* here is in the quality of service that they engender, and this for all who make them. That they are a school of prayer no one would question, but their chief thrust is directly related to service of the Lord, to which from the earliest days of Ignatius' conversion, when he experienced great familiarity with Christ in his prayerful reverie, he dreamed of devoting his whole life: to a service of that Lord who was beginning to grace him in rich, new ways.[12]

As a transition, the *Contemplatio* brings the *Exercises* out of the retreat into the workaday world, first by preparing the exercitant for it, then by an actual implementing in his life of service a facility for finding God everywhere. But before entering into the content of that contemplation, some ideas on how it can be made follow.

For the most part the *Exercises* call for the contemplation of only two mysteries from the life of Christ in one day although four or five full hours of prayer are devoted to this. So two or three of these prayer periods are given to repetitions of mysteries already contemplated, and the last repetition of the day is the "application of the senses." The *Contemplatio* is very much like the other contemplations in that the imagination is emphasized, and it is similar to the other repetitions in that it goes back to those points of singular religious

---

[10]Teilhard de Chardin, *The Divine Milieu* (NY, 1957, Harper Torchbooks), quoted in introductory article, "Teilhard de Chardin: The Man" by Pierre Leroy, S.J., pg. 13.

[11]William J. Young, S.J., pp. 27, 28.

[12]Luis Gonzales de Camara. (tr. by Young). *St. Ignatius' Own Story* (Loyola University Press, Chicago, 1956). ##7, 10, 11.

significance, whether of consolation or desolation, that were experienced before in the contemplation of the same mystery.

It is extraordinary, in view of the relative shortage of time—even in a thirty day retreat—that more mysteries are not proposed for the purpose of contemplation. Just two mysteries a day! And some days do not even have that since they are taken up with one or more of the typically Ignatian meditations. But what is sought in the *Exercises* is not an inventory kind of knowledge of the Lord but the knowledge that Mary had, that John had, that Peter had. They were not present at all the incidents of His life. None of them were. The sinful woman at the house of Simon had an abundance of love for the Lord but probably knew very little of what we would term the biographical details of his life.[13] But what Mary His Mother heard and knew, she dwelt on and went over and over. "As for Mary, she treasured all these things and pondered them in her heart."[14] The application of the senses goes back to what has already been experienced or contemplated. It presumes a great interest in the event and a delight at going back to it. In addition to the imaginative entering into the scene by contemplating persons, words and actions as is done in contemplation, there is applied a spiritual smell and taste of what is there. "The sense of smell St. Ignatius refers to the fragrance of a soul enriched with divine gifts, and the sense of taste to the interior savour of its sweetness, both of which exercises imply a certain presence of the thing or persons on whom we meditate, with a sweet and tender love of them."[15] One of the enriching features of this kind of prayer is that it mediates presence.

An example may clarify this. After World War II there was a spate of movies that had "flashbacks" to earlier times in the war. Some five, ten, and as the war receded into the past, fifteen and twenty years after, a soldier, often a pilot, would return to a camp or an airbase where he had been stationed. The base is empty now, the planes gone, the barracks vacated; only memories remain. But they are not empty; they have a content for him that was missing in the original events. Now from the vantage point of years later, the vicissitudes of the intervening years have brought him to a new appreciation of what transpired then. As he walks down the runway he sees again the planes departing, one after another in deafening crescendo, and then, almost immediately, sees those planes returning, fewer in number, some badly damaged, quieter now. As he looks into the barracks, the dining room, the officers' club, they come alive with singing and talking and shouting. Every doorway has a memory, each window a different story. It is a rich moment for him. There is an appreciation of what had happened there that was not possible when it first happened. The barren scene is alive with memories, and every look and every touch mediates presence.

In a somewhat analogous way the application of the senses brings the

---

[13]Lk 7, 36-50.

[14]Lk 2, 19.

[15]*Directory*, XX no. 1.

retreatant into touch with another dimension of what he has already contemplated earlier. There is something strangely uplifting and extremely therapeutic about sense experience that integrates into the person's total phenomenal field of knowing and willing and feeling when this is done in such a way that it gives body and tone to what is already possessed by the higher faculties. The *Directory* suggests as much when it talks of this exercise.

> The application of the senses differs from meditation in that meditation is more intellectual and more concerned with reasoning, and is altogether more profound; for it reasons concerning the causes and effects of these Mysteries, and traces out in them the attributes of God, as His goodness, wisdom, love and the rest. The application of the senses on the other hand is not discursive, but merely rests in the sensible qualities of things, as sights, sounds, and the like, and *finds in them enjoyment, delight and spiritual profit.*
>
> And so it is useful in two ways. For sometimes when a soul is unable to search into more profound things, while it dwells on these sensible impressions it is gradually disposed and raised up to those loftier thoughts. Sometimes, on the other hand, when it is already enriched and filled with devotion from its meditation on those profounder Mysteries, descending from them to the contemplation of these sensible things, *it finds in every one of them nourishment, and consolation, and fruit, because of the abundance of its love which makes every smallest thing, and even the slightest hints, to be of great value and to furnish matter for devotion and consolation.*[16]

Part of the enrichment of this exercise is that in sensible ways it mediates the "infinite goodness" and presence of divinity. There is a posture of reverence and awe that is engendered toward things which were graced by the presence, the actions and the words of the Incarnate Word. An atmosphere charged with sacredness can be felt, and suggests Ignatius' experience reported in his diary on March 30, 1544, where in the morning he was gifted with a loving humility for God but in the afternoon the grace was extended to include all creatures as the object of loving humility. This is a quality of the application of the senses, to get beneath reasoning and into the bodily senses and the feeling components of the person, where a loving reverence and a loving humility can establish a constant being in touch with the Divine Presence and the worth that it gives to all creatures. This can make the *Contemplatio* an extraordinarily apt training for finding God in all things. There is no indication in the *Exer-*

---

[16]Ibid., XX nos. 3, 4.

[17]Piet Penning de Vries, S.J. *Discernment of Spirits* (Exposition Press, New York, 1973). In this book de Vries defines application of the senses as "the exercising of divine life as if it were our own life, of divine perception as our own perception. There the sensory choice of words is a matter of course: it indicates the immediate and direct, simple and intuitive experience that can only be suggested by the force of the symbol of sensory perception." pg. 113. In this same paragraph he says: "This appropriation of divine life is the actual mystery of Ignatian repetition and therefore of Ignatian contemplation. For Ignatius it is easier to omit mysteries than to omit repetition (159, 161, 162). Because a repetition brings about God's presence through the force of God's words. In other words: God lives in us. He perceives in us, through us, and with us; and we perceive in Him, through Him, and with Him. We perceive God in our very perception. In the third and fourth week, after the unification through a common life-plan with God, Ignatius' sternness changes. He spares us both repetition and application of the senses (209)."

cises or in the *Directory* that the *Contemplatio* is meant to be treated as an application of the senses.[17] But the greatest difficulty in the *Contemplatio* is to make its idea of God present in all things, giving and laboring and seeking love, go to a depth beyond intellectual comprehension into the levels of full consciousness and awareness. For this the application of the senses is ideally suited.

As the normal retreat exercise at the end of the day, this application of the senses looks backward to the mysteries already contemplated. But used with the *Contemplatio* it looks forward to the time after retreat. As a matter of fact, it is probably a looking backward *and* forward, because it is the past that also acts as a guide. Using each of the four points of the *Contemplatio,* the exercitant brings into his imagination and consciousness those persons who will be in his life very shortly, the work that he will be doing, the places where he will be.

In all of the points he should visit those places where he will spend most of his time, the office or shop, the way to and from work. With his senses he can wander in and out, seeing and hearing, touching, growing in appreciation for these persons, this work, these places, now all seen as gifts coming from God, gifts for the exercitant. In an experience not unlike that of Scrooge with the ghost of Christmas Past, he sees anew. The beauty of the imagination is that it knows no limits of time or place. Mark Twain said it well: "The imagination was given us to make up for what we are not; a sense of humor was given to compensate for what we are." Neither humor nor imagination are out of place in prayer,[18] but the imagination especially, called by Coleridge a "repetition in the finite mind of the eternal act of creation in the infinite I AM," has a power to bring to be interiorly what is not yet totally and completely possessed. In the imagination, an act of loving forgiveness, completely sincere and with feeling, can be made before it is possible to make that same act to the person in question graciously and without awkwardness. And frequent similar imaginative repetitions of this act can in time extend this interior possession to the larger reality of the actual interpersonal relationship. A thought in the mind inclines toward the act of which it is a representation.

In these points the exercitant can begin to live his new resolutions not unlike the way that Ignatius, convalescing at Loyola, vividly imagined himself doing great deeds for the Lord. He let his thoughts run over many things that seemed good to him, always putting before himself things that were difficult and important but which seemed to him easy to accomplish in this grace-filled reverie. He would spend long hours in this, his remote preparation for a life of outstanding service. In this way he prepared himself to take the "warm" with him when he left Loyola, and also later, when he left Manresa.[19]

See footnote no. 17 on pg. 98 1

[18]Robert Ochs, S.J. *God Is More Present Than You Think* (Paulist Press, NY, 1970) c. 4, pg. 54: "Imagination, Wit and Fantasy in Prayer."

[19]Luis Gonzalez de Camara, ##7, 10, 11.

The first point of the *Contemplatio* recalls to mind the blessings of creation and redemption and the special favors the exercitant has received. This point can be used after the retreat, and of course during the retreat too, to recall any and all of the matter meditated, contemplated and reflected upon during the retreat. That is what the retreat is about, the blessings of creation and redemption. Each mystery of the life of Christ is a special blessing. If desired, the formal prayer after retreat could consist of a contemplation of some mystery in the life of Christ inserted into the framework of this "point," with the petition being that of the *Contemplatio:* for an intimate knowledge of all blessings received; and its colloquy could be the *Suscipe.* This would be a good way of continuing formal prayer very much in the spirit of seeking the love and the service that this *Contemplatio* and the *Exercises* ambition. It should be repeated that the content of these points should be pondered with "great affection" and the *Suscipe* made with great feeling. It is often necessary to rouse the emotions with the will when the affective response is inadequate to the matter contemplated.[20]

In the second point, the vision is that of God "who dwells in creatures: in the elements giving them existence, in the plants giving them life, in the animals conferring upon them sensation, in man bestowing understanding," as well as making him a temple by the divine indwelling. In this point the senses, which are the interior senses under the guidance of reason, reach out and in ways that will be different in each person mediate the divine presence and the infinite goodness in all that is contemplated. Of critical importance in this application of the senses is the affective element present which makes these images and these points come alive, and without which little more may happen than in the passive gazing at a dull TV show. This is true of any repetition.

> The third and fourth exercises (i.e. in the day) consist in repetitions of the first and second. These repetitions are of great value, for it often happens that in a first meditation upon such matters the understanding is stimulated by their novelty and by a certain curiosity, but afterwards, when its activity is moderated, the way is more open for the *exercise of the affections, in which the fruit chiefly consists.* Therefore in these repetitions we must avoid lengthy discourses, and only set before ourselves, and briefly run over the points on which we have before meditated, dwelling upon them with *our wills and affections.* And this is the reason why there are more colloquies here than in the former exercises.
>
> When it is said in the third exercise of the First Week that in these repetitions we should dwell especially on those points in which we have felt greater consolation or desolation, we must understand the meaning to be that we ought to repeat especially those points which have brought us *light and fervour;* but it is well also to repeat the points in which we have experienced *aridity,* because it often happens that in those very points we come afterwards to feel *a greater abundance of consolation.* Indeed the same meditation may be repeated twice if great consolation is felt, or any other good and spiritual affection, especially in the First Week.[21]

---

[20]*Exercises,* 16, 50, 51, 74, 206, 314.

[21]*Directory,* XV. 2, 3.

Notice how the exercitant, in retreat and out of it, can go to those thoughts or experiences that cause or have caused aridity and desolation, not avoiding them ostrich-like, but seeing them again in the presence of the Lord. In the context of the second point this aridity and desolation will concern difficulties in work, personality conflicts, ennui and boredom in work or in life, all that comes under the heading of the negative, the unpleasant and the difficult. In the vision at work in the second point, everything, whether the bleak or the bright, takes on the aura of the divine. Reverence is always one of the first responses felt; humility, too. The "senses" beautifully reach out, touch, embrace, permeate, come in contact with that which "does but sanctify and exalt what is of earth."

There is a striking example of the kind of thing that can happen when the *Contemplatio* is made as an application of the senses in this way. It is from a televised interview with a prisoner who had been jailed for armed robbery. While in prison he had become an artist, and had made $15,000 in the last few years from his work. He showed some of it: the ocean shore washed with waves, a scene in the woods, a self-portrait. He said, "I identify with what I'm doing with my painting. I am that ground, those rocks. When I am painting I am the waves of the sea, the sunlight in the air. And it makes me free. I am more free than you are. Not in the other times of the day, but when I am doing my painting, I am free!"

This is what the *Exercises* are about, making a person free, free to love. The application of the senses, which was very much what this prisoner was into, does not lead the exercitant to identification with what is out there, but to a loving reverence and a loving awe for it. And these dispositions permeate and perdure. It is not just a function operative when he is thinking of one or other of the points, it is part of him even when he is busily engrossed in a hundred and one details, unattentive and miles away from the intellectual awareness of the presence of God. There are levels and degrees of assimilation of this disposition, of course, but the whole experience of the retreat in addition to the exercitant's desire to make his day and his life come alive in rich new ways contribute to a heightened ability to find God in all things.

The third point of the *Contemplatio* sees God laboring in all things for the exercitant. "My Father goes on working, and so do I."[22] The implied question, "What return shall I make?" at the end of each point is most easily answered here. "I will labor. I will serve. No matter how insignificant my contribution, it will be a wholehearted gift of service. Love is a mutual exchange of gifts. God is laboring everywhere for me: giving me air, sustaining me in countless other ways, providing nourishment from the table but also the richer nourishment of joy and love and faith and peace, and the still greater nourishment of His own Son whose 'flesh is real food' and whose 'blood is real drink'.[23] I will offer my work in response to His ceaseless labor for me." Again, a new

---

[22]Jo 5, 17.

[23]Jo 6, 55.

aliveness can come into the life of the exercitant here, not only when he reflects on the presence of God working, but in his own working. It is a labor of love, and in it he is "making love."

The fourth point of the *Contemplatio,* although all points overlap, adds a new vantage point from which to view the presence of the God who continually gives, labors and seeks love. All blessings, including the good found in self and in others, is from above like rays from the sun. When you sense the warmth and the light of the sun's rays you are in touch with the sun itself. A few lines from Wordsworth's "Tintern Abbey" suggest the thoughts of this fourth point of the *Contemplatio.*

> A presence that disturbs me with the joy
> Of elevated thoughts; a sense sublime
> Of something far more deeply interfused
> Whose dwelling is the light of setting suns,
> And the round ocean and the living air,
> And the blue sky, and in the mind of man:
> A motion and a spirit that impels
> All thinking things, all objects of all thought,
> And rolls through all things.

Just as there is no place on planet earth completely bereft of the effects of the sun, so there is no facet of life ungraced by the blessings of the Son. The application of the senses again searches out this presence, and again it is in reverence and in humility that it will be found, a reverence and humility that can grow, that can become an enduring attitude toward work, persons, places, a posture that seeks and desires a deeper expression in love and service. From the lives of those who most often and most deeply experienced the transcendent, it is learned that the feelings most often evoked are those of humility, reverence and gratitude. Peter's "Lord depart from me for I am a sinful man" after the miraculous catch of fish[24] illustrates the reverence and the humility that this incident caused in him. And we know the quality of the love and service which followed.

So the exercitant makes this *Contemplatio* in the same way that he made the final repetition of the day during the retreat as an application of the senses. In just the same way that this sense-contemplation mediates the divine presence and goodness in the previously contemplated mysteries of the life of Christ, it now mediates that same divine presence and goodness in the persons, the work, the places soon to fill the exercitant's life in the humdrum and the hurly-burly of everyday living. But in this contemplation they come into his consciousness with all the sacredness and mystery that the previous mysteries of Christ conveyed. The same loving humility for the Divine Majesty that filled in various ways the last prayer of the day during the retreat now reaches

---

[24]Lk 5, 8, 9.

out again to the Divine Majesty found "present in all places and filling all things."[25] The future experiences, soon to be realized, become diffused with a radiance not unlike that found in the repetitions on the words and works of Jesus. In the final days of the retreat more and more the contemplation looks not only backward but forward, not so much to the Christ of the historical past, as to Him in mystery living in the here-and-now and the future soon-to-be. Of course, this exercise can and should be continued with great profit after the retreat. It can become an enduring contemplation in action as well as in private prayer.

To the extent that this contemplation takes hold, becomes interiorized, it prepares the exercitant for re-entry into the same hectic pace and schedule left a few weeks earlier. Perhaps there will not be very much more time that he will be able to give to God in formal prayer than he did before he began the retreat. His mind will not be on God in those occupations that demand mental attention and alertness any more than they were in the past. But there is a distinct possibility that deep down there is a realization that in all he does, however mundane and insignificant, he is making a return of a gift for precious gifts received, he is actually making love. There is a loving humility and a loving reverence for people, for work, for all things that did not exist in the same way before. There is an aliveness that rises out of this that is a new sharing in the life that Christ came to give, and to give in abundance. When one joins the application of the senses repeatedly to the Contemplation to Attain the Love of God in this way, after the many days of contemplation of Christ in His mysteries, the shock of going from the warm to the cold is largely circumvented, and to go out is also to go in.

---

[25] William G. Storey, *Praise Him!* (Ave Maria Press, Notre Dame, Indiana. 1973.) From Byzantine Liturgy, pg. 165.

My Experience of a Directed Retreat

Sister Margaret Baker, H.V.M.

Volume 31, 1972, pp. 573-577.

In trying to share with you my deep and beautiful experience of the *Spiritual Exercises,* I wonder how I will do this. I cannot help but think of Mary and her attempts to share the mystery of Annunciation that occurred in her. How do you describe in words the mystery of Incarnation, of Jesus coming alive within you?

Perhaps Mary will not mind if I borrow her words and say that the *Spiritual Exercises* were for me a time for the Holy Spirit to come upon me, when the power of the Most High overshadowed me. I like to say that the retreat continues, and so I hope I can say that a child is still being born, who is the Son of God.

As a beginning perhaps I can give you some idea of how I came to make a thirty-day directed retreat, where, under whom, and so on. I find these are some of the immediate practical questions people have.

I made the full *Spiritual Exercises* about a year and a half ago, in July, 1970. I would like to share with you how I arrived at this decision. In 1970 I had been in religious life fifteen years. For about seven years before this I had a growing desire for a longer period devoted to prayer and quite. Some communities at this time called this a tertianship or period of renewal.

This desire gradually became clearer and deeper. Perhaps I could describe it as desire for time for prayer; time to listen to God, to the Holy Spirit. I felt I was missing a lot He was saying. I had a need for time and help to sort out all the different "motions" within me and outside of me. I was also drawn to prayer and sacrifice for the needs of my own community and of the church.

However, although I had this desire and it kept getting stronger, I was unable to do this for seven years. I was involved in full-time apostolic commitments and there seemed no way to be relieved. Also, in the Home Visitors of Mary, a new, small religious community, a longer time of renewal simply had never occurred.

Gradually, though, the way became clear. In the very first chapter of our community, in August, 1969, a proposal passed encouraging longer times of prayer and renewal, without specifying type or length. Also my specific work situation had changed. Although I had a responsible job, the summer was somewhat lighter, and the person in charge was open to taking time off for renewal purposes.

I talked with my superior several times about the possibility. She was encouraging but asked that I discuss it with the entire community of twenty-two members. When I did this the main reaction of the sisters was that if someone sincerely felt God was asking this, after prayer and advice, she should go ahead. So I received permission for a long retreat in January, 1970. It was not until May of that year that things firmed up enough in my work situation, so I felt I could ask for the month of July off.

Now that I had permission for a month off, I still had to decide what to do with this time! I did not want to just go off by myself for a month; I knew I needed some kind of framework and guide. Actually I knew little about the *Spiritual Exercises* and was not particularly attracted to them.

However, I just happened to know a Jesuit priest, Father Nicholas Rieman, who said he gave thirty-day retreats. He had mentioned this casually several years before, and I had filed this mentally, thinking he would be a good one to ask when I was able to make a long retreat. In March I wrote to Father Rieman about this, and he agreed to guide me through the *Exercises* in July.

It didn't matter to me what kind of retreat Father Rieman would give, as long as he would work with me during the thirty days. However, those who know Father Rieman realize he would give only the *Spiritual Exercises* and give them very well, since he has had much experience in this area. I recall talking with the community about the *Spiritual Exercises,* just before my retreat, and some of their comments: "Why do you want to make the *Spiritual Exercises?* You don't have any big decision to make!" And: "The *Exercises* are so structured!"

In our annual community retreats in the past we had had six or seven given by Jesuits, all based on the *Spiritual Exercises*. These eight-day retreats were the usual "preached" retreat with about four group conferences a day. A big surprise was in store for me in making the thirty-day retreat—I was to discover what a real *Spiritual Exercises* retreat is like!

A final preparation for my thirty.day retreat was to find a place to stay. In 1970 Father Rieman was assistant at St. Mary's parish in Toledo, Ohio. I arranged to get a private room at nearby Mary Manse College in Toledo.

Also I was pleased to learn that Father Rieman would guide another sister through the *Exercises* at the same time, Sister Patricia Hughes from Cleveland. So as Father expressed it, the two of us made a private retreat together. That is, we met with Father individually for guidance, but shared liturgy, physical relaxation, and "break days."

In making the full *Exercises* I met with the director for material for meditation (called "points") and guidance in prayer on a regular basis. I met with Father every day for about the first two weeks, then on an average every other day, for about forty-five minutes to an hour. This individual guidance is how Ignatius always gave the *Exercises,* and is what is called a "directed retreat."

During the *Spiritual Exercises* I was asked to get in four to five hours of prayer a day if possible. This was a silent retreat; meals were in silence, and there was no unnecessary talking. I found this silence a great help in aiding interior awareness, a deeper consciousness and listening to the Spirit. I was asked to prepare each hour of prayer, and after each hour, to jot down reflections. Sister Patricia and I were fortunate to celebrate the Eucharist several times a week with Father. We found the dialogue homily a beautiful way to share the inspirations of the Spirit during the retreat.

During the thirty days we were asked to get some active physical exercise each day. Sister Patricia and I located a nearby indoor pool, and we were able to enjoy swimming almost every evening. We also looked forward to the three "break days" during the retreat, when we got outdoors for picnics and swimming for the whole day.

The description I have given so far are only the externals of the retreat, in a way. I would like to try to share with you some of the inner aspects of the retreat: "what was really going on," as a director would say.

Father Rieman described the retreat as a time to be alone with God; a great grace; a once-in-a-lifetime grace. When we began he told us there were three things we should do—God would do the rest. These were: silence, generosity, and the *Exercises.* By the *Exercises* Father meant fidelity to preparation and time of prayer each day.

I found that this was really true. My days were very full, with the hours of prayer, liturgy, meeting for direction, and swimming. In a real sense, I can say I never worked so hard, I have never been so active. Prayer is work; it is intense activity.

I found I had a tremendous need to be alone with God. I was hungry for this and had little difficulty in settling into a routine of silence and prayer. I think I might try to describe the entire experience as one of deep prayer, discernment, and decision, leading to a real conversion.

I consider the retreat one of the great graces of my life, comparable to baptism and religious profession, and really a continuation and deepening of these graces.

For me the experience of solitude and prayer is central in the *Exercises,* and is, I think, part of the genius of Ignatius, one of the reasons why the

Exercises are always contemporary and relevant. The Church will always need the value of prayerful confrontation with God, when I in my uniqueness stand alone before God. This seems to me to be especially significant and needed today, in this age of personalism and attention to individual and communal charisms.

One of my biggest surprises during the retreat was the deep psychological impact of the *Exercises*. I recall remarking half-way through the retreat: "Ignatius is a tremendous psychologist!" For me there was a real build-up during the *Exercises* which seemed slowly, gently, but surely to lead me to clearness of vision and openness to the Spirit.

This began with the meditations on sin in the First Week, which was for me one of the most beautiful experiences of the entire retreat. This week led me to deep self-knowledge, but *not* depression or self-pity. I seemed to come to a profound understanding of my own sinfulness, weakness, and limitations—much of which I was not fully conscious of before. But there was at the same time a profound joy, especially in the celebration of the sacrament of penance—and an abiding realization that, in the words of the blind man in the Gospel: "Before I was blind, but now I see." I realized as never before that in Christ, I am healed, re-created, made new.

I think perhaps this experience of the First Week is the basis and beginning of this clarity of vision I mentioned. With a much deeper realization of my need for Jesus, I was then able to move into the Second Week, meditating on the Infancy and the Public Life of Christ. Here too I experienced the advantage of a directed retreat, for I was able to spend more time praying over the mysteries in Christ's Life that particularly attracted me. For example I spent a short time on the Infancy and early life of Jesus, and most of the time on His Public Life. Here too I selected certain events and words in His Public Life I wished to dwell on. These meditations were for me a great source of light.

I found the director to be of tremendous help during the retreat, and might describe his role as guiding me along the path of the *Exercises* he had already traveled. He is really sharing a personal faith experience that has made a big difference in his own life. Father Rieman gave me helps for prayer, brief material for each hour, and watched over the entire retreat schedule and movement to be sure all was going well. He was careful to follow Ignatius' suggestion not to get in the way of the primary director, the Holy Spirit.

I discovered that another crucial role of the director is to aid me in discernment. This Father could tell through my sharing with him "how the hours of prayer are going." I found that as I calmed my everyday concerns, and listened deeply to God, the lights, attractions, insights, call, and demands of the Holy Spirit became clearer and more insistent. Through my sharing of these, Father was able to help me sift through the various movements and discern the action of the Holy Spirit.

Another major thing I learned from this retreat was that discernment takes much time and patience, prayer, and guidance. But once having had this experience it is the only way I want to make important decisions, and really to live my life. Ever since this retreat the discerning process has been a constant help to me in everyday life. I find myself much more attentive and able to listen, discern, and respond to the Holy Spirit in the daily events and situations of my life.

I found the direction during my thirty-day retreat extremely helpful and profitable. It seems to me that it fulfilled not only important ascetical and spiritual needs during such a deep prayer experience, but also psychological needs, to communicate, and to be guided with wisdom and skill.

In praying through several key meditations during the Second Week I became aware of the effort to bring me to openness to the Spirit and readiness to do whatever God would ask. There gradually developed a wonderful sense of freedom—to go wherever God wished. These areas of discernment and decision-making (sometimes called Election) seemed to come quite naturally for me during the course of the retreat, with no strain. I was *not* trying to arrive at any crucial decision regarding vocation or apostolate. However, while praying four to five hours a day, in solitude, for thirty days, something is bound to happen!

Perhaps I could express it in this way: God was calling me to a deeper commitment, a fuller living out of my religious life, especially greater trust and love. It seemed that when I gave Him the chance there was much God wanted to tell me about myself, His love for me, His needs for the building up of the Kingdom.

The meditations of the Third and Fourth Weeks on the Passion, Death, and Resurrection of Jesus seemed to me to strengthen my decision taken in the Second Week. I seemed to grow in a deeper determination to follow a Christ who serves and saves by losing His life.

Near the end of the retreat and afterwards I realized a clearness of vision, a singleness of purpose, and also a wholeness, and integration: it was like all the little pieces of a puzzle (my life) had finally fallen into place. It seemed I could say: *now,* I know myself, I know where I am going . . . because I know Christ, the power of His resurrection and the fellowship of His sufferings.

There was a real way that the retreat was for me a true community experience. I had the prayers and support of my own community, my friends and relatives in religious life, and the cloistered sisters of the Detroit area. Through Sister Patricia a letter was sent to a group of C.L.C. members, including some who had made the thirty-day retreat, asking for prayer and sacrifice for us during the retreat. I really experienced the power of the prayer of others for me, a real communion of saints, during this time.

I see the experience of the *Exercises* as apostolic and communitarian. This type of retreat should not cater to a selfish desire for solitude and prayer for itself alone. This time alone, and concentration on prayer, are *means* to form more effective apostles. This is precisely what Ignatius intends. The ultimate goal for active religious making this retreat is "apostolic service out of love in community." This intimate contact with the Father, Son, and Holy Spirit for thirty days forms men and women of deep prayer who know who they are, who God is, and where they are going.

In conclusion I would like to describe my experience of the *Spiritual Exercises* in the words of the prophet Isaiah about the Suffering Servant. In the Semitic mind this figure was a corporate personality, a fluid concept representing both an individual and the nation, the People of Israel. So it seems especially appropriate to express the individual and communal aspects of the thirty-day retreat: Yahweh speaks to His servant, Israel:

> Now, thus says the Lord . . . Fear not, for I have redeemed
> you; I have called you by name, you are mine . . .
> You are precious in my eyes, and honored, and
> I love you . . .
> You are my witnesses, says the Lord, and my
> servant whom I have chosen, that you may know
> and believe me and understand that I am He . . .
> I, I am the Lord (Is 43:1-11).

III. PRAYER AND DISCERNMENT

The Four Moments of Prayer

John R. Sheets, S.J.

Volume 28, 1969, pp. 393-406.

The religious life today presents many different faces to one who is trying to assess its mood, vitality, and direction. Sometimes we wonder how so many different (often contradictory) qualities can come under the same common denominator which we call the religious life. It is like watching the weather report on television. We see varying types of weather throughout the whole country, currents of air moving in different directions, high pressure in one part, low in another, rain in one place, snow in another, and sunshine in another. This suggests the picture of the various trends in the religious life at present, or for that matter in the whole Church.

It would be too ambitious a project to try to draw the weather map of the religious life. Like the weatherman we would very likely be wrong in many of our judgments. We would like to single out only one aspect of the religious life, the life of prayer.

Even here we find many conflicting currents. In fact the life of prayer is a small scale model of the whole weather map with the various currents running through the religious life. There is, on the one hand, great interest in prayer. This is very often manifest in the careful attention which many congregations are giving to the subject of prayer in preparation for chapter meetings. On the other hand, we have to confess that very often more time is spent in talking about prayer than in praying. As in the case of so many other religious values, discussion of the value has become a substitute for the value itself.

Even in the discussion of prayer there is often the feeling that one needs prayer if he is to be a *good* religious, while without prayer he is a religious, though perhaps not outstanding for his piety. It is extremely important for

163

us to recapture once again the New Testament mentality concerning prayer. It is simply this: to be a Christian in the true sense of the term one must pray. Prayer is not simply an accessory to Christian life, something superadded to make a better Christian out of a good one. A Christian is one who prays. This is the lesson which is brought home in every book of the New Testament. It is not something mentioned in passing. It is the milieu of Christian life as we find it described there. We have to question the seriousness with which we live our Christianity if one of the primary signs of our union with the Father in Christ is not present, namely, our response to this new fellowship through prayer.

There are basically two signs which manifest the nature of the new fellowship in grace. They are signs which manifest the new orientation which we have to God and to our fellowman. The new orientation to God is shown in our filial attitude, because we are sons with the Son and can say, "Abba! Father." Practically, this is shown in our life of worship and of prayer. The new relationship which we have to others is shown through charity: "By this love you have for one another, everyone will know that you are my disciples" (Jn 13:35). If these signs are not there, then our Christian life is like that of a retarded child, an unfortunate affliction in any family, but especially in the family of God. There are retarded Christians as there are retarded human beings.

We have to realize that prayer flows from the very nature of the fellowship we have with Christ, the Father, and with one another, through grace. It is not something extra. As we have said, the New Testament leaves no ambiguity on that score. For example, we see Christ praying and teaching his disciples to pray; the Christian community is a prayerful community; throughout his Letters Paul speaks of his own prayer and exhorts the Christian communities to persevering prayer; the book of Revelation shows the whole of creation, with the Church at the center, united in praising God and the Lamb.

There is a great need to recapture the New Testament notion of prayer and to see how it is integral to the life of the Christian. What was called the "Death of God" was simply the surfacing of the death of faith. In turn the death of faith has its roots in many cases in the neglect of prayer. It should be no surprise if we cannot see when all of the lights are turned out in a city or in a room. Again, it should be no surprise that there is a power failure in our faith and in our love if there is no effort to draw light and strength from God through prayer.

Christian prayer draws into conscious focus the whole of our Christian life. In our ordinary day-to-day life it is probably true to say that everything enters into the power we have to speak—our physical, mental, and social life. If we are weak, our words have little strength; if we have no ideas, our words have little meaning; if we are not interested in communicating to another, our words are movements of air. The same is true of our life of prayer. Everything in our lives enters into it. Like the point in the hourglass, everything from our life must pass through it into our prayer. It brings into focus the relationship we have to God and also to our fellowman. If God is remote and impersonal, then there will be no prayer. If God is dead, then prayer is dead. Similarly, if our relationship to others is unChristian, then our prayer will be like that described by the king in *Hamlet:* "My words fly up, my thoughts remain below: words without thoughts never to heaven go."

The First Moment of Christian Prayer

There are fundamentally four "moments" to Christian prayer: listening, seeing, responding, and translating what one has heard and seen into one's life. We are not using the word "moment" here in its specifically temporal sense. Rather it is used to describe the movement of Christian prayer, which like the movements of a symphony make one organic whole. We would like to comment on each of these moments of prayer, keeping in mind that, although there is a certain logical sequence in which one follows from the other, in practice they cannot be separated or schematized in an artificial manner.

First and foremost Christian prayer is *listening*. There is probably no other expression which so aptly describes God's relationship to us and ours to Him. It is based, like other expressions which we use to describe God's relationships to man, on man's relationships to other men. It will be helpful to comment on this. In human listening there are always three elements forming something of a triangular relationship: the speaker, the word, and the one listening. Where all three aspects are present there is communication through the word. If one or the other is absent, there is no communication.

We also know that there are different levels of speaking and listening. They are levels going from communication of information about things or about oneself to the deepest level, that of communication of *oneself* through words. Each level of communication corresponds to a level of giving on the part of the speaker and a level of receiving on the part of the one listening. The range of giving on the part of the speaker goes from giving information, all the way to giving himself. The range of receiving for the listener is the same. On his part there are degrees of openness ranging from an openness to information to an openness for communion with another person.

This relationship of speaker to listener very aptly describes God's relationship to man. It is not possible to develop this idea at length. If we did, we would see that it involves the whole mystery of revelation, culminating in the mystery of the Incarnation and redemption. God's words are really actions. They are the form or shape which His actions take when they are addressed to man's heart through his power to hear: "The word that goes from my mouth does not return to me empty, without carrying out my will and succeeding in what it was sent to do" (Is 55:11).

Concretely Christian prayer is listening to God's word in Scripture. It means opening oneself to God's will to communicate Himself through His word. What we could call the "mental shape" of His will for us is communicated to us in Scripture. The Scripture is the privileged *locus* of God's word.

It will be helpful if we can understand more fully the mysterious power that the word of God in Scripture has for us. The mystery of the power of the prophetic word is a mystery of how the power and wisdom of God can be articulated in human words in such a way that the words themselves mediate this power and wisdom. There is a power to these words which transcends their material and time-conditioned aspect.

This power is not the same that belongs to the artist's creation. His work also transcends to some extent the limitations of time and space and appeals to something perennial in human nature. He evokes hidden resonances with the human spirit which are timeless because they belong to the very nature of the human spirit. But the power of the word of God in Scripture is very different. We find there something analogous to what takes place in the Incarnation. In this mystery the Word in His power overspills and overflows His flesh which embodies this mystery. The artistic creation has a certain power for us because we share in a common humanity and common experiences with the artist. But the power of God's word, and in a special way, the power of Christ's word, comes from the fact that it belongs to the mystery of life for which we were made, a sharing in the life of the Son. If we are related to the artist's word and work through a common humanity, we are much more intimately related to the word and work of God because we were made for the purpose of sharing this mystery: "To have what must die taken up into life—this is the purpose for which God made us, and he has given us the pledge of the Spirit" (2 Cor 5:5). We were not made to share a common humanity but to share that for which a common humanity provides the foundation—a sharing in the life of the Son.

The word of God in Scripture is, then, closely related to the mystery of our own identity. It is no stranger to us. It is the mental shape which God's will takes because of His intention to share with us His life. The words of Scripture make up our "name." If we recall, for the Jew the name declares the meaning of the person. The words of Scripture declare the meaning of man in his relationship to God. For this reason the word of God is described as enveloped with a mysterious power which reaches right to our heart: "The word of God is something alive and active: it cuts like any double-edge sword but more finely: it can slip through the place where the soul is divided from the spirit, or joints from the marrow; it can judge the secret emotions and thoughts. No created thing can hide from him; everything is uncovered and open to the eyes of the one to whom we must give account of ourselves'' (Hb 4:12-3).

The prayer of the Jew is also a listening to the word of God. It differs from Christian prayer in the same way that listening to a musical note differs from listening to the chord which embodies and fulfills the note. The Jewish attitude is seen in the response of Samuel when the Lord called him: ''Yahweh came and stood by, calling as he had done before, 'Samuel, Samuel.' Samuel answered, 'Speak, Yahweh, your servant is listening' '' (1 S 3:10-1). The Christian response, however, is typified by Paul's words to Christ when He appeared to him on the road to Damascus: ''What am I to do, Lord?'' (Acts 22:10). Christian prayer is listening to the word of God given to us in Christ. The Christian listens to the words of the Old Testament only insofar as they are avenues directed to their fulfillment in the Word-made-flesh. For this reason, in the vision in which St. John sees Christ clothed as the High Priest, he describes the sword of God's word coming from the mouth of Christ: ''In his right hand he was holding seven stars, *out of his mouth came a sharp sword, double-edged,* and his face was like the sun shining with all its force'' (Rv 1:16).

As we mentioned, there are different levels of speaking to which there correspond different levels of listening. At the most profound level there is a communication of self through the word. At this level words become the expression not of knowledge but of love. On the listening side, there must not only be a hearing but a true listening which comes from love. There must be a loving-listening which corresponds to love-speaking.

We all know that we listen to the degree that we realize what is said is important for us. A student listens at different levels to what the teacher says. If he thinks something is going to be asked on an examination, he will listen more carefully. We listen to those things which involve us personally. If someone is talking about us, we are all ears. If someone is talking to us, our attention can be very superficial.

Theoretically we perhaps realize the importance of God's words for us. But practically speaking they are like projectiles which hit a hard surface and then ricochet off in the distance. While it is true that our very identity, our very purpose for being, is involved in the words of God and that these words are written about me and for me and to me, in practice they simply are not that meaningful.

A partial reason for this is that the word of God is not always easy to interpret. But this is not the main reason. The main reason lies deeper than this. It lies in the intention of the speaker and in the heart of the listener, not in the quality of the word which is spoken. The speaker's intention is to transform the listener. This means that the listener will have to give up his ways which are self-centered and become open to the ways of God. There is a basic unwillingness in the heart of man to listen to a word which asks him to center his life on God and to center all other things on the kingdom: ''Set your hearts on his kingdom first and on his righteousness, and all these other things will be given you as well'' (Mt 6:33).

This means that God's word is imperative, centering, transforming, judging, quickening. It is not easy for man to listen to such a word. His listening has to be *obediential*. He knows that his own life is a response to the word of God. His own words are not above the word of God. But his whole life, not only his words, lie under the judgment of the word of God. It is His word which interprets us, not our word which interprets Him. With the growing interest in the study of Scripture, there is the danger that under the critics' scissors the two-edged sword of God's word begins to look like Don Quixote's limp and battered lance. Without realizing it, one can develop the attitude that the word of God is like any other word, simply grist for the critics' mill. We have to remind ourselves constantly that we are dealing not simply with the inspiring words of men, but the inspired words of God.

Let us draw out some further implications involved in listening. In order to listen our whole being must be attuned. This means that *asceticism* is necessary if there is to be any real listening which is sustained in difficult circumstances over a period of time. This is true in any form of listening. If one wants to listen to a lecture, or music, or poetry, there has to be an asceticism of imagination, in fact of all our faculties. Hearing is not simply a power which belongs to one faculty. The whole body listens. This is especially true where the sounds are delicate and gentle and are competing with the clamor of other sounds. Asceticism is really a refining of our power to hear the word of God, the most delicate of all sounds, in a world filled with a thousand other sounds, most of them more flattering to our ears than the simple and chaste word of God.

In order to hear the sounds of silence there must be a certain inner disposition. There must be silence. We often confuse silence with not speaking. Rather it is the atmosphere for speaking because it is the atmosphere for listening. Every poet, artist, anyone who listens to the whisperings of beauty at the heart of reality needs the atmosphere of silence to listen. Similarly, and much more, there must be the asceticism of silence for the one who is opening himself to listen to God's word.

This sounds very uncontemporary to our ears today, even to many religious. Perhaps it is part of the reaction which comes from having things imposed from the outside. For many silence simply has been an external restriction on their power to speak, rather than an internal atmosphere to listen. Similarly, many identify speaking with communication. Where there is a great deal of talk, there must be a great deal said. We know, however, that silence does not mean a lack of communication, nor does speaking mean communication.

It is a favorite theme of the theater of the absurd that there is a real failure to communicate even though the media of communication are multiplied past all imagination. In fact, communication simply by multiplication of words has become a source of alienation, not of union. There is really not enough silence to listen. T. S. Eliot has touched upon this theme in one of his poems:

> The endless cycle of idea and action,
> Endless invention, endless experiment,
> Brings knowledge of motion, but not of stillness;
> Knowledge of speech, but not of silence;
> Knowledge of words, and ignorance of the Word
>
> —from *The Rock*

The artist and the poet do not need to learn silence as one learns a lesson. They realize instinctively that silence is the atmosphere for receptivity. That is what Dag Hammarskjöld describes in his diary when he speaks of silence: "To preserve the silence within—amid all the noise. To remain open and quiet, a moist humus in the fertile darkness where the rain falls and the grain ripens—no matter how many tramp across the parade ground in whirling dust under the arid sky" (*Markings,* p. 83). Again, Gerard Manley Hopkins speaks of silence as singing to him, beating upon his ear, piping to him, evoking from him both surrender and eloquence:

> Elected silence, sing to me
> And beat upon my whorled ear,
> Pipe me to pastures still and be
> The music that I care to hear.
>
> Shape nothing, lips; be lovely-dumb:
> It is the shut, the curfew sent
> From there where all surrenders come
> Which only makes you eloquent.

The first moment, then, of Christian prayer is listening. It requires an atmosphere in which the word of God can be heard. There is a fatal instinct in all of us to reduce the word of God to the words of men, as well as to reduce the presence of God and the presence of Christ to the presence of men. There is the tendency to confuse our own dreaming and fancies with that listening which comes from the Spirit of Son. This kind of listening is not always easy. It has little fiction, but much hope; little sentiment, but much love; little that is flattering, but much that is fulfilling.

The Second Moment of Christian Prayer

Christian prayer is also *seeing.* It is necessary not only to listen to the word of God; we must also see the word of God made flesh. The total mystery of God and the manner in which man is enveloped in that mystery is deployed in such a way as to grasp us not only through our power to hear but also through our power to see, while at the same time it works inaudibly and invisibly on our hearts through grace. By "seeing" we mean the whole range of knowing activity which can be described as various levels of seeing: the seeing which belongs to the eyes of the mind, that which belongs to our imagination and memory, and that which belongs to our physical sight. As seeing goes from what is purely physical reflection to mental reflection it becomes less and less passive and more and more an activity involving the concentration of all of the powers of the person. For prayer to be meaningful there must be a seeing on every level. The object must impress itself on our whole being so that our whole world is stamped with its image.

We can repeat the words of Teilhard de Chardin here to emphasize the importance of seeing: *"Seeing.* We might say that the whole of life lies in that verb—if not ultimately, at least essentially. . . . *To see or to perish* is the very condition laid upon everything that makes up the universe, by reason of the mysterious gift of existence. And this, in superior measure, is man's condition" (*Phenomenon of Man,* Harper Torchbooks, p. 31).

We are faced with an anomalous situation today. There is much emphasis on personalism and also on sacramentalism. But there is at the same time a real inner sacramental vacuum because the truths of faith do not find a sacramental stronghold in the memory and the imagination. Perhaps there is no greater necessity today than to sacramentalize the memory and imagination. This is the world in which men of flesh and blood live and move and have their being. It is the world which is co-natural to him, without which ideas and ideals are in peril of dying for lack of oxygen. If a person is to enter into the total mystery of Christ it cannot be done merely intellectually. The mystery has to grasp his image world. This brings out the necessity for good Christian art. Even more it brings out the necessity for those sense expressions of Christian faith which is to the faith what the body is to the soul. Man lives in his body, in his images. Ideas do not move a person unless they are transmitted through and rooted in images. Theoretically man might live his faith only through faith perception. Practically speaking unless his faith vision has its counterpart in the vision that belongs to his senses it will wither and die.

It is not possible to enter into this in great detail because of the limitations of space. It seems that we are at present going through one of those movements which strangely enough emerge at different periods of history. It is basically iconoclastic in the literal sense of the term. The word means "image-breaker." It is applied to a particular movement in the eighth century in the Greek Church which was directed against the veneration of icons. In a wider sense it is applied to those movements which tend to spiritualize Christianity to the point where the bodily aspect of Christianity is neglected. It shows itself in rejection of images, such as statues or pictures, in the elimination of external gestures such as kneeling, genuflecting, in the abolition of those devotions in which Christian faith has incarnated itself, or in a false mysticism characterized by a flight from man's real world. All we can do here is point out the danger, a danger which has become for many a fact. The liturgical movement can to some extent incarnate man's faith in his sense world. This has not as yet happened, however. At present the faith of many Christians is floundering because their image world has become desacramentalized, and as yet nothing has been given to replace his traditional images. Like Adam who, before the creation of Eve, could find no helpmate suitable for him, Christian faith is searching for its helpmate in the world of images. When Christian faith finds its world of images, it can also exclaim, as did Adam: "This at last is bone from my bones, and flesh from my flesh" (Gn 2:23).

Practically speaking it is through our contemplation of Christ in the Gospels that we begin to create the image of Christ in the chaos of our sense world. It is through our prayer that the words "Let there be light" are extended not only to the darkness of our minds but also to the darkness of imagination and memory.

The importance of seeing is a central theme in the writings of St. John. He is called the eagle. In ancient belief the eagle was considered to have special power to see. He could soar close to the sun without becoming blinded by the rays of light. St. John did in fact see, both with the eyes of the faith and the eyes of his senses. His seeing is the source of his Gospel: "Something which has existed since the beginning, that we have heard, and *we have seen with our own eyes:* that we have watched and touched with our hands: the Word, who is life—this is our subject. *That life was made visible: we saw it and we are giving our testimony,* telling you of the eternal life which was with the Father and has been made visible to us. *What we have seen and heard* we are telling you so that you too may be in union with us, as we are in union with the Father and with his Son Jesus Christ" (1 Jn 1:1-4). These words express the sense of the words spoken to the man whom Jesus cured of his blindness, when the man asked about the meaning of faith in the Son of Man. Jesus told Him: "You are looking at him; he is speaking to you" (Jn 9:37).

We sometimes hear today that we do not need to pray because our action is our prayer. We do not need to contemplate Christ in Himself because we see Him in others. If our action is our prayer and our contemplation of others really is our contemplation of Christ, this can come only because we take the time to pray formally. Unless there is formal prayer there is the danger of hearing only the echo of our own voice and seeing only the reflection of our own image in all that we do, while we are under the tragic illusion that it is Christ's voice and His image.

The Third Moment of Christian Prayer

The third moment of Christian prayer is the response. This takes various forms. It varies according to our many faceted response to the one fundamental truth: the love of the Father shown to us in the gift of His Son. "With this gift how can he fail to lavish upon us all he has to give?" (Rm 8:32).

Among the many forms which the response can take are those of gratitude, praise, sorrow, adoration, and petition. There is first of all the response of gratitude. This is the fundamental disposition of the Christian. It is one of the most common forms of prayer in the Letters of St. Paul. He begins all of His Letters with a prayer of thanks and frequently stresses the necessity of gratitude in prayer (1 Cor 14:17; 2 Cor 1:11; 4:15; 9:11-2). It would not be too much to say that to the extent that one is Christian he is also grateful. To be consciously Christian means that one is aware of the difference that the Incarnation and redemption have made in our lives.

When one is conscious of the great deeds of God for our salvation the response will be praise. The Christian, like the Jew, praises God not for His essential characteristics (at least not directly), but for what He has done for man in His saving deeds. We only learn what God is through what He has done. We praise God chiefly for what He has done for us in Christ. We find many examples of this prayer of praise for God's wondrous deeds in Scripture: the Psalms, the hymns of victory scattered throughout the Old Testament, the Magnificat of Mary, the doxologies of Paul, and the hymns in the Book of Revelation.

Where there is consciousness of the failure to respond in the past, then our present response takes the form of sorrow. We have failed to listen to the word. The light of our eye has become darkness. We have become deaf and blind, as Isaiah says: "You have seen many things but not observed them; your ears are open but you do not hear" (Is 42:20). For this reason Christian prayer will always take the form of sorrow.

As creature before his Creator the Christian will adore. The prayer of adoration is the prayer of Christian maturity. It comes only when one realizes that God is the incandescent source at the heart of all creation, infinitely removed from all that is created but at the same time intimately present to all things since only in Him does everything else live and move and have its being. Adoration is the prayer of honesty. It acknowledges the truth which is at the heart of existence, that man's whole existence is simply a breath sustained by the Spirit of God.

There is the response which we call the prayer of petition. It arises from the realization of our needs and from the fact that it is our heavenly Father who can fulfill all of our needs. It is not a lesser form of prayer. The prayer of petition is a high form of prayer because it involves a basic realization of the meaning of God's fatherhood and His divine providence over us.

It would be possible to comment at length on any one of these forms of response. Let us conclude by mentioning a special kind of prayer which is modeled on Christ's own prayer. It is the prayer of intercession. The deepest need which all men have is to know the Father and Him whom He has sent, Jesus Christ. Christians must always intercede for others. The exhortation which Paul gives to Timothy and to his community of faithful can be applied to all us: "My advice is that, first of all, there should be prayers offered for everyone—petitions, intercessions, and thanksgiving" (1 Tim 2:1). Our Christlike concern for others must show itself through our intercession for them. The prayer of intercession renders explicit what is implicit in all Christian prayer: it is apostolic, for the kingdom.

The Fourth Moment of Christian Prayer

Finally prayer must translate itself into action. This means that it must lead to a life of service and witness. In saying this, we should not forget that prayer is itself service and witness. It is not some form of pre-service, or pre-witness, waiting to be taken up into the social dimension of man's world. It is itself service and at the same time is the source of the love which sustains our service of God and our fellowmen especially when this service tends to flounder amid temptations. The words of Christ addressed to the Apostles have a perennial meaning: "Pray to be not put to the test" (Mt 26:41).

For many the authentic note of the Christian is found in service of others. This is essentially true. The Scripture tells us that our salvation depends on our service. Yet many have a very superficial idea of service. They see it only from the "outside" in terms of how much one is doing for another. They fail to realize that in this sense even unthinking nature and unloving animals and machines serve mankind. Unless the "outside" aspect of service flows from a Christian "inside" it is like a sounding gong or a clanging cymbal. It is difficult to measure the "inside" of service. For that reason we very often content ourselves with only the "outside" because it is so easy to measure. We tend to think that it is the "outside" aspect which has an existence all of its own and forget that it is the motivation, the heart, the "inside" of service which is really the mainspring. This is known only to Christ, as He also was the only one who could measure the service of the poor widow who put a penny into the treasury: "I tell you solemnly, the poor widow has put more in than all who have contributed to the treasury; for they have put in money they had over, but she from the little she had has put in everything she possessed, all she had to live on" (Mk 12:43-4).

It is only through prayer that we gain the strength to serve, not simply to serve in an external way but to serve as Christ served, with the "inside" of Christ's own service, coming from the love of the Father and love for mankind. This means that service will be sacrificial in giving oneself to others and for others in imitation of Christ's own service.

It is no secret that many leave the religious life and the priesthood today because they have stopped praying. It is not possible to sustain a commitment without listening to the word which clarifies all other words, contemplating the Word-made-flesh in His life and responding through our sorrow, petition, thanks, adoration, and praise. It happens very often that while the "inside" of prayer can become more and more shallow, the "outside" seems to be becoming greater and greater. No one of course can judge another's motivation. But it is possible that as the "inside" dries up, some people are like those desert plants which extend their roots over a large surface of the ground to try to draw a little moisture to sustain the life which could not be sustained through contact with the font of living water. The extent of their service is in inverse proportion to the depth of their motivation.

Summary and Conclusion

We have discussed the four moments of prayer: hearing the word, seeing the Word-made-flesh, responding to what we hear and see, and translating this audition and vision into action. We know that this sounds easy. In practice it is not easy. Like our faith and our hope and love and our service, prayer has its seasons, its own winter, spring, summer, and fall. Even Christ's prayer had its seasons. Perhaps our own prayer will most often be like the winter of His prayer, that of the Agony in the garden, where one can only pray that the Father's will be done. Our prayer like the rest of our life is not fully resurrected. It still has the marks of Christ's own death and resurrection. This means that our prayer is not only a seeing and hearing and responding; it is also always an overcoming. It is not only an action; it is also always a victory over all that is negative. For this reason our prayer will always take an effort, sometimes heroic effort, when there is so much in us and around us to be overcome. But even here we have our fundamental source of consolation in the fact that if we love Christ, we possess the Spirit of Christ. Then what St. Paul says is true of each one of us: "The Spirit too comes to help us in our weakness. For when we cannot choose words in order to pray properly, the Spirit himself expresses our plea in a way that could never be put into words, and God who knows everything in our hearts knows perfectly well what he means, and that the pleas of the saints expressed by the Spirit are according to the mind of God" (Rm 8:26-7).

Consciousness Examen

George A. Aschenbrenner, S.J.

Volume 31, 1972, pp. 14-21.

Examen is usually the first practice to disappear from the daily life of the religious. This occurs for many reasons; but all the reasons amount to the admission (rarely explicit) that it is not of immediate practical value in a busy day. My point in this article is that all these reasons and their false conclusion spring from a basic misunderstanding of the examen as practiced in religious life. Examen must be seen in relationship to discernment of spirits. It is a daily intensive exercise of discernment in a person's life.

Examen of Consciousness

For many youth today life is spontaneity if anything. If spontaneity is crushed or aborted, then life itself is stillborn. In this view examen is living life once removed from the spontaneity of life. It is a reflective, dehydrated approach which dries all the spontaneity out of life. These people today disagree with Socrates' claim that the unexamined life is not worth living. For these people the Spirit is in the spontaneous and so anything that militates against spontaneity is un-Spirit-ual.

This view overlooks the fact that welling up in the consciousness and experience of each of us are two spontaneities, one good and for God, another evil and not for God. These two types of spontaneous urges and movements happen to all of us. So often the quick-witted, loose-tongued person who can be so entertaining and the center of attention and who is always characterized as being so spontaneous is not certainly being moved by and giving expression to the good spontaneity. For one eager to love God with his or her whole being, the challenge is not simply to let the spontaneous happen but rather to be able to sift out these various sponta-

175

neous urges and give full existential ratification to those spontaneous feelings that are from and for God. We do this by allowing the truly Spirited-spontaneity to happen in our daily lives. But we must learn the feel of this true spirited-spontaneity. Examen has a very central role in this learning.

When examen is related to discernment, it becomes examen of *consciousness* rather than of conscience. Examen of conscience has narrow moralistic overtones. Though we were always told that examen of conscience in religious life was not the same as a preparation for confession, it was actually explained and treated as though it were much the same. The prime concern was with what good or bad actions we had done each day. In discernment the prime concern is not with the morality of good or bad actions; rather the concern is how the Lord is affecting and moving us (often quite spontaneously!) deep in our own affective consciousness. What is happening in our consciousness is prior to and more important than our actions which can be delineated as juridically good or evil. How we are experiencing the "drawing" of the Father (Jn 6:44) in our own existential consciousness and how our sinful nature is quitely tempting us and luring us away from our Father in subtle dispositions of our consciousness—this is what the daily examen is concerned with prior to a concern for our response in our *actions*. So it is examen of consciousness that we are concerned with here, so that we can cooperate with and let happen that beautiful spontaneity in our hearts which is the touch of our Father and the urging of the Spirit.

Examen and Religious Identity

The examen we are talking about here is not a Ben Franklin-like striving for self-perfection. We are talking about an experience in faith of growing sensitivity to the unique, intimately special ways that the Lord's Spirit has of approaching and calling us. Obviously it takes time for this growth. But in this sense examen is a daily renewal and growth in our religious identity—this unique flesh-spirit person being loved by God and called by Him deep in his personal affective world. It is not possible for me to make an examen without confronting my own identity in Christ before the Father—my own religious identity as poor, celibate, and obedient in imitation of Christ as experienced in the charism of my religious vocation.

And yet so often our daily examen becomes so general and vague and unspecific that our religious identity (Jesuit, Dominican, Franciscan, and so forth) does not seem to make any difference. Examen assumes real value when it becomes a daily experience of confrontation and renewal of our unique religious identity and how the Lord is subtly inviting us to deepen and develop this identity. We should make examen each time with as precise a grasp as we have now on our religious identity. We do not make it just as any Christian but as this specific Christian person with a unique vocation and grace in faith.

Examen and Prayer

The examen is a time of prayer. The dangers of an empty self-reflection or an unhealthy self-centered introspection are very real. On the other hand, a lack of effort at examen and the approach of living according to what comes naturally keeps us quite superficial and insensitive to the subtle and profound ways of the Lord deep in our hearts. The prayerful quality and effectiveness of the examen itself depends upon its relationship to the continuing contemplative prayer of the person. Without this relationship examen slips to the level of self-reflection for self-perfection, if it perdures at all.

In daily contemplative prayer the Father reveals to us at His own pace the order of the mystery of all reality in Christ—as Paul says to the Colossians: ". . . those to whom God has planned to give a vision of the full wonder and splendor of his secret plan for the nations" (Col 1:27). The contemplator experiences in many subtle, chiefly non-verbal, ways this revelation of the Father in Christ. The presence of the Spirit of the risen Jesus in the heart of the believer makes it possible to sense and "hear" this invitation (challenge!) to order ourselves to this revelation. Contemplation is empty without this "ordering" response.

This kind of reverent, docile (the "obedience of faith" Paul speaks of in Rom 16:26), and non-moralistic ordering is the work of the daily examen—to sense and recognize those interior invitations of the Lord that guide and deepen this ordering from day to day and not to cooperate with those subtle insinuations opposed to that ordering. Without that contemplative contact with the Father's revelation of reality in Christ, both in formal prayer and informal prayerfulness, the daily practice of examen becomes empty; it shrivels up and dies. Without this "listening" to the Father's revelation of His ways, which are so different from our "listening" to the Father's revelation of His ways which, are so different from our own (Is 55:8-9), examen again becomes that shaping up of ourselves which is human and natural self-perfection or, even worse, it can become that selfish ordering of ourselves to our own ways.

Examen without regular contemplation is futile. A failure at regular contemplation emaciates the beautifully rich experience of response-ible ordering which the contemplative is continually invited to by the Lord. It is true, on the other hand, that contemplation without regular examen becomes compartmentalized and superficial and stunted in a person's life. The time of formal prayer can become a very sacrosanct period in a person's day but so isolated from the rest of his life that he is not prayerful (finding God in all things) at that level where he really lives. The examen gives our daily contemplative experience of God real bite into all our daily living; it is an important means to finding God in everything and not just in the time of formal prayer, as we will explain at the end of this article.

A Discerning Vision of Heart

When we first learned about the examen in religious life, it was a specific exercise of prayer for about a quarter of an hour. And at first it seemed quite stylized and almost artificial. This problem was not in the examen-prayer but in ourselves; we were beginners and had not yet worked out the integration in ourselves of a process of personal discernment to be expressed in daily examens. For the beginner, before he has achieved much of a personalized integration, an exercise or process can be very valuable and yet seem formal and stylized. This should not put us off. It will be the inevitable experience in religious life for the novice and for the "oldtimer" who is beginning again at examen.

But examen will fundamentally be misunderstood if the goal of this exercise is not grasped. The specific exercise of examen is ultimately aimed at developing a heart with a discerning vision to be active not only for one or two quarter-hour periods in a day but continually. This is a gift from the Lord—a most important one as Solomin realized (1 Kings 3:9-12). So we must constantly pray for this gift, but we must also be receptive to its development within our hearts. A daily practice of examen is essential to this development.

Hence the five steps of the exercise of examen as presented in the *Spiritual Exercises* of St. Ignatius Loyola (#43) are to be seen, and gradually experienced in faith, as dimensions of the Christian counsciousness, formed by God and His work in the heart as it confronts and grows within this world and all of reality. If we allow the Father gradually to transform our mind and heart into that of His Son, to become truly Christian, through our living experience in this world, then the examen, with its separate elements now seen as integrated dimensions of our own consciousness looking out on the world, is much more organic to our outlook and will seem much less contrived. So there is no ideal time allocation for the five elements of the examen each time but rather a daily organic expression of the spiritual mood of the heart. At one time we are drawn to one element longer than the others and at another time to another element over the others.

The mature Ignatius near the end of his life was always examining every movement and inclination of his heart which means he was *discerning* the congruence of everything with his true Christ-centered self. This was the overflow of those regular intensive prayer-exercises of examen every day. The novice or "oldtimer" must be aware both of the point of the one or two quarter-hour exercises of examen each day, namely, a continually discerning heart, and of the necessary gradual adaptation of his practice of examen to his stage of development and the situation in the world in which he finds himself. And yet we are all aware of the subtle rationalization of giving up formal examen each day because we have "arrived at" that continually discerning heart. This kind of rationalization will prevent further growth in faith sensitivity to the Spirit and His ways in our daily lives.

Let us now take a look at the format of the examen as presented by St. Ignatius in the *Spiritual Exercises,* #43 but in light of these previous comments on examen as discerning consciousness within the world.

Prayer for Enlightenment

In the *Exercises* Ignatius has an act of thanksgiving as the first part of the examen. The first two parts could be interchanged without too much difference. In fact, I would suggest the prayer for enlightenment as a fitting introduction to the examen.

The examen is not simply a matter if a person's natural power of memory and analysis going back over a part of the day. It is a matter of Spirit-guided insight into my life and courageously responsive sensitivity to God's call in my heart. What we are seeking here is that gradually growing appreciative insight into the mystery which I am. Without the Father's revealing grace this kind of insight is not possible. The Christian must be careful not to get locked into the world of his own human natural powers. Our technological world can pose as a special danger in this regard. Founded on a deep appreciation of the humanly interpersonal, the Christian in faith transcends the boundaries of the here-and-now with its limited natural causality and discovers a Father who loves and works in and through and beyond all. For this reason we begin the examen with an explicit petition for that enlightenment which will occur in and through our own powers but which our own natural powers could never be capable of all by themselves. That the Spirit may help me to see myself a bit more as He sees me Himself!

Reflective Thanksgiving

The stance of a Christian in the midst of the world is that of a poor person, prossessing nothing, not even himself, and yet being gifted at every instant in and through everything. When we become too affluently involved with ourselves and deny our inherent poverty, then we lose the gifts and either begin to make demands for what we think we deserve (often leading to angry frustration) or we blandly take for granted *all* that comes our way. Only the truly poor person can appreciate the slightest gift and feel genuine gratitude. The more deeply we live in faith the poorer we are and the more gifted; life itself becomes humble, joyful thanksgiving. This should gradually become an element of our abiding consciousness.

After the introductory prayer for enlightenment our hearts should rest in genuine faith-filled gratitude to our Father for His gifts in this most recent part of the day. Perhaps in the spontaneity of the happening we were not aware of the gift and now in this exercise of reflective prayer we see the events in a very different perspective. Our sudden gratitude—now the act of a humble selfless pauper—helps make us ready to discover the gift more clearly in a future sudden spontaneity. Our gratitude should center on the concrete, uniquely personal gifts that each of us was blessed with, whether large and obviously important or tiny and apparently insignificant. There is much in our lives that we take for granted; gradually He will lead us to a deep realization that *all is gift*. It is right to give Him praise and thanks!

Practical Survey of Actions

In this third element of the examen ordinarily we rush to review, in some specific detail, our actions of that part of the day just finished so we can catalogue them as good or bad. Just what we shouldn't do! Our prime concern here in faith is what has been happening to and in us since the last examen. The operative questions are: what has been happening in us, how has the Lord been working in us, what has He been asking us. And only secondarily are our own actions to be considered. This part of the examen presumes that we have become sensitive to our interior feelings, moods, and slightest urgings and that we are not frightened by them but have learned to take them very seriously. It is here in the depths of our affectivity, so spontaneous, strong, and shadowy at times, that God moves us and deals with us most intimately. These interior moods, feelings, urges, and movements are the "spirits" that must be sifted out, discerned, so we can recognize the Lord's call to us at this intimate core of our being. As we have said above, the examen is a chief means to this discerning of our interior consciousness.

This presumes a real faith approach to life—that life is first listening, then acting in response:

> The fundamental attitude of the believer is of one who listens. It is to the Lord's utterances that he gives ear. In as many different ways and on as many varied levels as the listener can discern the word and will of the Lord manifested to him, he must respond with all the Pauline "obedience of faith." . . . It is the attitude of receptivity, passivity and poverty of one who is always in need, radically dependent, conscious of his creaturehood.[1]

Hence the great need for interior quiet, peace, and a passionate receptivity that attunes us to listening to God's word at every instant and in every situation and *then* responding in our own activity. Again in a world that is founded more on activity (becoming activism), productivity, and efficiency (whereas efficacity is a norm for the kingdom of God!) this faith view is implicity, if not explicitly, challenged at every turn in the road.

And so our first concern here is with these subtle intimate, affective ways in which the Lord has been dealing with us during these past few hours. Perhaps we did not recognize Him calling in that past moment, but now our vision is clear and direct. Secondarily our concern is with our actions insofar as they were *responses* to His calling. So often our activity becomes primary to us and all sense of response in our activity is lost. We become self-moved and motivated rather than moved and motivated by the

---

[1]David Asselin, S.J., "Christian Maturity and Spiritual Discernment," pp. 201-213.

Spirit (Rom 8:14). This is a subtle lack of faith and failure to live as a son or daughter of our Father. In the light of faith it is the *quality* (of responsiveness) of the activity, more than the activity itself, which makes the difference for the kingdom of God.

In this general review there is no strain to reproduce every second since the last examen; rather our concern is with specific details and incidents as they reveal patterns and bring some clarity and insight. This brings us to a consideration of what Ignatius calls the particular examen.

This element of the examen, perhaps more than any other, has been misunderstood. It has often become an effort to divide and conquer by moving down the list of vices or up the list of virtues in a mechanically planned approach to self-perfection. A certain amount of time was spent on each vice or virtue one by one, and then we moved on to the next one on the list. Rather than a practical programmed approach to perfection, the particular examen is meant to be a reverently honest, personal meeting with the Lord in our own hearts.

When we become sensitive and serious enough about loving God, we begin to realize some changes must be made. We are deficient in so many areas and so many defects must be done away with. But the Lord does not want all of them to be handled at once. Usually there is one area of our hearts where He is especially calling for conversion which is always the beginning of new life. He is interiorly nudging us in one area and reminding us that if we are really serious about Him this one aspect of ourselves must be changed. This is often precisely the one area we want to forget and (maybe!) work on later. We do not want to let His word condemn us in this one area and so we try to forget it and distract ourselves by working on some other safer area which *does* require conversion but not with the same urgent sting of consciousness that is true of the former area. It is in this first area of our hearts, if we will be honest and open with the Lord, where we are very personally experiencing the Lord in the burning fire of His Word as He confronts us here and now. So often we fail to recognize this guilt for what it really is or we try to blunt it by working hard on something else that we may want to correct whereas the Lord wants something else here and now. For beginners it takes time to become interiorly sensitive to God before they gradually come to recognize the Lord's call to conversion (maybe involving a very painful struggle!) in some area of their lives. It is better for beginners to take this time to learn what the Lord wants their particular examen to be now rather than just taking some assigned imperfection to get started on.

And so the particular examen is very personal, honest, and at times a very subtle experience of the Lord calling in our hearts for deeper conversion to Himself. The natter of the conversion may remain the same for a long period of time, but the important thing is our sense of His personal challenge to us. Often this experience of the Lord calling for conversion in one small part of our hearts takes the expression of good healthy guilt which should be carefully interpreted and responded to if there is to be progress in holiness. When the particular examen is seen as this personal experience of the Lord's love for us, then we can understand why St. Ignatius suggests that we turn our whole consciousness to this experience of the Lord (whatever it be in all practicality, for example, more subtle humility or readiness to get involved with people on their terms, etc.) at those two very important moments in our day, when we begin our day and when we close it, besides the formal examen times.

In this third dimension of the formal examen the growing faith sense of our sinfulness is very central. This is more of a spiritual faith reality as revealed by the Father in our experience than a heavily moralistic and guilt-laden reality. A deep sense of sinfulness depends on our growth in faith and is a dynamic realization which always ends in thanksgiving—the song of a "saved sinner." In his book *Growth in the Spirit*, Françqis Roustang, in the second chapter, speaks very profoundly about sinfulness and thanksgiving. This can provide enormous insight into the relationship of these second and third elements of the formal examen, especially as dimensions of our abiding Christian consciousness.

Contrition and Sorrow

The Christian heart is always a heart in song—a song of deep joy and gratitude. But the Alleluia can be quite superficial and without body and depth unless it is genuinely touched with sorrow. This is the song of a sinner constantly aware of being prey to his sinful tendencies and yet being converted into the newness which is guaranteed in the victory of Jesus Christ. Hence, we never grow out of a sense of wonder-ful sorrow in the presence of our Savior.

This basic dimension of our heart's vision which the Father desires to deepen in us as He converts us from sinners to His sons and daughters, if we allow Him, is here applied to the specifics of our actions since the last examen, especially insofar as they were selfishly inadequate *responses* to the Lord's work in our hearts. This sorrow will especially spring from the lack of honesty and courage in responding to the Lord's call in the particular examen. This contrition and sorrow is not a shame nor a depression at our weakness but a faith experience as we grow in our realization of our Father's awesome desire that we love Him with every ounce of our being.

After this description, the value of pausing each day in formal examen and giving concrete expression to this abiding sense of sorrow in our hearts should be quite obvious and should flow naturally from the third element of practical survey of our actions.

Hopeful Resolution for Future

This final element of the formal daily examen grows very naturally out of the previous elements. The organic development leads us to face the future which is now rising to encounter us and become integrated into our lives. In the light of our present descernment of the immediate past how do we look to the future? Are we discouraged or despondent or fearful of the future? If this is the atmosphere of our hearts now, we must wonder why and try to interpret this atmosphere; we must be honest in acknowledging our feeling for the future, and not repress it by hoping it will go away.

The precise expression of this final element will be determined by the organic flow of this precise examen now. Accordingly, this element of resolution for the immediate future will never happen the same way each time. If it did happen in the same expression each time, it would be a sure sign that we were not really entering into the previous four elements of the examen.

At this point in the examen there should be a great desire to face the future with renewed vision and sensitivity as we pray both to recognize even more the subtle ways in which the Lord will greet us and to hear His Word call us in the existential situation of the future and to respond to His call with more faith, humility, and courage. This should be especially true of that intimate abiding experience of the Lord calling for painful conversion in some area of our heart—what we have called the particular examen. A great hope should be the atmosphere of our hearts at this point—a hope not founded on our own deserts, or our own powers for the future, but rather founded much more fully in our Father whose glorious victory in Jesus Christ we share through the life of Their Spirit in our hearts. The more we will trust God and allow Him to lead in our lives, the more we will experience true supernatural hope in God painfully in and through, but quite beyond, our own weak powers—an experience at times frightening and emptying but ultimately joyfully exhilarating. St. Paul in this whole passage from the Letter to the Philippians (3:7-14) expresses well the spirit of this conclusion of the formal examen: ". . . I leave the past behind and with hands outstretched to whatever lies ahead I go straight for the goal" (3:13).

Examen and Discernment

We will close this article with some summary remarks about the examen, as here described, and discernment of spirits. When examen is understood in the light and so practiced each day, then it becomes so much more than just a brief exercise performed once or twice a day and which is quite secondary to our formal prayer and active living of God's love in our daily situation. Rather it becomes an exercise which so focuses and renews our specific faith identity that we should be even more reluctant to omit our examen than our formal contemplative prayer each day. This seems to have been St. Ignatius' view of the practice of the examen. He never talks of omitting it though he does talk of adapting and abbreviating the daily meditation for various reasons. For him it seems the examen was central and quite inviolate. This strikes us as strange until we revamp our understanding of the examen. Then perhaps we begin to see the examen as so intimately connected to our growing identity and so important to finding God in all things at all times that it becomes our central daily experience of prayer.

For Ignatius finding God in all things is what life is all about. Near the end of his life he said that "whenever he wished, at whatever hour, he could find God" (*Autobiography*, # 99). This is the mature Ignatius who had so fully allowed God to possess every ounce of his being through a clear YES to the Father that radiated from the very core of his being, that he could be conscious at any moment he wanted of the deep peace, joy, and contentment (consolation, see the *Exercises*, # 316) which was the experience of God at the center of his heart. Ignatius' identity, at this point in his life, was quite fully and clearly "in Christ" as Paul says: "For now my place is in him, and I am not dependent upon any of the self-achieved righteousness of the Law" (Phil 3:9); Ignatius knew and was his true self in Christ.

Being able to find God whenever he wanted, Ignatius was now able to find Him in all things through a test for congruence of any interior impulse, mood, or feeling with his true self. Whenever he found interior consonance within himself (which registers as peace, joy, contentment again) from the immediate interior movement and felt himself being his true congruent self, then he knew he had heard God's word to him at that instant. And he responded with that fullness of humble courage so typical of Ignatius. If he discovered interior dissonance, agitation, and disturbance "at the bottom of the heart" (to be carefully distinguished from repugnance "at the top of the head"[2]) and could not find his true congruent self in Christ, then he recognized the interior impulse as an "evil spirit" and he experienced God by "going against" the desolate impulse (cf. *Exercises*, # 319). In this way he was able to find God in all things by carefully discerning all his interior experiences ("spirits"). Thus discernment of spirits became a daily very practical living of the art of loving God with his whole heart, whole body, and whole strength. Every moment of life was loving (finding) God in the existential situation in a deep quite, peace, and joy.

For Ignatius, this finding God in the present interior movement, feeling, or option was almost instantaneous in his mature years because the central "feel" or "bent" of his being had so been grasped by God. For the beginner, what was almost instantaneous for the mature Ignatius may require the effort of a prayerful process of a few hours or days depending on the inportance of the movement-impulse to be discerned. In some of his writ-

---

[2]John Carroll Futrell, S.J., *Ignatian Discernment* (St. Louis: Institute of Jesuit Sources, 1970), p. 64.

ings, Ignatius uses examen to refer to this almost instantaneous test for congruence with his true self—something he could do a number of times every hour of the day. But he also speaks of examen in the formal restricted sense of two quarter-hour exercises of prayer a day.

The intimate and essential relationship between these two senses of examen has been the point of this whole article.

Praying the Gospels

Arthur F. McGovern, S.J.

Volume 36, 1977, pp. 450-454.

We can thank *Godspell* and *Jesus Christ Superstar* for one contribution they made to all of us. They reminded us that the person of Jesus is worth singing about, that his person can be an inspiration to the modern world. They helped many people to discover the attractiveness of our Lord. One of the sad paradoxes of our faith is that the *person* of Jesus Christ can remain little known and loved even by the most faithful of church-goers. He waits to be discovered.

For a religious who has (presumably) read lives of Christ and prayed over the gospels a somewhat different problem can arise. The stories of Jesus' life are all too familiar. We can turn to the gospels with a *déjà vu* feeling. What more is there to learn? No new passages to discover. We have heard the stories many times. How, then, do we make the gospels become alive? How can they become truly good "news" for ourselves, news that will then spur us to share him with others?

What I would like to suggest in these pages are some ways of praying the gospels that have been especially helpful to me. But I should emphasize at the outset that these have proven "helpful to *me*." My own approach to prayer is quite "active," a questioning and searching of the Scriptures. But this is only one way of praying. Others may find (and at times I also find) a more contemplative "resting" with the Lord more congenial. In both cases (active or more passive) I am convinced that God speaks to us through our own feelings and emotions (see Robert Ochs, *God is More Present Than You Think*). God has no "voice-out-there" which speaks to us; he communicates with us by evoking in us feelings of love, the desire to change, a sense of his presence. So for me at least the conclusion is that I must make a real effort to dispose myself for his grace. I cannot sit passively, reading over words and stories that are all too familiar, and expect God to work miracles within me. I need to approach prayer with desire, searching, questioning, longing (though being open to a more quiet resting in the Lord).

The "Words" of the Gospel

A basic pattern of meditating on Scripture passages should be familiar to all religious. You read a passage, reflect on its meaning, and then talk to God about the thoughts and feelings you have as you reflect on his word. But how can we make this a more meaningful prayer experience? Several things I have found to be helpful. One is to read the passage *aloud,* slowly and with feeling, as one might read poetry or read a story to a child. A second help is to express the *feelings* I have about the words, if only to express my *desire* to feel something. A third element is to believe, with real conviction, that Scripture is a *living* word, that God really wants to address me in a personal way. One need not be a Scripture scholar to pray the gospels. In fact the aims of study and prayer are quite different. The scholar tries to determine *the* meaning of the gospel; in prayer I am searching only for what God wants to say *to me.*

Let me illustrate some of these points by drawing upon a personal prayer experience. I prayed aloud Lk 24, 1-3: "On the first day of the week, at the first sign of dawn, they went to the tomb with the spices they had prepared. They found that the stone had been rolled away from the tomb." As I prayed over the words "at the first sign of dawn" I became filled with a longing. I remembered back to my days as a novice when I would awake in the morning truly eager to begin prayer. I prayed for that eagerness, that freshness of response, to be born again. "They went to the tomb." How often had I picked up the gospels as though they were a tomb, a story about the past instead of a living word addressed to me. I prayed for the grace to believe that the gospels really contained good *news.* "With the spices they had prepared." And I prayed: "Of course, Lord, it makes so much sense. I have to prepare, to dispose myself for prayer, and work to create a situation in which your word has a chance to speak to me. Don't let me be lazy; make me challenge the words until they reveal your word to me."

Obviously the above hardly represents a scholar's exegesis of Luke's gospel. But it does express the thoughts and feelings which God evoked in me as I prayed his word. And that is what prayer is about—letting God speak to me through the feelings and thoughts he evokes in me as I reflect on his revelation.

What is the gospel saying to me? We are all tempted at times to relate passages to *someone else* we think needs to hear it (e.g., when Jesus denounces hypocrites). But it can also happen that a passage doesn't seem to speak to us because we read it too literally. "That is why I am telling you not to worry about your life and what you are to eat, nor about your body and how you are to clothe it" (Mt 6:25). Few of us have to worry about food or clothes. But what is it that *I* am letting disturb me—a criticism, an unfair judgment, uncertainty about next year? In praying that passage we need to let God speak to us about our fears and anxieties, and to express them honestly. (Sometimes religious can pray what they feel "one should" say to God, not what they truly feel, especially if the feelings are strong anger or resentment.)

While still discussing "words of the gospel" let me also mention two suggestions given to me (and which I found enriching) for praying specific parts of the gospel. One suggestion concerns the beatitudes: think about members of my community or other friends and then about the particular beatitude which each person most expresses or reflects. Or I might pray for the spirit of the beatitude that I seem most to lack. The second suggestion was made in conjunction with Jesus' last discourse in John's Gospel (chapters 14-17), though it would seem appropriate also for other teachings of Jesus. Take one verse or two lines at a time, imagining Jesus addressing them to you personally, and then respond to him about how you feel when he speaks these words. "Do not let your heart be troubled, Sister Joan. Trust in God still, and trust in me" (Jn 4:1).

The "Feelings" of Persons in the Gospel

A familiar way of praying gospel "stories" is to picture the scene in one's imagination. Most of us learned in some retreat or other to make preludes, to enter into the story of Jesus' healing a blind man or forgiving a sinner. But because it requires a good deal of concentration and freedom from distractions, this form of meditation can be difficult. Or once again the story can seem all too familiar. Jesus heals a leper. That's nice, but what's new? Well, let me suggest a simpler way of using one's imagination which *at times* has proved helpful to me. It involves creating a "story" to dramatize the events of the gospel. Take, for example, the story of the cure of the leper in Luke 5. We can read the brief account and the leper may remain more an object to be pitied than a human person to be respected and loved. So I ask in prayer: Who was this leper? How did he feel? In praying this scene I imagine the leper as a husband and father. He might have been a metal worker respected in his trade but now struck down with a disease that forced him to ostracize himself from home and family. I imagine his feelings as he first discovered the disease, as he bid goodbye to his family, afraid to even embrace them for fear he would contaminate them. I imagine his thoughts years later as he longed for just a sight of his wife and daughter, as he worried about his son just coming of age. How did this leper (this human being made in the image of God) feel when he heard of Jesus of Nazareth? Was he eager and confident, or hesitant and even despairing? How do *I* feel about going to Christ when I feel disgusted with myself and ashamed? Do I pray, "Lord, if you want to, you can cure me?" or do I shun the light and remain hidden in a cave of self-pity? For the gospel was originally addressed to real human persons filled with hopes, doubts, and fears. And now it is addressed to me. Christ is calling me forth to present myself for healing as I pray the gospel.

One reason the gospel scenes can seem all too familiar is that we take so much for granted about Jesus and the people he heals and forgives. The character traits of Jesus are already firmly established in our minds. We know that he will act with compassion, courage, and love. We know that the blind, the lame, and the sinner will ask him for healing and forgiveness. So again we have to use our imagination, and challenge what we too easily take for granted. How *might* Jesus have reacted if he were I? How *might* the sick and the sinner have responded to him?

Jesus is seated at table with Simon and the Pharisees (Lk 7). A woman of notorious reputation appears at the door and runs to his feet. Christ *might* have reacted (if he were like us) with embarrassment or even hostility: "Get her out of here; she is ruining my chances for influencing these men" (you need money to save souls). Or if that seems too far-fetched I can certainly imagine myself responding: "Mary, I'm interested in your case, but you can see this is not a very good time." And then perhaps calling to the apostles: "Could we set up an appointment for this woman later this afternoon?" Only when we see what *might* have occurred does the real beauty of Jesus' love become fully evident.

This same approach can be taken in looking at those to whom Jesus responded. For every story of a blind man who asked to see or leper who asked to be cured, there may well have been untold stories of blind men and lepers who felt it was hopeless to ask. Jesus called forth Lazarus from the tomb. But what if Lazarus had responded: "Leave me alone. I prefer being dead!" Or if the paralytic, when told to "Get up and walk," said "I can't—there's no use even trying."

In praying this way we often discover a great deal about our own responses to Christ. Do we really want to be forgiven or healed? Do we really believe we can be changed? We must pray the gospels, and, for that matter, all of Scripture, with the conviction that God is speaking *to me,* calling forth generosity, confidence, self-acceptance, or conversion. This does not mean all prayer involves endless introspection. Often the greatest transformation occurs when prayer is given over to a self-forgetting admiration and praise of Jesus. But this, too, is a personal response to the word of God.

If we were to formalize this use of the imagination in praying the gospels, the steps might read as follows: (1) a reading over the narrative slowly; (2) entering into the feelings of the persons in the scene; (3) an imaginative effort to realize what might have been a different outcome of the gospel story; (4) a personal application or response so that I truly "take on the mind of Christ" when I pray.

One final suggestion can be helpful in striving to know more deeply the person of Jesus as he is revealed in the gospels. When we deeply love others we begin to become aware of their gestures, their moods, their favorite expressions; in short, how they act and speak. So in contemplating the life of Jesus what can often be most beautiful is the discovery of *how* he reacted to others. Often the most revealing traits of Jesus are contained in phrases that we might tend to pass over: "He touched him," "He gave the son to his mother," "He told them to give her something to eat." If we recognize in our own lives how much a smile, a compliment, a hug can mean, we may begin to realize how much of God's love was communicated by Jesus through very simple gestures and words.

The gospels are not stories and teachings addressed to a civilization now dead. They are the living words of Jesus spoken to us. Of the Blessed Virgin Mary, St. Anselm wrote: "She so listened to the word of God that it took flesh within her." We are called upon to listen, too, that his word may come to life within us.

Disappointment in Prayer: Prelude to Growth?

William J. Connolly, S.J.

Volume 32, 1973, pp. 557-560.

"I've put a lot of time and effort into prayer, but...."

"I thought talking to you about prayer would get me started again, and it worked for a few days, but then . . . ."

These words and others like them describe an experience that is at least as common as the buoyant successes described in some current books and articles on prayer. They are hard words: hard to say, dispiriting to hear, and they express an experience that a person of faith can find hard to understand. So it is not difficult to see why the literature does not give more attention to this experience of disappointment. Yet it is often a crucial experience, for it can lead to fixated bitterness or to great creativity.

Take the situation of a religious for whom serious prayer has had little meaning for several years. Influenced by the conviction and vitality of friends who have been affected by one of the current movements for the renewal of prayer, he decides he wants "to deepen in prayer." He will usually mean by this that he wants prayer to be more satisfying, more sustaining, a more significant reference point for his life. However, he is aware that when he last tried to pray fairly frequently, he became enmeshed in worries, plans, questions, anything but prayer. So he gave up. His first goal now will be to spend time in prayer without being constantly harassed by "distractions."

Prayer and Achievement Orientation

However, a person approaches prayer with the attitudes he has toward the rest of life. A person for whom trying to achieve is the basic approach to life will try to achieve prayer. He will come to it as he would come to a wall to be built, a room to be painted, logarithms to be mastered. He will put the latest methods to strenuous use, go out of his way to consult an expert, or take up with dogged regularity practices he learned in school, in the novitiate, or in the seminary. He will inevitably fail and experience disappointment. The higher his hopes were and the stronger his achievement orientation, the more bitter his disappointment will be.

The emphasis given by American Catholics in the past to formal ascetical practices and forms of prayer—most noticeable in religious communities, but not confined to them—suggests that there are few of us who do not experience achievement orientation to a high degree. The experience of disappointment will thus be frequently encountered, and at different times in a person's life it will signal that he is putting his faith in his own strength and must let himself be more receptive.

Because this achievement orientation is so usual among Americans, we probably should banish from discussions of prayer terms like "work at," "be faithful to," and "regularity." It is not that the seriousness they express has no place in a balanced consideration of prayer. Far from it. But the terms serve to strengthen our bias toward a spiritual work ethic, and for most of us that bias is already too strong, whether we actually work in response to it or merely feel guilty about the work we don't do.

Reaction to Disappointment

Whatever the reasons for the strength of this bias, the experience of disappointment itself is a crucial event. The person can retreat now from his desire to pray, or he can question his assumptions about prayer and consider new approaches.

It is the practical assumptions, not the theoretical, that should be questioned most carefully. The person is not likely to need new definitions, but insight into what actually happens when he tries to pray. Does he spend as much time thinking about God as he spends thinking about himself, for instance? When he uses Scripture for prayer, does he let the Word speak to him or does he become so introspective that he cannot hear the Word? Does he let himself live a relationship with God in prayer?

It can be helpful to compare our reactions to God in prayer with our reactions to other persons. I know that a person comes to mean something to me only if I let myself look at him or listen to him. I know that he cannot mean anything to me if I am so intent on my own moods and problems that I pay no attention to him. Nor can he mean anything if he is for me simply a function of my moods and problems. I do not begin to relate to him until I listen to him or observe him in action. In the same way, I let prayer develop only when I listen to God and look at His action. It is then that I can begin to realize who He is and can react to Him rather than to my own feelings.

No method, no spiritual director, no amount of effort will enable me to pray until I am willing to listen to the Lord.

Disappointment in prayer is an experience of our own inability to save ourselves. It piques, prods, and urges us to listen, to be receptive. We can theorize eloquently and endlessly about the nature of prayer and relationship with God, but disappointment will sour us like bile until we listen.

The spiritual work ethic, the achievement orientation can be overcome only if we decide to pay attention. This means that a person will let what he hears strike his feelings and confront his anger, beat upon his fears, wash against his guilts. He has to let the Word come upon him where he lives, and so it may take time for him to begin really to listen. If he is unaccustomed to letting his feelings be touched by the Word he may have to ask himself what he actually does feel when he reads a Biblical text, or when circumstances in his life speak to him. He may have to talk over his reactions with someone else before he can know what he feels.

Disappointment and Receptivity

Several other observations on the experience of disappointment may be worth mentioning. The experience is not a once-in-a-lifetime occurrence. It seems to be a normal accompaniment of a call to deeper receptivity, and a person may be called to deeper levels of receptivity on a number of occasions in his life. Acceptance will often be followed, sooner or later, by another call to be still more receptive, to be receptive in another area of his life, or to be receptive on a deeper level of his consciousness. The deep, clear realization that I am incapable of a goodness that means anything to me, incapable even of sincerely inviting God to enter my life, but that He enters anyway because He loves me, seems to be the typical level to which the disappointment-receptivity sequence finally leads.

It is important to remember that "receptivity" here does not mean passivity. A person may well become more active as he becomes more receptive. He will always become more responsive to the needs and the companionship of his brothers. It is not only prayer that is spoken to by disappointment, but the whole prayerful life. Prayer itself is a microcosm in which the forces that operate in the whole of life can be experienced more distinctly than they usually can in other experience. The disappointment of losing a job, of seeing a career come to an end, of losing a close friend often occasions a deeper receptivity in one's attitude toward life, whether or not this new receptivity appears explicitly in prayer. That such disappointments can also result in fixation is abundantly clear today, particularly perhaps in religious communities.

It is impossible to overestimate how tough-fibered our subconscious resistance to receptivity can be. This toughness is evident in the bitterness of our disappointment, and such bitterness often seems necessary if the resistance is to be overcome.

Conclusion

A spiritual theology that conceives of the Christian life in terms of static perfection will make little sense of the recurring disappointment-receptivity experience. But to a theology that shares Gregory of Nyssa's vision of Christian perfection as progress, growth, journeying, this experience is essential. The Christian is often in need of rescue from blind alleys and tributary paths on his journey. Traveling habits that were helpful at an earlier stage later become hindrances, and he needs rescue from them too. Disappointment is a vivid signal that the need for rescue is present.

Prayer: The Context of Discernment

Charles J. Healey, S.J.

Volume 33, 1974, pp. 265-270.

Discernment Today

In our attempts to seek and find God in our lives and to live out our Christian lives of faith, hope, and love, we are often involved in a process of
rediscovery. There is not that much that is new for us in the sense of discovering something for the first time. But often the conditions of the times
in which we live and our own felt needs combine to lead us to focus on a
particular aspect of the spiritual life. Such, I would suggest, is the case in
the area of discernment. It is certainly a term that has deep roots in the
history of Christian spirituality. But ours is a period that has seized upon
the process of discernment—perhaps too quickly and too glibly at times—
in the hopes that it might aid us in our efforts to love and serve God both
as individuals and as communities, and to seek and respond more generously to His will in our lives.

This renewed interest in discernment should come as no surprise. First
of all, there is the very visible desire of many to deepen their own union
with God, to establish or reestablish what they consider the essentials and
priorities in their lives, and to make any required decisions in a context
of faith and prayer. In a time of great change, many are seeking to find
strength and unity within themselves not only to cope effectively with their
lives and all their responsibilities, but also to maintain themselves as loving and productive persons. Secondly, many communities are turning to
the process of discernment as a method of helping them in their attempts
at renewal as a community and as a basis for group decisions. But whether

it is a case of individual discernment or corporate discernment, it is important to stress over and over that the basis of any discernment has to be the deep and intense prayer of the persons involved in the process. The context of any true discernment is prayer. The purpose of this article, then, is to offer some reflections on discernment, using the word in the broadest sense here and focusing on the intimate connection between discernment and prayer.

Context Is Prayer

Discernment really makes sense only when it is situated in the context of prayer. Unless there is a corresponding desire to seek and find God continually in our lives and to deepen our awareness of His reality and presence, discernment can end up just being talk. The seeking and yearning attitude of the Psalmist must penetrate our own lives deeply: "To you, my heart speaks; you my glance seeks, your presence, O Lord, I seek. Hide not your face from me" (Ps 27:8-9). There is, of course, a renewed interest and even a hunger on the part of many today in the area of personal prayer; and this accounts in part for the renewed interest in the area of discernment. There are many indications of this all around us at the present time; and many are definitely expressing a desire for prayer which springs from a felt human need and the presence of the Spirit in our midst, ever renewing, ever arousing.

Recently I was listening to a taped conference on prayer by Thomas Merton in which he mentioned at the beginning that he did not like to talk a great deal about prayer. This was certainly not from any disinterest, for if there is any constant preoccupation and interest that emerges in his life and writings, it would be with the value and priority he constantly gives to prayer. But he wanted to stress the point that prayer for us should be something simple and natural, something as simple and natural as breathing. It is hard for us to talk about breathing since it is such a normal process of our lives and one which we can easily take for granted. So, too, he feels should be the case with prayer. At times we can complicate it and make an issue or a cause out of it. But usually when we make a cause or an issue out of something, we oppose it to something else: "This is prayer, this isn't. This is something sacred, this isn't." The focus could then shift to the issue rather than the reality, and prayer could then be viewed as something complicated and artificial. Perhaps we can best consider prayer as the simple, natural, continual response of one who is convinced he belongs to God and seeks to grow in union with Him, and the response of one who realizes he is a person possessed by a loving God. And it is in this climate, this atmosphere of prayer that the whole process of discernment should be placed. The context is a very normal, full, and serious seeking after God.

The Process of Discernment

Discernment, then, should not be considered a cause or an issue nor even a method in itself. It is a process in prayer by which one seeks seriously to know and follow God's will, to hear His call and faithfully and generously respond in the very real life situation of the person concerned. If prayer should be a very human and ordinary experience, so too should be discernment. In this sense, it is a very simple process; and yet, on the other hand, it can be difficult in the sense that it presupposes constant efforts at a deep and continuous union with God through prayer. This requires perseverance, patience, and willingness to expend time and energy. It cannot be turned off and on like a water faucet if it is to be effective; it presupposes a firm basis of faith and the continuous seeking of the presence of the Lord.

Although discernment is a word that can come easily to the lips, it can still remain a rather elusive concept. Perhaps this is because it presupposes so much else. At any rate, we might recall Father Futrell's definition that discernment "involves choosing the way of the light of Christ instead of the way of the darkness of the Evil One and living out the consequences of this choice through discerning what specific decisions and actions are demanded to follow Christ here and now."[1] Thus discernment focuses on the ongoing attempts to clarify and ascertain God's will in our lives and seeks to specify what actions and decisions are required in the life of one who wishes to follow Christ totally. The process presupposes an intense desire, hunger, and willingness to seek God's will and to embrace it generously once one has come to a reasonable certitude regarding it.

We might say it all comes down to our attempts to hear and respond to the word of God in our own unique lives. But if we are to be sensitive to God speaking to us in the many ways He does in our lives, we must first hear His call; we must listen quietly and give Him frequent opportunities to speak to us. If we are to be sensitive to God's presence and attentive to His touch, there must be an element of stillness and listening. Since this listening aspect is so important for discernment, we should not be surprised to find this aspect of prayer being re-emphasized today.[2] Many are experiencing the need today to take time out from all their activities in order to turn within and seek God's presence within, to contemplate Him and to listen to Him in the stillness of their hearts. It is a kind of active receptivity as we let the radical truth of God shine forth with its own life within us. We seek to make the words of the Psalmist our own: "In your light we see light." It is in this atmosphere of stillness and presence that one can best determine God's call, God's touch, God's will.

---

[1] John C. Futrell, S.J., "Ignatian Discernment," *Studies in the Spirituality of Jesuits,* v. 2, no. 2, p. 47.
[2] See, for example, W. Norris Clarke, S.J., "Be Still and Contemplate," *New Catholic World,* November-December 1972, pp. 246 ff.

Building on the Past

As we seek to see clearly where God is touching us at a given time and where He is leading us and asking us to respond and follow, it is very helpful to grow in the awareness of where God has touched us and nourished us in the past. Each of us has his or her own unique history in the hands of a loving God, that is, significant events, persons, books, Scripture passages, and so forth, that have been a source of great strength and help. All of this constitutes our own faith experience of God; and the more it is brought to our conscious awareness, the more it becomes our own. Often in discernment workshops or faith sharing experiences, methods and opportunities are presented to help individuals grasp more explicitly what they uniquely possess of God in their lives. One can call this by various names: one's core experience of God, one's beauty within, one's name of grace, and so forth. But it all comes down to the same reality: we seek to realize what we already possess, what is uniquely ours, and where God has touched us and loved us significantly. Once we are more aware of how God has acted in our lives in the past, we can more easily return in a spirit of prayer to be nourished and strengthened and sustained. What has sustained us in the past and what has touched us before, can sustain us and touch us again. This conscious awareness also helps us to be more responsive and sensitive to where God is touching us now, where He is leading us. We can begin to see a pattern and a continuity in our lives of faith. Above all, we become more aware of the profoundest reality of our lives, namely that which we possess of the power and love of God that has worked within us in the past and continues to be operative in the present.

Discernment in prayer, then, is an ongoing process that seeks to find God and His will in our lives; it involves a constant seeking of God and an awareness of His presence in our lives. Through discernment one seeks to hear God's continuous call, to recognize it as clearly as possible in order to follow it as faithfully and generously as possible. It seeks to answer the question: How can I best love and serve God in the present circumstances of my life. It is an ongoing process because our lives, our experience, our work, our relationship with God is an ongoing process. His Word does not come to us in a vacuum but in the concrete circumstances of our everyday lives. As Thomas Merton says in one of my favorite passages from his writings:

> Every moment and every event of every man's life on earth plants something in his soul. For just as the wind carries thousands of winged seeds, so each moment brings with it germs of spiritual vitality that come to rest imperceptibly in the minds and wills of men. Most of these unnumbered seeds perish and are lost, because men are not prepared to receive them; for such seeds as these cannot spring up anywhere except in the good soil of freedom and love.[3]

[3]Thomas Merton, *New Seeds of Contemplation* (New York: New Directions, 1961), p. 14.

In a very true sense, it is only the faith-filled person, the contemplating person that is acutely sensitive to these seeds of God in his or her life. And for the soil of freedom and love to flourish in our own lives, we must constantly open ourselves to the Spirit of God through an abiding spirit of prayer.

Not only must we seek to grow sensitive to God's speaking to us in the external events of our lives, but we must seek to grow in an awareness and sensitivity to the movements within ourselves as we react personally to the signs of His will and presence. How do my present reactions correspond to the felt experience of God that has been so much a part of my life in the past? Are my present movements in resonance with that source of peace, that sense of oneness and wholeness before God that I have experienced before, that sense of belonging to God that has been so nourishing and sustaining in my life? Are they consistent with the normal signs of the Spirit working within us, the signs of "love, joy, peace, patience, kindness, goodness, faithfulness, humility and self-control" (Gal. 5:22-3)? These are some of the questions one seeks to clarify in order to fulfill the desire to seek and find the Lord and His will. The spiritual director can play an important role in assisting here, for at times we can be too close to ourselves to have the needed objectivity. The director can aid us in clarifying and objectifying our own experiences and interior movements and aid us to see where God is touching us, loving us, and indicating His presence and His will.

A Sense of Freedom

In addition to a deep and constant spirit of prayer, discernment also requires an attitude of freedom and detachment. The attitude of freedom I refer to is that which allows a person to give to God and His will the central place in one's life; it is a freedom and detachment from all other things that would either prevent or hinder one's striving to focus on God. It is the sense of freedom that allows God to become and remain the central reality in one's life. The Psalmist speaks of this centrality with the words: "As the eyes of the servant are on the hands of the Master, so my eyes are on you, O Lord." It is the freedom that allows one to respond generously to Jesus' invitation to Matthew, "Come, follow me," and His words to the disciples of John the Baptist, "Come and see." Come and see and taste the goodness of the Lord. It is the freedom expressed in the words of the prophet Samuel, "Speak, Lord, for your servant is listening" (1 Sam 3:10), and the words of the Psalmist, "Here am I, Lord, I come to do your will" (Ps 40:7-8). We might note in passing that there can be an intimate connection between this spirit of freedom and a lifestyle that is marked by a spirit of simplicity.

How does one grow in this spirit of freedom? Ultimately it is through a cooperation with the power of God's grace and love working within us.

But one important way is through a deepening realization that one is a loved sinner, that one has been touched and healed. A profound conviction of God's steadfast love and fidelity can be a very liberating force that enables one to turn to God and seek Him alone and His service in a spirit of simplicity and joy. This freedom grows in a context of lively faith and is nourished in prayerful reflection on God's goodness, mercy, love, and providence.

Conclusion

In general, discernment in prayer is an inward looking process; the focus is mainly on the movements and experiences of God within us. But the process must never stop here for there should also be an outward dimension of discernment. First of all, as in so many areas of the spiritual life of man, a healthy norm is: "By their fruits you shall know them." There is a confirmatory aspect of all discernment in the external fruits that are in evidence and the good works that are produced. Secondly, the great commandment of love must always be kept in perspective, and a deepening union with God should lead to a deepening union with one's fellow man. An increasing sense of compassion for one's fellow man and his needs should flow from one's union with God. Finally, the process should lead to an increasing sensitivity to life and all its mysteries, to an increasing awareness of God's presence in all things, and to our own growth as contemplatives in action.

Christian Maturity and Spiritual Discernment

David T. Asselin, S.J.

Volume 27, 1968, pp. 581-595.

My purpose is to situate personal spiritual discernment in the context of faith-growth, that is, Christian maturity. From this viewpoint, to educate the faith is less a question of theological instruction than one of guided spiritual experience. I am thinking of the *teleioi* of Hebrews 5:14, "the *mature* who have their faculties trained by experience to discern between good and evil," an excellent summary of the Spirit's work of restoration out of the chaos which resulted from man's original attempt to determine good and evil for himself and on his own. The term could also be translated "the perfect," or, perhaps, "the personally fulfilled."

Faith, throughout this discussion, should be understood in the sense of Vatican II's *Decree on the Apostolate of the Laity:*

> Only by the light of faith [the impressive word is "only"] and by meditation on the word of God, can one always and everywhere recognize God, in whom "we live and move and have our being," seek His will in every event, see Christ in all men whether they are close to us or strangers, make correct judgments about the true meaning and value of temporal things, both in themselves and in their relationship to man's final goal.

Except for meditation on Scripture nothing is said in this text about the means of maturing the faith. The Council simply outlines the content of adult faith. What I should like to explore is an indispensable element in the process of maturation of this content.

The truth of the matter is that faith is not primarily a source of answers to our questions but rather our answer to the Lord's question, "Lovest thou me?'' In other words, I take faith not as quest for answers (to our intellectual problems) nor as a set of answers (to the questions of others), but as the answer of the whole person to the Lord inserting His Person and Spirit, and thus articulating Himself as the divine Word, in human life.

My general proposition is that at the very heart of growing in faith we find, necessarily, a refinement and increase of the grace of spiritual discernment. Without discernment there is no growth in faith. Spiritual discernment, therefore, is less a question of being intellectually clever than of being graced and called by the Lord to grow in knowledge of Him. All things serve the Lord of history; all persons are called to be the vehicles of His creative will; all men willy-nilly serve the God of human history's purposes. Otherwise, they would not be introduced into ongoing incarnational history. However, not everyone, so far, seems to hear the call to *know the Lord he serves,* to know Him as a friend does a friend, as a son his father, a wife her husband. To *know* Him is the mark of spiritual growth and maturity.

Faith-growth is God's work. Man can do no better than collaborate with the divine initiative in his spiritual life. This seems to imply several things.

First of all, as the spiritual point of departure, it demands an openness to *being moved* by God. This is the key to obedience as well as to all spiritual encounter. The fundamental Christian attitude, then, is that of a listener, one who is open to divine initiatives whatever they might be. It is radically and essentially a prayer-attitude, one that continues, or ought to continue, beyond prayer into the apostolate and every other work or experience.

The second implication is a need for some continual scrutiny and reflection in regard to the experiences interior to oneself in prayer and in all life's situations. This self-examination is needed not merely to lay hold of juridically imputable faults but more importantly to grow in habitual discrimination and discernment-by-faith of the various interior experiences and personal spiritual calls—impulses, inclinations, attractions, repugnances, assaults—that occur much more frequently than perhaps we either admit or spiritually discern.

The third demand is a growing ability to recognize and respond only to those experiences which are discernibly from the Lord. Here, in the area of concrete affectivity, are the contacts with the Lord's divine initiatives guiding the individual person or community. The difference between personal spiritual direction and spiritual government of a community involves a difference in the mode of spiritual scrutiny and recognition of the divine will in the concrete. Whatever accidental difference may emerge in the mode of reflection on experience, both the community scrutiny and the individual scrutiny lead ultimately to the possibility of a response which we may call ''rightly ordered,'' a direct response to inner vocation that gives first place to answering the Lord's question, ''Lovest thou me?''

In brief, these three requirements—openness to spiritual experience, reflection on it, and response-ability to it—are basic elements in the growth of *personal sensitivity* to the initiatives of the Lord, or spiritual discernment.

Whether on the community or individual level, in order to achieve government, spiritual direction, or faith-growth, the cooperation of several is required. The director and the directed, the superior and the subject, the spiritual father and his "son," must both be humbly alert in a collaboration of listening to the Lord's Spirit. The basic relationship of spiritual direction and government is a structured team-work of director and directed in discerning the will of the Lord in concrete situations. Both, then, must be continually subordinated to the Lord's Spirit and His word as the principal director. The hierarchy of subordination, in the context of spiritual direction, is that of a human director who by his calling is the servant of a relationship growing between the one directed and the Spirit of the Lord. In a sense, then, the human director takes his stand, spiritually, in the lower, not the higher, place.

In this relationship of spiritual direction, destined to serve the Lord's creative work in the individual and in the community, the responsibility falls first on the Lord Himself, secondly on the group or the individual called to Him, and finally on the servant of their relationship, the spiritual director. If there is any subordination to human direction in responding to God, this subordination must be established by the Lord and guaranteed by Him (or by a convenant or pact freely entered into on the part of the subject).

Growth in discernment of the action of God's Spirit is, then, the thing which truly matures and establishes in the faith a spiritual person or community. An authentic spiritual community is one which can be described in terms of its real awareness of being moved and directed by the Holy Spirit, on many levels. This awareness is not just found vaguely throughout the community but according to the clearly defined functions of properly subordinated individuals. As we find in the Gospels, to be great in the community of the Lord is to be the least and servant of all. The work of the one whose responsibility it is to direct others is a work of assisting them, as individuals and as a group, to hear and respond better to the Lord's initiatives in every situation.

This direction or government is a spiritual thing precisely to the extent that it is collaboration with the Lord's Spirit, the ultimate director and superior.

The Lord's indications, leads, initiatives, must be discerned as coming from Him and then followed, if a man is to serve the Lord in a way befitting man, that is by *knowing the Lord he serves*. There is, then, a need today to respect the importance and centrality of interior, personal, spiritual experience without undue fear of false mysticism or of the folly of the enthusiasts, quietists, *alumbrados*. Moreover, we must investigate the area of spiritual experience today because the Church is not only inviting us but requiring us to do so, in the words of one who cries out: "He who has an ear, let him hear what the Spirit says to the churches" (Ap 2:11).

The word "maturity" has been aptly defined by the Swiss psychologist, Jean Piaget, who made extensive studies of children in their process of development. Maturity, he found, is simply an increase in the capacity to differentiate in a practical manner interior experiences and operations. If we adopt this definition, then the life of faith in a man is mature to the extent that it involves a capacity to reflect upon, understand, discriminate between, and respond to, the inner spiritual *stimuli* that he experiences within himself.

The Lord's Personal Call

It might be well here to suggest some relationships between general law or principle on the one hand, and individuated personal experience on the other. To divorce the two is to fall into legalism and moralism, or into a kind of situation-ethic. The problem is how to relate these poles.

It is true that general law and principle rightly and concretely circumscribe each personal situation. But they do so only to the extent that this situation is common to all men, and not proper to this person as such. I mean that the situations of Peter and of Paul are correctly guided by general principle only insofar as Peter and Paul are men, therefore impersonally considered, not insofar as they are distinguished from each other *by name*. Peter qua Peter is more than just *a* man.

In this regard permit me to draw attention to the perfect way of knowing a man, intimately and personally, which is the Lord's way of knowing him, that is, by name. We read in Isaiah 43:1: "Fear not, for I have redeemed you; I have called you by name: you are mine." Or again, in John 10:3: "The sheep hear his voice, and he calls his own sheep by name and leads them forth."

Scripture continually reveals the personal and intimate knowledge that the Lord has of each of His creatures: "Before I formed you in the womb I knew you, before you were born I dedicated you, a prophet to the nations I appointed you" (Jer 1:5); "Lord, you have probed me and you know me, you understand my thoughts from afar, with all my ways you are familiar, even before a word is on my tongue, behold, O Lord, you know the whole of it, where can I go from your Spirit, from your presence where can I flee" (Ps 138:139).

Just as it is clear that the Lord knows and calls each man by name, it is equally clear that man becomes spiritually mature to the extent that he can recognize and acknowledge who it is that is calling him, responding to the Lord by name in all things:

> The days are coming, says the Lord, when I will make a new covenant with the House of Israel and the House of Judah. It will not be like the covenant I made with

their fathers the day I took them by the hand to lead them forth from the land of Egypt. For they broke my covenant and I had to show myself their master, says the Lord. But this is the covenant which I will make with the House of Israel after those days, says the Lord. I will place my law within them, and write it upon their hearts; I will be their God, and they shall be my people. No longer will they have need to teach their friends and kinsmen how to know the Lord. All, the least to the greatest, shall know Me, says the Lord, for I will forgive their evil doing and remember their sin no more (Jer 31:31ff.).

It seems clear, here and elsewhere in Scripture, that God is establishing with each human person as well as with His community a new spiritual relationship of tremendous value which exceeds the expectations of authentic Christian personalism today.

In order to discover the meaning of Peter qua Peter, and of Paul as unique and distinct from Peter, in the context of universal salvation history (which, after all, is the task in which spiritual directors and superiors are, I believe, primarily intended to assist), it is necessary to discover the unique meaning, value, and orientation that is proper to Peter's spiritual situation precisely as distinct from Paul's before the Lord. By what kind of logic is this sort of knowledge attained?

Over and above the universal validity of general principle and law, Peter, as an unrepeatable, unique individual, must be guided by a logic that is other than the logic of general principle and universal law. In other words, there are two kinds of logic.

One logic, which we might call conceptual or propositional, is the basis for reasoning in universally valid terms. The point of departure, the principle or the foundation from which the successive insights and conclusions proceed according to this logic will be an axiom. It begins therefore with a self-evident proposition.

Logic of the Concrete

There is another logic, however, the logic of concrete, unique, and individual events and persons (which, incidentally, is the way God apprehends things). Here, the human foundation or first principle will no longer be an axiom but an experience. As the logic of conceptual knowledge is based on axiomatic propositions, so the logic of concrete knowledge is based on concrete experience. *Mature* faith-response to the Lord's word can emerge only from *personal* encounter with Him.

I think it is the job of superiors and spiritual directors to point to those authentic experiences whereby the Lord is communicating Himself to individuals and communities, thus guiding their spiritual growth and governing their development as Christian persons. This concrete knowledge of the Lord and of His ways can only be had, as the Vatican Council proposes, "by meditation on the word of God." Faith-growth is inseparable from prayer-life. Both are areas of fundamental concern to all who are called not only by the Lord's, "Lovest thou me?" but also by His, "Feed my lambs and sheep."

What, therefore, the individual *as such* ought to decide in the area of liberty and private responsibility cannot be fully determined by general principle or law. It is of vital importance, however, that what is decided be determined with spiritual certitude, not merely by guesswork, accident, or whim. This is precisely why reliable, that is, mature, faith-discernment of interior experiences and events is important. Otherwise, we run a risk of considering these experiences as mere psychological phenomena, avoiding the whole world of concrete events in function of which spiritual discernment and maturity can take place.

Rather, we must approach the world of private and group experience as filled with the glorious presence *(shekinah)* of the Lord, the indications of His will and concrete providence, and perhaps the presence of an adverse spirit. Hence, it is only a faith-awareness and discernment of these events which can lead to an understanding of the individual or community relationship to the Lord, an estimation of their spiritual maturity, and a reliable increase in their personal freedom and responsibility.

No concrete choice can be well ordered in the faith unless it coincides with the determinations of the Lord of all human history. To be aware of these things in the concrete is the only way for a man to be "with it" spiritually, or "where the action is." To be with the Lord of history, who revealed Himself as being so continually and intimately with us, we must be in personal communication with Him in all things. Therefore, the particular experience that functions as a self-evident first principle for the logic of concrete individual knowledge is nothing short of a real experience of the Lord communicating Himself and uttering His invitation and call directly to a person for his unique situation.

Growth in discernment presupposes several elements. There must be, first of all, inner experience; second, repeated reflection on this experience; third, a discrimination between various experiences, not from the point of view of mere natural causalities (psychological or otherwise), but from that of personal faith in the Lord of concrete history; fourth, an evaluation of these interior experiences from this faith-standpoint; finally, the capacity to receive and obey those movements which are discernibly from the Lord, or at least clearly not inspired by an adverse spirit.

This is the only way to be *with* the Lord, and where His *action* is, in reality. Only thus can a man truly grow as a mature person and find fulfillment. He must find his own personal relationship with the creator and Lord of all things, and place himself at His service unreservedly.

Experience, then, of encounter and contact with the Lord, of listening to and of being guided by Him directly, must lie within the capacities of ordinary Christian faith-maturity. Otherwise, how could an adult Christian enjoy an authentic spiritual calling? The only way a man can be divinely called to a personal vocation is "by name," which means by a unique and personal encounter with the Lord in terms of incommunicable inner experience. Surely our adult Christians, in the light of Vatican II, are not merely destined to serve the Lord, but intimately to know the Lord they serve. Surely their service must flow from a personal knowledge of Him, a concrete knowledge which cannot be grasped from theology or from psychology or even from the mere absence of "impediments to vocation," but from personal experience and prayer.

There is question here of something mystical, at least on an elementary level, in the ordinary faith-growth of a Christian—something entailing immediate conscious contact with the person of the Lord.

Hence, we confront today a mysticism that is to be recognized and fostered within the *ordinary* providence of God's grace for anyone called to *know Him*. This kind of knowledge is what specifies the relationship between God and His people, God and the individual, in the whole Judaeo-Christian history of vocation.

I submit that today the discernment of spirits, as it is called, is the most relevant focal point in our spiritual heritage, because it is the concrete logic of personal spiritual knowledge of *las cosas internas,* the "interior things," the life of inner spiritual experience. Only a refined spiritual discernment will guide a man to mature self-possession, freeing him from inner disorder in his choosing so that he may enjoy a growing, divine encounter of faith in all circumstances. In this way, his faith-awareness will envelop, enlighten, guide everything else in his life, so that he will not be able to love anything or anyone save "in the Lord." It is only within this world of each man's personal experience that his faith-response can be given to the evocative word on the Lord.

Today in this age of personalism, of self-discovery, of fulfillment, of communication and dialogue, there is a dying interest in any gospel that might limit itself to spiritual absolutes and generalities, to moralism or trite devotionalism, just as there is a reaction against the spiritual anonymity of the lonely crowd" and the impersonality of the "organization man" in our "secular city." Such labels indicate the personal alienation that threatens urbanized man today. We all know the reaction formation which arises against this situation, offering a purely secular salvation in terms of this-worldly fulfillment of man's four basic desires: his desire for security, affection, variety, and esteem. Man's real salvation today, however, according to our Christian world-view based on the new convenant announced in Jeremiah 31, 31 ff., entails being radically graced by God in such a way that the divine presence and will can be known and acknowledged personally by each man.

Confronted exclusively with general principles and laws, or the enunciation of general truths based upon them which do not focus on each man as a unique person but necessarily treat him merely as another instance of numerically multipliable human nature undistinguished by any name, modern man will remain deaf to his true personal call to greatness, spiritually immature. If the Christian logic of concrete personal vocation is ignored today, there is a growing danger that tomorrow both Peter and Paul will search for their identity outside the authentic Christian view of things, perhaps against it.

It is only through the gradual and inevitably painful education of a man's faith-view of concrete particulars, that is, the education of his capacity spiritually to discern concrete reality within himself or others, that he can be entrusted with the responsibility of personally determining the steps and measures which bear on his own salvation or that of others.

We are far from endorsing, therefore, an undiscerning confidence and blind acceptance of everything that a man spontaneously is inclined to think best. According to the view of some, everything is acceptable or good which inwardly attracts or moves a man, as long as it is not a clear inclination to sin. As a matter of fact, if it were all that easy it would hardly be worth discussing.

Spiritual responsibility is insured only by an authentic growth of the capacity to discern the personal word and will of Christ for oneself or for another. This merely reaffirms the central Christian position which is one of listening to and following the word of God addressed to man: "Blessed is he who hears the word of God and keeps it"; or again: "My mother and brothers and sisters are those who hear the word of God and keep it."

To some degree or other all of us have this problem of faith-maturity. Therefore, we must consider maturity not as a terminal achievement but rather as *maturation,* a continuum of emerging awareness of interior encounter and personal vocation initiated by the Lord. All this applies to community experience as well as to that of the individual, and it includes in its ambit the beginner as well as the *teleios* in the sense of Hebrews 5:14, "the one who has faculties trained by experience to discern good from evil."

This points to faith-guided discernment as the correction of Adam's fault who attempted, according to Genesis 3, on his own and independently of the Lord's personal indication, to "eat of the fruit of the tree of the knowledge of good and evil," that is, to discern for himself independently of God what was good and evil in the concrete.

Hence any education in the discernment of right from wrong must emerge from the radical faith-position of one who is a listener to the Lord: "All that is not of faith is sin" (Rom 14:23).

Structure and Individuation

We are always confronted with the necessity of admitting the young into formation structures in such a way as to allow for varying degrees of spiritual maturity already achieved and to foster further personal growth in the knowledge of God's will and love by discernment. Moreover, at the beginning of the process of formation there are two factors polarized, which, I feel, need to undergo considerable change in their basic relationship by the end of that formative process.

We can label those two factors "structure" and "individuation." Structure, here, means a generally predictable behavior pattern within which the individual and the group are directed to maturity in their encounter with the Lord. For beginners there is need of a meaningful and reasonable overall structure in which the young candidates are introduced to spiritual responsibility. This structure will be more extensive and more detailed in virtue of the greater need for assistance and protection required in the period of initial growth.

By individuation, in the context of formation, I mean everything that falls under the general heading of personal admonition, directive, prescription, correction, or guidance.

It is my general impression that we have not been afflicted so much with overstructure in formation (we have had much structure but I think much is needed to begin the process of faith-growth) as with a kind of reverence for this structure which tends to find maturity in terms of structural function and hence to preserve initial structures unchanged throughout religious life.

I also believe we have been afflicted with an anxious protection and maintenance of this structure by overstricture, so that the individual has been given to feel that the structure is an absolute value and that his least exterior failure or fault will be judged as maximal when, in fact, it might be objectively and spiritually minimal.

A process of destructuring must occur. But, more importantly, we ought to begin formation with complete gentleness, patience, and the allowance for personal uniqueness, in the application of strictures within the required structure.

With structure and individuation polarized in this way at the point of departure of formation, let me describe the general evolution which hopefully might occur with respect to the relationship between structure and individuation over the years. By its end a period of formation ought to reveal much less structure (because we can presume that with discernment the spiritual adult has become more personally aware of his Lord and has achieved a more refined sensitivity to the promptings of the Holy Spirit) and much more stricture (because he has grown in spiritual sensitivity, in his capacity for self-direction, for discerning the Lord in all things by faith and love, and is consequently more accountable, that is, responsible, for these things).

No community ought to aim at being completely unstructured or informal as long as men are mortal and original sin still affects their motivation, decisions, and efforts. But I believe much failure in formation is due to the initial overemphasis of both stricture and structure, producing a reaction against both. We often end up with serious difficulties not so much with the young as the old and religiously "formed," who, when it is safe to throw off structures, will no longer listen to stricture either. This, of course, reveals that their formation left them spiritually immature. How difficult it is at times to tell a man who has been twenty-five years in religious life what to do or not to do. It is not easy, if he is obstinate. It is not easy if he feels: "Now that I have gone through that formation bit, you don't push me around."

I think a lot of our scandal emerges precisely when the process of destructuring takes place revealing little faith-education or spiritual maturity to fill up the vacuum created by this process. It shows that no growth in spiritual responsibility has supplanted the firmness of protective structures.

By the end of our periods of formation, when the collective factors have been diminished on the level of structure, there ought to emerge a deeper spiritual relationship with the superior, confessor, personal director, on the individual level, that is, on the level of concrete prescription, spiritual direction, and discernment. I feel that little faults in mature persons are much more serious than little faults in beginners. Perhaps we ought to increase the importance of private direction for the mature, not only in the sense of reprehension and correction of faults, but also of more tailored discernment of the will of the Lord. Existentially, this continuum of formation ought to be a movement from external law to the interior law of love.

St. Paul had insight into such freedom. He claims that we are freed by learning to love like Christ. He does not mean by freedom that we are no longer bound by external law, but rather that we are no longer driven, captured, or urged by anything except by divine love: "Caritas Christi urget nos." To the degree that mature Christian love existentially directs a man's choices, his need for external law and direction is lessened. Only by the strength of the Lord's personal initiatives of love in his regard will he be stimulated to respond to the Lord's word calling him to share responsibility for his own salvation and that of others. This call in its fullness is identical with the vocation to enter the paschal mystery of the Lord's suffering service, death, and resurrection.

Hence, we can say with Vatican II that it is "only by faith and by meditation on the word of God" that we can find God's will in anything, discover Christ in our fellowman, or evaluate temporal things in their true light, that is, in the light of salvation history into which all things have happily been assumed by the risen Lord.

There is no possibility of mature faith-growth unless, between the beginning and the end of its spectrum, there is inserted personal, incommunicable experience of entrance into the mystery of Christ's dying and rising.

The problem today is a growing tendency to skip the passion and death in an attempt to establish the Resurrection. We need more than ever a spiritual awareness of the contemporary dimensions of the passion and death, such as you find in St. Paul who identifies the mystery of Christ's *nekrosis* with his own experiences of suffering, persecution, and rejection in the apostolate and ministry of the word.

The word "mystery" in this context means a human experience of the Word made flesh such as we imply when we speak of the "mysteries" of the rosary or when we contemplate the "mysteries of the public life of Jesus." The definitive mystery of the Word make flesh is His redemptive experience of dying and rising, which is the matrix of all Christian formation and maturity.

Growth and formation involve the development of a conscious love relationship with the Lord. Lovers are those who share intimately each other's experiences of joy and suffering and know by experience the depth and the breadth and the mystery of the unique other. The Lord has this kind of knowledge of us—a knowledge which can become the friendship of mutual love only if we dwell also in this kind of knowledge of Him. Therefore, our entrance into His mystery of passion and death implies, in the first place, a growth in our awareness of His complete entrance into our mystery, His complete appropriation of our personhood and life experience.

Neither this awareness nor the experience of entry into His mystery are vague abstractions. His definitive entrance into our present life was by a very real dying and rising. It is this experience of His that has become the key to our faith-awareness of Him. Thus, His suffering, dying, rising, unfold anew in our life experience because of our intimate, mutual involvement with Him, revealed by faith.

Conclusion

The real spiritual theology of action, of renewal, and of labor (including the labors of the apostolate and ministry of the word), centers on this contemporary sharing in Christ's redemptive death and resurrection. You will find this everywhere in St. Paul, for instance in I Corinthians 1:3 ff. and 4:7 ff: "The sufferings of Christ abound in us, the consolation in you"; or again: "We are continually carrying about in our bodies the dying state of Jesus so that the living state of Jesus may be manifest in our bodies too."

So, too, Paul speaks of the personal mandate through Christian baptism of entering into the mystery of Christ's death and resurrection, which implies finding the dimensions of His mystery as it is realized concretely in one's own. This will involve a personal sharing of the emptying-out or *kenosis* of Christ, an experience of human barrenness, agony and dereliction out of which alone can emerge the marvelous truthfulness of the Lord rising in our personal world, today.

I do not think this is going to be appreciated if it is merely described, as

I do here. It is something that must be learned from experience under the guidance of that kind of spiritual discernment that calls a thing by its right name, as it is occurring in a man's experience. No natural terms or categories are sufficient to capture the meaning of this experience of entry into the mystery of Christ that is ours. Hence, the *language of faith* is the principal language to be used in spiritual direction and discernment.

Nobody can accomplish for me this work of collaboration with Christ to which I am personally called. Without personal inner encounter I have knowledge only of a kind of "unknown God," which really is no knowledge at all; and the danger of not knowing God is of becoming *adokimos,* someone of an undiscerning mind, who knows created reality by experience without discerning the Lord and Creator. This was the failure of the pagans according to Romans 1:18 ff., where Paul describes their decline through various stages of degradation because they were unable to discern the will and love of the Lord of all creation.

The human conversation with God was broken off in the garden of Eden, not because God stopped speaking to man but because man stopped listening to God. All sacred history recounts the restoration not only in the individual but in the city of man of the ability to listen to the word of God articulated in the contemporary events and realities of each successive age, as in a continuing kaleidoscope of the Lord's presence articulated in the eternal "today" of man's relationship to his Lord.

The builders of the tower of Babel were dispersed by God because they attempted to build the city on their own, without His initiative, His word. Abraham, in the next chapter, is the one in whom the listening to God's word historically begins to be restored. Eventually, the city image of Babel in Chapter 11 of Genesis, the city which is almost a bad word in the early parts of Scripture, becomes the very end-time symbol of the awareness of God's intimate presence and conversation in Apocalypse 21, where the new city created by God, the new Jerusalem, needs neither temple nor source of light other then God Himself and his Son the Lamb. Eventually, the Lord who is Father and the Lamb will themselves be both temple of worship and source of light for the city of man. This symbol marks the terminal point of community salvation. If you read Apocalypse 21, you will find that the individual relationship to the Lord emerges as perfect along with the de-structured community relationship to the Lord: "He who overcomes shall possess these things, and I will be his God, and he shall be my son" (Ap 21:7).

There is no opposition, then, between the community-growth and individual fulfillment. We reach full personhood in the community of the Lord's people by sharing an awareness of God's personal presence and glory. We celebrate this in our daily Eucharist. We announce these Christian facts of life and we promote them, there. We increase and grow in our realization of them by listening privately and together to the word of God, and together and in private responding wholeheartedly.

In conclusion I should like to indicate a fundamental criterion by which the authenticity of faith-growth and spiritual discernment must always be measured. The fundamental attitude of the believer is of one who listens. It is to the Lord's utterances that he gives ear. In as many different ways and on as many varied levels as the listener can discern the word and will of the Lord manifested to him, he must respond with all the Pauline "obedience of faith."

Obedience always implies an attitude of listening, signified by the Latin *ob-audire* and Greek *hupo-akouo*. It is the attitude of receptivity, passivity, and poverty of one who is always in need, radically dependent, conscious of his creaturehood.

Freedom, faith-growth, and spiritual maturity must always begin with fundamental obedience to the Lord's laws, directives, and providence for the individual and the community. The evolution of faith to spiritual adulthood is measured not by neglecting or escaping these basic divine dispositions so as to be no longer bound by them, but rather by transcending external laws and prescriptions so as to be bound more deeply and intimately by the greater demands of an internal law uttered in the heart.

One is always *bound* by general law and principle and by external authority legitimately exercised, but one can transcend this dimension as the *motive* of response to the Lord to the degree that one can discern and obey the internal law of love imprinted in the heart by the Spirit, establishing the new covenant announced by Jeremiah 31:31 ff.

Bound by external law and authority, our faith-growth consists in being moved by the internal: "Caritas Christi urget nos!" No internal discernment of the Lord's will and vocation is valid if it disobeys or destroys the Lord's external dispositions exercised by legitimate authority and institution. There is only one spirit breathing on many levels where and how He wills.

The authentic maturity of faith by spiritual discernment will manifest itself in a fourfold reconciliation of man, matching the fourfold human conflict introduced by man's primitive disobedience: a reconciliation (1) with the Lord in a Spirit of prayerful sonship crying "Abba," (2) within oneself by the peace that replaces the shame of guilt, (3) with one's neighbor by the love that replaces anger and fear, (4) and with *ktisis* or physical creation by a resurrection.

Profile of the Spirit:
A Theology of Discernment of Spirits

John R. Sheets, S.J.

Volume 30, 1971, pp. 363-376.

For various reasons the subject of what is traditionally known in Christian spirituality as discernment of spirits is coming to the fore. The literature on the subject is growing.[1] Without pretending to discover something new we hope to add another point of view to the traditional way of looking at the discernment of spirits.

Ordinarily the idea of discernment of spirits is concerned for the most part with the interior motions in the individual.[2] With the help of prayer, purification, and spiritual direction one attempts to sift out the various movements to see what is genuinely prompted by the Holy Spirit from what is alien, in order to come to a decision in accord with the movement of the Spirit.

The emphasis in discernment has been located mainly in the individual subject and with the attempt to discern the various elements at work in himself. Today, however, it seems necessary to bring out other comple-

---

[1]See the excellent study *Ignatian Discernment* by John Carroll Futrell, S.J., "Studies in the Spirituality of Jesuits," N. 2 (St. Louis: Institute of Jesuit Sources, 1970). In the third footnote of this work there is a select bibliography of works on discernment.

[2]"Discernment . . . involves choosing the way of the light of Christ instead of the way of the darkness of the Evil One and living out the consequences of this choice through discerning what specific decisions and actions are demanded to follow Christ here and now. The *diakrisis pneumatōn*—discernment of spirits—is a 'sifting through' of interior experiences in order to determine their origin and to discover which ones are movements toward following the way of light" (Futrell, *Ignatian Discernment*, p. 47).

214

mentary aspects in order to do justice to a wider view of man. There has to be a broader view of discernment of spirits to keep pace with a developing Christian anthropology.

We would like to view discernment as the two mutually interdependent foci of an ellipse. Traditionally only one of the foci has received attention: the subject and the internal movements of his soul. This view has to be complemented with the other focus of attention which is concerned with what is "ahead of" the subject.

This takes into consideration the *term* of all discernment which is *closer union* while not neglecting the origins of the movement. It emphasizes discernment as a way of seeing the *convergence* of various elements to effect greater union. It lays stress on the "Spirit-ahead" of us, calling us, rather than concentrating only on the "Spirit-behind-us," moving us from within. Further, it brings out the fact that discernment is not simply a way for one's own spiritual advancement, but that it has a larger dimension. It is the way that *history* becomes weighed with the power of the Spirit, the way that the Spirit inserts Himself into the movement of history, giving it Christic orientation. Instead of what can often be simply self-analysis it puts the emphasis on the *characteristics of the Holy Spirit* which form a profile against which we project the incipient movements in ourselves.

Discernment, therefore, is a process of seeing incipient growing of the Spirit, distinguishing this from what is in reality incipient death. It is like trying to see the face of someone at a distance. That is only possible if one is well acquainted with the "face of the Spirit" before one attempts to recognize Him from a distance. For this reason in the last section of what follows we have tried to sketch the main features of His face.

Discernment, therefore, has to do with the pneumatic self, the spirited self, too often, however, it is looked upon as some kind of a supernatural psychoanalysis. We approach a spiritual phenomenon with an attitude and apparatus that are unspiritual, as if we had some kind of a water witch to detect where the genuine foundations lie. We must approach the spiritual spiritually.

Discernment is related to human prudence but is not identified with it. Through discernment we try to see how the Spirit-ahead is drawing things into a Christic focus. The place where all of these converge is the epiphany of the Spirit. The tighter the convergence the closer the union, and the more does the Spirit place His imprint on the self and on History. This type of discernment is not simply a good prudential judgment. It does not arise out of the data presented, though it makes use of all the data. It is a judgment which is the result of an encounter of the Holy Spirit from above with the human spirit from below. It is larger than the data though it makes use of all the data. It involves not only good sense but an affinity with the person of the Spirit and empathy with His goals.

Human prudence is also a judgment about convergence, but it arises entirely from a correct assessment of the data. There is not anything in the prudential judgment which was not in some way in the data before. Prudence draws the various elements into a judgment for action by drawing them into a human focus. Spiritual discernment draws them into a Christic focus. The two processes of judging are related to one another in a way analogous to the relationship of reason to faith.

This also helps us see how the Christic focus can be achieved even though, after doing all that is possible, the human focus fails. This is the mystery of Christ's Passion and resurrection. Failure, frustration, death of the human point of focus can be taken up into the Christic focus and result in an even greater epiphany of the Spirit.

Before we attempt to draw up some norms for the discernment of spirits, it will be helpful to present very briefly some preliminary ideas concerning (1) the need for discernment, (2) the difficulty, (3) the dynamics of discernment, namely, the presence of the Spirit in the Christian, (4) the moments and the modalities of discernment.

The Need for Discernment

Discernment is necessary to answer the fundamental question: Along which path does life lie, not life simply as existence, but life in greater abundance? All discernment is a matter of determining the path of life from the path of death: "And you are to say to this people, 'Yahweh says this: Look, I now set in front of you the way of life and the way of death'" (Jr 21:8). The difficulty comes from the fact that the path of death simulates that of life. The very first temptation presented in Scripture shows the need for discernment. The life offered by God is presented as death, and the death offered by the serpent is presented as life: "You would not die at all: for God knows that the very day you eat of the tree your eyes will be opened, and you will be like gods who know good from evil" (Gn 4:5).

In the Old Testament two main types of discernment are shown to be necessary: the necessity of the prophet to discern within himself what comes from God's word from his own "dream,"[3] and secondly the need for the people to discern the false prophet from the true.[4] The experience of Elijah is a paradigm for the discernment of spirits. He did not find God in any of the commotions ordinarily associated with a divine epiphany, the wind, earthquake, fire, but in the gentle breeze, which was the least likely form of God's manifestation (1 Kg 19:9-13).

In the New Testament there is much more stress than in the Old on the

---

[3]"The prophet who has a dream, let him tell a dream: and he who has a word, let him speak my word faithfully, says the Lord. What has the chaff in common with the wheat? says the Lord" (Jr 23:28). There are many places where the prophets distinguish what comes from them and what comes from God; for example, Am 7:2-9,15, 8:1-2; Mi 7:1-10; Is 6:5-12; 16:9-11.

[4]This is a favorite theme in the prophets Isaiah, Jeremiah, and Ezekiel. See, for example, Is 28:7-13; 29:15-24; 56:9-12; 57:1-5; Jr 5:4,31; Ez 13; La 2:14; Ho 4:5; Dt 13:2-3.

need for discernment. Christ Himself as filled with the Holy Spirit is the discerner: "And the Spirit of the Lord shall rest upon him, the spirit of wisdom and understanding, a spirit of counsel and power, a spirit of knowledge and of the fear of Yahweh. (The fear of Yahweh is his breath.) He does not judge by appearances, he gives no verdict on hearsay . . ." (Is 11:2-3). He discerns the temptation of the evil one in the desert, the activity of the devil in Judas, and the evil hearts of those who want to kill Him (see Jn 8:33-4). He discerns His own heart as always open to the Father: "I always do what is pleasing to him" (Jn 8:29). He stressed the need for discernment because there will be many who claim His own authority to speak (see Mt 24:6).

John stresses the fact that spiritual phenomena in the Church have to be discerned: "But do not trust any and every spirit, my friends; test the spirits, to see whether they are from God" (1 Jn 4:1). He goes on to describe the norm for discernment: "Every spirit which acknowledges that Jesus Christ has come in the flesh is from God, and every spirit which does not thus acknowledge Jesus is not from God." The Holy Spirit speaks one word which is rich in its tonality: Christ.

Both in his own life and in his instructions to others Paul emphasize the need for discernment. The point cannot be developed here, but it would be instructive to study Paul's own life as one who discerns the Spirit. Surely the advice he gave to the Galatians was lived first of all in his own life: "If the Spirit is the source of our life, let the Spirit also direct our course" (Ga 5:25).[5]

He insists constantly on the need for discernment in the lives of the Christians. Often he uses the word *dokimazo* which means to test, prove: "Try to discover what the Lord wants of you, having nothing to do with the futile works of darkness but *exposing* them by contrast" (Ep 5:10-1). "Bring all to the test" (1 Th 5:21). "Put yourselves to the test" (2 Co 13:5). "A man must test himself before eating his share of the bread and drinking from the cup" (1 Co 11:28). There is a very special gift of discernment which belongs to the charismatic manifestations of the Spirit: "There are varieties of gifts, but the same Spirit . . . and another the ability to distinguish true spirits from false" (1 Co 12:4-10). This is the gift of discerning whether the spirits are truly spiritual, or evil.

Finally he stresses the need for discernment in order to preserve the purity of the Gospel message: "The Spirit says expressly that in after times some will desert from the faith and give their minds to subversive doctrines inspired by devils . . ." (1 Tm 4:1). Paul sees that it is the evil spirits who are ultimately responsible for the defections from the truth of the Gospel

---

[5]Paul sees his own conscience as cooperating with the Holy Spirit in forming his judgment: "I am speaking the truth as a Christian, and my own conscience, enlightened by the Holy Spirit, assures me it is no lie: in my own heart there is great grief and unceasing sorrow" (Rm 9:1). The word he uses is "co-witnessing."

(see 2 Th 2:9-11; 2 Co 2:11).

The same idea is brought our when Peter speaks of the fact that there will be false prophets among Christians just as there were among the people of Israel: "But Israel had false prophets as well as true; and you likewise will have false teachers among you" (2 P 2:1).

The Scripture, therefore, in both the Old and New Testaments, shows the importance of discernment in two ways: first of all, by showing the *practice* of discernment in those who bring to us the word of God (the prophets, Paul, John, Peter, and in an eminent way in Christ Himself); and secondly by showing the *need for discernment* corresponding to three different ways in which the Spirit acts: through discerning His will for us in our personal lives, through discerning the true Gospel from the false, and through discerning a genuine charism from what is inauthentic.

The Difficulty of Discernment

Experience shows us that it is not easy to discern the spirits. This is the lesson we read in Scripture, in history, and in our own personal lives. This could be developed at length. For the present, however, we would like to comment briefly on the three main sources of the difficulty: from the *term* to which the Spirit is moving, from the *self*, and from the *circumstances*.

The term of all activity of the Spirit is toward greater union with Christ and through this toward union with one another. When the union which is aimed at is more personal, it is also more delicate and fragile. In love relationships the bond has more of invitation and less of physical force or compulsion, more freedom, less entrapment, more speaking through silence rather than through words, more awareness through mutual attunement than through external signs. This is the first source of the difficulty of discernment. We are trying to pick up signals that are invitations to a union that is deeper.

The second difficulty comes from the self. Before one can discern, he has to be discerned. He has to allow the Word of God to discern him. He must be purified by the coal from the altar of God's holiness. Religious discernment is not simply a matter of finding out right answers, as one does in mathematics: nor is it simply a matter of depth analysis practiced in psychology. Discernment implies the docility of heart which is the same as purity of heart. What is being discerned is not simply a truth as an abstraction, but a love-truth. For this reason discernment involves not simply knowledge but identification with the truth, and a desire for progressive assimilation. The Holy Spirit is the absorbing Spirit. To discern one has to open himself to allow death to be swallowed by life. The difficulty of discernment, therefore, comes from the human heart itself: "The heart is treacherous above all things, and desperately sick—who can understand it?" (Jr 17:9). We are all aware of the proclivity of the human heart to rationalize any position, to overlook whatever might direct our eyes to the truth, to adapt the truth to ourselves, rather than to adapt ourselves to the truth.

The third source of difficulty of discernment comes from the circumstances. Sometimes the issue is so complicated that even presupposing openness to the Spirit and purity of heart it is not easy to see where greater union lies. An obvious case is that of discerning one's vocation. After one has taken all of the steps necessary, with the proper consultation, he has to let his net down into the unknown with trust in the Spirit who is drawing him.

In describing the music of Beethoven someone wrote that when you hear it you have the feeling that the one particular note just had to follow the other, that it was, so to speak, made in heaven. No other note would have fitted the "logic of beauty." This remark about music can easily be applied to the discernment of the note of the Spirit that simply "has to" follow. It is not easy to discern it, but it does follow a sequence that is the "logic of the Spirit." If one is attuned to the Spirit he has a sense for the "logic of the Spirit."

The Dynamics of Discernment: The Presence of the Spirit in the Christian

We have to recover the New Testament sense of the role of the Spirit in Christian life. What the soul of man is to his natural life, the Spirit is to Christian life. The Spirit is the source, guide, atmosphere, tone, pattern of Christian life.

Once again we have to content ourselves in the interests of economy of space to some brief allusions to this important truth without developing it at length.

The gift of the Spirit sums up the whole purpose of the Messiah's coming (Jn 1:33). The Gospel of St. John stresses the fact that through Christ's passion, death, resurrection His own body becomes the source for the Spirit. Paul emphasizes the new life of the Christian, with the new dynamics of the Holy Spirit: "The love of God has been poured into our hearts by the Holy Spirit which has been given us" (Rm 5:5). The whole of Romans 8 is a description of the new spiritual order of man as contrasted with his old, unspiritual self: "So then, my brothers, there is no necessity for us to obey our unspiritual selves or to live unspiritual lives" (Rm 8:12). The Spirit we have received has made us sons (Rm 8:15). He has revealed to our spirit the deep things of God (1 Co 2:10-1). His presence is the proof of what we cannot see, that we are sons of God (Gal 4:6-7). Through him we are renewed (Tt 3:5-6).[6]

It is important, therefore, to recognize the encompassing role of the

---

[6]The Jerusalem Bible in footnote, Rm 5:5, gives an extensive series of references to the doctrine of the Holy Spirit in the New Testament.

Spirit. In discerning we are not only trying to discern the presence of the Spirit, but the very process of discerning is from-with-in-by-through the Spirit. It is Spirit as possessed and possessing attempting to discern "Spirit on the way," the movement toward greater and greater union.

The Moments and Modalities of Discernment

Finally, before taking up the norms for discernment, we want to say a word about the moments and modalities of discernment. By moments we mean the qualities that distinguish in importance different periods of time, either by reason of special gifts of the Spirit or special decisions to be made. Modalities of discernment refer to the various ways in which the spirits are discerned.

Not every human moment is a divine moment. Sacred history teaches us that there are certain moments which are *kairoi,* special moments of grace, where history receives a special impetus of the Spirit. This is true in one's personal life as well as the life of the Church. These are moments of special invitations by the Spirit, of special responses, and of special discernment.

Further there is a modality of discernment which belongs to the ordinary day-to-day living of our lives and one which belongs to special occasions. In the ordinary more or less routine events that make up our workaday world, discernment is not conscious or reflective but takes place through the vital dialogue between our new self as graced through the Spirit and the circumstances of our lives. The habitual "spiritual set" that comes from the Spirit equips a person with an instinct for the Spirit and spiritual values.

On other occasions discernment is conscious, reflective, prolonged, methodical. The rules given by St. Ignatius are among the best known help in this process of conscious discernment.

Under modalities of discernment we could also include *personal* and *group discernment.* Personal discernment takes place in dialogue with God, the self-as-graced, and the circumstances. Group discernment adds the social dimension. It can be imagined as a pyramid. Those involved have a common base, the dialogue is with God, one another, and the circumstances, searching for the point where all of these converge into the greatest union possible. The main examples of group discernment are the general councils of the Church (see the Council of Jerusalem, Acts 15:28 "It is the decision of the Holy Spirit and our decision"). Other groups with a common bond and goal can engage in discernment. This is different from *group discussion* because it takes place in a whole new order with conscious and constant reference to the communion with God and with one another in the Spirit.

We have spoken of the need of discernment, especially as this is brought home to us through Scripture, the various difficulties in discernment, the dynamics of discernment which come with a new existence in the Spirit, and the moments and modalities of discernment. With these thoughts as a background we would like to give some norms for the discernment of the presence of the Holy Spirit. They are not expected to be some kind of a handy kit for spiritual discernment. They are an attempt to present a profile of the Spirit so that we can recognize Him when we see Him. We cannot be expected to recognize Him in our inner selves unless we have some idea of what He looks like in Himself. We have taken thirteen characteristics as a help to discernment basing them on the nature of the Spirit Himself.

Some Norms for Discernment

1. The first norm comes from the fact that the Spirit is the *Holy* Spirit. He is the consecrating Spirit, drawing men and the world into the orbit of God's own life.[7]

Holiness is one of those rich words which defies adequate description. It means that one's life is inauthentic, no matter how good a person is, unless it is authenticized with the special life of God, that is, unless the ways of God are incarnated in the ways of man, so that man is not simply made to the image and likeness of God through creation, but is shaped to the inner life of God by becoming the incarnation of God's ways, that is, His holiness.

The sense of consecration has the concomitant feature of bringing an awareness of the desecration in our lives, a sense of sin: "He will confute the world, and show where wrong and right and judgment lie" (Jn 16:8). For this reason, the Holy Spirit will never be the in-spirit, the spirit of the times. Though He is the comforting Spirit, he will never be the comfortable Spirit. He has to illumine darkness, and men do not want their deeds illumined. Augustine's remark is perennially true: "They love the truth when it enlightens; they hate it when it reproves; they love it when it reveals its own self, and they hate it when it reveals themselves."

The first rule for discernment, then, is this: Does it bring a greater sense of consecretion, an integration of life through holiness, and at the same time the need for purification, the sense of our distance from God?

2. The second norm is drawn from the fact that the Holy Spirit is *Spirit*. Everything produces its own likeness as far as possible. The Holy Spirit by His very nature spiritualizes.

It is difficult to appreciate what spirit and spiritualization mean not only because of the depth-nature of spirit, but also because of the false impression most people have of spirit. For many spirit means non-human, or less than human, unreal, foreign to the world of man. In the Scripture, however, spirit connotes power that is creative, overpowering, sustaining, surprising, inspiring, gentle in its force, but forceful in gentleness (see Elijah, 1 Kg 19). The spirit puts life into the dry bones of humanity: "I shall put my spirit in

---

[7]The theme of the consecration of Christians is a common one in the New Testament. For example, Rm 15:16, where Paul speaks of his ministry as a life of consecration; 1 Co 6:11; 2 Th 2:13; Rm 8:1-13; 1 Jn 3:7,8; 1 P 2:5.

you and you shall live" (Ez 37:1).

How does an act that is merely human become spiritual? It becomes enveloped with, impregnated with a new life. St. Paul describes in detail the spiritual life of the Christian (Rm 8:1 ff): "The unspiritual are interested only in what is unspiritual, but the spiritual are interested in spiritual things. It is death to limit oneself to what is unspiritual; life and peace can only come with concern for the spiritual" (Rm 8:5,6).[8]

This provides us with the second norm for discerning the presence of the Spirit: is an act more spiritual, that is, does it bear the imprint of the Spirit? This is the same paradoxically enough as asking: Is the act more human, because it is the nature of Spirit through His creative power to make things more what they should be by drawing them into a new source of authenticity. A spiritual act bears the mark of the new creation. On the contrary, an act that is unspiritual is one that bears the marks of death, inversion, self-centeredness. Admittedly it is difficult to apply this norm in some sort of an empirical fashion. It is a norm which only a spiritual person can apply because he alone can pick up the signals of spirituality.

3. The third norm comes from the fact that the Holy Spirit is the *Spirit of Truth:* "If you love me you will keep my commandments, and I shall ask the Father, and he will give you another Advocate to be with you forever, the Spirit of Truth, whom the world can never receive since it neither sees nor knows him" (Jn 14:15-17).

It is not easy to express all of the nuances in the Scriptural word "truth." We often equate it with a mental category. In Scripture, however, it describes a way of being, or more explicitly, a way of living. It is being-faithful or living faithful. In God's providence there are four notes that make up the one chord of fidelity: first of all, God's faithfulness to Himself or to His promise, which incarnates itself in Christ who is the manifestation of the Father's fidelity, whose fidelity in turn is poured out among men through the Spirit, who is the Spirit of Fidelity, who in turn creates the Church, which is described as the "pillar and foundation of the truth" (1 Tm 3:15).

Fidelity is a way of being where one's being and acting are shaped by a relationship to a person. The real, the unsubjective, what is there, is allowed to shape one's choices. Fidelity means that the past-self is not a matter of memory but is the present-self. It is the way past identity shapes present and future identity. In philosophy being is the highest expression of what existence means. In Christianity fidelity is the highest expression of the real.

In the discernment of spirits it is important to look for the note of fidelity, the degree to which we allow the word of God and His will to shape

---

[8]In the footnote to Rm 1:9 the Jerusalem Bible presents an extensive list of references to the word "Spirit" in the New Testament both as it pertains to man's spirit and to God's Spirit.

each moment of our lives, the extent to which we allow the Church as the pillar and foundation of fidelity to mediate to us God's word and will. As a negative norm for discernment any act is to be rejected which makes us less faithful, which loses the sense of the absolute, reducing everything to what is relative, seeing truth in terms only of opinions like conservative, liberal and so forth, embodying an attitude which sees truth only from a subjective point of view—all of these are signs that point out the spirit of infidelity, "in whom there is not truth" (Jn 8:44). The Spirit of Fidelity leaves his own stamp of fidelity.

4. In the fourth place, the Spirit of Christ is the *eschatological* Spirit. He is the Spirit of the Christ-who-has-come and the Christ-who-is-to-come. He is the personal tension of that which is already done in Christ and that which is yet to be done in His members. His whole purpose is to pour forth the gifts that are in Christ: "Ascending on high he gave gifts to men" (Ep 4:8).

The Spirit as eschatological gift is the Spirit of Perspective. He gives us the vision of the relationship between the past event in Christ, or present living out of this event, and the future fulfillment. He gives, then, a sense of the direction of time and its relationship to eternity, of this world to the next, a sense of what is simply means and what is goal.

This serves as a norm for discernment of spirits. Is there a sense of value of eternal life over temporal life, of what is permanent over the transient, of the presence of Christ as the absolute over the relative, of awareness of the overplus of meaning over non-meaning, of direction over drift in history?

Negatively, is there a loss of perspective? Are means made into ends? Is eternal life seen as the climax of love or as an abstraction? It must be confessed that internal life does not play too large a part in our contemporary mentality. We are like people who keep throwing life jackets to pull those who are drowning into a sinking ship.

5. In the first place, the Spirit of Christ is the Spirit who creates the *Christian community*. The various terms used for the Church in the New Testament bring out the aspect of community: one body with many members, family, people of God, temple, vineyard, city, spouse. The Holy Spirit creates community by creating unity: "Do all you can to preserve the unity of the Spirit by the peace that binds you together. There is one Body, one Spirit, just as you were called into one and the same hope when you were called" (Ep 4:3).

The unity of the Church is not based on common interests, bonds of blood, or even a common goal. The bond is the Spirit who draws the members together through their faith, which is the this-side expression of the inner union of the Spirit with the Father and the Son.

This serves as a help to discern the spirits. Does an action tighten the bonds of unity in the community? Negatively, does it bring about division and fragmentation?

6. In the sixth place, the Spirit of Christ is the Spirit of the *Word made flesh*. He is the sacramental Spirit, the incarnating Spirit, the "material" Spirit. Proceeding from the flesh of Christ He draws all flesh into the flesh of Christ: "On the last day and greatest day of the festival, Jesus stood there and cried out: 'If any man is thirsty, let him come to me. Let the man come and drink who believes in me.' As Scripture says: 'From his breast shall flow fountains of living water.' He was speaking of the Spirit which those who believed in him were to receive; for there was no Spirit as yet because Jesus had not yet been glorified" (Jn 7:37-9).

Here we see the importance not only of the sacraments formally so called, which in reality are points of Christic concentration, vortices drawing men into Christ, but the drawing presence of the Spirit through all that is material—other people, circumstances, the sacramentals of the Church. In this connection we cannot emphasize enough the importance of sign and symbol as vehicles of the Spirit. The Spirit is a hungry, thirsty Spirit. He draws men through every pore of matter into the flesh of Christ.

As a norm, then, to discern the presence of the Holy Spirit we should see to what extent His sacramentalizing presence is brought out. Negatively, the Spirit is absent where there is a tendency towards desacramentalizing, a false depreciation of matter, or a false internalization that devalues the drawing power of sign and symbol.

7. The Spirit of Christ is the *Family Spirit*. The same Spirit of Christ animates Christians of all centuries, creating a kindred Spirit. He creates a basic identity that transcends difference of culture, philosophy, manners, and customs. The Christian is at home with the prophets of the Old Testament, the Apostles of the New, the fathers of East and West, and so on through history.

As a norm for discernment of spirits it is helpful to ask to what extent some mode of action bears the marks of the kindred Spirit.

8. The Holy Spirit is the *charismatic Spirit*. There are two ways in which He distributes His gifts: to the person for the social, and to the social for the person. He gives His gifts to individuals to build up the Church for the person. He gives His gifts to individuals to build up the Church, and gifts to the Church to sanctify persons. He is the author of both types of charism: institutionalized charism, which is the Church, with the special role of the pope and the college of bishops; and the personal charism, given to an individual for the whole Body.

It is a sign of the presence of the Spirit where there is due respect for both modes of the Spirit's charismatic presence. Negatively, any spirit which puts these gifts in opposition is not the Holy Spirit.

9. The Spirit of Christ is the Spirit who opens us to the *will of the Father:* "He will not speak on his own authority, but will tell only what he hears" (Jn 16:14). The Spirit is "all ears" for the will of the Father. He tries

to open our ears to hear His voice. Paul makes this one of his main concerns, that the Christian seek the will of God (Ep 5:17: Col 1:9; 4:12; Ph 1:9; 2:13).

This acts as a norm of discernment: the extent to which we are concerned with the discovery and the living out of God's will.

10. The Spirit of Christ is the *Liberating Spirit:* "now the Lord of whom this passage speaks is the Spirit; and where the Spirit of the Lord is, there is liberty" (2 Co 3:17; see Rm 8:1-13). Much has been written about freedom. Unfortunately we have to limit ourselves to a few observations. Freedom is that mysterious power at the heart of a person by which one can open oneself to other selves. It is a power of excentration, by which the self is given, and other selves are received, It is the way in which life becomes a sharing of persons, not simply a sharing of things. Christian freedom is a share in Christ's own freedom through His Spirit, a power to open oneself to the Self of the Father and the Son, and to love others as Christ Himself has loved.

It is a sign of the Spirit's presence where there is genuine growth in freedom, which manifests itself in a greater sense of responsibility to the Father and to others.

11. The spirit is the *Spirit of Christ*. His whole work is to reproduce the image of Christ (2 Co 3:17ff). If something leads to a greater awareness of Christ, then it comes from the Spirit of Christ.

12. The Spirit of Christ is the *Organic Spirit*. He is the Spirit who creates unity through variety. He is the Spirit who gives not only His gifts, but shares His own power to give: "There are varieties of gifts, but the same spirit" (1 Co 12:4).

There are two ways to destroy an organic unity, either through dismemberment, or by reduction of differences to make one homogeneous mass. The true Spirit is present where there is respect for the distinctiveness of His gifts and their complementarity. The evil spirit destroys either by dividing or by reducing everything to an undifferentiated mass.

13. Finally the Holy Spirit is present where he produces the symphony of His life in the Christian: "What the Spirit brings is very different: love, joy, peace, patience, kindness, goodness, trustfulness, gentleness, and self-control" (Gal 5:22). This is another way of saying that He creates the image of Christ. The Spirit is present to the extent that a spiritual harmony is found in one's life.

Discernment of Spirits

Herbert F. Smith, S.J.

Volume 35, 1976, pp. 432-454.

This text is part of the *Pilgrim Contemplative* (pp. 69-97) and is used with permission of The Liturgical Press (Order of St. Benedict, Inc.), Collegeville, Minnesota. All rights reserved.

The Need for Discernment

The briefest of reflections should elucidate the need every human has to discern spirits, and the special need for discernment in the life of the agent contemplative.

Every human being experiences the driving force of thoughts, sentiments, desires, and random impulses so diverse—so holy and so satanic, so wise and so insane, so good and so evil—that if he acted on them without some objective or subjective norm for sorting them out, he would destroy himself. One poll indicated that seventy-five percent of young people consider suicide. And speaking on behalf of every man, St. Paul wrote: "I cannot even understand my own actions. I do not do what I want to do but what I hate" (Rom 7:15).

The agent contemplative[1] is not spared this human experience. Yet not only must he sort the good impulses from the bad, but he must discern the divine impulse from other sources good or bad.

This need to recognize divine impulses introduces a faith-dimension into the problem of sorting out human thoughts and impulses. Psychology gives names to these human impulses, but Revelation names their sources: they commonly originate from a man's own self, but they also come from other

---

[1]"Agent contemplative" is used here to designate a soul in progress towards the realization in his spiritual life of the ideal of contemplation in action.

persons: from other human beings, from angelic messengers, from fallen angels, and from God himself directly. This is the biblical data.

The complexity of the origin of human impulses poses a problem for the agent contemplative. Speaking ontologically, he is an instrument joined to God, but speaking psychologically, he is an agent at God's disposal. His intelligence is put to work by faith in the service of love. He is not satisfied with *any* act of charity, but only with the most discerning act of charity. This discerning charity leads to discretion in the choice and execution of ministries, and in everything else. How is he to make sure his discernments are guided by God?

We answer this question by warning that it is not easy, and by pointing to some of the pitfalls. Let us consider first the sheerly human problem of establishing a stable norm for human value judgments apart from faith. One atheist was asked how this could be done. He responded that the choices which made him feel better were good and the ones which made him feel worse were bad. But he added that he had to test this norm against authority—the authority of accepted social mores, religion, and so forth—since he had to guard himself from personal quirks, and he had to recognize that his real good lay in a good relationship with the community. Thus, this atheist recognized that to discern between his good and bad impulses he needed a subjective norm but he also needed an objective one. So, too, the agent contemplative, when he discerns, needs both subjective and objective norms for his discernments.

The subjective norm for true discernments given by right reason and by the Scriptures and the saints is peace and joy. Man was made to find peace of mind and joy of heart in God and his will and purposes. In theory this is simple, but in practice it is not. Let us consider some of the problems.

Few things are simple in life, and most paths we pursue bring us a mixture of joy and sorrow: joy in what the course of action is bringing us, and sorrow or sadness at what it is costing us. The Scripture says: "Even in laughter the heart is sad, and the end of joy is grief" (Pr 14:13). The result is often difficulty in saying whether we feel more joy and peace or more sadness and unrest when we consider a certain course of action. And when we are sick or in pain, it is frequently impossible to use the norm of peace and joy in discerning, for we often feel neither. Pain obscures both. When the body is shouting with pain the whispers of discernment are drowned out.

For the unmortified man, the problem is even worse. He loves his own ease more than he loves God. When he considers the right but difficult path he feels sad, and when he considers the wrong but pleasant path he feels pleasure. So he trains himself to believe that whatever displeases him displeases God, and whatever pleases him pleases God. He does this without testing his subjective state with Revelation and other legitimate authorities. This man is capable only of the grossest rudimentary discernment, which will lead him to penance and mortification before it leads him higher.

The mortified man has his own problems. The passion of a good man to do good—to create goodness in the likeness of God—is so intense that it requires consummate self-control to rein in his own godlike impulses until he is certain that here and now they fall in with the will of God. Thus it is that St. John of the Cross writes: "It is concerning good things that the soul that is good must ever have the greatest misgivings, for evil things bear their own testimony with them" (*Ascent of Mount Carmel,* III, 37).

Despite problems and difficulties, there is no room for doubt that God does speak to man by directly stirring up appropriate thoughts and affections, as the Christian faith teaches, and as this treatise has repeatedly shown. And whatever the dangers of error, the Christian must learn to discern spirits. It is the only way he can live in the Spirit, and life in the Spirit is the only Christian life there is.

One thing that remains for us to do here is to state emphatically what discernment of spirits is *not*. It is *not* the abandonment of intelligence, experience and good judgment to walk by some magic rite that preempts our autonomy the way a trance preempts the autonomy of a medium. It is not life lived by a set of enigmatic taboos; it is not alien impulses constantly seizing and directing us apart from our own human efforts. True discernment, although it is mystical and supernatural, is so normal and human on the face of it that the difficulty lies precisely in detecting whether one is truly being divinely guided. The Son of God became a man both to live humanly himself, and to live a human life that transcended human nature without suppressing humanity. Jesus is the model for authentic discernment of spirits. The gospels show Jesus blaming his apostles more for failing to use their intelligence faithfully in faith than for any other sin.

The divine aid that makes discernment of the divine will possible generally operates at the roots of the human mind and heart, so that the thoughts and impulses which arise from the divine input are truly the product of both God and of the person in whose nature they are implanted. They aid human discernment by surreptitiously illuminating the mind, or by stirring in the heart an impulse to respond with love to precisely that course of action which falls in with God's plan. This is seen in the inspired writers of the Scriptures. They communicated God's word in a style and a manner that flowed from their own depths in accord with their own personal uniqueness. Discernment of spirits is a cooperative venture of God and man working as one. It is a co-seeing and a co-willing, in many instances at least. That is, the human person reads out the situation, and creatively responds to it in precisely the way that falls in with the purposes of God, who created the person to be what he is, and to freely do what he is doing. Discernment flows out of the way God has created a particular individual, and out of the way he has graced his faculties; and something, out of the way he illumines and moves those faculties through an angelic messenger or through his own direct divine action.

To be even more concrete: the discernment of spirits is not a matter of *hunches,* but of the very human operation of one's own intelligence and affects and affections working in subtle cooperation with grace. St. John of the Cross teaches that God communicates to us through our affections, which he sometimes has an angel stir in us. Of our affections St. John writes: "Without them his communications are slight" (*The Spiritual Canticle,* Stanza 2, Commentary).

Some pilgrim souls hear of discernment of spirits and want to live in the way of discernment. Not knowing how to go about it, they begin responding to every random hunch, intuition, and impulse as the will of God. The result is that their good desire enslaves them to their own stray and neurotic impulses, and perhaps to impulses of evil spirits. The considerations made in this chapter are meant to ward off so mistaken a concept of living in the Spirit. I will close this section with experiments designed to raise one's consciousness concerning the nonsense-value of many so-called hunches and intuitions.

Experiment One: Take an ordinary deck of cards. Try, without looking at the faces, to sort the cards out according to the four suits. Sort them according to your "hunches," without looking at any of the faces until you have sorted the whole deck. When you finish, see if you have done any better than chance. You will probably learn from this exercise that such "hunches" are completely worthless. If your score is consistently better than chance, then it is ESP at work, and this too must be distinguished from discernment.

Experiment Two: Repeat the first experiment, but this time when you feel a particularly strong hunch, put the card in a special pile, one special pile for each suit. When you finish, count the results. Again, you are likely to learn that even these strong hunches are completely misleading, because they are only stray irrational impulses having nothing to do with true intuitions. Learn from these experiments that discernment of spirits does not operate on these worthless and misleading hunches, but relies on our most genuine thoughts and feelings. By these exercises learn to break free of slavery to stray impulses which confound discernment of spirits rather than serve it. Learn to distinguish readily these stray impulses from true spiritual ones. A spiritual impulse is a feeling of connaturality for a specific decision to be taken or an action to be done. It is a creative urge to grow personally in some explicit way, or to contribute to the growth of the Kingdom through some specific course of action.

The two experiments just presented dealt with false knowledge. They exposed as false and irrational the feeling that one has knowledge which is in fact not possessed. We must also contend with false impulses of the will. We are all subject to irrational impulses to change the unchangeable laws of nature. We must learn to grow instantly aware of and reject such irrational and rebellious impulses of the will. The following experiment is designed to help us gain that awareness and to promote rational control of the will.

Experiment Three: Take an ordinary deck of cards and play a game of solitaire. The moment you feel any anger that you do not "win," stop and reflect on your goal and your attitudes. Are you playing to "win" in a sense contrary to the laws of nature dealing with chance? That is irrational and can only lead to a lifetime of wasted psychic energy. Try to adjust your goal until your purpose is to cooperate with the laws of nature (the laws of chance) so that you will lose no opportunity to forward the game in accordance with the rules. That is the only goal within your power, and therefore the only rational one. Should you feel frustration that your luck is not better, stop and reflect that instead of serving God by cooperating with the laws of his creation, you are irrationally rebelling against laws on which you can in no way infringe or change in the least. Then renew your desire to serve God ,in all things— even in the games you play, by serving him through his laws of chance. Over the weeks, you should find frustration dissipating and attacks of anger diminishing, both in and out of the game of solitaire.

By these exercises and the attitudes they produce, a pilgrim soul can be helped to purge false and irrational impulses of mind and will. With his psychic life thus purified, he will be better disposed to live in the way of discernment of spirits—a way which is at the heart of the life of an agent contemplative.

The Nature of Discernment

The *art* of discernment of spirits cannot be learned from a book, but the *science* of discernment can. The Scriptures and the saints have formulated something of that science, and I will attempt to draw together here its major premises and principles for the guidance of the agent contemplative.

Our procedure will be to begin with a vague description of discernment of spirits, and then to proceed to refine that description through information gained from scriptural cases of discernment. We will also formulate the principles of discernment as we discover them.

Discernment of spirits is the attempt to deal in faith with the sundry emotions, feelings, stimuli, sentiments, mental and emotional states and tendencies, and action-oriented ideas, all of which tend to influence the shape and direction of our lives. Discernment of spirits is a sorting out of this mélange of thoughts and impulses to locate and reinforce those which are leading us to God and to his will, and to suppress or at least refuse to act on those which contaminate or dilute our commitment to God.

The first thing we should attempt to do is to define the arena within which this individual and personal Christian discernment ought to take place. Consider the rich man who came to Jesus and asked: "Teacher, what good must I do to possess everlasting life?" Jesus answered: "If you wish to enter into life, keep the commandments" (Mt 19:16-17). What becomes manifest here is that the question of what constitutes the fundamental obligations of the life of a believer is a question to be answered by the clear teachings of Revelation, not by personal rumination and discernment. "Yes, your *decrees* . . . are my counselors" (Ps 119:24). This consideration invites us to formulate our first principle:

1. *To circumscribe the arena of legitimate freedom for personal discernment, and to obtain the necessary guidelines for Christian discernment, know the Bible and the tradition.*

The rich man's problem was one that called for a responsible knowledge of the Revelation, and not for personal discernment. We do not ask God to reveal to us personally what he has already revealed to all who will take the trouble to ponder his revelation.

In the ninth chapter of Matthew we have an event which defines another limit to discernment: "As he moved on, Jesus saw a man named Matthew at his post where taxes were collected. He said to him, *Follow me.* Matthew got up and followed him" (9:9). Let us accept the sensible traditional interpretation of this event, which is that Matthew was illumined with such a flood of divine light and impelled with such devotion that there was no confusion, no doubt, and no hesitation about his course of action. What God wanted him to do was so clear it needed no discernment, and so holy and attractive to him it required no struggle for him to say *yes*. This leads us to our second principle:

2. *At times God reveals his will to us so personally and so clearly that we carry it out spontaneously without discernment or struggle because we experience neither doubt about it nor resistance to it, but only a loving impulse to do it at once.*

These first considerations have clearly delineated for us the arena wherein personal discernment legitimately operates: *For the mature Catholic, the sphere of personal discernment of spirits is confined to those impulses and courses of action which are not already judged by the definitive Revelation, or directed by prior private inspiration.*

Mary of Nazareth has much to teach us about discernment of spirits. On the day of the annunciation, an angel came to Mary and greeted her: "Rejoice, O highly favored daughter! The Lord is with you. Blessed are you among women." On receiving this greeting from the angel, Mary "was deeply troubled by his words, and wondered what his greeting meant" (Lk 1:28). The Greek word translated "troubled" also means "confused" and "perplexed," and the word translated "wondered" might better be translated "tried to figure out" (what his greeting meant). "To be confused" means "to be moved in diverse directions by various impulses and considerations." Mary was thus in the grip of diverse impulses, and tried to reason out what was going on and what she should do. This leads us to a rather surprising realization, which we can formulate as our Third Principle of Discernment:

3. *A private revelation does not necessarily eliminate the need for discernment, for the revelation itself may need to be discerned as to its authenticity.*

Mary's reaction to this confusion was to try to escape it by examining the matter in reason and come up with an answer. This leads us to our Fourth Principle of Discernment:

4. *Reason informed by faith must play its proper role in every discernment of spirits.*

The difficulty remains that reason alone is not an adequate judge of divine matters. Reason must look to God's help and be guided by it. Accordingly, Mary received further information from the angel: She was to be the mother of Jesus. She asked a question: How did this role of motherhood relate to her virginal state? She received an answer: The two were compatible, for her motherhood was to be a work of God, not of man. Mary related this data to the whole sweep of her previous life—to the identity it had given her before God—and recognized the harmonious relationship of this new call with *who she was in faith*. This helps us to enunciate our Fifth Principle of Discernment:

5. *The basic interior measuring rod for discerning spirits is the whole history and shape of a person's relationship with God. This relationship must therefore be known by constant prayer and meditation and return to the springs of first graces.*

What is really being said here is that God is revealing a person's grace-identity to him in events throughout the course of his life, and this self-identity is a key datum of every discernment he makes. Therefore, the pilgrim who does not, like Mary, constantly ponder the mysteries of his own life with God and man, will suffer from subjective spiritual amnesia. And a subjective spiritual amnesiac is not capable of right discernments. He has lost contact with the personal identity which is the God-given subjective measuring rod for measuring and recognizing and embracing new divine sendings as they come along. He cannot walk in a straight line to God because he has lost his grace-identity and therefore his sense of direction.

The pilgrim who neglects pondering not only his own personal history with God, but even the history of God's dealings with the whole people—the Revelation—will suffer from both subjective and objective spiritual amnesia, and has no adequate foundation upon which to develop a mature ability to discern spirits.

Of course, the compatibility of the new call with one's own grace identity need not be lucidly clear, and in some matters it is not clear, as one person has testified: "I am often drawn convincingly to what seems to make no sense and then the light dawns and the path is clearly opened." But in cases where the compatibility is not clear, two conditions ought to prevail before one acts: The call to the new action is not *incompatible* with one's firm commitments (as motherhood seemed at first hearing to be incompatible with Mary's way of virginity), and the *certitude* that it is God who is leading me outweighs the ambiguity in that to which he is leading me.

The fact that a beckoning course is compatible with one's grace-identity is an argument in its favor, but not a *decisive* argument by itself. There are often many paths compatible with one's grace-identity. *Is this beckoning course the one that pleases God?* This was the question that still faced Mary, just as it had faced Zechariah six months before when the angel visited him with a message about a son to be born of his sterile wife (Lk

1:5ff). At this point Zechariah's discernment broke down, and Mary's went on to a successful conclusion. What was the difference in the way they proceeded?

The external evidence and message for God's plan in each case had been given at this point. From this point on, it was what took place *within* Zechariah and Mary, respectively, that completed their discernment, Zechariah's wrongly, and Mary's rightly. Whatever happens in the external world, it is in the interior that man's communication and communion with God finds its center and its certitude: "No one can come to me unless the Father who sent me draws him. . . . It is written in the prophets, *They shall all be taught by God.*"[2] Mary settled the discernment of the authenticity of the angel by turning in trust to her habitual prayerful relationship with God, and learning through the peace and joy with which God spoke to her within as the angel spoke to her without, that all was from God. Zechariah, on the other hand, was defeated by fear and distrust, and so failed to discern the truth of the angel's message. This leads us to formulate our Sixth Principle of Discernment:

6. *Discernment of spirits is founded on the belief that, as regards private revelation and inspiration, God reveals himself and guides us individually and personally more through interior states and affective experiences than through clear and distinct ideas.*

At this point we can update our definition of discernment: *Discernment of spirits is the effort interiorly to experience God's exact purpose for us as that purpose comes exteriorly to our attention through the direction of events.*

Any agent contemplative who has spent years in a constant quest for God's purposes in his life knows that we need yet more refined and helpful guidelines to avoid befuddlement in our discernments. Let us consider certain discernment mistakes which Scripture recounts for us. Saul of Tarsus made the mistake of believing he was doing God's will by persecuting and punishing Christians, only to learn that he had to do *all* discernment *in Christ and according to Christ.* That Christ would one day be the formulary for discerning God's will in everything was foretold by the prophet Isaiah: "I have given you as a covenant to the people" (42:6). And so Paul came to know and to teach us that we discern rightly only when our will and affections are devoted to our one Lord, and our mind is obedient to him in the one faith, and we are joined to his one body the Church through one baptism.

We are in the rudimentary stage of Christian discernment when we are still living in accord with the revealed Christian *do's* and *don'ts* as external norms of our conduct; we advance a stage when we put ourselves under a capable spiritual director who individualizes and personalizes the applica-

---

[2]Jn 6:44-45; cf. also Jn 7:16-17; 1 Co 2:6-13.

tion of these norms to us, and teaches us to do it for ourselves; we advance further when we assimilate the Revelation so that we think and evaluate with the mind of Christ. In accord with this Christ-centered mentality we further modify our definition: *Discernment of spirits is the effort to see the truth of the Way, in some particular, in the Son, and to experience being drawn to it as God's will for me as that will comes to my attention in connection with actual exterior events.*

We can think we are very familiar with the mind of Christ, but actually be misinterpreting it. St. Peter lived with Jesus, and yet made the mistake of trying to make Jesus change his mind, for St. Peter felt he had detected Jesus discerning wrongly (cf. Mt 16:21-23). The two disciples on the road to Emmaus made the same mistake, and for the same reason: They had set their hearts on an uncrucified Christ, and so they did not recognize God's anointed in the only Christ he sent (Lk 24:25-27). Without the cross, discernment goes astray. This leads us to enunciate a Seventh Principle of Discernment:

> 7. *Discernment of spirits must be done in the shadow of the cross of Christ and in the hope of resurrection with him, or it will lead to error after error* (cf. Phil 2:5-11).

This principle leads us to further advance our definition: *Discernment of spirits is the effort interiorly to experience God drawing us to do his will in the likeness of Christ* slain and risen, *as that will comes to our attention through exterior events.* This means that a mature Christian discernment-spirituality is a passion-resurrection spirituality.

Let us return to the rich young man who asked Jesus the way to life, for he can further instruct us in discernment. When he had given witness to his faithful keeping of the commandments—and not before—Jesus invited him to the perfect way in his personal company. This leads us to a further principle of discernment:

> 8. *Since a wise leader rarely promotes a man who is doing poorly in his present responsibilities, entertain grave doubts about the accuracy of a discernment that leads you to more difficult enterprises if you are already failing under your present obligations.*

The rich man was succeeding in his present obligation, and Jesus loved him and called him not just to perfection (all are remotely called to that) but to the way that provides *outstanding means to* perfection: life in his immediate company. The rich man declined the offer, but what instructs us is that we are told: "The young man went away sad" (Mt 19:22). Was the rich young man so attuned to his interior state that he could immediately be aware of his inner condition and say to himself: "I'm losing my joy. Is it because I am making a wrong discernment, a wrong decision—doing something wrong"? This consideration of the rich young man's interior state on refusing Jesus leads us to formulate our Ninth Principle of Discernment:

9. *Before a pilgrim can gain expertise in the discernment of spirits, he must develop the habit of habitual attunement to his own psychic and spiritual states, for they are the instruments of discernment.*

St. Paul teaches that the first fruits of the Spirit are love, peace and joy (Ga 5:22). Thus when we discern and decide rightly we should normally have our act corroborated by peace and joy, since a right discernment is a work of the Spirit. When we discern and/or decide wrongly, we will normally experience unrest and sadness (unless we are hardened by habitual resistance to God's will). The case of the rich young man, then, helps us to refine further our definition of discernment: *Discernment of spirits is the art of experiencing God drawing us in love, joy, and peace to do his will in the likeness of the slain and risen Christ, as that will comes to our attention through exterior and interior events.* The mature discerner not only has the mind of Christ, but he enjoys a lucidity and wholeness of his interior life, and a constant recollection and attunement to his interior states. He knows at once what is happening to him interiorly, and he senses at once whether this happening is a harmonious growth experience or an alien incursion upon his grace-identity and his personal religious history.

Joy and peace, if they persist after some discernment is made, are a reliable confirmation of the rectitude of the discernment and consequent decision. One veteran agent contemplative, when asked whether he was in the right work, wrote:

> I think the happiness I have in the work (hospital chaplaincy) is a fair indication that it is what our Lord wants me to do. I look forward, every morning, to getting to the hospital, arriving usually almost an hour earlier than I have to. I have a month vacation. Every year, for five years, I have found the last week of my vacation too long because of my anxiousness to get back.

St. Paul's vision on the road to Damascus calls our attention to another aspect of discernment. Jesus spoke to him by private revelation, but then sent him to the Church (in the person of Ananias) to learn what he must do (Acts 9:6). Later, when Paul's doctrine conflicted with that of other apostles, he traveled to Jerusalem to consult the Twelve, and it was the Church hierarchy at the highest level who conducted a communal discernment there to arrive at the truth (Acts 15:1ff). This leads us to our Tenth Principle of Discernment:

10. *Individual discernment of the Catholic is limited and guided by hierarchical authority.*

Paul's words to Jesus ("What is it I must do, sir?" Acts 22:10) remind us once again that the objective of discernment is not simply to distinguish good from evil, or the better from the good, or even the most suitable course for me that human wisdom can select. The object is *to do God's will*. Let us formulate this in our Eleventh Principle of Discernment:

11. *The object of discernment of spirits is to employ all my*

ingenuity in determining upon what course to which I am guided by the best use of my own wisdom responding to the inspiration and confirmation of divine wisdom. Discernment therefore seeks an illumination, a rightness, and a certainty which God alone can give (cf. Gen 3:22 with Col 1:9).

It is time to update our definition again: *Discernment of spirits is the art of disposing ourselves to experience the Father drawing us by peace and joy to that course of action which more fully incorporates us into the slain and risen Christ and his body the Church.*

It would be difficult to overstress the fact that discernment never searches for the best course of conduct in the abstract. Discernment seeks the path to which God is guiding me in the concrete with all my personal limitations, responsibilities, sins and graces. Contrast this with the man who invited himself to join Jesus' personal apostolic team (Mk 5:18). In the abstract, it was the best course, but it did not belong to him because the Father had not drawn him to it—he had chosen it when it had not been given. Jesus sent him on a different mission.

That God really does at times give illumination concerning, and certainty about, a course of action that we could not arrive at by any human means is not only taught by Revelation, but confirmed by the experience of many. One veteran agent contemplative writes:

> There has been no special "sense" of the supernatural in my choice of my life's work, or in any of my subsidiary activities during my life. My choice of state of life, and all of the changes during its working out have been the result of hard thinking, planning, "wanting to do" certain things, and being able to do them. Plans and decisions have always been weighed carefully, and prayed over, but I cannot recall a single instance when I "felt" that God was guiding me or was present to my actions.
>
> The only time I definitely feel the presence of God is in visits to the Blessed Sacrament. There I can almost always feel myself most powerfully influenced. I have seldom any trouble in engaging in direct dialogue with God, and I mean dia-logue; I get answers as well as pose questions. Some of my toughest problems have been solved this way, and not all of them to my liking. However, I fortunately have had the sense to follow out the divine guidance; as far as I can tell, it invariably works. In this you might say that my apostolate and mission have been guided and influenced by inner inspiration. I have always looked upon it as the working out of actual grace.

This testimonial makes it evident that its author, in the course of writing it, came more clearly to the realization that he makes his choices in two different ways. In the first way, all that is evident is that his choices depend on his human industry; in the second way, grace is clearly breaking into consciousness. In the first way, the discernment and choice seek divine guidance ("prayed over"), and no doubt receive it, but it does not break into consciousness; it is subliminal. This is the more common form of discernment. On the conscious level, it need be distinguishable from an atheist's decision-making only by the faith and prayer that go into it. In the second way, there is a sense of communion with God and of divine influence upon the discernment and decision. This second way is the preferred way and the objective of discernment, for it provides more assurance that God has guided the decision.

To further this development, I would like to refer to one other actual case of discernment, this one reported not by the Scriptures, but by St. Ignatius Loyola, in whose life it occurred. The setting: he was a soldier downed by a shell, and reading to while away the time of convalescence. He read an adventure story and dreamed dreams of gallantry to win the hand of a noble lady of very high rank. He read a book of lives of saints, and dreamed of becoming another St. Francis or St. Dominic. Both dreams gave pleasure, but Ignatius (speaking of himself in the third person) records the following discernment of spirits:

> There was, however, this difference. When he was thinking of the things of the world he was filled with delight, but when afterwards he dismissed them from weariness, he was dry and dissatisfied. And when he thought of going barefoot to Jerusalem and of eating nothing but herbs and performing the other rigors he saw the Saints had performed, he was consoled, not only when he entertained these thoughts, but even after dismissing them he remained cheerful and satisfied. But he paid no attention to this . . . until one day his eyes were opened a little and . . . step by step he came to recognize the difference between the two spirits that moved him, the one being from the evil spirit, the other from God.

This experience was a watershed for Ignatius, one of the springs of his first graces. It led to his conversion to holiness and a lifetime of expert discernment of spirits in a life of agent contemplation.

This Ignatian experience points out the fact that discernment of spirits should not be reserved for important matters; discernment is a way of life; it is a dynamic process co-extensive with our waking hours; we ought to discern everything, at all moments. Discernment can become as habitual and as spontaneous as maintaining our balance while we walk. Perpetual discernment alone harmonizes all our actions with our growth pattern in Christ, in accord with the will of God. Perpetual discernment is the soul of the life of a mature agent contemplative. One agent contemplative writes:

> Years ago I learned how to discern spirits in critical matters, but it is only in recent times that I have learned to live at such a depth of ongoing self-awareness that I discern rather continually and habitually. It is also significant that many small but important discernments have to do with what TV programs I watch and what books I read. More and more the Lord is showing me what to avoid and what to enjoy, and how these entertainment inputs are immensely powerful in their effects on me and my apostolate.

This factor of perpetuity leads us to formulate our Twelfth Principle of Discernment:

    12. *Discernment of spirits in the veteran discerner is a spontaneous and ceaseless process that instantaneously guides his conduct in everything in accord with the desire to find and do God's will.*

We ought to add that this process can proceed without any formal reference to God, just as a fluent person can speak flawlessly without conscious recourse to the rules of grammar. The man of the Spirit acts out of his own depths in spontaneous identification with God in purpose and work: "Whoever is joined to the Lord becomes one spirit with him" (1 Co 6:17).

Our Thirteenth Principle of Discernment is also occasioned by the Ignatian experience:

    13. *Discernment of spirits will not proceed in the wisdom of Revelation unless it takes into account the fact that in addition to human and divine impulses, man is influenced by the devil.*[3]

One problem remains to be considered here: What is a pilgrim to do when there is a decision he must make, and yet none of the alternatives stirs in him any vital impulses of peace and joy or unrest and sadness? He should begin by following the normal procedure of collecting all the facts relevant to the matter and drawing up the possible alternatives. If he still experiences no spiritual impulses, he should weigh the alternatives according to the best judgment of reason guided by faith (Cf. *The Spiritual Exercises of St. Ignatius,* Nos. 178-188). When he has come to a tentative decision based on reason, he should offer it to God in prayer, but not finalize the decision until it has been confirmed by peace and joy—or until he *must* act.

To extricate himself from a situation in which neither reason nor spiritual impulses help him to decide on the right course, he should carefully consider the relevant practices of saintly men and women of good judgment and *evident* devotion to truth and to Revelation. If possible, he should also consult such people.

We are now in a position to finalize our definition of discernment.

Discernment of spirits is the happy experience of being led by the Spirit to deeper union with the Father in conjunction with a particular course of conduct joining me more intimately to the slain and risen Son in his body the Church (cf. 1 Jn 2:27; 4:17-18; 5:6-9).

The mature discerner has put on the mind of Christ and become one in heart with him; he has become attuned to his own interior impulses and those of the Spirit, and learned to discern between them; he has broken free of slave impulses and become docile to those of the Holy Spirit (Ps 119:32). He is sensitive to the direct impulses of the Divine Adviser

---

[3]Cf. Mt 4:1ff; 1 Pt 5:8-9.

whether they lead him along the path of his own spiritual growth or direct his apostolic action to advance the Kingdom.

No agent contemplative is mature until he is a mature discerner.

The Steps of Discernment

The act of discernment of spirits is the process of *experiencing* the harmony between God and oneself in his spiritual identity and history, his informed faith, his will and feelings, and a reasoned course of action. More descriptively, discernment of spirits is the passive or intuitive sensing of the most harmonious and suitable response I can give to my present life situation. It is a sensing of the response which would, in the concrete situation, be most true to myself, my God, to my vocation and my commitments.

The act of discernment, in its broader sense, includes the gathering of all the data necessary properly to inform the mind of the one doing the discerning, followed by a period of time spent in adequately assimilating the data; in its more immediate sense, it is simply the passive and intuitive sensing of the appropriate course of action one ought to take. Thus the purpose of discernment of spirits is *to learn what God wants*. A discernment is properly followed by the decision it calls for, and the action necessary to execute the decision.

There are three things in the foregoing consideration which ought to be observed more carefully. The first is that the *essential* act of discernment of spirits is totally interior and totally passive—as passive as the act of *seeing* with the eyes. We are free to enter the light or to shun it, but the eyes cannot see when there is no light, and they cannot *not* see when there is light. There is no forcing of sight—and there is no forcing of discernment. In the case of bodily sight, there are the objects to be seen and the light by which we see them; in the case of discernment, these "objects" are the various ideas, alternative courses of action, and impulses and affections diversely related to them. There is also the self, God, and the relationship between all of these. What we are attempting to discern or "see" is the *right relationship* between all of these elements—the relationship which I ought to choose and promote. The inner "light" by which I hope to see this relationship is composed of my reasoning, intelligence, self-knowledge and knowledge of God, faith, love (with its rich spontaneous feelings and volitional impulses) as a source of connatural knowledge, and above all, *grace* as divine illumination of my intellect and a divine impulsion of my will and affections to the right course of action. Thus, to discern is to *see* the truth of the way, in *some particular,* in the Son, and to *feel* the impulse of the Spirit to live it.

The second thing to be observed is that while I cannot force the essential act of discernment, since it is passive, I can actively gather the *data*—the objects to be seen—and I can enter the *light* by thought, meditation, and prayer.

The third thing to be observed is that I am seeking God's will by seeking the course of action which my intelligence, experience, and knowledge of faith and the world tell me is the one most suited to me as *this Christian, this agent of God.* Thus I do not seek God's will simply passively and supernaturally. I rather seek that creative course of action which becomes me as a free and intelligent being who am also an agent of God in the work (his and mine) of establishing the Kingdom of God in the world. I pursue *my longings and my will and vision* as long as discernment tells me I am in harmony with God's will and vision; I renounce my will and vision only when I discern that they are in conflict with God's. This reliance on the Christ-character of our own thoughts and affections is valid only if it is preceded by prolonged mortification, purification, and experience in sorting in a practical way our various inner impulses, so that we are not easily seduced into calling holy what is only a base inclination or a clever diabolical temptation.

Now let us turn to an actual formal discernment undertaken to help decide on some course of action which must soon be taken. The question that arises is this: How do I manage the balancing act of bringing into play simultaneously all the elements of the discernment process? If we think of the many discernments which are made informally, spontaneously, and instantaneously in the course of a day, we have a partial answer: All the elements of discernment *need not* be brought formally and consciously into the discernment process, any more than I need to be formally and conciously thinking of my hands to use them, or formally and consciously aware of the position of the letters on a typewriter to type. I need not even be formally aware that I am seeking the will of God to discern the will of God: My habitual orientation to believe, to obey, to serve, to do the will of God, comes into play whether I advert to it or not—just as long as I do not deliberately exclude it. This is true, of course, only of one who *has* such a habitual orientation. Whether the elements of the discernment process are operative explicitly or implicitly, all authentic discernments follow basically the same structure as I will describe here.

To better perceive the discernment process, let us divide it into: A) The Preludes; B) The Actual Discernment.

A) *The Preludes.*

1) A confusion of mind arises as to the right course of action, because both thoughts and feelings are ambiguous.

2) I begin to reflect on the issue.

3) I spend the requisite time gathering the information necessary to clarify the issue and formulate the various alternatives.

4) I try to reduce the alternatives to two: I will follow course of action X; I will not follow course of action X.

5) If I am aware that my feelings are enslaving me to one course of action so that I am not free to make a true discernment, I begin a program of

spiritual exercises designed to help me break free of my addictions and uncontrolled affections (*The Spiritual Exercises of St. Ignatius* are admirable for this purpose). Only when I am free do I go on to the actual discernment.

B) *The Actual Discernment.*

1) I seek the presence of God just as I do in my ordinary prayer.

2) I try to become consciously aware of who I am in my grace identity and personal Christian history: of my basic way of relating to God, and my fundamental way of going to God through my state of life, responsibilities, personal religious experience and attractions, etc. (just in a global sense: no particulars).

3) I try to sense my I-Thou relationship with You, God (I don't try to *reflect* on it, I try to *experience* the relationship which makes you and me *us:* experience it about the way I do in my normal prayer).

4) In Your Presence, I bring forward the first alternative. I try to make its effect on me and on us as concrete as possible. I offer to You the alternative and its effects on our relationship.

5) I attend to the consequences. What emotions, affections, thoughts and impulses are stirred? Do I feel closer to you or more distant from you? Do I sense you are pleased—or displeased? Do I feel increased peace, joy, and consolation, or an onset of unrest, sadness and desolation?

6) After carefully attending to these effects, I now offer you the other (contrary) alternative, and once again note the effect on our relationship. Does this alternative produce reverse effects?

7) Thus I try to *experience* which proposed course of action makes me grow into a deeper, happier relationship with you—and which interferes with our relationship. Our grace-filled relationship itself should tell me, for grace does break into consciousness (cf. Gal. 5:22-25).

8) If one alternative clearly enhances our relationship, and the other disturbs it, I have discerned which to adopt, and which to reject.

9) If I feel either alternative equally enhances our relationship, I can securely put either into practice.

10) If neither alternative enhances or disturbs our relationship, I am not able at present to settle the matter through the discernment process. It may be that neither alternative is right. I have to go over the possibilities, perhaps gather new data, and so forth.

11) If I discern one course to be the right one, I choose it and act on it. Should the results show that I seem to have made a wrong discernment, I must first discern this new supposition, and not readily abandon a decision I have so carefully made. Only when the evidence that I have made a mistake is more compelling than the evidence of the original discernment, should I bring the original discernment under review by repeating it in the presence of the new evidence. I may then learn:

a) that I am simply growing tired of sticking to the right course;

b) that the course has now to be modified but not abandoned;

c) that new circumstances require a new course;

d) that my original discernment was deceptive because I was the slave of some passion, or blinded by some bias, or careless in collecting the information necessary before I could draw up the real alternatives. I correct the disorder as best I can, and repeat the discernment.

The Tactics of Discernment

We have defined the discernment of spirits as *the consoling experience of being led by the Spirit to a deeper union with the Father in conjunction with a particular course of conduct joining me more intimately to the slain and risen Christ in his body the Church.* This definition encapsules the strategy of discernment. We drew up the principles of that strategy in the course of formulating our definition.

Strategy, however, deals only with the overall management of the art and science of discernment. There can be no real skill in discernment without a knowledge of the specific *tactics* needed to deal with typical discernment situations. That is why we are here considering *discernment tactics:* that is, defined methods for dealing with specific problems of discernment.

Tactics are devised in the course of dealing with such problems, and so we will approach our consideration of discernment tactics by considering the common problems of discernment which crop up in the lives of all of us. The fact is that the study of the strategy of discernment which we have just completed should make the answer to many questions about discernment quite evident. At any rate, let us proceed with some questions:

1) *Is sorrow a sign something has gone wrong between God and me?* The answer to this question is *No.* Sorrow *can* be a sign that something has gone wrong, but it need not be. Sorrow, like joy, is the fruit of love. It is related to the delay of enjoying one's love, and is even subtly marked with the pleasure of love, as Shakespeare noted: "Parting is such sweet sorrow/I could say good night till morrow." Contrast sorrow with *sadness,* which is the fruit of desolation with its hopelessness and meaninglessness and lack of purpose or direction.

Since the enjoyment of God is delayed even for the just man in this world of sin, sorrow is a part of the Christian life even as joy is. The more we love, the more joy and the more sorrow we will experience. Think of Mary's seven sorrows, and of the fact that Jesus is sometimes called "The Man of Sorrows." St. Paul says of himself that he is in constant sorrow for his unconverted fellow Jews: "My conscience bears me witness in the Holy Spirit that there is great grief and constant pain in my heart" (Rom 9:1-2). The discerner must learn to distinguish carefully between sorrow and sadness. Sorrow is related to the burdens of love, but sadness is related to the meaninglessness of a life without love. If the rich young man had accepted Jesus' invitation to follow him, he might have felt sorrow at leaving all else behind, but he would not have felt the sadness with which he departed.[4]

2) *Does God sometimes send sadness and unrest when I fail him in little matters?* No. Sadness and unrest have no direction and lead to despair. They are the work of the devil. To the unrepentant sinner God offers the grace not of sadness but of grief and repentance; He also withdraws grace to let the sinner experience the unrest and meaninglessness of his life. It is true, however, that God corrects and chastises us even in lesser matters, and if we receive correction with a bad grace we can fall into sadness of our own making. The author of the Letter to the Hebrews cautions us against this very thing: "My son's, do not disdain the discipline of the Lord nor lose heart when he reproves you. . . . For what son is there whom his father does not discipline? If you do not know the discipline of sons, you are not sons but bastards" (12:5,8).

Sadness and unrest involve some lack of hope, and the same letter tells us to avoid this as Jesus did, who kept his eyes on "the joy which lay before him" (12:2) and thus were able to bear the cross [314, 329].

The main caution here is that we ought not to visualize God as a slave-driver who is forever relentlessly goading us to perfection. Many people project on God the impulses of their own neurotic scrupulosity and ambition and perfectionism. They will have no peace until they are able to discern the difference between divine inspiration and these impulses of their own imperfect psyches. We can be helped to avoid this pitfall by knowledge of the real nature of the discernment process (as it has been presented in the last several chapters), by a realization that the devil may plague us with deceptive impulses to what seems to be good (see the answer to Question Six), and above all by a conviction of the *kindness* and *love* of God our Savior (Tt 3.4). God is not a slave-driver, not a nit-picker, not a perfectionist, not a nagger. None of these things are compatible with love, which is patient, kind, not rude, not self-seeking, not a brooder over injuries (1 Co 13). Once we have a conviction of the *kindness* of God, we have a new, exhilarating freedom and a superb help for discerning between God's loving impulses in us and our own neurotic drives and naggings.

3) *Are there ways for an individual person to learn directly from God himself what God wants him to do in certain matters?* The answer is *yes;* this effort to learn directly from God is at the heart of discernment, as we have already seen. This is so common a teaching in Scripture that references seem almost superfluous. Before Jesus chose the Twelve he spent the night in prayer. Abraham, Moses, Mary, and innumerable others

---

[4]For those who are interested in a corroboration of these answers through relating them to "The Rules for the Discernment of Spirits" in *The Spiritual Exercises of St. Ignatius,* I will append after each answer a number in brackets which will refer to the relevant rule in the *Exercises.* In this case, cf. [317] to see that *desolation* is not the same as *sorrow.*

were clearly called by God. Religious and priestly "vocation" is a "call" from God. But we should not restrict divine calling and guiding to special persons or we will be opposing the Revelation, which calls us all to life in the Spirit—that is, to learn God's will in individual matters from God himself: "All who are led by the Spirit of God are sons of God" (Rom 8:14) [330; 336; 15].

4) *Are sadness and unrest signs that something has gone wrong between God and me?* The answer is *no, not necessarily.* Both Mary and Zechariah at first felt unrest when the angel of God addressed them. In general, the visitations of the good spirit begin that way, and the visitations of the bad spirit end that way.

Sadness and unrest are signs we are confused about purposes and direction. The confusion *may* be caused by sin—that is, we may have deliberately chosen a wrong direction, and are now suffering from the consequent darkness. The confusion may also be caused by new information we have not yet been able to assimilate, or new circumstances we have not yet been able to manage, or by the darkness of temptation. Jesus himself felt troubled before his passion (Jn 12:27), and he certainly felt darkness, sadness, and unrest in the course of the passion (Jn 14:21; Mt 27:46).

Sadness and unrest are part of the burden of life, even for the just man. When they strike, we should examine ourselves for fault, but we should not peremptorily conclude that we have abandoned God—and certainly we should not believe that God has abandoned us [322].

5) *Can sadness and unrest come from my own spirit only?* The answer is *no,* in accord with the answer to the last question. Both other men and evil spirits can drive us to sadness; and good spirits can *occasion* sadness due to our fears and confusion and weakness, and may even cause sadness to lead us to give up habitual sin.

6) *Should I always be at peace if I always do God's will?* The answer is *no.* Even Jesus was not always at peace. We can maintain that deep down the just man never loses his peace entirely, of course; but on the level of immediate experience every man knows what it means to lose peace. The search for peace is a constant work. Peace is fundamentally *a right relationship with God,* so that doing his will guarantees our peace in the long run; but more broadly, peace is *the tranquillity of right order,* and that order can be disturbed by anyone.

We conclude, therefore, that we should generally experience peace so long as we do God's will, and only if we do God's will, for peace is God's gift alone: "Peace is my farewell to you, my peace is my gift to you; I do not give it to you as the world gives peace. Do not be distressed or fearful" (Jn 14:27).

Just as Paul had perpetual sorrow (Rom 9:1) as well as perpetual joy (Ph 4:4), all of us have the roots of perpetual peace but we must fight against unrest (Ph 4:6) or it will destroy our peace [322].

7) *Do evil spirits sometimes try to make us feel happy and sometimes sad?* The answer is *yes.* As God sends peace to the just man, and stings the conscience of the sinner, Satan tries to bring the just man to despair, and lull the sinner into complacency. Satan follows the principle of adapting his tactics to circumstances to produce the effect he wants: "Sometimes a way seems right to a man, but the end of it leads to death" (Pr 16:25). He bade Jesus to feed himself (Mt 4:3), which is ordinarily a good thing to do—but not when one needs to fast. Satan is capable of inspiring us to good works, but only so he can twist them or us to his purposes: "For even Satan disguises himself as an angel of light" (2 Co 11:14). The serpent of Genesis employed deceit in tempting Eve; the deceitful allurement of spurious happiness is Satan's greatest lure, for every man wants to be happy [332].

One of Satan's most effective temptations of the good man is to inspire him in the name of God to works beyond his power which will end in failure and sadness and perhaps despair. Another is to sap a man's drive to please God by leading him to the joyless and depressing conviction that God is always nagging him to do better and can never be pleased: "A joyful heart is the health of the body, but a depressed spirit dries up the bones" (Pr 17:22) [329].

8) *Can evil spirits directly affect me and the way I feel? Yes.* This is the teaching of Revelation and the tradition in the Church. It is also a perduring human tradition.

The Scriptures in many places recount this direct influence of evil spirits on men, from the Book of Genesis to the Book of Revelation. Jesus himself was tempted directly by Satan (Mt 4). Of Judas the traitor we are told: "Satan entered his heart" (Jn 13:27). It is the contemporary penchant to demythologise this scriptural teaching covering Satan, but demythologizing founders on the clear teaching of Jesus: "The Prince of this world is at hand. He has no hold on me . . . " (Jn 14:30). The magisterium always insists on the real existence of Satan. The *Pastoral Constitution on the Church in the Modern World* teaches that Jesus "was crucified and rose again to break the stranglehold of personified Evil" (in the Latin: *Malignus*) (#2; cf. also #13, 22).

The work of discernment, however, is not wasted on the difficult task of detecting diabolical influences; it is always directed to seeking only that path which accords with the will of God. Evil influences are rejected without expending energy distinguishing their sources. But Revelation tells us of the devil so that we will take warning that we cannot deal with the deceits of evil by our own weak minds and wills: "Put on the armor of God so that you may be able to stand firm against the tactics of the devil. Our battle is not against human forces but against the principalities and powers, the rulers of this world of darkness, the evil spirits in regions above" (Ep 6:11-12). The agent contemplative who draws up his strategy for work in the Kingdom without taking into account the one whom Jesus called "this world's prince" (Jn 12:31), will too often be thwarted because he will not understand the real nature of the struggle for the advance of the Kingdom [325-327; 136ff].

9) *Is it true that God himself only makes people feel happy, never sad or troubled?* The answer is *no*. From the lowest sinner to the highest mystic, the religious experience involves not only happiness but sadness, trouble, and desolation. Many of the reasons have already been discussed in this section.

Perhaps we should safeguard one principle here. God is the perfect cause, and thus when He acts personally without secondary causes, he can cause only perfect effects—and sadness and troubled feelings are not perfect effects (though they may serve good purposes, as when they lead a man to give up evil ways). If we speak in the strictest sense, therefore, it seems we ought to say *yes* to this question, but all the time remember that the onset of the self-manifestation of God can occasion (but probably not cause) a reaction of fear and unrest even in the saints [314].

10) *Is it always easy to distinguish between the action of God and that of an evil spirit on the soul? No.* If it were easy, discernment would not be such a problem. We know how readily evil men can deceive us by posing as good men; we know how easily we deceive even ourselves concerning our motives. Without divine light, then, how readily can we be deceived by Satan, whom Jesus called "a liar and the father of lies" (Jn 8:44).

Still, the more we grow into the likeness of Christ, the more readily and spontaneously will we recognize what is of Christ, and what is contrary to Christ and therefore of Satan. This power of recognition works according to the *principle of connaturality,* which states that every living thing readily recognizes its like, and readily perceives its contrary, by the effects they produce. Fire can be mixed smoothly with fire, and water with water, but the mixing of fire and water produces a sputtering, a noise, and even an explosion. Thus the man full of light and truth will easily detect a diabolical influence in ordinary circumstances. And he will easily recognize the influence of Christ according to his own words: "I know my sheep and my sheep know me" (Jn 10:14; cf. also 10:4-5) [335].

11) *Is it much better if I try to solve all my own problems than go to another for advice since God will help me directly? No.* Just as it is wrong to think the individual can learn nothing directly from God, it is wrong to expect to learn everything directly from him. Furthermore, those who will not believe the teaching Church will not believe the inner inspirations they receive. Their own spirits will concoct what they wish to believe.

Revelation makes it clear that we must seek guidance not only from God directly, but from the Church and one another—else the Bible itself would be unnecessary.

To rely on God and self alone is to open oneself to diabolical deceits

and other delusions, as we have often observed already. The objective revelation belongs to the Church. Personal inspiration should be tested (with
the help of a spiritual director) for its compatibility with the faith and
morals of the Church [326; 17].

12) *When I feel sadness and unrest about some decision I have just
made, is it a pretty good sign it was the wrong decision? Yes,* it is a *pretty
good sign,* but not a *certain* sign. Jesus' experiences are normative, and he
was consoled in confirmation of his rejection of temptation (Mt 4:11), and
in confirmation of his choice of the apostles (Lk 10:21). On the other
hand, Jesus' resolve was greatly tried in his agony.

Peace and joy are the signs we are making a right decision, and the
peace will normally continue, but trials in carrying out the work can de-
press us in our weakness: "Whoever puts his hand to the plow but keeps
looking back is unfit for the reign of God" (Lk 9:62). Also, Satan will
attack our good resolves and change our peace to unrest if he can. Therefore we should expect times of trial after any great resolve.

In short: Only prolonged sadness and unrest should cause us to review
our decisions, and only if our commitment was not irreversible. In the
latter case we should trust ourselves to God's providence for he who called
will provide. If we do not believe this, we lack the authentic motive for
discerning spirits.

13) *Is peace and joy the ordinary condition of a faithful Christian?
Yes.* Jesus gave us a share in his joy at the Last Supper (Jn 15:11). But
sometimes we must find our joy in persecution and suffering—so taught
Jesus (Mt 5:12). So we should not have a naive conception of Christian
joy. Our joy will be like that of Jesus, rich but shot through with sorrows
—as is the joy of every great lover in a sinful world full of enemies of God
and true love [329].

14) *If the individual pays close enough attention to the teaching of the
Church, shouldn't this make personal discernment unnecessary? No.* God
reveals the general Christian path to us through the Church, and he reveals
to each of us individually our own personal path in the Church. That there·
is a sacrament of the priesthood I know from the Church, but that I was
called to it I knew only through God's call and communication to me
personally. So with other matters.

15) *Isn't great zeal one of the best signs a person is rightly discerning
God's will? No.* A passion to produce results can come from pride, ambition, jealousy, greed, lust for power, and other evil motives. Of the Pharisees' zeal Jesus said: "You frauds: You travel over sea and land to make
a single convert, but once he is converted you make a devil of him twice as
wicked as yourselves" (Mt 23:15). Recall, too, Paul's distorted zeal prior
to his conversion. Since "zeal" is a product of many passions, it is itself
in need of discernment, and is no ready measure of discernment.

Since a good discernment is the work of the Spirit, better signs of a good discernment than zeal are the specific signs of the Spirit at work in us: "The fruit of the Spirit is love, joy, peace, patient endurance, kindness, generosity, faith, mildness and chastity" (Ga 5:22-23).

Let us close this treatment on the discernment of spirits with a comprehensive description of the discernment process:

Discernment of spirits is the consoling *experience*
of being impelled by the Spirit
to a deeper union with the Father
in conjunction with a particular course of action
which is judiciously sensed through discernment strategy and tactics
to be the course which the Father wills me to adopt
because it most intimately joins me
to the slain and risen Christ
in his body the Church,
and most effectively advances the Kingdom.

Discernment in the Director

Judith Roemer, O.S.F.

Volume 34, 1975, pp. 949-956.

The focus of this paper is on the spiritual director: what does such a person experience within himself or herself as he or she works with another person in the directing situation? My observations come out of a few year's experience with direction in the *Spiritual Exercises of St. Ignatius*. Many of the references are to the *Exercises* themselves or at least to directing situations that have taken place within the Ignatian tradition. Because of the Ignatian setting, the role of discernment within the spiritual directing situation takes on added importance, for I look upon spiritual direction not so much as a counseling or information-giving or therapeutic session but rather as a communal discernment session wherein two persons, director and directee, seek to discern "spirits" (affective movements) in order to find the *Spirit* and thus listen to the Word of God to them here and now.

The most helpful description of discernment for me in the directing situation is Karl Rahner's. "Discernment is an experiential knowledge of self in the congruence of the object of choice with one's fundamental religious orientation." Herein is described what happens in good direction: two adult Christians, formed within the Christian community, listen to the prophetic Word of God in tradition and scripture and listen to the existential Word of God in the reality about them. In that milieu, the person being directed makes his choices that will better bring about the Kingdom as he responds to God's call for him. The spiritual director accompanies him in this process and acts as a reality check along the way.

In the discernment workshops given by the Center here, we talk about seven elements that go into any discernment. These elements are not steps in the sense of a chronology, but rather they are elements present in any good discernment. Since directing is a discernment situation, speaking of the seven elements in discernment can be a very fruitful way of exploring what is present in a director during spiritual direction.

The first important element for a director is an attitude and atmosphere of faith within the interview situation. If the purpose of direction is to help someone to grow in the God-life, to bring forth the Kingdom, and to heal non-freedoms, then whatever I as director do within this interview situation, any clarification, any discernment, takes place within this context of the God-life being brought forth, the Kingdom coming and the non-freedoms being healed. This means that I myself am living the Christian life. Specifically, not merely my keeping the commandments or doing "nice things" but that as the faith grows in me, I am experiencing what it means to be loved by God and by my associates, what it means to be redeemed personally and communally. This life is a reality now: not just something that happened once. At present I am being drawn into life with God as I accompany another person in his process towards God.

Further, it is important although not essential, that I as director am living within a vital Christian community as this happens. I don't mean by that, living on some mission with seven Sisters who are Catholic and Christian, or living in some neighborhood or parish where many are Catholic or Christian. It is not merely that kind of living in a Christian community. Rather, I mean I am living with people who are learning with me what it means to love, what it means to forgive. As director, I know from experience what love and forgiveness mean. The community is part of my challenge, my reality check. In it I watch what other faithfilled persons do as they make decisions for the Kingdom. I watch to see what people do when they decide, how they seek God in the peace and joy of their lives.

Living within Christian community also means that I submit my own self to spiritual direction as an individual, and that as a member of a group I submit myself to some kind of supervision periodically, checking out with other experienced directors what I am doing. Ideally I am willing to be tutored, learning from others what direction entails. Working on a directing staff is a particularly helpful community check. When the Center Staff meets everyday in the summer, we get the richness of twelve people sharing on some aspect of directing. This professional sharing, coupled with the day to day process of being loved and redeemed, provides a rich opportunity for growth. As I watch and participate, a background is forming out of which I will be directing.

As a director then, I am talking from a background of personal experience. I see this experience as a kind of touchstone. This living experience saves me from a formalism which could reduce discernment to a technique. I do not go into the interview with predetermined answers. I do not go in to manipulate the person to be directed nor to be manipulated myself. I am uneasy in the face of some questions that inevitably come up after a discussion on giving spiritual direction. When a would-be-director stands up and says, "What should I do if this happens in this situation?" My answer to that is, "I don't know." In each situation I have to listen to my directee, put my heart, head and faith together and make a decision about what is most appropriate for him at this time.

A second element of discernment within a director is that of prayer, prayer which is deep and consistent. First of all, I need it myself even as a director. I have a life that is separate from the person I am directing. For that reason, I simply cannot be praying with one person on the resurrection and with somebody else on the hidden life and with someone else on the passion. Because my life is separate from the person being directed, I do my own praying as I feel called. Further, beyond the personal I need prayer for the quality of the interview situation so that I am sensitive and responsive to what God is asking. I need prayer because I need the clarity to be saved from my own blindness, remembering I am not the Messiah and Savior of the person I direct. Solid personal prayer reminds me of the instrumentality of my role.

Just as I need prayer, the person being directed also needs my prayer. I need to ask God's blessing on that person and the grace to share out of my own experience. In other words, I am not just handing him something from a book but something from a real life situation, often something of my own experience. As he experiences difficulty in prayer, he may come to know that I, too, have experienced difficulties. Furthermore, not everybody is going to pray in the same way. If I as director am familiar with many different methods and degrees of praying, I am in a better position to appreciate someone's prayer even though I myself may not pray in his way.

The third element of discernment in the director is the recognition of my own sinfulness: my hang-ups, addiction, and personal lack of freedom. I always carry my usual limitations to each interview, but there are certain kinds that seem to come out more particularly as I direct someone else. They form an occupational hazard for me as director. I would like to suggest some out of many possibilities.

One of them is: "I want to be helpful." At times my own need to help a person gets so high that it becomes a professional disorder. If I am not careful, my need-to-be-needed moves me into problem-solving, giving advice, and making decisions for the person I direct. I end up being paternal or maternal, creating dependencies that do not foster freedom and maturity.

In directing situations I need to be very careful to distinguish my needs from the needs of the person I direct. I have a serious obligation to keep my own needs very low so that I do not impose them on others. For example, if as a talker, I have not had a chance to chat with someone during the day, whoever I happen to be interviewing that afternoon is likely to hear all about the rabbit that is eating my petunias, about the arthritis in my finger that is bothering me today, about my poison ivy, etc. A little chattiness is not going to hurt anyone; but on the other hand, the person being directed is not there to take care of my social needs. To give another example, if I let myself get too tired so that I can't go into the interview and listen carefully, I am imposing my needs. Somehow I have to be physically and psychologically ready so that

I do not impose my physical and psychological needs on the unsuspecting person being directed.

A second kind of hazard is the possibility of having false expectations about certain categories of people. At times there are some irrational things that I tell myself about persons I direct. "Be very gentle with the old ladies because they can't take much." Yet my experience says, "They can take plenty." Sometimes I think, "Priests know everything." (I grew up this way and I hate to admit that I still believe it a little.) When I am in an interview situation, I have to keep reminding myself that this is an irrationality. Or, I think, "Contemplatives are too sacred to handle." That too, is a kind of irrationality. If I have a young person, "He must be a beginner"; if I have an administrator, "He must be very decisive." In all these examples, I have let my expectations of the stereotype color my directing. In reality my experience has disproved the categorizing, reminding me to deal with this person as he is.

My very first retreatant taught me a great lesson about stereotyping. I had been at the Center only a few months when a man applied for a retreat. No one was available to direct except me, but I was not yet fully trained for directing. Although the man was told my situation, he insisted on having me direct him in the retreat despite the limitations of my experience. When he arrived, my very first retreatant was a priest, a Jesuit, who himself was a retreat director with a doctorate in the *Exercises*. Here I was . . . a nun, non-Jesuit, woman, who had no advanced degree in theology and who was very scared. Yet what happened in this situation was that both of us tried to listen to each other. I was sensitive to what he was saying and reflected to him what I prayerfully thought about his situation; he listened and in deep faith responded to what God was calling him. Happily, he had a marvelous retreat.

I am not implying by this example that a director does not have to know anything, that he has only to go in to the person being directed with gentleness and sensitivity, and it will all work out. What I am trying to say by that example is that a lot of reading and academic training do not necessarily make a person a good director either. I need both the learning and the experience and the willingness to work through what is at hand.

A third hazard is the whole area of transference. As director I am aware of the fact that when I am in an interview situation, there is going to be a certain amount of love and hostility that is going to move out of me and back to me that has little to do with things that happen within a conference situation. I once had a man on retreat to whom I gave a passage in Jeremiah about the potter's wheel as a background for his praying on creatureliness. He came back the next day absolutely furious saying, wasn't that just like a woman to want to do something on ceramics. I could have taken his upset as an indication that I had done something wrong. It was, in fact, a problem of his transferring some hostilities about women to me. Sometimes, if I am working with a vibrant young Sister who I think is being oppressed, I play "Madam Liberator." Something happens to me with superiors as well. If I have a few resentments about my own, I can transfer my resentments to the one being directed. Yet he does not need to be told off. I have those things within me that I am transferring onto him. Another common transference happens when a directee "gets a crush" on the director or vice-versa. Rather than shun it or get upset, a good director is aware of these transferences and can see a way to work through them.

A fourth hazard in directing is having personal "causes" that I now impose on the person I am directing. There may be certain things that are very dear to my heart. I feel that everybody ought to be a mystic, and my directee is going to be a mystic come hell or high water, or I'm going to know the reason why. Or, I feel concerned about social consciousness. Every suggestion I give has a social-consciousness twist to it whether this slant fits or not. Or, I think everybody ought to live in overt poverty. Every resolution is now aimed at material poverty. Obviously, I have no right to impose my causes on others; and I need to be highly sensitive to what each person's call asks of him while at the same time widening the vision and raising the awareness of Christian responsibility.

The last hazard I will mention is wanting results. Needing results is vicious in the directing situation especially if I as director am a person who has high needs for closure, seeing that all loose ends are carefully tied. If at the end of a particular amount of time, I want to make sure that all is put together in a neat package, I am asking for trouble. It can be very frustrating. If I insist that a person come to a decision or if I insist that some process be quickened because I, not the person being directed, needs to have it finished, I am possibly deaf to the way God is working with him. I once worked with a lady who could not get into the fourth week of a 30-day retreat. (She came back a year later for the fourth week.) I could have had some anxiety feelings because she was leaving the retreat "unfinished." On another occasion, somebody else spent three days on the Kingdom. I caught myself fretting, saying to myself "This is ridiculous, everybody gets through with that in a day or less—and here we are three days on it." Had my need for closure gotten too high, I could have rushed in where I didn't belong and spoiled the unique workings of the Spirit.

There are other hazards, I am sure. As director, I constantly need to sort out these limitations and non-freedoms within me so that I do not stand in the way of God's grace in someone else.

The fourth element in a director's discernment is freedom and indifference. In the Ignatian tradition "indifference" is that attitude of mind and heart that says, "Dear God, I want what You want. I will take poverty or richness or illness or health or whatever. If You just let me know what You want, I would like to do it." What I am asking for as a director is to be free from and indifferent to possessiveness. This person is not *my* possession. My life and my status do not depend on whether he is successful or not. He is not an indicator as to who I am. I am not his Savior. On the contrary, I am merely here to facilitate his response to God's call.

Secondly, I want to be free from a certain formalism. Imagine the difficulties if in anticipating the interview, I figure out beforetime what is going to happen in the interview and have my papers lined up before the first meeting. In such a case I may not even listen to what the person is saying. It doesn't matter because I have these papers according to a preconceived plan. On the contrary, I want to be sensitive to what is going on and to work with each one where he is.

Further, I want to be free from being too much in awe. At times I may work with someone whose faith experience and dedication is far beyond my own. I could want to withdraw and not contribute to his direction. Yet, as the director, I must be willing to maintain my role and offer my limited expertise in simple spirit. Fear, as well as awe, can prevent a lot of good from being accomplished. If I am not willing to acknowledge my own strengths, my fears will limit the potential for good.

Whether in awe, in fear, in peace and joy, I try to remember that the purpose of spiritual direction is: to clarify and to discern. What I am doing as director is setting an atmosphere in which the directee can find both clarity and discernment and then can move out to participate more fully in the Kingdom.

In the event any of this should sound too lofty, I would like to put in a special plea for the fifth element. I need facts: plain, ordinary and commonsense facts in a direction situation. What kind? First of all, I have to know the faith. Catholic, Christian faith has a content, a tradition, a context which I need to know. My directing is done within this scope. Occasionally I meet someone who does not have the basic content of faith. I have come across persons who are doubtful about the divinity of Jesus, the reality of sin and sinfulness, the three-ness of the Trinity, etc. Obviously, this presents a difficulty, even an obstacle to serious direction. Part of my role as director is to be that reality check for content for the person. I have to know what kind of reality I am dealing with in the Catholic faith.

Further, I need a sense of tradition: knowing what is generally considered to be Catholic. If somebody talks about the will of God in a static way, I can say to myself, this is within the tradition. Or, if someone views the will of God in a dynamic way, that, too, is within tradition. Some would say that Jesus knew everything from the first moment of His birth; while others hold that Christ grew into the consciousness of His mission. Both are within the tradition. I find myself having to rely on good commentaries, having to grow in a sense of what is in the church, scripture, tradition, and what is generally understood by reputable theologians.

I also need to know what is generally considered prayer so that I don't get prayer mixed up with yoga techniques, altered states of consciousness or the like. I am not against any of these things; but they are not necessarily prayer, and I need to have a sense of what is considered prayer in the Church. It is very helpful to do some reading in the classic writers in prayer such as John of the Cross, Teresa of Avila, Bonaventure, Francis De Sales' *Treatise on the Love of God;* bibliographies are endless. It is important to touch some of the classic writers. The *Exercises* themselves and commentaries on them are another source.

Besides seeing what prayer is in the written tradition, I watch to see what it is like in the people around me. If I want to know how to pray or what prayer is like, I ask those who pray. I have learned what a saint prays like because I have listened to present-day saints tell me what it is like through their faith-sharing. This lived experience of them, coupled with some basic theory and my own reflections is a marvelous source of knowledge for me as a director. It broadens my touchstone for what good discernment and direction mean.

There are other facts I will merely note. Knowing basic psychological facts is important. The reality of fear, insecurity, and ignorance that are going on in an interview situation both in myself and the person that I am directing, knowing that people have personal griefs or personal hang-ups which color very much what is going on. I have to be very careful that I don't try to please my directee, and I have to watch that his response is not merely to please me. There are subtle things that need watching.

I need to know facts of physiology, too. I have a private theory that about 75% of problems could be solved if people had decent "soup and sleep." As director, I have to watch that tiredness or poor diet doesn't dictate what is going on in someone. If a person is on heavy medication, how can he or I be very accurate about discerning desolation or consolation? If the person has been drinking or is on drugs, his "spontaneous affections" unfortunately are being artificially and chemically produced. Undoubtedly there are many other facts of psychology, physiology, sociology, etc., that I should know and use, but these examples give a director an idea of the importance of looking at as much information as the situation permits.

The sixth element that comes into discernment in a director is my looking at something from both sides. Looking at the pros and cons of something, sifting out what is good, what is valuable, what leads me to God, what leads the other person to God, getting rid of what leads us away from God. Within the interview situation itself, I listen to what the directee is saying in terms of who he is. I can't do this entirely, but I make an effort to "get into his skin," to listen to what he is saying in his framework, I then take this information back into who I am and listen to the response of my own organism with that information. It is not only what I, as director, am thinking about as I listen but also what I am feeling. How does what the person says fit and feel to me the director, as I listen to it in view of what facts, faith, and feelings I have.

During that reading of my organism, I have to sift out my own non-freedoms, my own fears because this is the pastor or "he is going to get angry with me." I have to sift that out and put what the person says in the light of faith, making a decision as to what is most appropriate to say to the directee at that time. Actually I take time to reflect on that, and to see if what I think and what I believe and what I feel can somehow come together. My head, my heart, my faith have to come together in my reflected reply. When I can get that together, I offer my observation to the person I am directing provided the timing is right. He then must integrate my observation with his own head, heart and faith. It is in those terms that I discern with him. I sort out, I give prayerful consideration to what he has said. I give that information back to him and it becomes his decision what he does with it. Here in particular the "experiential knowledge of self in the congruence of the object of choice with one's fundamental religious orientation," comes into play. In good direction, both director and directee experience the congruence of what is decided.

Lastly, the seventh element of discernment in a director is the confirmation of the discernment. As a director, when I work with someone, I should experience some kind of togetherness, some kind of rightness about what is being said and concluded. Intellectually, affectively, in faith this fits. I am with God, the directee seems to be with God as he makes that decision, and together we experience some kind of peace and joy and rightness about what is being decided. Together we rest in the congruence.

Besides this interior confirmation there is also some kind of an external confirmation of what is being decided. This decision fits well within the context of the directee's life. There is a continuity with the way God habitually calls to him. The decision helps him grow in God's love. It helps him further the Kingdom. It helps him to be freed from his unfreedoms. He manifests peace and joy. Furthermore, the decision works out over a period of time. When we look at this a month from now, two months from now, three months from now, the decision continues to fit. That is confirmation of time.

A second exterior confirmation is the confirmation of authority: the broad authority of the Church and of tradition, the other legitimate sources of authority within a particular person's life. All of these: personal congruence, peace and joy, the working out in time, the approval of authority blend together in a confirmation.

At the beginning of this article I suggested that discernment within the director was not a methodology whereby one checked off seven steps to find success in directing. Rather, discernment in a director is an art and grace and a process in which several elements interplay. All of them are "essential" in various degrees. Some attempt was also made to suggest that spiritual direction is not simply a matter of being given a director's position or having credits in psychology and theology. Rather giving good direction is a matter of being co-operative with grace, being sensitive to persons and circumstances, being disciplined not to get in the way so that God can work with His people, being smart enough to know what I don't know, being willing to study and learn, and growing in an ever-deeper listening to the Spirit.

Good discernment demands of a director a great amount of energy and discipline. Even if only a very small part of a day or week is given to direction proper, discernment demands of the director a continuous life of prayer, study, "holy leisure," a reflective attitude towards life. However demanding other aspects of daily life might be, a good director is always learning to listen more and more to the rhythms of life, the sighs of humanity, the movements of his interior, the whispers of the Spirit. By comparison the occasional directing session is merely the tip of a huge iceberg.

IV. APOSTOLIC IMPLICATIONS

The Ignatian Method and Social Theology

John J. English, S.J.

©*Soundings* (Washington, DC: Center of Concern, 1974).

The developing struggle over justice and peace has produced in the Church a whole range of documents dealing with social, economic and political issues. Outstanding here are the teachings of Vatican II and an impressive series of Papal encyclicals. Synods, regional councils of Bishops, theologians and committed social leaders have kept these burning issues alive in the changing situations of our day. Not only the Church's credibility but her very *raison d'etre* requires that the significance of this social teaching be realized concretely in the lives of her members. Unfortunately the vast majority of Catholics are scarcely aware of such concerns, let alone committed to action. Even many Church leaders, although they may have studied the documents and agreed with their contents, cannot find time nor energy to devote to their implementation.

Clearly, the causes behind this impasse are complicated and many-sided. Apart from what may be attributed to age-old human weaknesses, to concupiscence and to covetousness, to the sheer inertia of unwieldly structures in the Church, to complacency, to vested interests, and to so many other obstacles, the problem of educating leaders and followers deserves, I think, very serious attention. One aspect of that educational process is exclusively my concern here: How are the social teachings, dynamic and developing as they may be, to become "real knowledge" for members of the Church?

The knowledge needed is not merely a knowledge of abstract truths that satisfy the mind or of lengthy discourses on the principles of social justice and peace. The knowledge needed might be described as a deep-felt knowledge that stirs one's whole being to awareness. It has affective and passionate dimension to it. It means that the truth of this social teaching is appropriated in a way that makes it so much a part of a person's inner self, that he or she urgently desires this teaching to become enfleshed in his or her own life and in the whole world.

Here the task confronting social theologians runs parallel with that of catechists, liturgists and other educators in the Church. This is to present their teachings in a way that will achieve the deep-felt knowledge mentioned. The task is made more difficult because the Popes' encyclicals and the documents of Vatical II are sometimes written in a style that may prevent the student from obtaining any real awareness of their personal and social significance.

If part of the difficulty has to do with the style of these documents, then a contrast between the overall *genre* of these documents and the *genres* found in sacred Scripture and even in certain spiritual writings will be helpful. Of course, the inspired character of Scripture enables it to influence readers deeply, but its concretely personal *genres* surely contribute to this effect. The *genre* of certain spiritual writings helps some people to achieve a deep-felt knowledge of Christ that leads to commitment.

When the *genre* of sacred Scripture, or of certain ascetical works, for example, the Spiritual Exercises of St. Ignatius, does not seem helpful for obtaining an affective appreciation or deep-felt knowledge of the truth presented, then demythologization is in order. But the result of this is often only "head-knowledge." The further step of remythologizing, that is, of presenting the truth in an affective, imaginative way, becomes necessary.

But evidence indicates that, not only the style and content of sacred Scripture and ascetical writings, but the very context in which they are read is significant in achieving this deep-felt knowledge and change of heart. A study of the kinds of contexts that bring about a knowledge that leads to commitment will be fruitful. One such context is that required for the Spiritual Exercises of St. Ignatius as they are now experienced in the personally-directed retreat. (On the special character of the Full Exercises, please see Appendix.)

In this paper I wish to suggest that the methods (including the whole context) given by St. Ignatius in the Spiritual Exercises for obtaining a free, personal response to God's invitations may be useful for promoting a self-appropriation of the truth presented in the social teachings of the Church. With this aim in mind, I will begin with an analysis of the methodology of personally-directed retreats and of the Spiritual Exercises themselves.

But before beginning let me emphasize my conviction that recent developments in the personally-directed retreat and the Exercises are closely linked with the insistence of the Vatican II upon humanity's responsibility for building-up the kingdom of Christ on earth (tr. Abbott, pp. 218, 219, 232, 233). This doctrine takes seriously human responsibility and human freedom. It also acknowledges the central role of God's love and truth flowing into the mind and heart of people. Although people are free and fully responsible, they can choose to rely on God's enlightment in tackling current problems and on God's strength in carrying into action whatever solutions they may find. God's revealing love and truth, both historical and present, provides the religious context in which persons freely learn and decide in any particular instance. Their free response and their concerned action in love and truth will promote the kingdom of Christ. Their free rejection of the loving, truthful inspirations of the Holy Spirit will delay the kingdom. Yet, whatever course is chosen, God is alway loving, inspiring and strengthening the members of Christ's body. The kingdom develops in compliance with human freedom. Hope is to be found in the faithful love of God (cf. Rom 5:6-11) expressed in the triumph of the man Jesus Christ, the Second Adam (cf. Rom 5:12-21; 1 Cor 15:20-28, 44-58).

It seems right, therefore, that education in the social teaching of the Church should proceed in a manner that enables a free exchange between God and people to flourish. I think this is the manner, the basic dynamic, proposed by Ignatius in his Spiritual Exercises.

The Method of St. Ignatius

By "method" I mean, not only the form of prayer and sequential design, but the whole context in which the specific Exercises are made as distinct from their content and matter. Method includes the overall thrust, the climate, the atmosphere for the Exercises. It includes the attitude of the director, the dispositons of the retreatant, and the directives for prayer, reflections and sharing provided by Ignatius. Of course, the content is important, for personal truth carries within itself an appeal to the person who ponders it. Nor can these aspects of the Exercises be separated in practice. But my discussion will limit itself to the methodological matrix that makes possible the self-appropriation of the truths presented. In the discussion which follows, I rely upon the experience of persons who have made retreats and have directed others in the present method of the personally-directed retreat, and I associate this experience with the directions given by St. Ignatius in his Spiritual Exercises.

Five factors, I think, require special attention — the same factors which, in the second part of this paper, will be brought to bear on the problems of educating Catholics in the social teachings of the Church. I begin first with the context of faith and prayer. This will lead, secondly, to the whole atmosphere of free response which is so crucial to spiritual growth. A brief comment will then be made on the cyclical movement that spirals upward through different levels of awareness. The fourth factor includes Ignatius' directives for both retreatants and directors, and the fifth considers communal, solitary, and shared activities.

1. Faith-Prayer Context

Present day directed retreats are based on the belief that the Holy Spirit meets each person in prayer. The Exercises of St. Ignatius are founded on this belief: God will indicate to the retreatant what his will is, he will answer the request of the generous and persistent petitioner, and give the retreatant sorrow, knowledge, love, indifference, desire, strength, or whatever is needed. Events of Christ's life and truths of the faith are considered in this prayer context. In such a context the knowledge gained is grasped and appropriated personally and not only conceptually.

In both the present day personally-directed retreats and the Exercises, the person prays during a number of separate periods each day. These periods of prayer are under the guidance of a director. The director is basically a discerner of what is happening in the retreatant. With this knowledge of the "movement of spirits" he or she decides, together with the retreatant, what the material for the next exercise (prayer period) will be.

It is highly significant that one prayer period is built up from the findings in the previous review period. The second, third, fourth, and fifth prayer periods are repetitions. These may be continued until the retreatant, in consultation with director, thinks new matter is in order. Thus, once or twice a day the retreatant discusses with the director how he has progressed, or better, what has happened. This articulation brings understanding of the Lord's activity and a degree of objectivity, appropriation and commitment to the findings of prayer.

The method of repetitions helps the retreatant focus in on a truth or personal experience of the Lord until it becomes a part of his very being or until the Lord has freed him from a disorder, fear, or inordinate attachment. Further, this concentration differs from intellectual concentration in that the retreatant becomes sufficiently poised, relaxed, balanced, so that he can allow the Lord to elicit a response to the truth or consolation he is dealing with. Even the relaxed balancing itself becomes the work of God's freeing action.

Scripture has become the chief matter for consideration in present day retreats (cf. Vat. II, pp. 125-127). The approach used follows one or other of the many methods of prayer given by St. Ignatius in his Exercises. Ignatius' method of contemplation, for example, brings an horizon of reality to the retreatant that the ordinary study and discussion of Scripture do not provide. This method of being present to the mysteries of Christ's life brings about a deep-felt understanding of the Lord which leads one to love and to follow him better. The combination of Scripture and the Exercises seems to make a deeper impact than either of them alone. When used together, the prayer becomes very personal and permits continually growing knowledge of self, of Christ, and of companionship with him.

2. Liberating Atmosphere

Thus, the retreatant communicates with the Christ-mystery in mind and heart. Communication with God is an essential part of the learning process, but it requires a liberating atmosphere. Such retreats are not instruments for teaching catechetics or theology, or what we might describe as technical understanding. Nor are they moralistic in the sense of indoctrinating rules of action or imposing images of God that have a deterministic effect. Rather, they are instruments for disposing the person to meet the Lord. This means that the context in which this intimate knowledge is gained must be a free one. The whole person must be able to respond freely. Since genuine results are dependent on the free action of the Holy Spirit, both the director and the retreatant must follow the Spirit's lead and not introduce new matter or new dimensions of challenge until the retreatant is ready. Otherwise, resistance, alienation, or a psychological determinism can result.

The experience of those making and directing personally-directed retreats is that the desired context of freedom is established through a growing awareness of God's accepting and forgiving love. This awareness brings with it a trustful desire to know and serve the Lord and his people. The retreatant then becomes open to discern the signs of Christ's presence and to meet his challenges in our present-day culture. The retreatant is also free to discover the ways he or she can be controlled and deceived by the disordered elements of our culture.

The director (another believing, praying person) plays a key role here. He is a relaxed observer confident that the Lord will reveal himself and his true will to the retreatant. He can help only in so far as his questions and directions help to free the retreatant and to reveal the Lord. He cannot be making moral judgments. When he is truly supporting the one at prayer, he can present very difficult doctrines to the retreatant. The Ignatian method of contemplation, which puts the retreatant before Christ speaking and acting, is very helpful for this purpose.

The process is simple to describe but very sophisticated in application. Since it requires freedom for its fulfilment, it must take place in the matrix of free relationships between the Trinity and human persons. The dependent but free relationship (loving and truthful) between the director and the retreatant is one aspect, a social one. The dependent and free relationships with the Trinity for both the retreatant and the director is another, a spiritual one. Relationships with other free beings and with the cultural and cosmic structures in which they are involved are also present. This context of free relationships is essential for acquiring knowledge and for entering in to the decision-making process needed to meet our culture and its challenges. This freedom is necessary both for discernment and for commitment.

3. Cyclic Movement

What is the dynamic as it is now being experienced in personally-directed retreats of eight and thirty days? How does this dynamic relate to the dynamic of the Exercises of Ignatius? Aspects of both can be expressed in the figure of a spiral composed of cyclical movements, each cycle beginning at a new level of the spiral. We can think of the classical purgative, illuminative, and unitive ways in terms of purification, orientation, confirmation, of the cycle of disposition, appropriation, and conversion, or that of knowledge, affection, and commitment.

One form of the cycle occurs in each Exercise and its review. There is another level of the cycle for each day and each "week." In the Exercises as a whole the three dimensions of each cycle are sought in the extended period of the First Week, the Second Week, and the Third and Fourth Week combined.

4. Ignatian Directives

The attitudes of the retreatant and the director during the prayer experience is important for understanding this method of educating to a deep personal conviction. The directives given by St. Ignatius in the Spiritual Exercises have proven indispensable in all personally-directed retreats. Both the retreatant and the director are to be free and easy before the Lord.

The retreatant is to be generous in prayer (*Sp. Ex.* tr. Puhl [5, 12]). Ignatius takes seriously a person's response to the urging of the Spirit for he outlines in great detail the preparation for prayer, recollection, review of prayer and practice of penance [73-90]. The retreatant is to strive earnestly to learn his disorder and to struggle to overcome it [12, 16]. He is to trust the director [22, 3, 326]. He is to be grateful and not attribute grace to himself [324]. This means that the knowledge and appropriation gained is grasped as grace. It is something so freely given by God that no human effort could achieve it.

Ignatius also insists that the retreatant should be open to the urgings of the Spirit. He is to discern whether there has been consolation or desolation in prayer, to go back to those experiences and seek to realize their full significance [62, 2, 334]. These frequent repetitions in the presence of the Lord help to appropriate a much deeper knowledge of self and knowledge of the truth embodied in Christ Jesus.

The directions given by Ignatius to the director are also illuminating. The director is to believe that God will show his presence and approval or non-approval by consolations and desolations. He is to question the retreatant accordingly [6, 17]. "Therefore, the director of the Exercises, as a balance at equilibrium, without leaning to one side or the other, should permit the Creator to deal directly with the creature, and the creature directly with his Creator and Lord" [15]. He is to give short points so the retreatant can relish what he finds himself [2]. He is to encourage the retreatant to make repetitions, returning often to that prior moment or point of consolation [6, 318].

Desolation and difficult challenges are also to be investigated carefully [62, 319, 333, 334]. In general, the director's role is to help the retreatant to find meaning in life and to meet its radical challenge. By questions and answers he can help the retreatant to become aware of the different horizons of meaning in our universe. He hopes that through his prayer experience the retreatant will reach that spiritual horizon of meaning which gives perspective to all the other horizons of life.

5. Activities

In the present personally-directed retreat movement, there are two new factors that were not present in Ignatius' day. Both are communal. The first is that today a number of persons make personally-directed retreats *together*. The second is the phenomenon of a group of directors working as a team. Both of these communal aspects are important elements of today's methodology.

These communal aspects bring a social dimension to the retreatants that they would not receive if they were alone. In the liturgy they experience a sense of solidarity with the other retreatants and directors in communal worship, especially through the shared petitions, but also from the various styles of homilies from the concelebrating team. When relating with their directors, they experience the effect of the team and its interchange at team meetings. The remarkable freeing influence which the director gains from the support and shared prayer of the team meetings reaches the retreatant in significant ways.

Despite such communal features, in the personally-directed retreat the person remains alone with the Lord for most of each day. This experience of solitude is of great significance for the success of the retreat—for the self-appropriation of the truths he is meditating on and for his developing relationship with the three divine persons. The routine is recollection (silence, etc.), matter for prayer (points, petitions, etc.), then one hour of prayer, fifteen minutes spent in reviewing this prayer, followed by a period of relaxation—the whole set repeated four or five times a day.

In addition, once or twice a day in short meetings, the retreatant shares with his director what has happened to him in prayer. Even this articulation of his prayer experiences and his specific exchanges with God helps bring about the deep-felt knowledge that is sought.

If consolations of the retreatant indicate it (cf. [318]), the retreatant and his director decide whether it is time for new matter. This would mean that the retreatant now desires to overcome himself and is ready to meet a deeper truth or make a deeper commitment to the Lord. Figuratively, the retreatant is moving vertically in the spiral movement from one level of truth and freedom to another. His prayer with the Lord has been disposing him for the moment when he and his director judge the time is at hand for his decision. It is in the free atmosphere of the changing levels of spiritual awareness that the implications of doctrine are presented. Only as he grows in his response to the steadfast love of God can a person grasp the deep significance of a truth and freely commit himself to it, or rather to the person of Jesus Christ who is the Truth.

Application to Social Theology

As in the Exercises, the knowledge of social theology that we are seeking is not simply conceptual nor just some matter to be memorized. It must become personal and call forth a genuine response. The methodology of the personally-directed retreat and of the Exercises will not easily be applied to social teachings. Nevertheless, we can consider possible applications under the five headings we have treated above. Thus a faith-prayer context, a liberating atmosphere, a cyclical movement, dispositions of the participant and of the director, and appropriate activities will all need serious attention if what we are looking for is an authentic commitment to these teachings.

1. Faith-prayer Context

Clearly, it will not be enough to explain the principles, cite the documents which set them forth, and apply these to particular cases. Even workshops devoted to specific issues would not likely get beyond a certain degree of head-knowledge. But a setting which stimulates the students' faith and calls them to prayer and conversion to the Lord's will might afford an opportunity for deeper understanding.

In a faith-prayer context, people can relate to the Church's teaching in a much more personal way. They will see the relationship between the Church's teachings and their own union with the Trinity and with other persons. They can then grasp the doctrines in any effective way. This assumes, again, that communication with God in prayer is a crucial part of the learning process. And so a prayerful context in which the Holy Spirit can operate freely seems essential for the purposes intended here.

The question of literary *genres* will have to be faced. My only suggestion, in general terms, is that the instructors of such programs study the relationship of these teachings to sacred Scripture and combine them in a way similar to the combination of Scripture with the Spiritual Exercises in today's personally-directed retreats.

2. Liberating Atmosphere

The prayerful study of the Church's social teachings, then, would take place in the context of God's goodness, his forgiving love, his concern for mankind, and the support he gives to persons who desire social justice and peace. Directors must be careful lest they create an atmosphere of moral judgment. It is important that the challenging and accusing aspects of the social documents come to participants amid their awareness of God's encouraging love.

In order to maintain a liberating atmosphere, instructions on the different levels of relationship (individual, social, public) and levels of awareness or conscientiousness (sinful structures, cultural addiction, power structures) would be given in a context of support and encouragement. The awareness of graced structures is important as part of the realization of the overall freedom and love poured into our world by God loving us (cf. Rom. 5:5; 8:38,39).

3. Cyclical Movement

The cyclical movement found in the Exercises might be realized in this instruction on the social teachings if the pattern of the personally-directed retreats were followed. This pattern begins with the awareness of God's love, then moves to the sense of creaturehood with its accompanying wonder and its desire for indifference (Principle and Foundation). From this level the pattern moves to the experience of sin and mercy and the sense of amazement that I am still alive with its accompanying hope in the strength of Christ to save (First Week). After this, the pattern moves to the experience of desire and weakness when called by Christ, and it soon rises to the act of response and commitment (Second Week). The final movement is to the sense of confirmation (Third and Fourth Week).

This would require a great deal of study of the social documents in order to arrange them in the sequence of themes suggested in the above paragraph. At the same time, methods of presenting new material together with sacred Scripture should be carefully organized.

Perhaps a few particular suggestions might at least clarify what I have in mind here. Equivalent to the Principle and Foundation might be themes dealing with divine Providence in the social world, the purpose of economic and political structures, human responsibility in the use of natural resources, and the like. First Week themes might include social evils both in the historical experience of mankind and in comtemporary conflicts, exploitation and violence; it should be emphasized, however, that sinful structures should always be seen in the light of Christ's crucifixion. Themes patterned after the Second Week, the place of social commitment in the kingdom of Christ, and the ways of confirming and strengthening such commitments along the lines of the Third and Fourth Weeks might be conceived more easily.

4. Dispositions of Participants and Directors

As a participant dialogues with his/her director, both should become conscious whether the social themes are being understood and truly appropriated. Together they will decide whether it is time to change the matter of prayer or meet a new challenge presented by the social documents.

The use of the review of prayer and the practice of making repetitions in terms of consolations and desolations, as described in the Exercises, could be very helpful. The method of examination of conscience may be very important both for meeting the challenges of the Church's teaching and for self-appropriation.

The spiritual state of the director is very important. How does he relate to God in terms of the social doctrine of the Church? Is he relaxed with the Lord? How does he relate to his own sinfulness and limitations and to those of other men and women? How does he feel about his own and humanity's responsibility for building up the kingdom of Christ? Does he transmit a peaceful, free, yet responsible attitude to the person he is directing?

Following the example of the personally-directed retreat, the director's main role is to relate to his participants with sympathy and love, even as he encourages them to pray and to open themselves more unselfishly to the realities of social need. As he questions the person about his prayer and understanding of these teachings, he must be careful not to judge moralistically. He has to maintain an equilibrium and not be anxious about a student's slowness in responding to any particular challenge.

5. Activities

While instructing and praying over the social themes, some form of communal activity will be necessary in order to realize the social dimension more effectively. This can be done in silence through the liturgy, and simply by living together; but some form of group sharing may be more helpful here than in a retreat situation. Naturally, experiments have already been made in this direction (I shall return to this below).

As with personally-directed retreats, there is a great advantage in having a team of directors both for the well-being of the directors themselves and for the participants they are guiding through the social documents. What holds for retreats would apply here as well.

A good deal of solitary reflection and prayer which relates the social teachings with the sacred Scriptures in a very affective and personal way seems necessary for the kind of self-appropriation and deep-felt knowledge that will lead to commitment. Here the method of repetition should be taught to the person; and this, not in the manner of a student learning and memorizing for exam purposes, but in terms of consolation and desolation experienced when he considers the Church's social teaching. Consolation might be expressed as his/her sense of being united with Christ while reflecting, whether this is a union in joy or in suffering. Desolation, on the other hand, is the experience of self as alone, anxious, etc. (cf. [316, 317]). Now, repetition places and emphasis upon such experiences, and their significance can be appreciated especially when they are shared with another.

Shared activity (that is, between a director and his/her participant) is very important for developing the kind of knowledge that is needed today in working for social justice and peace. There are two ways in which this sharing can take place, one in a setting modeled on retreats and the other in a form of group dynamic that I will return to below.

In the sharing between director and participant, I think the most important element in the methodology of the Exercises is the significance of spiritual consolation in appropriating of knowledge and making decisions.

Spiritual consolation for Ignatius is present "when an interior movement is aroused in the soul, by which it is inflamed with love of its Creator and Lord, and as a consequence, can love no creature on the face of the earth for its own sake, but only in the Creator of them all" [316]. Tears and sorrow for sins, or for the sufferings of Christ, all interior joy that invites and attracts one to peace and quiet in the Lord are also consolation according to Ignatius. Its presence signals the time of true knowledge and of personal appropriation of knowledge. This is the experience Ignatius considers necessary for decision making. He says: "In time of desolation we should never make any change, but remain firm and constant in the resolution and decision which guided us the day before the desolation, or in the decision to which we adhered in the preceding consolation. For just as in consolation the good spirit guides and counsels us, so in desolation the evil spirit guides and counsels. Following his counsels we can never find the way to a right decision" [318]. If this attitude of Ignatius is to be applied to the promotion of social teaching, it means that the director must try to search out and discover with each of his/her participants what brings consolation in reflecting upon the social themes. When the Lord has given such consolation, the director can proceed to introduce new matter (which always involves a new acceptance, commitment or decision) from the social teachings of the Church. The pattern the director might follow has already been indicated. But the knowledge is gained in a time of consolation and this makes possible its real appropriation.

This methodology allows for the action of the Holy Spirit to cooperate with social teachings (already under God's inspiration) as presented by a trained instructor. The Spirit will give love (consolation); this, in turn, leads to freedom and to the possiblity of accepting the truth and the commitment it involves. The individual now realizes that the truth of God's love is found only in terms of the Church's social doctrine.

Group Dynamic

Can this methodology be used to help groups gain an awareness of social theology that will move to action? A number of experiments have already been made in this field. When a large enough group is involved, the social dimensions of the present day personally-directed retreat will naturally emerge, but a specially designed group dynamic might add something more than the awareness that comes in the silence of a retreat situation.

When a team of directors is available, a group dynamic might be organized in the following manner. Themes from the social documents of the Church might be presented in the morning as matter for personal prayer. These points could be very brief since the documents themselves could be distributed for reading. Each members of the group is then urged to pray over the documents alone and in silence. Following this period of prayer, he should review by himself what happened. Next, he joins a group of six to eight, together with their director, in order to share his new awareness. After this sharing, he goes to his room for a further period of silent reflection on what happened to him in the group sharing and on what further insights he gained into social teaching. The same procedure might be repeated in the afternoon, and thus leave time for personal direction with a member of the team in the evening.

Such a procedure takes seriously the need for prayer in grasping social teaching. It gives the persons involved an opportunity to discern the consolations or desolations experienced privately or in the group. The team of directors can discern the movements going on in the group and in individuals, and they can adjust their program accordingly. Because a dynamic of this sort is more public, it can bring into the open all the joys and pains of breaking out of disordered structures, of receiving deeper insights, and of making personal commitments to social values.

Conclusion

This has been a very simple introduction to what could become a very profound study. Much more work has to be done on precisely what the Ignatian method is. For example, what is the relationship between recollection, composition of place and appropriation? How does the review of prayer give the person enough distance to determine that he/she now grasps a truth as grace-given? Beyond this, we may ask, what is the difference between the Ignation method and modern educational methods? What does the new dimension of the communal, yet personally-directed, retreat signify for social theology? What aspects of the method are to be used at what times and how? I am well aware that I have done no more than point to the method itself and suggest possible applications.

Appendix

It is my conviction that the Full Thirty-day Exercises of St. Ignatius should be kept and used as they are for those special occasions when a retreatant is seeking to know the Lord's will concerning a state of life or some all-embracing new apostolate—that is, for a serious personal decision. I distinguish the Thirty-day "Full Exercises" from preached retreats, however long, and from other personally-directed retreats, even those of thirty days duration, which might follow the pattern of the Exercises. I consider the Full Exercises to include both the method and the matter as given in the book The Spiritual Exercises of St. Ignatius. They should be given only to those with the dispositions outlined by Ignatius and as exemplified in his treatment of Faber, Laynez and Xavier at Paris.

Ignatius says that the exercitant should be generous and magnanimous [3], educated or talented [19], desirous of making as much progress as possible and willing to go into thirty days of seclusion to be united with his Creator and Lord [20], cooperative and more "ready to put a good interpretation on another's statement than to condemn it as false" [22].

Persons who were desirous to determine the will of God as to their state of life were considered apt subjects for the Exercises, as the Directories make clear: "He should be a person about whom a judgment can be made that he will be not a little productive in the house of the Lord, should he be called to it...that at least he should have a maturity and native competence so as to be able to make progress" *(Autograph Directories of St. Ignatius.* Pamphlet from Program to Adapt the Spiritual Exercises, Jersey City, N.J., No. 394, p. 19). St. Ignatius also indicated that the choice of a way of life was a part of the context of the Full Exercises (A.D. No. 420, 421, pp. 27, 28).

The *Constitutions of the Society of Jesus* speaks as follows about the candidates for the Spiritual Exercises: "The Spiritual Exercises should not be given in their entirety except to a few persons, namely, those of such a character that from their progress notable fruit is expected for the glory of God" *(Const.* tr. Ganss, [649]). In another place Ignatius says: "That he should not be so attached to anything that it would be hard to bring him to the attitude of placing himself in an equal balance before God" (A.D. No. 394, p. 19).

For those who are not capable of the Full Exercises, Ignatius gives instructions in No. 18 of the Spiritual Exercises: "Thus exercises that he could not easily bear, or from which he would derive no profit, should not be given to one with the little natural ability or of little physical strength...one who wishes no further help than some instructions and the attainment of a certain degree of peace of conscience may be given the particular Examination of Conscience...(if) the exercitant has little aptitude or little physical strength, that is one from whom little fruit is expected...should be given some ways of examining his conscience, and directed to confess more frequently than was his custom before" [18]. Ignatius also considers obstinate and immature persons unfit for the Full Exercises. He says: "And he who is known to be very obstinate in this way before entering the exercises, should not be encouraged to make them, nor admitted to them until by frequent confessions, as has been said, he should become more mature" (A.D. No. 417, p. 26).

Summing up the dispositions that Ignatius expects in the exercitant for the Full Exercises, we find these qualities: he is to be magnanimous, generous, an apt and mature subject; he is to be free and willing to offer himself to whatever the Lord asks of him; he should have sufficient awareness of himself; he should be capable of judging in relation to God's commandments, the precepts of the Church, and the works of mercy, so that he can seek forgiveness and amend his life [18]. Preferably, these dispositions should exist before he enters the retreat. When this is so, he can do the Principle and Foundation and the Five Exercises on sin rather quickly, that is, in four or five days. But, if he is obstinate and lacks docility, he should be given considerable preparation before doing the Five Exercises on sin (A.D. No. 418, p. 27).

I suppose in modern terminology this would mean that only persons at a certain level of social, psychological and spiritual awareness should enter and do the Full Exercises. I think of one who has a deep awareness of Christ's forgiving and accepting love for himself/herself personally and for the whole human race. He/she is a person who has some knowledge of the social, psychological, and public determinants in his/her life and has a desire to achieve personal freedom in these areas. But he/she is also a person who follows the doctrine of Vatican II and the Church's social teaching, who accepts his/her responsiblity for building up the world into the kingdom of Christ and who wishes to serve the Lord in this work no matter what the cost.

Persons with this awareness, freedom, and understanding are rare. The practice of the personally-directed retreat according to Annotation 18 would seem to be a good preparation for the Full Exercises for those persons from whom "notable fruit is expected for the glory of God."

Social Consciousness in the Ignatian Exercises

William J. Byron, S.J.

Volume 32, 1973, pp. 1365-1378.

M y opening thesis is not calculated to shock or offend those who have been formed by the *Spiritual Exercises* of St. Ignatius. Let me state it first and then explain. In simplest terms, I would argue that the *Spiritual Exercises* are individualistic, not social in content. Put another way: Ignatian spirituality, as an immediate expression of the *Spiritual Exercises,* is a self-interested spirituality.

The fullness of Christian spirituality is social, of course, centered in charity which embraces the proper love of self, the total love of God, and the dedicated love of neighbor. But Ignatian spirituality, in its primitive expression in the book of the *Spiritual Exercises,* is not the fullness of the Christian message, not the fullness of Christian spirituality. The *Spiritual Exercises* are a preparation, a conditioning process leading to a fuller participation in the Christian life. The *Exercises* are Christocentric but they emphasize a dimension that is not explicitly social; they emphasize an interpersonal relationship between the exercitant and Christ. I am not, however, asserting that the *Exercises* are narrow in their scope. I would rather want to suggest that they are wisely selective and, given their purpose, decidedly short of the full Christian message of social charity.

Perhaps the development of my thesis would benefit from a textual overview.

The Foreword and Purpose of the Exercises

The foreword in the book of the *Spiritual Exercises* is the *Anima Christi,* a prayer recommended but not composed by St. Ignatius, and not prefixed to the autograph copy.[1] In this keynote prayer, the word "me" appears eleven times. "My" and "I" once each, and the plural pronoun "they" appears not at all. Moreover, this prayer is repeated at critical junctures in the *Exercises*—in the triple colloquy of the First Week, and in the colloquy of the Two Standards, for instance, as well as in the second and third methods of prayer.

The purpose of the *Spiritual Exercises,* the text reveals, is "the conquest of self and the regulation of one's life in such a way that no decision is made under the influence of any inordinate attachment" (no. 21). The exercitant reads in the First Principle and Foundation (no. 23) of the means whereby he may "save his soul." Nothing is mentioned there, possibly for reasons that respect sequential growth in spirituality as well as for reasons of sound soteriology, of saving the souls of others.

The Particular Examination of Conscience

The Daily Particular Examination of Conscience is outlined for the exercitant (no. 24) so that he may set out to "improve himself." Introducing the General Examination of Conscience (no. 32) to the exercitant is the statement: "The purpose of this examination of conscience is to purify the soul and to aid us to improve our confessions." Covered in the General Examen are thoughts (no. 33), words (no. 38) and deeds (no. 42). In the section on words, the case where "one speaks of matters that do not pertain to his state" is illustrated by Ignatius with the example of a religious speaking "of wars or of commerce" (no. 40). He makes it clear, however, that such words are not "idle" and can be meritorious. Presumably, however, statements on the social issues of war and business do not pertain to the religious state as understood by the author of the *Exercises* when he wrote the book. In this same discussion of sinning by word, Ignatius does provide us with a principle of adaptation that is important for a director who would want to bring the exercitant to a consideration of the social implications of Ignatian-Christian spirituality: "Among sins of the tongue may be considered ridicule, insults and other similar sins, which *the one giving the Exercises may discuss if he judges it necessary"* (no. 41:2, emphasis added). Today, the "one giving the *Exercises"* would surely want to incorporate the developing theology of social sin into the awareness of the retreatant. Another adaptation principle, this one derived from the Eighteenth Introductory Observation (Annotation) in the text of the *Exercises,* is pertinent here. "The Spiritual Exercises must be adapted to the *condition* of the one who

---

[1]The text from which I shall be quoting is Louis J. Puhl, S.J., ed., *The Spiritual Exercises of St. Ignatius* (Westminster, Md.: Newman Press, 1951). Fr. Puhl notes (p. 162) that the *Anima Christi* first appeared at the beginning of the *Exercises* in an edition printed in 1583.

is to engage in them . . ." says Ignatius. And he illustrates this with the phrase, "that is, to his age, education and talent." Again, the frame of reference is individualistic. However, it seems to me appropriately Ignatian to regard the word "condition" (which, of course, was not emphasized in the original text) as having central importance, and without losing sight of the centrality of the individual in the experience of the *Exercises,* deal with that individual in the context of the question: What is the *condition* of contemporary man?[2]

Meditations on the Three Sins

Continuing with the textual overview, we come to the First Exercise (no. 45), a meditation on the first, second, and third sin. The introductory prayer, never to be omitted throughout all the subsequent exercises, is a prayer for self, not others: ". . . that all my intentions, actions and operations may be directed purely to the praise and service of His Divine Majesty" (no. 46).

In the Second Prelude, "I will ask God for what I want and desire . . . . Here it will be to ask for shame and confusion . . ." (no. 48).

In the Second Point of this First Exercise, the reminder is given that a "great corruption" came upon the whole human race on account of the sin of Adam and Eve. In outlining this case study, the socially conscious director might call the retreatant's attention to the notion of human solidarity, evident in the shared effects of original sin, but not so evident in the shared responsibility any single human being has with the rest of human nature with whom he stands, linked and locked hand-in-hand, so to speak, all around the world. Without in any way encouraging slippage from the awareness of personal sinfulness, the director can at this point sharpen that awareness by commenting upon sinful contemporary man's unnoticed complicity in structural or social sin where, for example, surplus and need co-exist under a theoretical blanket of solidarity. This is, in fact, the "condition" of man in the modern world. The shock of recognition following upon such a consideration may generate the "shame and confusion" the exercise is designed to produce.[3]

---

[2]See also, the *Directory* of 1599, Ch. 8, no. 5.

[3]For more on the concept of social or structural sin, see: Peter J. Henriot, S.J., "The Concept of Social Sin," in *Sourcebook on Poverty, Development and Justice* (Campaign for Human Development, U.S. Catholic Conference, 1312 Massachusetts Ave., N.W., Washington, D.C.), 1973, pp. 63-82. The same author has an article on "Social Sin" in *Chicago Studies,* Vol. XI, no. 2, Summer, 1972. See also Patrick Kerans, S.J., "Theology of Liberation," *Chicago Studies,* Vol. XI, no. 2, Summer, 1972, for an excellent treatment of social sin.

I am grateful to Dominic W. Maruca, S.J. for sharing with me his recognition of the opportunity in this exercise to direct the retreatant away from a self-conscious "Nathan-like" attitude toward sin and encourage a socially-conscious reflection on the

Many retreatants have been troubled and confused in a quite counter-productive way by the insistence in the Third Point of this exercise that they meditate on "a particular sin of anyone who, because of one mortal sin, went to hell" (no. 52). William Peters offers an interpretation of the text which not only helps one avoid the theoretical problems of mercy, justice, and the mystery of mortal sin in this case, but also opens another avenue for socially conscious reflection. Peters argues that "pecado mortal" should be translated "capital sin."[4] One capital sin, not one sinful action, is the object of consideration. Capital sin is major sinfulness. It is deep disorientation, habitual insensitivity to the things of God and the needs of neighbor. Such deep-down disorder stems from one of the seven "capital" roots. Reflecting upon such major disorder and its inevitable consequence, the retreatant is better able to see, for instance, that the sin of Dives (Luke 16:19 ff) is his insensitivity to the dying poor, an insensitivity rooted in pride and greedy self-indulgence. Such insensitivity, it should be noted, had developed to full maturity long before Lazarus ever appeared at the rich man's gate.

In the Third Exercise, a repetition of the First and Second Exercises, we have three colloquies. In the first, I ask, among other things, for "a knowledge of the world, that filled with horror, I may put away from me all that is worldly and vain" (no. 63:3). This need not present a difficulty to the socially conscious director if he interprets it in the light of the Johannine and Pauline understanding of "the world," but distinctions and discussion are needed to bring this part of the Ignatian text comfortably into line with the ecclesiology of the Second Vatican Council's *Pastoral Constitution on the Church in the Modern World* where the line between sacred and secular is far thinner than it was in the lifetime of Ignatius.

In his "Notes" following upon the discussion of "Penance" (no. 87), Ignatius misses the opportunity to include apostolic penance (that is, penance for others) in his list of the principal reasons (all individualistic) for performing exterior penance.

The Director and Social Consciousness

If the textual evidence thus far supports the thesis that the book of the *Spiritual Exercises* is not explicitly a social document, it might be well to

---

content of this particular text, thus stimulating quite early in the retreat, the desired social awareness.

The same objective may be pursued by inviting the retreatant to take something like Bernard Haring's discussion of the seven capital (principal, root, source) sins (cf. *The Law of Christ*, Vol. I, Newman, 1961, pp. 374-82) and meditatively read the selection in the light of Thomas Clarke's remark that "concupiscent man projects his addictions into concupiscent social structures."

[4]My thanks to William J. Walsh, S.J. for calling my attention to this point. See William Peters, S.J., *The Spiritual Exercises of St. Ignatius: Exposition and Interpretation* (Jersey City, N.J.: The Program to Adapt the Spiritual Exercises, 1968), p. 62.

pause to make the point that the intensive, possibly individualistic experience of the *Exercises* can still include and maintain a social vision, if the exercitant finds *in the director,* a man who has himself been formed by the *Exercises,* an embodiment of social consciousness. The primal experience of the *Exercises,* it would seem, brings one who is less spiritually and socially sensitive (one who is not yet aware of his inordinate attachments) into contact with a director who is presumably more spiritually and socially aware. This somewhat unbalanced relationship would, I should think, ordinarily hold in the *primal* experience of the *Exercises.* The point to note is that intensive individualism may be just what the exercitant needs at the time of the retreat. As his spiritual vision begins to clear during the retreat, he is unlikely to read social directives in the text of the *Exercises.* He must find them (read them, as it were) in the life of the director, whose social consciousness has developed not in spite of but because of the same primal experience. Moreover, a supportive, trusting, properly affective relationship normally develops in the interpersonal relationship that is the personalized, guided retreat. In such an environment, the sociological dictum that values are "caught" rather than "taught" may well apply. But the director must *have* a social consciousness if the retreatant is to catch any of it.

Meditation on the Kingdom

Returning to the text, we pick up with the meditation on "The Kingdom of Christ." Here the vision of the exercitant is widened. He is invited in the First Prelude "to see in imagination the synagogues, villages and towns where Jesus preached" (no. 91). In the First Point of the Second Part (no. 95), an explicit worldview is presented to the retreatant who sees "Christ our Lord, the Eternal King, before whom is assembled the whole world." And a reference—no more than that and therefore not to be made too much of—a reference to a social problem is made in the famous oblation at the end of this meditation: "Eternal Lord of all things . . . it is my earnest desire and deliberate choice . . . to imitate thee in bearing all wrongs and all abuse and all poverty . . ." (no. 98). But even here, it should be noted, poverty is mentioned as an individual, not a social condition.

The Incarnation and the Nativity

An even wider vision is opened up for the exercitant on the First Day of the Second Week in the First Prelude of the contemplation on the Incarnation, a locus in the book of the *Spiritual Exercises* which I regard as the social cornerstone of Ignatian spirituality: "Here it will be to see how the three Divine Persons look down upon the whole expanse or circuit of all the earth, *filled with human beings* . . ." (no. 102). True, no social problem, only the severest of their spiritual problems ("going down to hell") is mentioned as the text continues; this is interpreted to mean that they are out of touch with God. But the exercitant, nevertheless, is asked to look not at himself but at humanity in need of help. This is a vision to be retained throughout the retreat.

The First Point (no. 106) provides an international outlook ("behold all nations"). The same outlook carries through the Second and Third Points. In the colloquy, however, I pray for *myself,* not for the nations of the earth! Still, a qualitative improvement has been added to the vision of the exercitant—a worldview.

It is of utmost importance to note that no. 130 of the book of the *Exercises* (Note IV after the First Day of the Second Week—the day on which the contemplation on the Incarnation is made) instructs the exercitant to take his Incarnational worldview forward to every "place or mystery I am about to contemplate" throughout the *rest of the retreat.*[5]

In the Third Point of the Contemplation of the Nativity (no. 116), the exercitant sees our Lady, St. Joseph, and "the maid," all mentioned earlier, "making the journey and laboring that Our Lord might be born in extreme poverty, and that after many labors, after hunger, thirst, heat and cold, after insults and outrages, He might die on the cross, and all this *for me.* Then I will reflect and draw some spiritual fruit from what I have seen" (emphasis added). The literal direction is again individualistic but now necessarily filtered through the enlarging prism of the Incarnational view of humanity. Some of the "spiritual fruit" is likely to be social. This will be the work of the Lord who deals directly with the soul during the retreat. It is work, however, to be assisted by the director.

The Two Standards

Just before presenting the Meditation on the Two Standards, Ignatius gives an "Introduction to the Consideration of Different States of Life" (no. 135). Referring here to the meditation to be taken up next (The Two Standards), Ignatius writes: ". . . let us consider the *intention* of Christ our Lord, and on the other hand, that of the enemy of our human nature" (emphasis added). It seems perfectly legitimate, if not necessary, therefore, to think of the Two Standards as representations of two intentions, two mind sets, two mentalities, ideologies, value systems, and ultimately as two cultures.[6]

Equipped with the worldview garnered and brought forward from his reflections on the Incarnation, the exercitant notes in the First Prelude to the Two Standards that "Christ calls and wants all beneath His Standard, and Lucifer, on the other hand, wants all under his" (no. 137).

The Third Prelude, significantly and most importantly for the exercitant

---

[5]This important instruction was first pointed out to me by George A. Aschenbrenner, S.J.

[6]My thanks to Fr. George Aschenbrenner for indicating to me the strategic position of the emphasis on "intention" in no. 135.

now turned outward from himself toward the world, calls for the grace of discernment of spirits: "Here it will be to ask for a knowledge of the deceits of the rebel chief and help to guard myself against them; and also to ask for a knowledge of the true life exemplified in the sovereign and true Commander, and the grace to imitate Him" (no. 139). Karl Rahner sees a sequential strategy in the Standard of Satan who tempts one first with the "desire to possess" and then with the "desire to *be* somebody," and then on to a self-identification with the things possessed. This shift goes on almost unnoticed. Imperceptibly, the standard of values is changed: "The desire to be somebody leads ultimately to the desire to exist absolutely for self, and to the attempt to assert oneself unconditionally through an existential identification of self with one's possessions and capabilities."[7]

Culture and Counterculture

When he considers the Two Standards, the retreatant is sorting out elements of the mentality, ideology, or intention of Christ and comparing these with the mentality, ideology, or intention of Satan. The exercitant is dealing now with value systems. By this very fact, he is dealing with two cultures, for a culture, as I understand it, is characterized and identified by its dominant values. Rooted in any set of values is a design for living. The values become normative of behavior.

If the dominant values of "the world," as considered in the Third Exercise of the First Week (no. 63:3), are the riches-honor-pride values of Satan (no. 142), then the dominant values of Christ, namely, poverty, insults, humility (no. 146), form the basis of a counterculture. The director must help the exercitant discover which value system runs deeper in him. No need for us to apologize for the fact that this is focused on the individual. This is moving toward a moment of personal conversion. Once a man is converted or reconverted to the mentality and intentionality of Christ, he is ready for action, ready to build the counterculture which is the Church, in the world, and *on the way to* the kingdom.

To illustrate my point that these who choose the Standard of Christ thereby choose a countercultural stance in contemporary America, let me offer the following observation of psychologist Kenneth Keniston:

> This [the fact that today's youth may be able to perceive the gulf between principle and practice, between creed and deed, more clearly than previous generations have done] points to one of the central characteristics of today's youth in general and young radicals in particular: they insist on taking seriously a great variety of political, personal and social principles that "no one in his right mind" ever before thought of attempting to extend to such situations as dealings with strangers, relations between the races, or international politics. For example, peaceable openness has long been a creedal virtue in our society, but it has rarely been extended to foreigners, particularly those with dark skins. Similarly, equality has long been preached, but the

---

[7]Karl Rahner, S.J., *Spiritual Exercises* (New York: Herder and Herder, 1965), p. 175.

"American dilemma" has been resolved by a series of institutionalized hypocrisies that exempted Negroes from the application of this principle. Love has always been a formal value in Christian societies, but really to love one's enemies—to be generous to policemen, customers, criminals, servants, or foreigners—has been considered folly.[8]

Ignatian principles require us to prefer "folly" and to choose what "no one in his right mind" would regard as wise. Some of the issues which Keniston alludes to remain with us as unsolved social problems because the dominant values of our society, populated in the main by "right minded" and "wise" people, tolerate a coexistence with such problems and often consign them to a category of "benign neglect."

I regard the Meditation on the Two Standards as a personal exercise in conscientization, the process of consciousness-raising, written about by Paulo Freire[9] and concerned essentially with the dawning awareness of dominant values which can, in fact, be oppressive forces. Once aware of the dominant values of Satan and of their oppressive, destructive force in my life and my world, I pray for the courage to choose and be chosen for the dominant values of Christ. I elect identifiable membership in a counter-culture.[10]

Third Degree of Humility

The Third Degree of Humility (no. 167) puts before the exercitant the choice of *being with* the poor because Christ was poor. He chooses in this way to *be with* Christ. Poverty is not chosen for itself; the choice is to be with and like Christ. Once there, what does the exercitant *do?* Presumably, he uses his wisdom and prudence (which, as the text suggests, the world no longer recognizes in him) to meet the needs he finds around him. A fuller understanding of social needs will await development outside the school of the *Exercises* which deals more immediately with the understanding of self. How he will meet those needs and, indeed, which of those needs he should attempt to meet, will be the work of discernment—another skill acquired in the school of the *Exercises*. After the retreat (out of school, so to speak) the Incarnational viewpoint will be retained, the habit of discernment will continue, and the social-spiritual awareness will grow with the flow of Ignatian spirituality into the fullness of the Christian vision. But the full flow

---

[8]*Young Radicals: Notes on Committed Youth,* A Harvest Book of Harcourt, Brace & World, Inc., 1968, p. 238.

[9]Paulo Freire, *Pedagogy of the Oppressed* (New York: Herder and Herder, 1970).

[10]The contemporary relevance of the Ignatian perception of the riches-honor-pride interlock is unwittingly demonstrated by economist John Kenneth Galbraith who asserts in his most famous book: "Broadly speaking there are three basic benefits from wealth. First is the *satisfaction in the power* with which it endows the individual. Second is the *physical possession of things* which money can buy. Third is the *distinction or esteem* that accrues to the rich man as a result of his wealth" (*The Affluent Society* [Boston: Houghton-Mifflin, 1958], p. 88; emphasis not in the original).

is, in my view, only initiated by, not contained in the book of the *Spiritual Exercises*. The life of the graduate should exceed the reach of the student, else what's a diploma for? The Ignatian diploma is discernment, a special tool for the successful practice of life. My contention in these pages has been that in the school the emphasis is on the preparation of the student, not on the practice of life. Direct his vision to social problems, of course, but don't instruct the exercitant in detailed remedies. Instruct him instead in how to choose what God wants to be chosen.

Seeking God's Will

In the Fourth Point in the first of the "Two Ways for Making a Choice of a Way of Life in the Third Time," Ignatius says that "this will be to weigh the matter by reckoning the number of advantages and benefits that would *accrue to me* if I had the proposed office or benefice solely for the praise of God our Lord and the salvation of my soul" (no. 181; emphasis added). Benefits *to me,* not to others! God will care for the others, I interpret Ignatius as saying, perhaps through me, perhaps not. The important thing in the mind of Ignatius is that I choose what God wants me to choose now, that I know his will and do it.

The Will of God and the Good of Mankind

"But the will of God is identical with the good of mankind," observed Walter Rauschenbusch, the Social Gospel writer who died in 1918.[11] Commenting on this remark, James Gustafson interprets Rauschenbusch in these terms: "This means that what we can know about the good of mankind is knowledge about the will of God. What we can know about the will of God is knowledge of what is good for mankind. Everything turns on this hinge."[12] With this insight, are we any better off? We can agree, I suppose, that what is good for mankind *is* the will of God. If we have agreement on this point, then we have discovered a social theme at the core of the quest which is the *Spiritual Exercises,* the quest for the Divine Will. But to admit this is not to say that the man of the *Exercises* has the solutions to social problems. It simply says that his discernment is much more crucial, risky, and difficult than may have been previously recognized. For only the arrogant and spiritually insensitive man would want to claim flatly that his view of what is good for the world is identical with the will of God. Yet true knowledge of what is good for mankind is, if you accept Rauschenbusch's insight, a source for knowing God's will.

What is good for mankind? To answer this question is a lifetime's labor. But not to so labor is to abandon the quest for God's will. Hence the experience of the *Exercises* propels a man into social involvement.

---

[11] Walter Rauschenbusch, *Social Principles of Jesus* (1916), p. 128.
[12] James M. Gustafson, "From Scripture to Social Policy and Social Acion," *Andover Newton Quarterly,* Vol. 9, no. 3 (January, 1969), p. 162.

Social Specification of the Exercises

I was struck by the echoes of Rauschenbusch in a recent essay by George Dunne.[13] In discussing social change, the gospel, and Ignatian spirituality, Father Dunne takes a few paragraphs to present a self-defense against the charge filed against him in 1943 by Father Zacheus Maher, American Assistant to the Jesuit General. In giving a retreat that year to the theologians at Alma College in California, Father Dunne had, in the judgment of Father Maher, "ignored the *Spiritual Exercises* of St. Ignatius and substituted instead a series of brilliant talks on social subjects." Fr. Dunne, thirty years later, has this to say:

> It was impossible for me then—as it is now—to reflect upon Christ's predilection for the poor, his warning to the rich, his parable of the Good Smaritan, his commandments of love, his Sermon on the Mount, his at once terrifying and inspiring parable of judgment narrated in the 25th chapter of Matthew's Gospel, and much else besides, without seeing their bearing upon a host of "social subjects," such as the sin of segregation, anti-Semitism, the migrant farm workers, the second-class citizenship of Latin Americans, rats in the tenements, racial ghettos, the *favelas* in Rio, the slums in Calcutta, the gap between rich and poor, property claims and human claims, war, violence, etc. This also raises questions about the economic and social structures of our society and our tendency to regard them as God-given, binding the church to the support of the status quo and of the privileged and powerful.
>
> Here was the fundamental difference between us. To me all of these concerns arose directly out of the Gospel and, since with few exceptions the *Spiritual Exercises* of St. Ignatius are reflections upon the Gospel, were related to those *Exercises*. To Father Maher they had nothing to do with the Gospel nor with the *Exercises*.[14]

Directors of the Exercises have many well-known sources of help for the effective use of Scripture in an Ignatian retreat. The texts referred to by George Dunne in the above quotation are well suited for social specification in the prayer of the retreatant. It is noteworthy that all of the Scripture texts suggested by Ignatius in the book of the *Exercises* are apostolically oriented. He seemed anxious to give the process of individual liberation, well begun in the experience of the First Week, a clear apostolic specification in the subsequent weeks of retreat. The socially sensitive director will bring to this desired apostolic specification a pronounced social dimension. But how?

Previous Literature on the Subject

The literature on the social dimensions of the *Spiritual Exercises* is not extensive. What I have presented here differs from but does not necessarily contradict earlier discussions of the topic. The difference, as I see it, is that

---

[13]George H. Dunne, S.J., "The Winds of Change: A Personal Memoir about the Gospel and 'Social Subjects,' " *Commonweal*, January 26, 1973, pp. 372-5.

[14]Ibid., p. 373.

I have restricted myself to the personalized, one-on-one, directed Ignatian retreat. Although other Jesuit writers like Gordon George,[15] Theodore V. Purcell,[16] Thomas J. Casey,[17] and Patrick J. Boyle[18] mention the director and his responsibility for making the *Exercises* socially relevant, they seem to be working more from the model of a preached retreat. This is not surprising since few men of their generation ever gave or made individually directed retreats until quite recently. Gordon George, writing in 1950 as a young graduate student in sociology, argued that the integration of magisterial statements on urgent, contemporary social problems in no way devalued the text or experience of the *Exercises*. Writing in 1963, Theodore Purcell offered a twofold thesis: "The heart of the *Spiritual Exercises* is charity, the love of God and neighbor. Secondly, the social sciences, perhaps more than any other discipline, can help both director and exercitant to understand what really is charity in practice."[19] In other words, social science helps the director *define* charity.

A Digression

I would like to digress for a moment to consider the desirability of bringing the *Exercises* to social scientists. The directed retreat movement today in the United States is not, in my judgment, taking adequate initiatives toward laymen. I fear that some who are devoting full time to this apostolate of the directed retreat, but whose clientele is predominantly women religious, will develop a style and vocabulary that will make it difficult for them to reach active, influential laymen who could profit from the experience of the *Exercises*. In terms of reaching social scientists, it must be said that the *Spiritual Exercises* will not solve the social problems of our day but they can motivate competent specialists to work, for the love of God and man, on the solution of especially complicated social problems, or in meeting particularly urgent social needs.

Modification of the Original Thesis

Before offering some rather general and certainly insufficient "how to" advice to the director, I think my opening thesis should be reconsidered. A slight modification will be helpful, and then the modified thesis may serve as

---

[15]Gordon George, S.J., "Can and Should," *Social Order*, Vol. III, no. 10, December, 1950, pp. 450-460.

[16]Theodore V. Purcell, S.J., "The Social Sciences and the Spiritual Exercises," in Robert F. Harvanek (ed.), *Contemporary Thought and the Spiritual Exercises of St. Ignatius Loyola* (Chicago: Loyola University, 1963), pp. 3-14.

[17]Thomas J. Casey, S.J., "Resocialization through an Ignatian Retreat," *Review for Religious*, January, 1971, pp. 85-105.

[18]Patrick J. Boyle, S.J., "The Social Consciousness of the Spiritual Exercises," *Woodstock Letters*, April, 1957, pp. 127-131.

[19]Theodore V. Purcell, S.J., op. cit., p. 3.

a useful reminder to the director as he offers suggestions for the prayer of the retreatant.

Originally, I said: "The *Spiritual Exercises* are individualistic, not social in content." Now I would phrase it this way: The *Spiritual Exercises* are personal, not social in content. The social *content* comes from the suggested Scripture texts, from the recommended reading, from the faith experience and worldview of the director, and, last but by no means least, from divine activity in the soul of the retreatant. By social content, I do not mean detailed information about social problems, I mean instead the cultivation of that personal attitude like the attitude of Christ Jesus (Phil. 2:5 ff), a social perspective like that which Ignatius built into his exercise on the Incarnation. Emphasis on the personal need not in any way detract from a concern for the social. It may in fact be the best antidote to the inevitable discouragement social reformers must face. It may moreover be the surest route to the resolution of social problems. As Paul Evdokimov has written:

> Since the end of the nineteenth century and especially after the Soviet experience, the mystical belief in the *utopia of an earthly paradise* has given way to disillusionment and deep discouragement. It has become clear that the perfect society is unattainable because evolution will always go on. Only Christian personalism has a chance of resolving the problems; for unlike capitalist individualism and Marxist collectivism, it insists on the basic worth of the human person as subject (not object) and seeks his fulfillment only in communion with all other individuals *(sobornost)*.[20]

No need, therefore, to apologize for an absence of consciously social references and specifically social content in the book of the *Exercises*. But this does not excuse the director from recognizing and accepting his responsibility, during the personally guided retreat, of maintaining an environment of truly Christian personalism. This means turning neither to the right of capitalist individualism, nor to the left of Marxist collectivism; it means as well no solipsistic U-turns into self. The socially sensitive director will do all he can to move the work of the retreat to the higher ground of Christian community consciousness.

Suggestions to the Director

Today's director will enhance his own social consciousness by being with the poor,[21] being open to other cultures, by reading books like René Lauren-

---

[20]"Social Dimension of Orthodox Ecclesiology," *Theology Digest*, Spring, 1970, p. 46.
[21]I was impressed many years ago to learn that Alfred Marshall, the great neo-classical, late 19th-century British economist, walked regularly through the slums of London to maintain his motivation for continuing his relatively isolated and indirect theoretical work which he hoped would contribute in some way to easing the burdens of the poor. Whatever the verdict might be on the place of Marshall's work as part of the problem or solution of poverty, the conscious exposure to the poor is surely a good thing for men whose professional energies are spent in libraries, offices, and conference rooms.

tin's *Liberation, Development, and Salvation* (Orbis, 1972), or Gustavo Gutierrez, *Theology of Liberation* (Orbis, 1972). Robert Heilbroner's *The Great Ascent* (Harper, 1963) is still quite useful in getting a sense of world poverty. So are books by Barbara Ward, Gunnar Myrdal, and many others. Abundant bibliography is available elsewhere on domestic and international social issues like racism, poverty, unemployment, crime, and the multiple forms of injustices and inequality.

The socially sensitive director will select and study and offer, where appropriate, for the consideration of the retreatant parables like that of the Good Samaritan, the unjust steward, the judgment parable of Matthew 25. He might want to supplement his exegetical studies with reading of the so-called Social Gospel writers like Walter Rauschenbusch. And, to put a good focus on a legitimate extension of the gospel message by means of a responsible hermeneutic, he will want to stay alert to developing news of current social issues like tax reform, busing, resistance movements, industrial strife, and so many others that crop up regularly in the headlines.

A Sampler of Texts

Finally, I would like to offer a sampler of texts, ancient and modern, that can serve to cultivate a social sensitivity during time of retreat.

> So you are not a miser, nor do you rob, yet you treat as your own what you have received in trust for others! Do we not say that the man who steals the coat of another is a thief? And what other name does he deserve who, being able to clothe the naked yet refuses? The bread you keep belongs to the hungry; the clothes you store away belong to the naked; the shoes that moulder in your closets belong to those that have none; the money you have buried belongs to the needy. Therefore, you have wronged all those to whom you could have given and did not. (St. Basil, *Homily on Avarice*).

St. Cyprian spoke of sharing with the poor in the context of reparative penance. His people failed to flee the persecution of Decius, he says, and abandoned their faith instead because they were too attached to their possessions.

> What deceived many was a blind attachment to their patrimony, and if they were not free and ready to take themselves away, it was because their property held them in chains. That is what fettered those who remained, those were the chains which shackled their courage and choked their faith and hampered their judgment and throttled their souls, so that the serpent, whom God had condemned to eat of earth, found in them his food and his prey, because they clung to the things of earth. (St. Cyprian, *De lapsis,* no. 11).

An early illustration of structural, social sin is seen in remarks by St. John Chrysostom on the institution of slavery.[22]

---

[22]I am grateful to Carlos de la Cruz, S.J. for providing me with these and other selections from Chrysostom. On the important issue of social sin, see the references in note 3 above. For a fuller presentation of Chrysostom's views on slavery, see his commentary on Paul's Letter to Philemon, Homilies No. 3 and No. 4.

And if someone asks from where does slavery come and why was it introduced into human life, I will tell you. Avarice, covetousness, ambition engendered slavery. Noah did not have slaves; neither did Abel, nor Seth, nor his descendants. All of this was the product of sin.

And in another place on the same topic:

If he who had the form of God has emptied himself taking the form of a slave so as to save the slaves, is it strange, then, that I, who am no more than a slave, make myself the slave of my fellow slaves?

A direct line back to the beginning of the Christian tradition is visible in the person and audible in the words of Cesar Chavez, national leader of the farmworkers, who in 1968 at the end of his 25-day protest fast against unjust working conditions for agricultural laborers in America, said:

When we are really honest with ourselves, we must admit that our lives are all that really belong to us. So it is how we use our lives that determines what kind of men we are. It is my deepest belief that only by giving our lives do we find life. I am convinced that the truest act of courage, the strongest act of manliness, is to sacrifice ourselves for others in a totally non-violent struggle for justice. To be a man is to suffer for others. God help us to be men.

"God Help Us to Be Men"

The *Spiritual Exercises* try in every way to help us become "really honest with ourselves." If there is any truth, or any suggestion of the possibility of truth in film director Luis Bunuel's belief, as reported in the words of Robert Lauder, that "the cleric is the man who has totally conformed to an unjust social situation,"[23] then the custodians of the powerful apostolic instrument that is the book of the *Spiritual Exercises* must push themselves toward greater honesty. They must examine their conformities to see if they are free enough to use the *Exercises* for the liberation of others. If there is no social consciousness in the experience of the *Exercises,* it is because there is no social consciousness in the person of the director. As each of us works through the problem of his own complex conformities, infidelities, and deep social sinfulness, we can pray for all in the words of Cesar Chavez: "God help us to be men."

---

[23]Robert E. Lauder, "Luis Bunuel: The Surrealist as Moralist," *America,* February 3, 1973, p. 94.

Social Action and the Directed Retreat

William J. Connolly, S.J.

Volume 33, 1974, pp. 114-118.

The renewal of prayer that has been developing in the American Church for the last three or four years has aroused concern among some Catholics dedicated to reforming unjust social structures and serving the needs of the socially deprived. This concern seems to stem primarily from the fear that a disproportionate amount of the energy generated by Vatican II is being diverted from attempts to deal with the complexity of social, economic, and political issues and devoted instead to the less frustrating task of putting our spiritual lives in order.

This fear is not baseless. The Christian desire to reject sinful values can easily become an excuse for a flight from the complexity of life, and religious movements concentrating on prayer and ritual have tended to thrive in disjointed times. There has been, too, in the last year or so a tendency in some religious communities for significant numbers of members to opt for explicitly spiritual work while few choose ministries to the socially deprived. The problem, it seems, is not that many choose a spiritual ministry, but that despite Church and community declarations on deprivation in our society, so few are choosing a ministry that will do something about it. When this has consistently happened in communities where such decisions are made by discernment, the validity of the means used to recognize the action of the Spirit has been called into question.

This article proposes to reflect on the question of the relationship between social action and the renewal of prayer in terms of the experience of the directed retreat as that form of help in prayer has been practiced at the Center for Religious Development in Cambridge for the last two years.

286

It will not attempt a resolution of the question, but will try to suggest some dimensions that will have to be taken into account before a resolution is achieved.

Meaning of Directed Retreat

Many forms of prayer experience are now sharing the term "directed retreat." Indeed, usage varies so widely that it can be misleading to employ the term without describing the practice to which it refers in a given instance. At the Center, typical practice stresses the indispensability of personal freedom in all decisions made during the retreat.[1] "Direction" tends to be non-directive, encourages individuality, suggests three to five hours a day of private prayer, avoids imposing structures, usually gives attention to life problems only when they arise in or otherwise affect the experience of prayer. It is assumed that authentic prayer will increase a person's ability to discern the action of the Spirit in his life and develop his readiness to respond to that action. If this does not occur, the authenticity of the prayer is re-examined.

A considerable number of the people who have sought this kind of help have already been engaged in some form of work for the socially deprived, and they have tended to be among those who have benefited most from the experience. It is reflection on the typical retreat experience, however, rather than on that of people already committed to social action, that can tell us most about the relationship developing between prayer and social action.

Retreats and Openness to Reality from the First Week

An experience of authentic prayer in the First Week of the *Spiritual Exercises*[2] leaves a person more open to reality and therefore to the needs of the people around him. Such an experience frees him from control by anger, fear, or a sense of inadequacy, and makes him less vulnerable to group pressure. For example, a person who lacks initiative because experiences of repression have left him angry and bitter should be freed in prayer from control by his bitterness and so regain his initiative. A fear-dominated person becomes hopeful. A person who has let his life be structured by the approval or disapproval of his peers begins to decide for himself.

These experiences open a person outward. Freed from the control of forces that have tended to close him in on himself, he becomes more aware of the reality and needs of other persons and more able to react to them. Without this freeing experience, a person prays "with his head" or his more

---

[1]William J. Connolly, S.J., "Freedom and Prayer in Directed Retreats," pp. 61-67.
[2]William A. Barry, S.J., "The Experience of the First and Second Weeks of the *Spiritual Exercises,*" pp. 95-102.

superficial feelings, and, preoccupied with the tangle of pressures within him, cannot be attentive to the Lord. In particular, he cannot give prolonged attention to the values and priorities of Jesus. Thus it is essential to a prayer that sets out to understand Jesus and respond to His invitation to share His values and mission. Many people need six or seven days or more on this phase of the *Exercises*. It is time well spent as the depth of their later response to the values of Jesus demonstrates.

But the freedom that comes as a result of the First Week also has apostolic value in its own right. The retreatant usually begins to reach out in apostolic action at this point if an opportunity presents itself. The personal awareness of God's love gives him at the same time freedom and the incentive to use it. Rarely does the result of the First Week seem to be purely interior, and rarely does it lack an apostolic thrust. Far from withdrawing the retreatant from action, the First Week experience frees him for it and urges him to it.

Effect of the Second Week of the Exercises

The Second Week of the *Exercises* is a sharply different experience from the First. In this phase the retreatant, now free to listen, is invited to share the mission of Jesus. He contemplates Him, His values and priorities, and lets himself be drawn into an interior association with Him. Through this association he comes to be convinced of the values he wants to live by and the direction he wants his life to take.

A decision to work for the deprived or for the reform of social structures that comes during the *Spiritual Exercises* will generally come during the Second Week. However, the directed retreat as it has been described here has only recently come into frequent use in North America, and the contemplation and freedom on which its success depends are very new to most American priests and religious. Thus many who have made very helpful directed retreats have not yet experienced the whole of the Second Week. Most retreatants seem to need at least two eight-day retreats, often three or four, with frequent prayer between them, before they complete this phase of the Exercises. This does not mean that they are spiritually retarded, but that they need time to be themselves before the Lord and let Him be Himself to them.

The Work of the Retreat Director

Does the lack of more obvious social results point also to a lack of social awareness on the part of directors? The question is not easy to answer. The director is not a teacher; and, in the practice of the Center, his task is one of evoking rather than instructing. Because the person's own freedom and initiative are essential, the retreatant is encouraged to see himself as a peer of the director, not his pupil. Anything that would remind him of homework or class assignments is avoided. He is expected to see himself as an equal responsible for his own life, able to let himself meet the Lord with the knowledge he has already assimilated. Instruction on social issues would conflict with this attitude by placing the director in the role of a teacher, "one who knows."

In this perspective, a good director works with a retreatant as he finds him. He does not set out to teach him the psychologist's or the political scientist's view of reality. He helps him to recognize and respond to the reality he sees for himself when the scales of his anger, fear, and guilt drop away, and when he has committed himself to the mission of Jesus. The director carefully avoids, then, imposing his own view of reality, because such imposition could not fail to obscure the retreatant's view. Especially in the early stages of a retreat, his task is to help the retreatant to develop clear sight. In a sense, it does not matter what he sees, as long as he sees it, and knows that it is real.

In order to perform satisfactorily his essential task, then, the director refrains from trying to perform other tasks if he believes these may clash with it. This means that he will be content to leave areas of ignorance, but unwilling to leave a fear of expanding horizons or a lack of concern for God's People. A directed retreat that ended with a person knowing nothing about economic determinism or the welfare system might be completely successful, but a retreat that gave a person much knowledge of both, yet left him afraid to let the creative action of God touch him, or too angry to let the Spirit invite him to a new direction in his life would not, as a directed retreat, be successful at all.

Individual and Social Dimensions of Meditations

With these reservations stated, however, it is clear that such key themes of the *Exercises* as Sin in the World, the Kingdom, and the Two Standards should be presented with a social as well as an individual emphasis. Cultures and nations sin, and individuals become both victims and accomplices of their sin. A retreat director either accepts or ignores this fact. A director aware of the entangling and destructive nature of both individual and social sinfulness can, by stimulating the retreatant's awareness of what he already knows, present both dimensions without imposing undigested knowledge. Many retreatants can rather easily become aware that the King comes to rescue societies as well as individuals, and that the Two Standards involve choices between social good and social evil.

In the same way the deeds, teaching, debates, and death of Jesus have a social as well as an individual dimension. He struggled with and was killed by a poltical, religious, economic system. The socially aware director can call attention to the pertinent gospel data without burying the retreatant's consciousness under a mound of new facts and viewpoints.

The core of the directed retreat experience is personal dialogue with the Lord. If a person wants to deepen his prayer and life experience, there is no substitute for this personal dialogue. From it there will develop an increasing receptivity to reality; and if the person's experience is not to be truncated, this will include social reality.

Authenticity of Renewal and Social Action

The question of the relationship between social action and the renewal of prayer is of crucial importance to those who promote contemporary Ignatian spirituality. For this spirituality, when it is genuine, leads generally to apostolic action; and if a widespread renewal of the *Spiritual Exercises* leaves unaffected so central an area of apostolic endeavor as social action, the authenticity of the renewal must be questioned. Like any spiritual movement the Ignatian contribution to the renewal of prayer must be judged by its fruits. By Ignatian standards the fact that this contribution helps people to pray is important indeed, but not enough. The Lord reaches through authentic prayer to grasp a man's life; and if the life of a praying person remains untouched, there is something wrong with the prayer. In the same way, if a spiritual movement leaves central, obvious, and critical needs of God's people untouched, there is something wrong with the movement.

Social Action from Love, Not from Anger

On the other hand, the experience we have had of directed retreats may have much to say to social action. For instance, this experience has revealed the surprisingly deep and varied influence of anger on the prayer and life attitudes of American Catholics, and the startling extent to which it can control both. Social action, because it sees so much to be angry at, will have to be particularly wary of this control. Anger against all authority and any establishment, which accumulates to some extent in every life, may go too long unrecognized and uncriticized in the social activist's life because the critical and surgical function so necessary to the curing of sinful structures affords him a handy outlet for it. If, however, his action is finally to proceed from love, and not from a desire to destroy, he must submit his anger to the Lord in extensive and profound inner dialogue. And anger has so many disguises, especially zeal, that for many people the directed retreat may be the best way, even the only way, to detect its real force and place it before the Lord.

POSTSCRIPT

Notes on Adapting the Exercises of St. Ignatius

David T. Asselin, S.J.

Volume 28, 1969, pp. 410-420.

The book of the *Exercises* is not monolithic. It contains, according to nos. 18, 19, 20, more than one series of spiritual exercises, demanding adaptation by the one who gives them. In the concrete, it is the director's responsibility to tailor the content, order, and method of these exercises to the spiritual and natural capacities, needs, and dispositions of his retreatants. Even within the 30 days' Exercises careful selection and adaptation are not infrequently indicated, for instance in nos. 4, 17, 72, 129, 133, 162, and so forth.

The conclusion seems inevitable that adaptation is proper, even essential, to any authentic tradition of the *Spiritual Exercises* of Ignatius. To give them without careful adaptation to the retreatant's concrete circumstances might gravely reduce, even eliminate, their genuine Ignatian character.

However, nowhere does the author of the *Exercises* deal directly with the kind of adaptation that is commonplace today, namely, the annual abbreviated (anywhere from two to eight days) Exercises given to a group; moreover, those Exercises that are made by private individuals are rarely guided by a director in the Ignatian manner. Such casually accepted adaptations of the Exercises involve considerable departures from their original concept, judged by the writings of their author and the first century or more of their practice. It would seem to be a basic rule of any adaptation that the essence or substantials of the original be preserved in the adapted form. It seems that on several points many modern adaptations fail in this regard.

First, the most accepted tradition involves telescoping all four Weeks of

292

the Exercises into about a quarter of the time originally devoted to them, the point being that this abbreviation is usually achieved by omitting all or most of the repetitions that appear essential to the original Ignatian method. Second, the Exercises today are frequently experienced as a kind of annual "refresher" for those who have made them at least once already in one form or another. Third, these annual abbreviated Exercises are usually the only form in which most retreatants have any experience of them. The fourth and fifth points have already been mentioned, namely, that almost invariably the Exercises take the form of a group experience, and finally that those who make them privately usually make them without genuine Ignatian direction—whereas the authentic Exercises on the human level seem to have been conceived as a dialogue not, mind you, between the retreatants themselves, but between the retreatant and the director. Although privately directed Exercises are doubtless the ideal, it may not be practical to suggest the immediate elimination of group retreats today. Let us content ourselves with a few suggestions about how to give or make them in a more authentic manner.

We might begin with some remarks about the Ignatian repetition. Although he never considers a group repetition of the Exercises, such as the annual retreats common in our day, Ignatius does not leave us without considerable evidence about his notion of repetition within the Exercises themselves, for instance in nos. 62, 118, 119, 121-126, 204, 226, 227, and elsewhere.

For Ignatius, a repetition is never the simple reduplication of a prior exercise. Perhaps it is on this point that we have made our greatest mistake in conceiving the annual repetitions of the *Exercises*. The activity characteristic of an Ignatian repetition is not a simple review of matter covered in a previous exercise; rather, it means returning to and dwelling on those points in that exercise where affective responses or spiritual experiences were stimulated in the retreatant, consolations, desolations, inspirations, and so forth (see no. 62). In the Ignatian repetition it is not so much the points of subject matter as the points of personal sensitivity that are revisited, so as to reinforce, deepen, or better appreciate them. The process might be compared to focusing closely with a zoom-lens, which eliminates large areas of the original picture so as to concentrate on points of particular personal interest.

Ignatian repetitions, therefore, imply considerable abbreviation of the prior prayer matter, together with concentration on points of personal spiritual experience, which are most unlikely to coincide in any two individuals. Moreover, true to the general principle enunciated in no. 2 of the *Exercises:* "It is not much knowledge that fills and satisfies the spirit, but to feel and taste things inwardly," Ignatius does not aim in his repetitions at expanding concepts, spiritual theology, or noetic faith, but rather at simplifying and intensifying an awareness of spiritual realities, especially personal presence to and service of the Lord. What counts in repetitions is not new content, but renewed encounter—not just repeating an old acquaintance with the things of God, but discovering deeper levels of friendship with Him. Over the period of a typical day of the *Exercises,* Ignatius usually insists on four or five hours of contemplation, of which three or four are repetitions of the first hour, in the manner described above. This is perhaps one of the most characteristic aspects of authentic Ignatian prayer. To drop it from plans for adapting the *Exercises* is no minor omission.

By dint of these repetitions, Ignatius expects a characteristic development to occur in the retreatant's daily prayer; there is a pattern of simplification and spontaneity, there is a penetration of the true meaning and relevance of the mystery contemplated, there is an increased realization of the contemporary actuality of that mystery in the world of the retreatant's experience, finally day by day there grows a cumulative sense of the interdependence and relationship of the mysteries of the Word make flesh. By virture of repeatedly entering the mysteries of the Lord at successively more intimate levels, a man can be expected to see, savor, and know the Word in a new and wholly personal way—eventually, to borrow Ignatius' favorite prayer phrase, to "find the Lord in all things."

The retreatant does more than appropriate a mystery of the Lord; rather, he begins to appreciate how completely his own mystery has been appropriated by the Lord.

It is clear from the days described in the book of the *Exercises,* that what began as meditation and rumination of a mystery of the Word is designed to conclude with intimate contact, spontaneous response, and personal colloquy. Day by day facility in entering the mystery of the Lord should grow, which implies a growth in faith, hope, and love, or, essentially, a growth in consolation according to Ignatius (see no. 316 of the *Exercises,* and no. 11 of the *Autograph Directory*). This results in a growing realization of the Lord's presence and dynamic involvement in the entire world of one's everyday experience, and an integrating overview and comprehension of the Lord's concrete engagement in all contemporary reality. This cumulative integration of the Lord's mysteries is explicit in the book of the *Exercises,* for instance both in prospect (in no. 116) and in retrospect (in no. 130). When the Word of God becomes enfleshed anew ("nuevamente," no. 109) in the retreatant's world of experience, contemporary reality takes on incredibly new value and significance for him: his faith view of events interior and exterior to himself deepens and matures. Really, it is only in virtue of such repeated contemplation of the mysteries of the Word of God that one can personally discover the full and real significance of the events of human history and one's own existence. "Only by faith and by meditation on the word of God can one always and everywhere find God . . . seek his will in every event, see Christ in all men . . . make correct judgments about the true meaning and value of temporal things," as we read in the decree on the laymen in the Church, of Vatican II (see Abbott's edition, p. 493).

If what is known as the "lectio divina," or meditation on the word of God, is a kind of common denominator of authentic Christian prayer (see J. Leclercq, O.S.B., "The Unity of Prayer," in *Worship*, v. 32, # 7, p. 408 and "Meditation as a Biblical Reading," by the same author, in *Worship*, v. 33, # 9, p. 562 ff.), we should be able to discern its essential elements in the typical prayer form of the *Exercises*. We submit that the text reveals the pattern of the "lectio" in several ways, at least in its three basic phases: first, the reading or listening to the word of Scripture; second, the personal appropriation of this word in a concrete, contemporary, and meaningful way; third, the spontaneous response, personal contact, colloquy, or prayer, which emerges by grace and the action of the Lord's Spirit ("who teaches all things and brings to your mind whatever I have spoken to you" [Jn 14:26]) out of the preceding phases of the "lectio." In the *Exercises* the director's role touches all three phases: he is to feed the word of God to the retreatant, guide the method of prayer and repetition, and discern the action of the Lord's Spirit. The *Exercises* are a school of prayer on Scripture and of discernment of the initiatives of the Spirit, which is of course why they are ideally dispositive for one confronted with making a decision, if personal circumstances call for one.

The Scripture-centered character of the *Exercises* is not difficult to determine from a simple perusal of the text where the focus for thirty days is almost uniquely on the word of God introduced daily in the so-called History Preamble—a fact that was formally recognized by the late Father J. B. Janssens, General of the Society of Jesus, in an instruction of May 7, 1964, declaring that "masters of novices and spiritual directors should draw their teaching and their direction principally from Holy Scripture, from which St. Ignatius drew the matter of the *Exercises*."

If we examine the historical beginnings of the *Exercises*, which, according to no. 99 of Ignatius' autobiography, occurred on his sickbed at Loyola, it is not difficult to discern the basic phases of the same "lectio divina," at least in their rudimentary forms. His spiritual experience began with a kind of Scripture reading (the *Vita Christi* and the *Imitation of Christ*; it was the words of Christ and Mary that he transcribed carefully in a copy book, from which the book of the *Exercises* apparently evolved). Secondly, there followed long hours of rumination and personal appropriation of what he read, imagination and affectivity reducing his discoveries to their contemporary implications for him. Finally, from this emerged notable peace, a taste for prayer and spiritual things, and a consuming desire to change his whole way of life so as to please and serve his Lord in all things, a decision that took many forms but was never retracted. This, as he notes in the same autobiography (no. 100), was the beginning of the characteristic trait of his lifelong spiritual development, a growing facility in finding God in all things.

We also discover the same basic phases of the "lectio" in Ignatius' so-called preambles to each of the contemplations of the *Exercises* (see 102-105). These are more than mere preludes to Ignatian contemplation: they are integral parts of it, providing its fundamental structure and essential movement. What is known as the "Historia" is designed to begin invariably (see no. 105) with the eye of faith focused on the heart of the divine Trinity as it contemplates man's spiritual plight and total helplessness and determines to take salvific initiatives by sending the divine Word into the world; every History Preamble begins this way and leads to reading a selection from Scripture; thus it corresponds to the first phase of the "lectio."

The second preamble, known as the "Composicion," is designed to assist the concrete and personal appropriation, or (as J. Leclercq puts it) the embodiment of the Scripture just read, so that somehow it is realized more deeply and translated into more contemporary spatial-temporal dimensions for the retreatant. The process of rumination is designed, to our mind, for realization, that is, to see, hear, grasp with greater effect, the contemporary relevance and reality of the mystery, truth, or event revealed in Scripture. In this way, revelation takes place anew, as it were, within the retreatant's consciousness of reality. Just as the "Historia" focuses on a Biblical event as one in a series of points of entry of the divine Word into human history, so the "composicion," by image, symbol, or parable, lends that event an actuality in the retreatant's present world.

It is both natural and effective to communicate great truths in concrete symbol and image, to capture the importance of events in dramatic portrayal, to point a great lesson in graphic parable. It is this kind of experience of things that touches more than the mind—it moves the whole man, head and heart, to spontaneous reaction and response. In our culture of communication arts and imagery these remarks are almost trite, but they illustrate the importance of the second preamble of Ignatian contemplation whereby an invisible salvation event or truth is translated into concrete image or symbol to convey it to the heart and imagination that govern man's responses.

The third Ignatian preamble brings us to the point of personal contact and response, prayerful petition and colloquy, which characterize the third phase of the "lectio." It would be incorrect to consider this preamble as a mere prelude to spiritual encounter; it is already the first effect of it.

In his own particular manner, we feel Ignatius has reformulated the age-old method of prayer on Scripture. If this is true, then the preambles are more than introductory steps; they provide the basic structure and frame of reference for all that follows in the contemplation of the *Exercises*. The first step is taking up the word of God in Scripture as a revelation of the intimate concern and engagement of the Trinity on the history of man. The second step is realizing the contemporary actuality of this divine involvement in the world of human experience; and it is precisely at this point that many have found an apt use of short films, slides, symbols, and so forth, to be effective in stimulating realistic contemplation of the word of God and mature response to it. If appropriate, these parables, images, symbols function as vehicles of the divine word into the affectivity of the retreatant, deepening realization in and stimulating response from the whole man.

What are usually referred to as the "points" of Ignatian contemplations are really, as a glance at nos. 106 ff. will reveal, nothing more than *repetitions* in greater detail of the three preambles we have been discussing. The content of the "Historia" is unfolded more graphically; the function of the "composicion," which is to grasp the mystery more concretely in contemporary terms becomes, in these so-called "points," simply "to see . . . to hear . . . to observe closely" what the "Historia" presents. And it is not difficult to see how the closing colloquy of Ignatian contemplations both continues and expands the third preamble or petition for "lo que quiero y deseo." It is in the colloquy that the contemporary dimension of the salvific events or mysteries is indicated by Ignatius (see no. 109) as well as their cumulative integration (see no 116). Everything centers around the presentation of the Scriptural word. By insisting on such repetitions within each exercise and within each day, Ignatius hopes to plant the word of God in the inner man to transform and move him entirely.

It would appear superfluous to submit by way of conclusion from the preceding observations that the director of annual repetitions of the Exercises might consider it his primary job to suggest apt selections from Scripture touching on a single theme of the *Exercises* for prayerful contemplation over each day of the retreat. If his remarks are appropriately brief leading the individual to find for himself what spiritual fruit he can, more time can be devoted to the private discussion and direction of his personal prayer experience according to the norms of discernment carefully outlined and emphasized by Ignatius. If the number of retreatants is large, the principal reason for a team of directors is to assure this daily guidance to each retreatant.

A careful use of short films and slides in conjunction with the director's remarks introducing Scripture, for the purpose indicated above, can be very helpful in a group retreat, but its importance is quite secondary. In general, films do not substitute for or contain the word of God proposed by the director; rather, they are meant to concretize it, to convey it to the affectivity, bringing home its full meaning and contemporary relevance to the retreatant's heart and mind. Needless to say, such communication aids should be very carefully selected in view of the purpose they are meant to serve. They are not intended in the *Exercises* of Ignatius as points of departure of group discussion; and it is a misguided hope, to say the last, to search for films and slides that will substitute for the director's role of proposing Scripture for private contemplation.

In the course of annual repetitions of the *Exercises,* one should expect not only a simplification of prayer method, an abbreviation of subject matter, but especially an increase of personal individuation and responsibility in determing the structure, manner, and movement of the exercises, always, of course, in private dialogue with the director. Only in this way, it seems, can we permit the Spirit to breathe when and how he wills. Spiritual maturity cannot be orchestrated for a group in the same direction or at the same speed. Greater room for authentic repetition must be allowed for the individual to return to points of personal spiritual sensitivity; increased private direction must be provided so as to tailor the movement and content of prayer to the spiritual capacities and needs of each; greater respect must be had for the uniqueness of the inner inspirations and vocation of the individual, his personal spiritual maturity, his own relationship to the Lord.

Over a period of time, the emphasis should move from "lectio et meditatio" to "oratio." One of the principal purposes of repetition in the prayerful rumination of Scripture is precisely to increase the facility of this "oratio" or finding the Lord in things (which, incidentally, is Ignatius' definition of the word "devotion," see *Autobiography,* no. 100).

Such a movement or development is discernible on the whole within the *Exercises* themselves. The emphasis of the first two weeks seems to be rather on carefully structured meditation and contemplation, which, as the author notes in no. 162, is merely an introduction and model for better and more complete prayer later on. The last two weeks are distinguished by a personal penetration of and identification with the Lord's own experience of dying and rising, the focal point of the Gospels and the key to spiritual life. In the final contemplation of the *Exercises* ("to attain love") Ignatius accumulates in four points the progressive modes and levels of finding the Lord which were characteristic respectively of the four preceding Weeks. By then he expects the retreatant's sensitivity to have matured with respect to the Lord's presence and initiative in all things. In a word, what is anticipated as the fruit of each hour, each day, or of the many days of the *Exercises,* is essentially the same thing—an increase of Biblical peace or "shalom," which is an experience not merely of the absence of inner conflict but of the presence of the living Lord. In Ignatian terms, it implies finding God in contemporary reality.

This shift from "lectio" to "oratio," from rumination to colloquy, from meditation to spiritual contact, in the *Exercises* as a whole, does not imply that Ignatius expects the earlier weeks to be entirely discursive and experientially dry; quite the contrary, in every exercise spiritual experience is both the goal and criterion of progress (see nos. 2, 4, 15, 48, 76, and so forth).

Throughout the Exercises, whenever a moment of spiritual contact is attained, the retreatant is instructed to pause until the experience is exhausted before returning to meditation on new matter (see no. 76). The *Spiritual Exercises* have this in common with the ancient tradition to the "lectio divina," that meditation and rumination on the word of God do not aim at what might be called faith education but rather a faith experience—"no el mucho saber . . . mas el sentir y gustar las cosas internamente" (no. 2). But if we stop at the point of spiritual satisfaction and experience we inadequately express the purpose of both the Ignatian *Exercises* and the "lectio." Both, it seems, aim at achieving prayer experience not merely to satisfy the soul for the moment, but hopefully to have the experience somehow overflow into daily life. By habitual and varied repetitions, the spiritual impression and awareness of the Lord's presence and engagement in realities will linger afterward, return more spontaneously, become an abiding awareness that accompanies both the events of life within oneself and those in the world around. This begins the spiritual maturity of finding the Lord not only in the exercises of prayer, but in all things. This, perhaps, is what it means to "pray always."

It is not surprising to read in the opening lines of the first charter of the Society of Jesus (the *Formula* approved by Paul III in 1540), that the Jesuit "is part of a community founded primarily for the task of advancing souls in Christian life and doctrine, and of propagating the faith *by the ministry of the word, by spiritual exercises . . .*" (emphasis added).

It may be interesting and relevant at this point to indicate how the first group adaptations of the *Exercises* were conducted. About the middle of the 17th century near Vannes in Brittany, a certain Father Vincent Huby, S.J., and others had been granted the use of a house for the purpose of directing the *Exercises*. At first, all who came were directed privately, beginning from the day on which they happened to arrive. After a while it was promulgated throughout the parishes that any wishing to make the *Exercises* should apply on either of two designated days each month. When the first of these days arrived, a large crowd of all sorts of people came and the first group retreat on record began (see Watrigant, "Collection de la bibliothèque des exercises de s. Ignace," no 2) about a century after the death of St. Ignatius.

From the detailed description provided in the source mentioned, we might draw attention to several points. First, these earliest group retreats were conducted by a team of about five priests, principally for the purpose of providing adequate private spiritual direction. Moreover, in the evening, the "points" for contemplation were given in the chapel completely darkened except for a large translucent picture, lit by candles from behind, presenting a scene concretely illustrating the "points" being given. Short of improvements in the field of communications at our disposal today, this technique of about 1660 might well be suggested as a considerable improvement over the method of presentation so many retreatants have been subjected to since that time. These pioneers in group retreats were thus attempting to communicate the word of God in conjunction with an image whereby the message was conveyed not merely to the mind but to the heart, to the whole man. It was an attempt to translate into a group situation the composition preamble, and appears as the legitimate ancestor of the modern use of slides and films in the *Spiritual Exercises* of Ignatius, as we have described it.

It is not for group discussion, but as a part of the contemplative prayer experience itself, that the best use of these media of communication is made during a retreat. They are not teaching aids, nor need they carry an explicit spiritual message in themselves. In point of fact, it is more important that they be works of quality and strength in their own right than bearers of a moral or spiritual lesson. The role of communicating the Scripture, of introducing the retreatant to the gospel mysteries for private contemplation, and of guiding and instructing him in his personal spiritual experiences, remains the principal work of the director. Whether or not he uses modern communication media will depend on whether he can find and employ in his approach some that are effective supports for his main task, not substitutes for or distractions from it.

The importance that Ignatius places on the use of images and parables for the essential functioning of the *Exercises* is not difficult to illustrate from the text. We have already seen this emphasis in the composition preamble (see no. 47) which he felt could never be omitted. In number 74, in a set of instructions about the immediate conditions and preparation for contemplation, he emphasizes the connection between the use of brief parables (in themselves purely secular) and the spiritual fruit desired in a particular exercise. The exercitant rising at midnight is instructed to turn his attention to the subject of his contemplation, moving himself toward the desired grace experience of that prayer, not by adding thoughts, ideas, resolutions, and so forth, but, by using examples, proposing to himself a little parable about a knight arraigned before his king and stricken with shame and confusion. In the following exercise he is told to identify with the image of great culprits going loaded with chains to appear before their judge. We find the same emphasis in the famous parables of the temporal king and three pairs of men. The connection between the use of these images or examples and the specific spiritual fruit and grace desired in the exercises ("drawing myself to confusion for my many sins *by setting before myself examples*") is quite explicit. Today, a short film can play, perhaps even more effectively, the same role. In point of fact it can serve many purposes.

First, the film can portray some part or aspect of the real world which the director desires to impress upon the retreatant precisely as he invites him to contemplate that real world from the viewpoint of the word of God. This word thus unfolded works in him as he views concrete realities, helps him to see and evaluate everything anew from the standpoint of the gospel: a dynamic composition of the word of God and a human reality begins to occur in the retreatant, which can dramatically alter his whole attitude to the world, and his posture in making decisions for the future.

Moreover, the film can act as a meaningful and effective symbol or parable, with similar effect on the retreatant's response to the word of God with which he has been confronted. It is clear, too, that some films may effect a certain atmosphere or mood desirable in view of more fruitful receptivity of the word of the Lord. Finally, a second or third screening of films can be useful in bringing about, at times, the desired effects of repetitions in a retreat. Clearly, all these film uses call for greater explanation and discussion.

These pages have been entitled deliberately and, it is hoped, not ineptly, mere "Notes." They do not pretend to be more than observations which are pertinent to the basic problem of adapting the *Spiritual Exercises*. Perhaps they may contribute something towards a renewal that will insure their continued effectiveness in an age of spiritual search and crisis.

Hopefully, further and more penetrating study will prompt concrete and detailed suggestions with regard to resources and techniques for group *Exercises*. But these would correspond rather to the second of three stages of renewal of the *Exercises* proposed by both Pope Paul VI and Father Pedro Arrupe, General of the Jesuits, namely, the practical reworking of the *Exercises* in the light of Vatican II and the spiritual needs of modern man. Such concrete efforts should be undertaken only on the basis of a more penetrating study of the documents and history of the *Exercises* themselves as the only solid ground for experimentation in adapting techniques for giving them today.

The Nineteenth Annotation Retreat: The Retreat of the Future?

Mary Sullivan, r.c., and
Dot Horstman

Volume 36, 1972, pp. 277-285.

Many busy wives and mothers would like to make a retreat but find that their responsibilities make a traditional retreat impossible. One solution to this problem has been found on Long Island, New York, where, over the past four years, over seven hundred married women have made a nineteenth annotation retreat according to the *Spiritual Exercises of St. Ignatius*.

The introductory observations of the *Exercises* (sometimes called the annotations) provide ground rules for the director/directress of an Ignatian retreat. Ignatius' nineteenth annotation provides for the person who is preoccupied with "necessary business" and unable to get away for a strict retreat: the retreatant may make the *Exercises* over an extended period of time as she remains in her ordinary life-situation.

The nineteenth annotation retreat does not separate a retreatant from concrete, ordinary life experiences; it plunges her further into them as she prays each day. During the retreat she is continually invited by her God to surrender to him. She begins to realize that God is always with her, always present in the daily exigencies of her life. Her surrender to him in prayer is instantly experienced in her day-to-day living. Her prayer teaches her to be as present to her God as he is to her.

Four years ago we were responsible for bringing a group of ten married women together to make this type of retreat. Since then the retreatants have grown from ten to more than seven hundred. We have grown from one team of directresses (always including a religious and a married woman) to twenty-two teams.

Among the many things we have learned are three major points: the nineteenth annotation retreat works well with a group, the combination of lay and religious as a team of directresses is beneficial; women religious find it feasible to be trained in this spiritual ministry while continuing their other apostolic involvements.

Beginnings

The hunger to experience Jesus Christ in a retreat has been very evident in our area for some time, and the growth of that hunger has far outstripped the availability of traditional retreat modalities.

Long Island's Diocese of Rockville Centre is the fastest growing in the U.S. In Suffolk County, the eastern part of the diocese, growth is particularly rapid. New families move in each week; parishes have neither the time nor the money to build parochial schools for the education of the children. Most parishes have instead constructed parish centers, and the children's religious education goes on in parishioners' homes.

In order for their children to receive religious training, Catholic parents have had to become involved in the teaching of religion. The parents who wish to teach—most often the mothers—are required to take an updated doctrine course given by the diocese. Many continue in this program for advanced study.

As these women learn, they find themselves wanting to know God, not just to know about him. They are ripe for growing in prayer, ready to make retreats.

The desire for a retreat is present in these women. They lack free time to make a traditional retreat. How were these women to be served? Obviously, the retreat would come to them.

We began with ten women. They instantly recruited ten more, who instantly recruited ten more. The nineteenth annotation retreat in the home environment was responded to, was needed, was effective. We gave this type of retreat in our area a new name: "At Home Retreats" was launched.

Our rules are simple. We keep the groups small—no more than a dozen. We limit the time commitment each retreatant makes to two hours once a week and fifteen minutes once a day—we must be mindful that these retreatants must attend to "necessary business." Each team of directresses spends time together in prayer and preparation, and they make themselves available to the retreatants for consultation in addition to the formal meeting times. We base our retreat on the Ignatian *Exercises,* and give it over an extended period. And, as we'll explain later, we insist that each retreat team include both a lay person and a religious.

In 1974 we incorporated "At Home Retreats" in order to codify the training of retreat teams and to insure fidelity to the concept we were developing.

Expectations

We are continually reminded of the effectiveness of "At Home Retreats." As the retreat begins, each person shares her expectations with the team and with the other retreatants. Each week, as the retreat unfolds, we see something happening with these expectations.

Expectations are typically stated in one of these general ways: "I used to know God better as a teenager. He seems to have slipped from my life. I'm faithful to the Church, teach CCD, am active in some parish organizations. But God is no longer a person to me. I want to know him again, but this time as an adult." Or, "My husband's so at ease in his relationship with God. I envy him that. I want to know God that way." Or, "I don't know why I'm here. But when Suzie told me about this terrific experience that she had I thought that maybe I'd like to make an 'At Home Retreat.' Maybe, just maybe, the peace that I saw literally grow in her will grow in me. I sure could use it." Or, "I want to grow in my faith so that I can pass it on to my children."

Each woman may come with a different set of expectations, motivated by a different set of felt needs. But underlying all of these there is a basic desire for God, a trust that he can come, and a belief in him.

Prerequisites

We feel very deeply that unless there is this basic desire, trust and faith in God on the part of the retreatant, the person should not make the retreat. We have learned this from experience. The retreat cannot be a time of Scripture study, or a doctrinal refutation, or theological discussion.

When we began giving retreats in the home, we felt that anyone who wished to come and make one should do so. We soon learned that those who thought a retreat was to solve problems, or *discuss* God, or to nit-pick Scripture points was not looking for a retreat experience. We then discovered that such women hinder the retreat experience of the others in the group.

We now ask that each prospective retreatant believe in her God, desire him, trust him. She is asked to pray daily over material presented to her. She knows that she will share with the whole group just what is happening within her prayer and how it is overflowing into her family and other concerns. She makes a three and one-half month commitment to meet weekly with the team and the other retreatants. We also ask that the sharing in each of the sessions be kept within the group. This principle of confidentiality, beautifully adhered to by all the retreatants, enables the whole group to relax and be themselves.

An "At Home Retreat" has thirteen sessions. The structure of the first twelve is the same. One of the team members opens with a prayer. She then asks the women to share what has happened in their periods of prayer during the previous week. Then the team, through talks, a film, a record, or slides, presents the material to be reflected on during the week. The two-hour session concludes with shared prayer.

Each retreatant leaves for home with Scripture passages for daily prayer and some tangible object that is the outgrowth of the session's consideration of Ignatius' *Spiritual Exercises.* The principle of the "Application of the Senses" comes alive for them in this way.

The time for the weekly session depends upon the team's scheduling and the best time spot for the retreatants. Some women find it convenient to meet one morning a week when their children have all gone to school and they can be free for two hours. Others with very young children rejoice in spending a retreat evening together while their husbands can be home to baby-sit.

Patterns

As each retreatant begins to ponder the "Principle and Foundation" of Ignatius' *Spiritual Exercises,* she seems to enter what might be called a honeymoon stage of her relationship with God. He becomes so tangible, so evident, so necessary in everything—nature, her husband, her children, her own uniqueness. She can't wait for the fifteen minutes of daily personal prayer. It is too short a time to spend with him. She knows with certainty that she has been created uniquely by God for himself. She is happy.

The session after the women have prayed on the "Principle and Foundation" is their first opportunity to share with each other about their prayer. They are excited, realistic, and truly spontaneous. As they share their lived moments of personal realization in their prayer, they begin to notice how alike they are. A bond begins to form, and the bond is that God is present in the life of every woman in that room.

We have discovered that as the retreatant continues in this prayer she begins to find that the time for prayer drags. Suddenly fifteen minutes is much too long to pray. Maybe, she suggests to the group the following week, it would be better to pray for five minutes three times daily. There are simply too many distractions at home to pray there. There is always the telephone, the children asking questions, things to do. Maybe, just maybe, she should make the retreat at another time.

At this stage of the retreat we have begun to notice a variety of responses within the group. Those who are praying deeply begin to feel discouraged in their prayer. Those who are not being faithful to their times of daily prayer find that everything's going "great," "beautiful," "wonderful." The victory bulletins tend to be false at this point. Why is this so? What's begun to happen here? The group explores obstacles to prayer, fears, struggles. The lay member of the team tells how she has had to find a place at home for prayer, a definite time that was best for her to pray, and ways of letting in-beween periods of prayer prepare her for her time of daily reflection. The retreatants are able to grasp so much from her honest sharing that they feel renewed.

We then ask the retreatant to trust God, to pray faithfully, to wait upon him. As she does so, she begins to realize deep within herself that she has been unfaithful to this God who has given her so much. She experiences again, very tangibly, that her God loves her and is with her. No matter how much she has turned from him, he is still there calling her back to himself. She is happy that she never left the retreat.

First Fruits

She has arrived at what we feel is the most necessary, most important, most crucial "moment" of the whole retreat. God is faithful. He asks that she be generous, open, and responsible to him. At this time of retreat she *feels,* she *knows,* she *experiences* herself as loved by God. She *loves* and *accepts* all others as loved by God. It's a time of acceptance, of peace, of relief, of joy, of love. It spills out everywhere. Because she is changed, she views her husband, her children, the other retreatants, her neighbors as God would view them: lovable! The retreat experience integrates very nicely with life experience.

The daughter of an "At Home" retreatant put it beautifully, "You know, Mom, there hasn't been a single fight between you and Dad. You're not hollering all the time at us kids either. I sure like your retreat!"

Hearing of reconciliations, of the lightness, the joy, the peace that each of the retreatants are experiencing at this moment in the *Exercises,* another bond forms to bring the retreatants closer to each other. The bond is the knowledge that each one is a sinner but a loved sinner. They accept each woman in that room as who she is.

The "Call of the King" is felt as surrender in very practical terms. We have found that at the end of this session the group is extremely quiet, pensive, thoughtful. The joy, the laughter, the lightsomeness of the previous prayer is still there, but now it is a basis for something new. All during the week that follows the presentation on the kingdom, the team is busy with outside consultations. Each retreatant has need to share how she hears the call, how she hopes to respond, how she needs help to respond.

The awareness of a common struggle to respond, a common desire to be of service, a common fear of giving themselves to God draw the group out of themselves. The team members spend individual time listening to the retreatants. The latter spend more time daily in prayer and begin to seek out the others in their group and share prayer with them in between the weekly sessions.

Midpoint

The retreat group has now been meeting for about one and one-half months. Much has drawn them together—their daily prayer, their sharing of struggles and joys in prayer and life, their acceptance of themselves and each other, their awareness of who they really are. And so the contemplation on the Incarnation is easy to understand. The Word has become flesh for them in this very group, in their own families, in themselves. They are filled with a keen hunger to know Christ intimately, to love him ardently, and to serve him. And so for the next month they ponder him growing within Mary's flesh (as their own children grew within them), growing in Nazareth's family, reaching adulthood and the time for service. They simply walk with him, marvel at his words and deeds, and ultimately face Jerusalem with him.

More than one month is spent praying over the life of Jesus. Scripture comes alive for them as it never did before. The realization that Jesus dwells within each other is newly evident to them. But somewhere during the contemplations on the Life of Christ, it seems that struggle seems to set in again. And it does so for the whole group, though not at the same time for each of them. They begin to seek excuses not to pray; they would prefer more discussion than prayer at the weekly sessions. At this point the team purposely makes the sessions shorter. They wish the retreatants to be face-to-face with God and to experience him, not them.

Each retreatant ultimately has to say, "But, for me, who is Jesus?" As she ponders this question, as she faces who he is and what he has done, she finds herself telling the group that he is continually calling to her in her life. They all experience this and marvel at his way with each of them.

The time to enter Jerusalem has come. The time of his passion has arrived. The time of compassion with him is now. We have found this to be one of the most supportive, encouraging times of the retreat. Each realizes that Jesus has died for her. Each realizes that she is able to participate in his passion. Each realizes how each of the others is participating or has participated in Jesus' passion. They are compassionate toward one another through their sharing, their prayers, and their deeds for others during the week. This time of compassion for others' passions is new for many of them. For the first time they are drawn out of themselves to enter into his passion and the passion of others.

He is risen! They enter into the newness of his life rejoicing. They are ready to speak his love not only with words but with actions to others. Three and one-half months are over; at the final session, celebration of the Eucharist brings the retreat to a close and to a beginning.

Why It Works

The growth, the realness, the tangibleness of change is so evident in an "At Home Retreat" that we have often asked ourselves "why?" To put it simply, we believe that all this happens because the retreatant prays daily over an extended period of time. The very intimacy of her relationship with God has to overflow, has to be evident, has to be tangible. It is also because she prays with others who are living her life style and who are called by him, as she is, in the midst of diapers, cooking, ringing telephones and all the rest. There is a mutuality between her prayer at home alone and her weekly prayer with the others. She finds both supportive.

The Lay Directress

We have discovered that the lay member of the team brings an important dimension to the retreat. She brings herself, her own prayer, her expertise as a lay woman living as the retreatants are living, her ability to articulate back to them what they have experienced because she herself has experienced God as they have.

We cannot emphasize strongly enough the necessity of having a lay member on the retreat team. From 1968 to 1972 we gave retreats in the home with only religious as the retreat team. It was only with the added in-depth dimension of the lay person that the idea took hold, caught fire, and moved.

We have learned a lot from experience about the selection of the lay member of the team. We have found that women over thirty, married for at least ten years, who have made an "At Home Retreat" and have been changed by this experience are the best potential lay retreat directresses.

We have discovered that women who have been recommended to us because they have a master's degree in theology or are CCD coordinators, or are "pious" or "a friend of Sister's" are usually not the people for whom we are looking. Suffice it to say that we have learned this through actual experience.

We have learned that if a directress has not experienced herself as loved, as lovable, as acceptable by her God she is judgmental of her retreatants. She is not able to recognize all that is happening within them of God and tends to move them at her rate rather than at his. We no longer have lay persons recommended by sisters as good potential retreat directresses. We wait, we pray, and as we see someone develop during a retreat we ask her if she would like to be trained to give "At Home Retreats."

The most effective lay people in our "At Home Retreat" movement have a sense of humor, a good marriage, are able to listen, to discern, to empathize, and are experiencing Jesus Christ as alive and well in their married lives. This is what we look for in our selection of an "At Home Retreat" lay directress.

The Religious Directress

More and more we find that women religious are seeking to expand their present ministries in the Church into more pastoral areas, into a more spiritual ministry. Giving "At Home Retreats" is one way they can fulfill this desire.

Many of our religious team persons are active either in the formation of their own religious, or are members of a parish pastoral team, or are CCD coordinators or parochial school teachers. They are able to be active in their present ministries and give one "At Home Retreat" at a time.

One of our team members told us that working with lay women in their own homes has taught her that "I've not been at all realistic in working with our novices. This is the real world and I'm just beginning to experience it. I've not prepared them to be effective in ministry." She found her participation as a retreat directress had an added benefit to her formation work in her own congregation.

Another sister, active in teaching adult religious education courses, mentioned experiencing a hunger for God among her students. She found that giving "At Home Retreats" was a ministry which flowed naturally from the work she was already doing. "Through giving retreats, I'm now able to bring some of my own parishioners to that deep level with God that they wish to experience."

None of the religious involved with the program is involved full time. We think this has been an advantage. The sister may give her full attention to the ministry for which she is primarily responsible. Meanwhile, she is not bound to seek "success" in retreat work. She is free to let God be with his people and she follows them through their retreat.

We require the same qualifications for the religious directress as for the lay member of the team. She must be a woman of prayer; she must have made the *Exercises;* she must be stable in her religious life, mature, with a sense of humor, a listening ear, an ability to articulate and to discern.

The hunger and desire for this type of retreat experience has been so keen that the religious does not have to spend time "recruiting" women to make the retreat. Waiting lists have formed all over the Island and the harvest is ripe.

Training

Teams complete a three-month training course together before giving their first "At Home Retreat." Weekly supervision, days of input, and evenings of evaluation add to their skills.

The training course is wide-ranging. The future teams study *The Spiritual Exercises of St. Ignatius,* receive communication skills, explanations of spiritual direction, the use of current audio-visual aids to bring out into contemporary form what Ignatius sets forth—all the tools we can give them.

In our first training sessions we learned that the religious and laity were leery of one another. As they worked together, learned together, shared together and prayed together, they began to recognize the talents that such a team would bring together to complement one another. Once they begin to give a retreat together, they say that they would only give a retreat this way—each brings something to this type of retreat experience that is necessary and would be missed were the retreat given *only by* a lay person *or only by* a religious.

The Need

There have been sixty-five "At Home Retreats" for married women in this diocese alone. In the beginning of 1977, "At Home Retreats" will begin in a neighboring diocese. As this year closes, we find ourselves expanding to provide programs for other groups of retreatants. We plan a retreat for widows (the team: a religious and a widow), a retreat for A.A.'s (the team: a religious and a recovered alcoholic), a retreat for couples (the team: a religious and a married couple), a retreat for the Spanish speaking, and others. We still have so much to do, so much to learn!

We know that the nineteenth annotation retreat with a group does work. We know that a lay person brings a dimension to a retreat team which is lacking without her presence. We know that the religious finds that her role as a retreat directress adds a depth, an assurance to her other ministries.

We would like to explore other possibilities: perhaps a priest and a layman in his parish working with lay parishioners . . . an elderly sister and an elderly lay woman in a nursing home . . . a novice or a seminarian with teenagers . . .

We hope that our learning has helped you.

The Danger of Faddism and the Thirty-day Retreat

David L. Fleming, S.J.

Volume 33, 1974, pp. 97-101.

Within the past few years, there has been a great interest in both men's and women's religious congregations to a renewal through a more intensive prayer experience. The focus is correct, but at times its implementation is not well thought out. A good example of such implementation, fraught with potential disaster, is the often enthusiastically hailed practice of a 30-day retreat.

Possible Dangers in the 30-day Retreat Movement

Many groups who previously have had no tradition of this kind of an intensive period of prayer have suddenly embraced this practice as if it were commonly desirable for all persons or at least for all religious. That assumption needs to be far more carefully examined in terms of the prayer-life charism of the particular group. For some religious groups, to have spent thirty days in prayer has become a certain mark of elitism. A new distinction is being imbibed, after older ones of teaching vs. working brothers and sisters and professed vs. non-professed members have broken down. The accomplishment of having spent thirty days in prayer can easily be set up as a false criterion for determining who the really renewed religious are. It is not so much a conscious putdown of the "have nots" (those who "have not" made a 30-day retreat), but rather a whole atmosphere is being created for the desirability and even necessity of being among this new elite in order to be *the good religious.*

Then, too, there are always people who look to any of the latest fads to answer all problems. For example, we find this true in the sales of the latest diet book as well as the most recently publicized practices of the Eastern guru. In religious life, this kind of person looks to the 30-day retreat as the cure-all for all spiritual difficulties. Undoubtedly such an intense experience can effect some radical change, especially in view of cooperating with the richness of grace offered at this time. But the living out of any retreat is always the necessary process of a gradual healing or making one's life whole. Religious, above all, should not be people who hunt for the latest cure-all. Yet often the panic situation of a renewal not yet begun or one moving all too slowly forces measures to be taken that go far beyond realistic hope.

A variation on this theme of a cure-all comes usually from the side of superiors who give orders to one of their religious subjects to make a 30-day retreat as a last desperate measure. The subject is often reluctant if not outright antagonistic because this last desperate measure falls usually into the category of "saving a vocation" or "a last chance at getting a spiritual life." Again there is no doubt that, with a certain minimal good will and effort at prayer, a more balanced attitude and a real openness to the movement of God's grace can result from such a making oneself available to God and reflection on His action in one's life. With God, however, respecting and reverencing man's freedom, a certain degree of cooperation and desire on man's part is essential for this time to be truly fruitful. We cannot expect that the necessary quiet and space for prayer is even minimally attainable if the person's turmoil runs deep. Psychologically, there are times in a man's life when lengthy prayer periods are more a hindrance than a help in fostering his relationship to God.

Dangers on the Part of Retreat Directors

Although so far we have considered the problems only of those making an extended prayer experience, just as much concern should be exercised for those who are directing such retreats. In the wide search for more directors today, some put themselves forward whose action can only be described as tempting God. While it is true that spiritual directors and retreat directors must start somewhere in their work, as much prudence as possible in the selection of capable directors must be employed. Current practice often has young men and women religious in their mid-twenties or less directing people their own age and those far older. Despite the possible precociousness of their own spiritual growth, what these young people lack is the life experience which is essential for direction work. Good will, lofty idealism, and even a rather solid prayer life for their own age and level of maturity do not supply the necessary experiences of life and deep reflection upon it which have been the recognized criteria for direction work throughout the history of religions, including the desert father tradition within Christianity.

Guidelines to Be Observed

Looking back over the experience of a certain spiritual tradition, we find some guidelines which are especially helpful in our present situation. First of all, let us consider that particular 30-day prayer experience which follows the method of the *Spiritual Exercises* of St. Ignatius Loyola. Ignatius considered the 30-day retreat experience to be a primary formation tool for the members of the Society of Jesus. From the very beginning, a necessary part of a Jesuit vocation was the potential and readiness to make a 30-day retreat. Today we have more clearly identified this potential and readiness as the recognition of and sharing in the particular charism of a founder—Ignatius Loyola—for a Jesuit candidate. While it is assumed that all Jesuits make the 30-day retreat, it cannot be a criteria foisted upon any other religious tradition for all its members. This is not to respect either the charism of that particular founder or the kind of person drawn by inclination and God's grace to a particular religious family. It is obvious from the Church's approval that the *Spiritual Exercises* are an instrument of God's action and grace meant for the whole Church and not just for the Society of Jesus. But the *Exercises* are only *an* instrument. Just as there are many devotions and pious practices as well as methods of prayer within our Christian tradition, so no one of them stemming from personal charism is suitable and appealing to all members in the Church. If it were otherwise, we would wipe out all distinctions of spiritualities along with the idea of a vocation call particularized to one religious family.

Caution and Prudence of Ignatius Loyola

For Ignatius, the instrument of the *Spiritual Exercises,* which he developed over long years under the inspiration of God, had a real dynamic. The prayer periods had a movement and a clear direction; it was not just a "time for prayer." As a result of this dynamism, Ignatius realized the power present here and was extremely cautious in approving directors of such an experience. Although he encouraged the scholastics in training and the young priests to be active in directing and conducting shorter prayer periods as a part of their apostolate—particularly those exercises which are basic to conversion and are sometimes described as First Week exercises—he was very selective in allowing his priests to conduct the total movement of the *Spiritual Exercises.*

Ignatius' own prudence is what is often lacking in the formation of many retreat "teams" in our present-day situation. While the monitoring by an experienced director is the model of the Ignatian training of directors, he demanded of each potential director a certain lived experience which comes only with a maturity of years. The early *Directories* of Ignatius are all witnesses of his monitoring a particular director in the course of conducting a 30-day retreat. It is clear that he gives great freedom to the man who is conducting the retreat because he expects a discretion which allows him to adapt to the retreatant and to the particular circumstances. We should be far more critical of those who attempt to be directors of the 30-day Ignatian retreat; we need to inquire whether they possess this kind of experiential discretion.

Modified Versions of the Ignatian Exercises

Alongside the strict dynamics found in the *Spiritual Exercises,* there has grown up today a retreat, often of 30 days, which is modeled after the *Exercises* but definitely drops its peculiar movement and direction. It becomes a much more generalized "intensive prayer period." No doubt there is a real thirst for a "desert experience" in our rushed and overactive lives. Such an intense time of prayer can be most attractive for both younger and older religious. But a few cautions are in order.

First, as we mentioned, such a period of prayer is not the *only* way of renewal and cannot be set up as a necessity for a whole group who has never had such a prayer tradition. It should not become the point of a possible elitism charge. Secondly, even for this kind of prayer experience, there should be some selection process for both those making such a retreat and those conducting it. Thirdly, both retreatants and directors should consciously be aware that they are involved in a 30-day prayer experience and that no false expectations of entering into the full dynamics of the traditional Ignatian *Spiritual Exercises* be built up.

Criteria for Retreatants and Directors

The criteria which I would propose for selecting candidates for such an intense prayer experience would be as follows: (1) the continuous experience of regular spiritual direction for about a year preceding the retreat; (2) a prayer life that has a certain consistency which the person is able to describe to a director; (3) the desire or at least the positive openness to making such a retreat, along with some reflection on what is the motivation for it *at this time;* and (4) usually a previous experience of a shorter directed retreat period sometime in the past.

In terms of the directors, too, certain criteria should be followed. A director should have had (1) a deep and mature personal experience of such an intense prayer experience; (2) a fairly long exposure to personal spiritual direction; (3) a certain preparation through reading, instruction, and reflection for conducting this kind of prayer experience (for those who desire to conduct the strict Ignatian *Spiritual Exercises,* a much deeper knowledge and appreciation of their structure and movement is essential); and (4) a certain reflective exposure to life for which all the youthful zeal, fervor, and piety cannot supply or substitute. In summary, the director should be a mature person of prayer, prudence, and true discernment.

Many good results have already flowed from the renewal of religious life in terms of intense prayer periods. It would be a sign of our human pride if we did not try to take the necessary human precautions to allow God to work with both the retreatant and the director. Both of them should find themselves open and ready to listen to God because they have done their human part to prepare and meet Him along the way.

A *Directory* for the Use of Scripture in an Ignatian Retreat

Paul G. McCormick, S.J.

Volume 38, 1979, pp. 223-228.

How does a director properly use Scripture in a directed retreat? I think most directors would agree that Scripture is not to be carelessly cut up to serve a theme or point in a retreat. Scripture has an integrity and a message of its own and this must be respected and heeded. Moreover, Scripture contains works that were carefully composed as wholes so as to carry thematic as well as topical meanings. The true and complete meaning of Scripture takes in the thematic as well as the topical messages and thus it is not best understood by chopping it up into topical chunks. Modern exegesis, then, seems to demand some modifications in the way Scripture has been traditionally handled in directed retreats. This short directory will suggest some ways of using Scripture in a retreat that will hopefully avoid a "goulash" approach that deforms or impoverishes Scripture.

Directors acquainted with the *Spiritual Exercises* of St. Ignatius may also ask, how does one use Scripture in the context of a retreat based on the *Spiritual Exercises* so as to give each their due respect and power? I think the best attitude towards resolving this is that of Fr. Jerome Nadal who regarded the Exercises as a means to help people receive and listen to the Scripture. The Exercises are not an end in themselves but are a tool ordering and selecting Scripture for a retreatant. Scripture is foremost and the Exercises are an aid for listening to it.

Practically, this use of Scripture during a retreat which is schematized by the *Spiritual Exercises* is what the remainder of this article describes. From many people and sources I've gathered a number of principles concerning the use of Scripture in an Ignatian retreat that is given to adults in an eight or thirty day period. These directives are most surely not absolute or the final word. They are a beginning to which each is encouraged to add his own additions and amendments.

The Purpose of Scripture for Us

1. The earliest Christians first experienced Jesus and his Spirit, then they reflected upon their experience, and then formulated that theological reflection into the writings we call the New Testament. The proper, prayerful use of Scripture involves the reverse of this threefold process—moving from the formulation back to the reflection back to the experience.* Scripture is to become an experience for each person of the saving action and love of God in Jesus Christ. The Scripture is to work on each person and become a transforming influence in one's own personal experience. This is the rationale for the use of Scripture during retreat.

2. Authentic prayer based on the Scripture renders the individual more willing to heed God's word, more dedicated to service in love, more obedient and responsive to God's will, more in communion with God and the Body of Christ. This is the fundamental test for prayer based on the Scripture; the end is service, love, obedience to God's will and not a narcissistic enlightenment or aesthetic experience. The director must lead a person to the Scripture for this purpose and caution the person when he veers from this course.

3. Scripture has its own integrity and dynamic and this must be respected by the director and retreatant. It is improper to manipulate Scripture to fit a need or an interpretation. Scripture is not to be used as "proof texts" for theology. The director must respect and uphold this integrity in his or her use of Scripture.

4. The director must accept and recognize the often radical, harsh demands of the word of God in Scripture. It is dishonest to "water down" the gospel message and its demands. Scripture is a two-edged sword and must be allowed to cut as it will.

The Role of the Spiritual Exercises and the Director

5. The Spiritual Exercises are not meant to compete with Scripture for the retreatant's attention. The Exercises are rather a means, a tool, a hermeneutical key to Scripture and the gospel message. The Exercises are a program for ordering and selecting Scripture for one's experience and greater profit. The Exercises dispose and aid the individual to receive and

---

*This threefold schema of Scripture's origin and use in prayer has been borrowed from David Stanley, S.J., "Contemplation of the Gospels, Ignatius Loyola, and the Contemporary Christian," *Theological Studies*, 29, (1968), pp. 417-443.

listen to the word of God by not only arranging Scripture to be experienced but by stripping the person of masks, distractions, and supports so that he meets Scripture with his real, true self. The director must never set one up against the other but use the Exercises as an aid for the reception of the word of God.

6. All Scripture culminates in the revelation of God in Jesus Christ. Christ is the center for the interpretation of all Scripture. The Exercises themselves also focus on Jesus Christ as the center of our existence. The director seeks above all else to aid the formation of an intimate, personal relationship between Christ and the retreatant. Hence, the director will wish to highlight this goal and to reorient the retreatant to this goal if it becomes forgotten or lost.

7. In a retreat as well as everyday of our lives, the primacy of work is given to the Holy Spirit. The ministry of the director, then, must be seen as service in docility to the Spirit. The director serves the Spirit in the Spirit's transformation of a person. This should inspire an attitude of awe, humility, and respect in the director. The director personally must ever cultivate prayer and openness to the Spirit not only during retreat but throughout his life.

8. The director's first task is to encourage and aid the retreatant to prepare himself to receive the word of God, especially as found in Scripture. This includes not only the proper selection and introduction of Scripture texts, but also the encouragement and assistance for achieving a proper climate for prayer. A climate that fosters relaxed prayer, silence, recollection, and sensitivity to the word of God should be developed. The director should also encourage and foster the retreatant's generosity and docility by penances when deemed desirable.

9. The director needs a sound, extensive knowledge of Scripture. Both personal and academic study of Scripture must be complemented by frequent reading, relish, and personal prayer based on the Scripture.

Selecting Scripture for a Retreatant

10. In selecting a text for the retreatant's prayer the director must bear three things in mind: a) the intention of the writer in a given text; b) the need of the retreatant; c) the goal and current dynamic of the Spiritual Exercises as this applies to the various stages of an Ignatian retreat.

11. The director should select a text with a specific grace or purpose in mind. The *id quod volo's* of the Exercises are invaluable in this regard. After first determining an objective, the director is then ready to select a Scripture text to match.

12. Although the desired fruit of a text and prayer period is important, the director and retreatant must both remain open and docile to the movements of the Spirit, for in all things the Spirit leads.

13. The director may profitably receive suggestions from the retreatant regarding the selection of texts or specific graces to be sought. However these suggestions are not to be taken as absolutes or necessarily adopted.

14. The director will be wise to select texts in relation to a retreatant's consolations and good inspirations. If a pattern or area of Scripture has brought consolation and fruit, then it should be continued. (For example, if a retreatant experiences God's love while praying 1 John, it would be inadvisable to move him to Genesis texts on the same day.) Stay in the area of Scripture in which fruit is experienced. A director may also profitably select texts that will counter temptations or illusions that the retreatant experiences. In addition, texts that bring desolation may be continued if the action of the Good Spirit is discerned in the experience.

15. A director must not weigh down a retreatant with too much matter from Scripture. Depth is desired, not breadth. Passages should not be too long either. Because many passages are little "gospels" wherein the retreatant is able to perceive the entire mystery of Christ, a couple of texts done slowly and with repetitions can fill a whole day. Do not overload a person with texts; this especially applies for task-oriented retreatants for whom the temptation is to "get a lot done." The director should encourage retreatants to move slowly, deeply, restfully through few texts. In short, deeply felt knowledge and appreciation are more to be desired than width and flashy insights.

16. For a retreatant who is a "busy" person, repetitions should be introduced gradually in the course of an eight or thirty day retreat. Such retreatants need a director who will gradually wean them of "getting things done" in prayer, of the need for new matter to "work on." Repetitions are important but should be introduced gradually. As the retreat progresses, then, the amount of Scripture given may be decreased as this seems suitable.

17. In an eight day retreat it is advisable to select "mysteries of Christ's life" from one Gospel. Because the different Gospels involve different theological visions and purposes, it is best for clarity's sake to stay with one perspective and set of themes in a shorter retreat. An eclectic, pick-and-choose approach may obscure and confuse the thematic meanings of a writer's work in Scripture. This principle applies especially to the second and third weeks.

18. The director should be cautious of mixing Old and New Testament texts. Many themes of the First Week are suitable to the Old Testament, whereas the remaining three weeks seem most suited to the New Testament. Although New Testament texts can be used to enrich the Old Testament texts of the First Week and center the retreatant on Christ and the mercy received through him, it is generally inadvisable to hop back and forth between the two Testaments in too short a time.

Presenting Scripture to a Retreatant

19. The director's role is to point to the places in Scripture in which a person may meet God. In presenting Scripture to a retreatant the director should avoid the two extremes of merely dumping texts of chapter and verse on a retreatant or of presenting a homily or exegetical lecture to the person.

Rather, the director should comment briefly upon a text in view of the retreatant's particular need at the moment. The need of the retreatant should never be overshadowed by the director's fervor, over-solicitousness, or desire to preach. Let the director err on the side of being too brief rather than too lengthy.

20. The director's comments on a text should help open up a text for a retreatant. The director should point to the various issues, themes, concerns that are apparent in a text. Such themes are sometimes only apparent when viewed in the writer's overall context and purpose; here is the value of a director's exegetical background. The director must be sensitive to feedback from the retreatant to discover what any given individual finds helpful, for needs will vary as will effective techniques from person to person. Again the director is to mediate a text to the retreatant, not drain it dry by lengthy explanation nor so rigidly interpret it so as to enclose the person's experience in a straightjacket.

21. The director may also need to remove certain obstacles or misunderstandings of a text so that it can be properly understood by a retreatant. Here the director must be cautious in the effort not to propose obstacles that do not actually exist for the retreatant, yet he must be sensitive enough to clear away those that do exist.

22. In presenting a Scripture text in conjunction with the dynamics of the Spiritual Exercises the director will do well to note what Ignatius selects and subtracts from his points on Scripture texts. This can clue the director into what themes in Scripture are important for the various moments in the Exercises.

23. The director should seek to have the retreatant reflect on the word of God in Scripture rather than on the word of the director. Occasionally the director will find that a retreatant has derived great profit from something he has said; this is well and good for the word of God comes in many ways. The issue, however, is that the director should not seek to supplant the word of God in Scripture with his own word.

24. The director should encourage the retreatant to personally apply the gospel message, to ask "How is this passage a message to me to follow Jesus in poverty, humility, and suffering?" The retreatant can go overboard, laboring to moralize every phrase in the Scripture and so turn the focus from Christ to himself. Yet, at the other extreme, the prayer of

Scripture could turn out to be merely an intellectual, abstract experience that yields no fruit of conversion in attitude and life.

25. To certain retreatants who can easily, without undue distraction, do it, the director might suggest memorizing of passages from Scripture. Memory more than reading could be emphasized,

26. At all times the director should allow freedom for the person to hear and respond to the impulses of the Spirit. This delicate balance between direction and freedom in the Spirit must be maintained.

Additional Instructions

27. The director must evaluate the effectiveness of his approach, words, and suggestions throughout the time of retreat. If a technique bears good fruit, then stay with it. If a technique bears poor fruit, then modify it. For example, some retreatants may need more help in the opening up of a Scripture passage, and some less. A director must be sensitive enough to read feedback and modify technique when necessary. The director must be flexible and adaptable to the implications of the retreatant's feedback.

28. The director need not provide the retreatant with a text of the *Spiritual Exercises*. He might also want to be aware of whether a retreatant is using a commentary to Scripture. Often such aids provide a block to the retreatant's genuine and deep-felt experience of Scripture. Ordinarily, commentaries should be used sparingly, if at all, by the retreatant.

29. The director should encourage the retreatant to remain with and relish the momentary fruit found in a given phrase or sentence. There is no need to hurry, or to "finish" the whole passage. Nor is there need to "complete" all the texts given by the director.

30. The director should also encourage the retreatant to read and pray the scriptural passage slowly, restfully, and simply. He should not strain to moralize over it or to "work it over." Let the text speak to each individual. Often a person cannot hear the gospel message because he is trying to fit it into his own categories. Often the director must encourage each one to let the text and the word of God work on him. It is the Spirit of God's love sent into our hearts that wishes to do far more in us than we can ask or imagine.

31. After finishing a retreat, or on a break day, the director may find it profitable to review a listing such as this one so as to evaluate his directing. This practice will provide an opportunity to increase his skill as well as to add any new insights he may have found.

The Limits of the Adaptability of the *Spiritual Exercises*

Donald W. Reck, S.J.

Volume 39, 1980, pp. 906-915.

One of the side effects of the general upsurge of interest in prayer and spirituality in the United States over the past decade has been a broadening of interest in the *Spiritual Exercises* of St. Ignatius of Loyola. More and more priests, religious men and women, and laypersons have in one way or another been introduced to the *Exercises* and have made them in their full month-long form or in some shorter adaptation. Moreover, as the demand for the *Exercises* has grown, more and more Catholics of all walks and stations, of all spiritual formations and backgrounds have sought to learn more about them and, in many cases, to be prepared to give them. Whereas previously the making and especially the giving of the *Exercises* had been an activity of interest chiefly to members of the Society of Jesus, Jesuits are finding themselves being called upon more and more to share this specific part of their heritage with the larger Church. And as the field of those who are making and giving the *Exercises* widens, so too does the number and breadth of questions that are being asked regarding the limits of the adaptability of the *Exercises*.

The question of adapting the *Exercises* is not new. It was addressed by Ignatius himself in the eighteenth annotation or prenote in the book of the *Exercises*.[1]

> The Spiritual Exercises must be adapted to the condition of the one who is to engage in them, that is, to his age, education, and talent....

[1] *The Spiritual Exercises of St. Ignatius*, edited by Louis J. Puhl (Chicago: Loyola University Press, 1951), no. 18, pp. 7-8.

> Similarly, each one should be given those exercises that would be more helpful and profitable according to his willingness to dispose himself for them.

This principle of adaptation is subsequently applied to specific questions which arise in the giving of the *Exercises*. Thus, for example, in regard to the arrangement of the hours of prayer in all four weeks (SE 72); the choice of a prayer posture which helps the retreatant gain the grace he is seeking (SE 76); making changes in the amount of penance employed in order to discover what is most suitable for the individual retreatant (SE 89), and so forth.

Thus it is clear that questions regarding adaptation have been asked as long as the *Exercises* have been given. My impression is, however, that there has been an increase in the extent and depth of the sort of adaptations being suggested. From being questions merely as to how to make use of the *Exercises* as they exist, the questions have moved more in the direction of challenging what I would call the idiom and mode in which they were composed. Thus I have encountered such questions as whether one might change the sequence of the individual exercises, starting, for example, with the life of Christ or his passion, or even with the Contemplation to Attain the Love of God; whether the so-called "key exercises," such as the Principle and Foundation, the Kingdom, the Two Standards, and the Contemplation to Attain the Love of God are indispensable; whether it would be legitimate to substitute scriptural texts for some of them; whether it is necessary to touch upon the material of all four weeks in the course of a thirty-day retreat, so that one might not get further than the first and second weeks, or even spend the entire thirty days in union with the crucified Lord; whether one could drop entirely the structure of petition for specific graces, leaving the choice of the grace to be given entirely in the Lord's hands; and ultimately whether one might begin with any element of the *Exercises* which the director might feel appropriate for this retreatant, and then simply go in pursuit of those graces which seem appropriate and helpful for the directee.

My interest in asking the "boundaries" of the *Exercises* is much more than verbal or legalistic. It is tied in rather with the conviction, gained through experience in both making and giving the *Exercises,* that they normally evoke a dynamic of spiritual conversion and growth which is closely related to the different meditations, contemplations, petitions, etc., presented by Ignatius. My desire is to preserve and utilize that dynamic. Therefore I am interested in knowing when the term "Ignatian Exercises" can or can no longer be used, primarily in the sense that I want to know when the structure and dynamic which Ignatius experienced in living the *Exercises* and intended in giving them is or is not any longer present in a specific manner of adapting them.

In the reflections which follow I am less interested in deciding specifically what may or may not be omitted in giving the *Spiritual Exercises* without loss of their basic content and dynamic than in setting forth an understanding of the *Exercises* which I have found in workshops and discussions to be helpful in addressing such questions of radical adaptation as I have cited. My contention is that the *Exercises* as we know them are the result of the interweaving of three "elements." The first is that of the Christian faith heritage; the second that of the dynamic of Christian conversion and growth; and the third that of the specifically Ignatian "mode and idiom" of expressing, in terms of the Christian faith heritage, the dynamic of Christian conversion and growth. Unless the distinction and interrelationship of these three elements is clearly seen, the questions of radical adaptation of the *Exercises* become, I believe, either unanswerable or else lead to overly simplistic and detrimental answers.

The Elements of the Exercises

1. *A Basic and Common Christian Heritage*

As Christians we hold in common a history and a body of beliefs and convictions. Most briefly they may be found expressed in the *Apostles' Creed* or, scripturally, in the various catecheses set forth, for example, in the *Acts of the Apostles,* as in Peter's speech (1:14-36), or in Stephen's defense (7:2-60), or Paul's address (13:16-41). We believe there is a God—Father, Son and Spirit—who is the source and goal of all that is. He is infinite love. He has gifted the human race with all that exists and wishes to share with us even his own life, initially through faith, trust and love, and eternally in the possession of himself. The depths of God's love are made known and available in a unique manner through the life, death and resurrection of Jesus Christ, the eternal Son of God and yet a human being like ourselves in all but sin. Jesus continues his presence and his mission through his Spirit, which works in the hearts of all humankind, but in a special manner through the community called Church. Each of us is called personally to respond to the Spirit of God at work within us and thereby to be shaped into other Christs, to continue his presence and work in our world.

This common heritage is obviously the possession of every Christian, even though not known or lived. It is expressed in Scripture and the doctrinal teaching of the Church across the ages. It is common to every state of life and to every "school" of spirituality.

This common Christian heritage forms, if you will, the beams and bricks and mortar of which the *Spiritual Exercises* are built. They make it identifiable as a Christian document and explain why it is immediately intelligible to Christians. On the other hand it is clear that not everything in the Christian heritage is included in the *Exercises* or assigned equal importance. Ignatius did not include, for example, all of the mysteries of Christ's life. Some of them he includes in the text of a specific week, others he merely includes in the reference guide at the end of the *Exercises* (SE 261f). Pierre de Bérulle, to use a frequently cited contrast, writing within a hundred years of Ignatius and using the materials of the same Christian heritage and life of Jesus, put emphasis on entirely other aspects of the same mysteries.[2] In an analogous manner, St. Benedict or St. Francis or St. Dominic were selective in writing their rules. Already at this level of selectivity and emphasis we can see an Ignatian distinctiveness about the *Exercises*. And yet we must go further and look at two other "elements" before we can answer our question about the limits of adaptability.

2. *The Dynamic of Christian Conversion*

The *Exercises* had their origin in the experience of St. Ignatius himself. The patterns of his conversion and subsequent Christian growth found their way into his ubiquitous notebooks. As he attempted to respond to the needs of those who, already in Manresa, came to him for direction, he noted a parallel between their experience and his own. Gradually he seems to have identified certain patterns which he had come to expect to find in the midst of the mysterious, grace-inspired process of conversion and Christian growth: consciousness of personal sinfulness seen against the backdrop of God's love and leading to a call to repentance; ever further calls to a deeper knowledge and following of Jesus Christ; a development in prayer life from a heavily discursive meditation form to a simpler contemplative focus upon the events and words of Jesus' life, and in many cases finally spreading out into an ability to experience the presence and activity of God in all of creation.

This dynamic of Christian conversion and growth, of moving toward a "conquest of self and the regulation of one's life in such a way that no decision is made under the influence of any inordinate attachment" (SE 21), this growth towards "spiritual freedom," is the dynamic which directors have learned to expect to occur in one seriously making the *Exercises*. Obviously spiritual conversion and growth is the fruit of grace, and grace suited to the individuality of this retreatant. But the discovery of Ignatius and of many others who have attempted to assist individuals in their prayer or to preach a mission or retreat of any sort, is that there are fairly regular *patterns* of growth involved. A knowledge of these patterns and the attempt to take them into account in the selection of material for days of prayer and in the direction of individuals, while certainly not forcing the hand of God's grace or constraining the freedom of the individual, does allow for a more conscious cooperation with divine grace and the human factors at work. The manner in which Ignatius expressed and attempted to facilitate this common Christian dynamic of conversion and growth by a selective use of elements of a common Christian heritage is what is most distinctively Ignatian about the *Exercises*.

3. *The Specifically Ignatian Expression of the Process of Christian Conversion and Growth*

Simply expressed, then, the *Exercises* are a series of reflections, meditations and contemplations selected and arranged by Ignatius, through which the retreatant proceeds under the guidance of a director, who, in company

---

[2] See for example, Aelred Squire, *Asking the Fathers. The Art of Meditation and Prayer* (New York: Paulist Press, 1976), pp. 155-156.

with the retreatant, attempts to discern the Lord's present call to conversion and growth.

There has been a good deal of discussion as to how much of the *Exercises* are original to Ignatius, which parts are adapted from other authors, and which are simply copied.[3] For the purposes of our study here, it would seem to me that this discussion is irrelevant. The fact is that in 1548 Ignatius published the *Exercises* in almost exactly the form in which they are today. Regardless of the source of the materials included, if there is anything clear in even a casual study of the *Exercises,* it is that whatever the context in which the rocks and timbers previously were, they have been woven together anew by Ignatius.

There are various ways of describing Christian conversion and growth. St. Theresa spoke of successive "castles." Alan Jones has given many illustrations of the use of the "journey" theme.[4] Ignatius' conception of the process is present in the *Exercises*. If I had to identify the heart and core of the Ignatian symbolization of conversion and growth, I would point primarily to the series of progressively fuller "calls" addressed to the retreatant through the course of the *Exercises*. The so-called "key" reflections or meditations or contemplations tend to crystallize this call at specific moments of the retreat. The other hours of prayer in some sense prepare for the key moments of call, but also allow these calls and their implications to be more deeply assimilated and affirmed by the retreatant. To illustrate this Ignatian symbolization of Christian growth more clearly, I would like to compare briefly the call made in the Principle and Foundation, the Kingdom, the Two Standards, the Three Kinds of Humility, and the Contemplation to Attain the Love of God, and to show how these calls are bound together by the other materials in the *Exercises*.

The "Principle and Foundation" for entering fruitfully into anything contained in the *Exercises* is the Christian conviction that all is created by God with the purpose of bringing the human person back to him, and hence ought to be used accordingly (SE 23). One might speak of this as the call of reason and of creation itself. It is the first call within the context of the *Exercises*.

To what extent have I as an individual lived according to this call? This is the question which the first week is equivalently asking (SE 45f.). The admission sought is the faith response, but confirmed by personal experience, that the retreatant is a sinner, but a sinner supported and surrounded by the love of God, especially as manifested in the crucified Jesus (SE 53).

If the retreatant, despite his shortcomings, is still willing to say "yes" to the call through creation to use all to the praise, reverence and service of the creator, he arrives at a further call, that of the eternal king (SE 91f.). The most obvious difference between this call and that of the Principle and Foundation

[3] See, for instance, Joseph de Guibert, *The Jesuits. Their Spiritual Doctrine and Practice* (St. Louis: Institute of Jesuit Sources, 1972), pp. 152-167.

[4] *Journey into Christ* (New York: Seabury Press, 1977).

is that this one is personal — it is given by "Christ, Our Lord, the Eternal King" (SE 95) to each individual in particular. The response called for is certainly one of 'judgment and reason'' (SE 96). But beyond that it is also a uniquely individual and affective response: "those who wish to give greater proof of their love, and to distinguish themselves in whatever concerns the service of the eternal King and Lord of all... " (SE 97). The grace asked for is not to be deaf to Christ's call but prompt and diligent to accomplish his most holy will (SE 91). Ignatius suggests by means of his prayer "Eternal Lord of all things... " (SE 98) the way in which such a personal love might express itself.

Having been presented with the King and his call, and having been invited to respond with a global and somewhat generic "yes," the retreatant is invited during the second week to enter through contemplation into various events in the life of Christ, asking for "an intimate knowledge of our Lord, who has become man for me, that I may love him more and follow him more closely" (SE 104). These contemplations of the second week do not proceed in a random or meandering manner, however. Their objective seems to be to concretize the call of the Eternal King by helping the retreatant come to know him more fully and deeply but also by helping him see and accept the personal implications of following such a leader. Consequently, within a few days after beginning the second week, reflections are introduced regarding "making a choice of a way of life" (SE 169); or, if this choice is not in question, at least of reforming one's manner of living in the present state (SE 189).

In the "Meditation on Two Standards," (SE 136f.), the retreatant is presented with a second leader in the person of Satan, whose values are contrasted with those of Christ, and is instructed to pray for "a knowledge of the deceits of the rebel chief and help to guard myself against them; and also... a knowledge of the true life exemplified in the sovereign and true Commander, and the grace to imitate him" (SE 139). This is an attempt to clarify the call of Christ and deepen the retreatant's response to it by contrasting it with a rival call which each human being hears.

The reflection on the "Three Kinds of Humility" carries the implications of this call of Christ still further, for here Ignatius presents as the fullest response that of a personal attachment of such an intensity that it brings one to desire to be as personally like Jesus as possible. Thus "whenever the praise and glory of the Divine Majesty would be equally served" by either choice, A or B, the basis of choice becomes "to imitate and be in reality more like Christ our Lord." Consequently "I desire and choose poverty with Christ poor, rather than riches; insults with Christ loaded with them, rather than honors; I desire to be accounted as worthless and a fool for Christ, rather than to be esteemed as wise and prudent in this world." The basis of such a choice stated simply is: "So Christ was treated before me" (SE 167).

What is the depth of the retreatant's response to the call of Christ as it emerges and takes on personal dimensions during the days of the retreat? Is it a merely verbal response, not moving from words into action? Or does it set some conditions? Or is it a total, whole-hearted, and unconditional "yes"? This is the question of the meditation called "Three Classes of Men" (SE 149f.).

The centrality of "call" in Ignatius' view of the spiritual life I would see as further confirmed by the importance given to the rules of discernment— "rules for understanding to some extent the different movements produced in the soul and for recognizing those that are good, to admit them, and those that are bad, to reject them" (SE 313). Everything for Ignatius depends upon our accurately hearing the call and wholeheartedly responding to it.

Having attempted during the second week to hear as clearly as possible the Lord's specific call to him or her and to respond to it as fully as possible, the retreatant is confronted in the third-week contemplations with the experience of Jesus responding to his call and is encouraged to enter into that experience— "to consider what Christ our Lord suffers in his human nature.... Then I will begin with great effort to strive to grieve, be sad, and weep" (SE 195). The reverse side of the Passion of Christ is his Resurrection—and the retreatant is asked to pray for the grace to enter into this also— "to ask for the grace to be glad and rejoice intensely because of the great joy and glory of Christ our Lord" (SE 221). What is the cost and what the reward of responding to the Lord's call to me? Something very close to the Passion and Resurrection of Jesus.

In the "Contemplation to Attain the Love of God," the call of "reason and justice" and that of a personal God are combined and seen as voiced forth by all of reality. The retreatant is asked to pray for "an intimate knowledge of the many blessings received, that filled with gratitude for all, I may in all things love and serve the Divine Majesty" (SE 233). The blessings in question are all of those "of creation and redemption, and the special favors I have received" (SE 234). God is seen not merely as having gifted me with so many created objects, but even with himself—dwelling in all creatures, endowing them with their existence, life, sensation, understanding, making of me a temple, created in the likeness and image of the Divine Majesty. The picture given is that of God laboring in the process of continuing creation—which I often suggest to my retreatants might be translated into the more concrete and imaginative Eastern image, that of the dancing Lord, without whose presence and constant activity the dance of created reality would cease. Consequently the final reflection of the contemplation is to see all creation as a participation in the qualities of its creator, "all blessings and gifts are descending from above," and thus all things are mirroring the wonder of its creator and source (SE 237). The appropriate response, it is suggested, is that of one "moved by great feeling," possibly speaking in the words of the prayer, "Take, Lord and receive..." (SE 234).[5]

---

[5] For another mode and idiom of expressing the spiritual journey and of assisting those who travel

The Limits of Adaptability

In terms of our reflections up to this point, then, we might say that the *Spiritual Exercises* are one specific expression of the dynamic of Christian conversion and growth towards ever fuller spiritual freedom. They are also a pastoral tool given to aid people in moving towards that freedom.

One word of caution before we go further. My attempt has been to illustrate how in the *Exercises* St. Ignatius presents his vision of Christian conversion and growth by means of the materials of our common Christian heritage. I have chosen to emphasize a conception of the Ignatian vision which centers upon call and response to call. Although I suspect my choice of this conception is based ultimately upon my own experience of the *Exercises,* I believe I have shown that this view is supported by the structures themselves. I do not propose this as the only understanding which is possible. Several years of working with a variety of retreat directors with a wide range of training and experience has taught me the difficulty — and, I believe, lack of necessity — of establishing any one exclusive understanding of the *Exercises*. For the purposes of this article, however, I am presuming that the *Exercises* are an organic unity around the specific theme of "call," as I have attempted to illustrate. When I speak of "radically adapting the Exercises," I am speaking of modifying for whatever reasons this specific view of Christian life and growth. Those who would argue for a different understanding of the *Exercises* will have to determine for themselves how they would address the question of radical adaptability, if indeed, according to their view, it is a significant question at all.

Thus we have come far enough that we may ask what are the limits of adaptability of the *Exercises,* in the sense of to what extent one might make substitutions in their specifically Ignatian mode and idiom (the "third element," according to my model), and still preserve their distinctive dynamic and in this sense be able to speak of "giving the *Exercises.*" I would like to propose a few rather generic conclusions or principles, in the light of which the sort of questions regarding adaptability raised at the beginning of this paper might be addressed.

1. In light of our reflections, we may conclude that "to give the *Exercises*" must mean two things: to promote the dynamic of Christian conversion and growth which they intend, but also to promote it by means of the Ignatian "Idiom and mode," that is to say in accordance with the specific reflections, symbols, and so forth, which direct the retreatant to an ever fuller response to Christ's call to him or her. From all we have said, it should be clear that *all* spiritual ministry is aimed at promoting Christian conversion and

it, see Raymond Studzinski, O.S.B., "The Directed Retreat — A Monastic Approach," REVIEW FOR RELIGIOUS 38 (1979): 571-577.

growth or at least some aspect of it. Ignatius experienced the path to this growth in a specific manner and proposed that a retreatant be helped accordingly. Obviously to help someone to spiritual growth is not necessarily to "give the *Exercises.*" To assist the person *in the manner proposed by Ignatius* is to do so.

2. Obviously to bring one's directee to spiritual growth is far more important than to use a specific manner of doing so. Presumably, then, the question of how far radical adaptability of the *Exercises* may go is being asked by someone who recognizes the value of the *Exercises* as a pastoral tool and is interested in knowing how adaptable that tool is to meeting new situations and new challenges, or whether it would be better to put them aside in favor of finding or creating some other tool. As a matter of fact I find that the question of radical adaptabiltity of the *Exercises* is most insistently raised by individuals who know the *Exercises* and find that they are being repeatedly brought back to them by their personal and pastoral experience and being aided by the reference. They are usually also individuals who have become aware that many interpretations and manners of giving the *Exercises* in the past were far more rigid than what Ignatius seemed to intend and are therefore looking for a manner of employing them which is both more pastorally beneficial and authentically Ignatian.[6]

3. In light of our reflections, it should be clear that I would see the most critical and therefore most difficult questions of adaptability as those dealing with the modification or omission of the "key" meditations, petitions, and so forth, which support the progressively fuller structure of "call," as I have presented it.

4. The critical nature of such modifications becomes clearer since the *Exercises* are an organic whole - tested and refined by Ignatius in his own personal experience and in that of his early pastoral companions. Practically anyone who has made the *Exercises* and certainly everyone who has given them is aware of this organic quality. As I have interpreted it, this organic quality would be the result primarily of the superstructure of key meditations, reflections, petitions, etc., which support the progressive "calls." Hence any change on this level will have implications elsewhere in the course of the *Exercises* given in their totality.

5. Yet the *Exercises* are clearly written to assist in the direction of the type

---

[6] Themes relevent to this question of the adaptability of the Exercises are taken up by Joseph Veale, "Ignatian Prayer or Jesuit Spirituality," *The Way*, Supplement 27 (Spring 1976), pp. 3-14, and also by Joseph Hitter, in "The First Week and the Love of God," *The Way*, Supplement 34 (1978), pp. 26-34, especially pages 26-27. Other articles in both of these *Supplements* discuss questions which are very significant for a contemporary understanding of the *Exercises*.

of retreatant whom Ignatius felt could be profitably given the *Exercises* in their totality. But as everything which is measured in terms of "types" or "averages," the *Exercises* are therefore in need of adaptation whenever they are used. Of this fact Ignatius was clearly aware, as indicated at the beginning of this paper. I do not find the limits of this adaptability clearly set forth by Ignatius. In any case, there is no possibility of using the *Exercises* as Ignatius clearly intended them to be used, namely in view of a specific concrete existing retreatant, *without* adapting them.

6. Since adaptation is therefore of the very essence of giving the *Exercises,* the prerequisite to any use of them at all would seem to be as deep as possible a practical and theoretical knowledge of their content and dynamic, gained above all through personal experience in making and in giving them. I would suggest that this experience is especially valuable when it is gained as a member of a retreat team, or at least when working in consultation with experienced directors.

7. Presuming this experience and knowledge of the *Exercises,* the only practical measure in most cases of whether a specific adaptation destroys their dynamic or enhances it must be, it would seem to me, the spiritual and pastoral sense of the director. I would suggest that the director who approaches the *Exercises* with a conviction of and a reverence for their organic efficacy, supported by personal and pastoral experience, and at the same time a realization that the supreme norm for every pastoral decision must be Christian tradition as addressed by the living Spirit, has the greatest chance of using the pastoral guidebook of the *Exercises* as it was intended by Ignatius to be used. To such a one I would not hesitate to say that there is nothing in the *Exercises* which could not, under specific circumstances, be altered. For I would know that he or she is aware that there are vast implications to *any* change in the specifically Ignatian element of the *Exercises* as we have identified that in this article.